Changing Practices of Tourism Stakeholders in Covid-19 Affected Destinations

ASPECTS OF TOURISM

Series Editors: **Chris Cooper** *(Leeds Beckett University, UK)*, **C. Michael Hall** *(University of Canterbury, New Zealand)* and **Dallen J. Timothy** *(Arizona State University, USA)*

Aspects of Tourism is an innovative, multifaceted series, which comprises authoritative reference handbooks on global tourism regions, research volumes, texts and monographs. It is designed to provide readers with the latest thinking on tourism worldwide and in so doing will push back the frontiers of tourism knowledge. The series also introduces a new generation of international tourism authors writing on leading edge topics.

The volumes are authoritative, readable and user-friendly, providing accessible sources for further research. Books in the series are commissioned to probe the relationship between tourism and cognate subject areas such as strategy, development, retailing, sport and environmental studies. The publisher and series editors welcome proposals from writers with projects on the above topics.

All books in this series are externally peer-reviewed.

Full details of all the books in this series and of all our other publications can be found on http://www.channelviewpublications.com, or by writing to Channel View Publications, St Nicholas House, 31–34 High Street, Bristol, BS1 2AW, UK.

ASPECTS OF TOURISM: 97

Changing Practices of Tourism Stakeholders in Covid-19 Affected Destinations

Edited by
**Erdinç Çakmak, Rami K. Isaac
and Richard Butler**

CHANNEL VIEW PUBLICATIONS
Bristol • Jackson

Dedicated to our wives, Ömür, Liga and Margaret

DOI https://doi.org/10.21832/CAKMAK8755
Library of Congress Cataloging in Publication Data
A catalog record for this book is available from the Library of Congress.
Names: Çakmak, Erdinç, editor. | Isaac, Rami K., editor. | Butler, Richard, editor.
Title: Changing Practices of Tourism Stakeholders in COVID-19 Affected
    Destinations/Edited by Erdinç Çakmak, Rami K. Isaac and Richard Butler.
Description: Bristol; Jackson: Channel View Publications, [2023] | Series: Aspects
    of Tourism: Volume 97 | Includes bibliographical references and index.
    | Summary: "This book employs epistemological, methodological and
    discursive approaches to explore the practices of tourism stakeholders
    in Covid-19 affected destinations. It discusses the changing practices
    of tourists and stakeholders at both micro and meso levels and provides
    a range of case studies offering insights into supply and demand"—Provided by publisher.
Identifiers: LCCN 2022045964 (print) | LCCN 2022045965 (ebook) | ISBN
    9781845418755 (hardback) | ISBN 9781845418748 (paperback) | ISBN
    9781845418779 (epub) | ISBN 9781845418762 (pdf)
Subjects: LCSH: Tourism—Management—Case studies. | COVID-19 Pandemic,
    2020—Case studies. | Tourism—Health aspects—Case studies.
Classification: LCC G155.A1 C43 2023 (print) | LCC G155.A1 (ebook) | DDC
    910.68—dc23/eng20230111 LC record available at https://lccn.loc.gov/2022045964
LC ebook record available at https://lccn.loc.gov/2022045965

British Library Cataloguing in Publication Data
A catalogue entry for this book is available from the British Library.

ISBN-13: 978-1-84541-875-5 (hbk)
ISBN-13: 978-1-84541-874-8 (pbk)

Channel View Publications
UK: St Nicholas House, 31–34 High Street, Bristol, BS1 2AW, UK.
USA: Ingram, Jackson, TN, USA.

Website: www.channelviewpublications.com
Twitter: Channel_View
Facebook: https://www.facebook.com/channelviewpublications
Blog: www.channelviewpublications.wordpress.com

The policy of Multilingual Matters/Channel View Publications is to use papers that
are natural, renewable and recyclable products, made from wood grown in sustainable
forests. In the manufacturing process of our books, and to further support our policy,
preference is given to printers that have FSC and PEFC Chain of Custody certification.
The FSC and/or PEFC logos will appear on those books where full certification has
been granted to the printer concerned.

Typeset by SAN Publishing Services.
Printed and bound in the UK by the CPI Books Group Ltd.

Contents

Contributors

Zahra Behboodi graduated in Strategic Management from the School of Management, Kharazmi University, Tehran, Iran. She has published two book chapters related to her master studies. Her research interests include crisis management, organisational learning and organisational resiliency in tourism.

Richard Butler, PhD, is Emeritus Professor at Strathclyde University and former Visiting Professor at Breda University of Applied Sciences. He has published over 20 books and over 100 papers and chapters on tourism. He is a past president of the International Academy for the Study of Tourism and was awarded the Ulysses Prize by UNWTO in 2016 for 'excellence in the creation and dissemination of knowledge'.

Erdinç Çakmak, PhD, is a senior lecturer at the Academy for Tourism, Breda University of Applied Sciences. His research focuses on practices and power relations in tourism, informal economies, conflict-ridden destinations and tourism paradoxes. He has published in leading tourism journals, (co)-chaired international conferences and special sessions and serves as an editorial member on several tourism journals. Since 2014, he is the current vice president of the international tourism group RC50 at the International Sociological Association.

Heidi Dahles, MSc, PhD, Radboud University, Netherlands, is an adjunct professor at the School of Social Sciences, University of Tasmania. Prior to this appointment, she held academic leadership positions at Griffith Business School (Brisbane) and Vrije University Amsterdam (Netherlands). She was also a visiting professor at the Cambodia Development Research Institute (Phnom Penh) and a member of the Griffith Institute for Tourism (Gold Coast, Australia). Her research interest is in local livelihoods, resilience and social enterprise, in particular in the tourism industry, in Southeast Asia.

Phoebe Everingham, PhD, is an early career researcher/consultant and sessional staff member at the University of Newcastle, Australia. She draws on multi-disciplinary perspectives from human geography, sociology/anthropology and tourism management. Phoebe is committed to ensuring that tourism and recreation can be enjoyed by all and is passionate about working towards sustainable/regenerative models for more inclusive and environmentally sensitive tourism futures.

Maree Gerke is an experienced educator, who has held senior roles within the Tasmanian public service in training and education, working closely with the tourism and hospitality industry to identify and implement strategies and initiatives to address industry and workforce needs and challenges. This research at the centre of this chapter was undertaken as part of a Masters of Tourism, Environmental and Cultural Heritage programme at the University of Tasmania.

Zahed Ghaderi, PhD, is an assistant professor in the Department of Tourism, College of Arts and Social Science, Sultan Qaboos University, Muscat, Oman. Zahed has over 20 years of experiences in the field and has published extensively in top-tier tourism and hospitality journals. He has conducted and led many research projects in different parts of the world. His research interests include organisational learning, strategic management in tourism, sustainable tourism, tourism crisis and disaster management, etc.

C. Michael Hall, PhD, is a Professor Ahurei in the Department of Management, Marketing and Entrepreneurship, University of Canterbury, Christchurch, New Zealand. He has visiting positions at Oulu, Linnaeus, Lund and Taylor's universities. He has published widely on tourism, regional development, global environmental change, sustainability and food.

Rami K. Isaac, PhD, is a senior lecturer at the Academy for Tourism, Breda University of Applied Sciences, The Netherlands. In addition, he is an assistant professor at the Faculty of Tourism and Hotel Management at Bethlehem University, Palestine. Currently, he is the Vice President of the Research Committee 50 on International Tourism, International Sociological Association. He published numerous articles, book chapters and edited volumes around tourism conflict-ridden destinations, critical theory and political aspects of tourism.

Gauthami Jayathilaka, PhD, is a former Sri Lankan travel writer and journalist whose experience inspired her academic research on the cultural significance of tourism and the way populations, nations and subcultures are represented through tourism and associated projective fields. Her doctoral research critically examined the ways English language and social class shape the worldmaking agency of travel writers in Sri Lanka. She is currently the Dean of the Faculty of Indigenous Social Sciences and Management Studies, Gampaha Wickramarachchi University of Indigenous Medicine, Sri Lanka.

Marion Joppe, PhD, is a Distinguished Professor Emerita in the School of Hospitality, Food and Tourism Management, University of Guelph, Canada. She specialises in destination planning, development and marketing, and the experiences upon which destinations build. Marion has extensive private and public sector experience, having worked for financial institutions, tour operators, consulting groups and government, prior to joining academia.

Maximiliano E. Korstanje, PhD, is a senior professor at the University of Palermo, Buenos Aires, Argentina and the editor in chief of *International Journal of Safety and Security in Tourism* (UP Argentina) and Editor in Chief Emeritus of *International Journal of Cyber Warfare and Terrorism* (IGI-Global US). He has co-edited almost 10 specialised journals and takes part of almost 30 journals associated to themes as human rights, mobility, tourism and terrorism. He has also recently been selected to take part of the 2018 Albert Nelson Marquis lifetime achievement award.

Meghan L. Muldoon, PhD, is an assistant professor in the School of Cultural Geography at the University of Groningen in the Netherlands. Her research interests include feminisms, mobilities, identities, arts-based methodologies and the intersections of tourism and poverty.

Daniel H. Olsen, PhD, is a professor in the Department of Geography at Brigham Young University in Provo, Utah, USA. His research interests revolve around pilgrimage, tourism and spirituality. He has published over 70 articles and book chapters and is the co-editor of *Tourism, Religion and Spiritual Journeys* (2006), *Religious Pilgrimage Routes and Trails: Sustainable Development and Management* (2018), *Dark Tourism and Pilgrimage* (2020), *Religious Tourism and the Environment* (2020) and *The Routledge Handbook of Religious and Spiritual Tourism* (2022).

Can-Seng Ooi, PhD, is an anthropologist/sociologist and a professor of Cultural and Heritage Tourism at the University of Tasmania. Besides interest in critical and responsible tourism studies, his research interests include cultural tourism, destination branding, cross-cultural understanding, art worlds and the tourist experience. His three-decade long research career spans across Australia, Denmark, the UK and Singapore. His comparative studies cover these places and others, including Malaysia and China. His research profile is available at www.cansengooi.com.

Ian Patterson, PhD, is Head of School of Tourism Management at the Silk Road International University of Tourism in Samarkand, Uzbekistan. Previously, he was an associate professor in the School of Business (Tourism) at the University of Queensland, St Lucia campus, Queensland, Australia between 2001 and 2015. His research interests include senior tourism, social-psychology of tourism, tourism management, accessible tourism, health psychology and qualitative analysis. He has published over 100 publications in textbooks, book chapters and peer-reviewed journal papers.

Ricardo Nicolas Progano, PhD, is a lecturer at the Center for Tourism Research, Wakayama University, Japan. His research interests include religious tourism, heritage management, regional revitalisation and cross-cultural studies. He has carried his fieldwork on the tourism development of Japanese pilgrimage sites, such as Kumano Kodo and Koyasan, combining his backgrounds in Asian Studies and Tourism. His recent research projects include guiding activities of religious figures of Katsuragi pilgrimage, and the impacts of the Covid-19 pandemic on Koyasan's tourism activities.

Faraz Sadeghvaziri, PhD, is an assistant professor at Kharazmi University. He has published over 15 articles in academic journals such as *Eurasian Business Review*, *Journal of Business Economics* and *Quality and Quantity*. He has also translated two books and authored another one in the area of qualitative research. Dr Sadeghvaziri has more than 12 years of teaching experience at both undergraduate and graduate levels, as well as for executive development programmes. His research interests include branding, business administration management, etc.

Manoj Samarathunga, PhD, is a qualitative research expert, particularly with N-Vivo software. He has contributed to the capacity development of many academic staff members in Sri Lanka on qualitative data analysis. Additionally, he is the President of the 'Sri Lanka Research Community' which is aimed at supporting early-career academics in Sri Lanka. He has also served as a reviewer and as an editorial board member to many indexed journals in the world. His research interests are tourist gaze and power, tourism planning, tourism anthropology, post-war tourism, and tourism and reconciliation.

Siamak Seyfi, PhD, is an assistant professor at the Geography Research Unit of the University of Oulu, Finland. Using a multi-/interdisciplinary approach and informed by diverse disciplinary perspectives, his research focuses on critical tourism geographies, impacts of tourism, resilience, sustainability and politics of tourism and peace through tourism. Siamak has published in leading tourism journals and serves on the editorial boards of several tourism journals.

Nitasha Sharma, PhD, is a tourism geographer and her research broadly examines the multiple and contested representations of place and spatial behaviour through projects situated in critical tourism studies. She specialises in the perception of authenticity, dark tourism, spectral geographies/haunted heritage, folklore and supernatural tourism, rituals and sacred spaces. Her other research interests include moral and ethical issues in tourism, and decolonial studies.

Kiran A. Shinde, PhD, is the Convener of the Planning programme at La Trobe University, Australia. Combining research training of an academic and the professional practice of a planner, he has extensively published on topics related to religious and cultural heritage and tourism, urban planning and destination management. Some of his recent publications include *Buddhist Tourism in Asia: Towards Sustainable Development* (UNWTO, 2020), *Religious Tourism and the Environment* (co-edited with Daniel Olsen, CABI, 2020) and *Sacred Sites, Rituals, and Performances: New Perspective for Religious Tourism Development* (MDPI, 2021).

Philipp Wassler, PhD, is an assistant professor at the Department of Management at the University of Bergamo (Italy). He works in both, the Management and Foreign Languages, Literatures and Cultures departments. His primary research interest is in tourism management with a particular focus on sociological perspectives. He has also worked on other tourism-related subjects, among which tourism marketing and sustainable development.

Alexandra Witte, PhD, is a research assistant professor at the School of Hotel and Tourism Management at the Hong Kong Polytechnic University where she is involved in the tourism sub-alliance research group of the University Silk Road Alliance. Her research interests include tourism mobilities and their links to questions of identity, culture, geopolitics and more, as well as ethnographic research in tourism, and sustainable tourism.

Yu-Hua (Melody) Xu, PhD, is a lecturer in the School of Community Resources and Development at Arizona State University. Her research focuses on destination planning, tourism crisis and risk management, sharing economy and community resilience. She is dedicated to finding sustainable solutions for destinations and communities in face of various turbulence and crises.

Acknowledgements

We would like to thank all the people who partook in pulling this volume together. First of all, we are greatly indebted to the contributors who have produced thought-provoking and challenging ideas on the changing practices of tourism stakeholders in Covid-19 affected destinations. We very much appreciate their efforts, time, assistance, understanding and patience at times with our requests for details and adjustments. Their breadth of viewpoints, together with stimulating and detailed knowledge of their very different subject matter, has provided us with a unique and wide range of topics related to the subject of this edited volume. We are also grateful to all at Channel View for their support and cooperation throughout the preparation of the book proposal and submission of the manuscript, and in particular, Sarah Williams, for her continued encouragement, support and patience.

Eindhoven, Breda and Prince Rupert
January 2023

1 Introduction

Over the past 50 years, tourism has shown continuous growth, albeit with slight fluctuations, particularly in the 1970s and in the early years of the 21st century. While international tourism has shown slightly less consistency and has been more responsive to specific global events, domestic tourism, the larger part of the industry, has remained buoyant and constantly growing, despite wars, depressions and natural disasters. However, the advent of what became the Covid-19 pandemic marked a major diversion from what had been normal overall growth. As noted below, the effects of this health-related crisis, which also became an economic disaster for the tourism industry throughout the world, have been unparalleled, not least because they brought both international and domestic tourism to an almost complete halt globally. Tourism has always been potentially vulnerable to disasters of all kinds, partly because it represents an optional expenditure of time and money for those fortunate enough to be able to take holidays, and partly because many of the locations visited by tourists are coastal, many of the activities involved are weather dependent, and all require the movement of vast numbers of people, often over long distances. Thus, natural disasters such as tsunamis, floods, heat waves, wildfires, atmospheric pollution and earthquakes can have dramatic effects on tourist visitation to destinations affected by such problems. Economic recessions, such as in 2008, can lower the amount of discretionary income available for leisure-related expenditures, reducing international, and sometimes domestic tourism, while human disasters such as nuclear power explosions, terrorism and conflicts of any kind will deter tourists from visiting specific locations because of concern over security, or simply result in them not travelling at all. Disasters related to health, with the exception of Spanish Flu a century ago, have generally resulted in tourists avoiding specific locations of outbreaks of the disease, but virtually all forms of disaster have been followed by tourism recovering and returning to the affected destinations fairly rapidly.

The current Covid-19 pandemic has proved to be a radically different disaster, both in terms of the scale of its coverage and the level of its impacts upon virtually all forms of economic activity, with major political and social consequences also. Such has been the level and form of these impacts that unusual and sometimes unique steps have been taken in response to this disaster. It is these measures that represent the focus of this volume, illustrating how stakeholders have modified their behaviour, their offerings, their facilities and services, and their marketing in efforts to survive the economic and health problems that have resulted from the pandemic, and which are still continuing in many locations. These modifications have often been novel and untried in specific situations; some have been successful in ensuring survival, both in economic terms and health-wise, while others have not prevented enterprises going out of business. Some have been encouraged and assisted by the public sector, some represent individual changes in behaviour in the absence of such support, and all represent what are generally seen as short-term solutions to an immediate crisis that has already lasted two years or more in some places.

The probability of a return to pre-Covid-19 levels of visitation in all locations is unlikely, and as is discussed here and elsewhere (e.g. Callot, 2021), where recovery occurs, the changed underlying situation may be very different to what existed before 2019, in terms of opportunities, attitudes and behaviours of residents and visitors. Whether the modifications that have been undertaken will prove to become permanent or disappear with the end of the pandemic remains to be seen. Societies tend to develop long-term patterns of established practice, or habitus (Bourdieu, 1977), and the impact of the pandemic and adjustments to it may change such patterns on a permanent basis, with consequential impacts for cultures and communities. To provide an appropriate context to the chapters that follow, this chapter first provides a background to the relationship between tourism and crises such as disasters, and then reviews some of the major issues that have arisen in the past years and the responses from tourism stakeholders in a range of settings, followed by an explanation of the structure of this volume.

Tourism and Crises

Tourism seems to be susceptible to negative events and, since there is always a crisis somewhere in the world, the industry would appear to be under an almost permanent threat with the certainty of yet another crisis already emerging somewhere (Pforr, 2006). As McKercher and Hui (2004: 101) point out, crises are inevitable, 'episodic events that disrupt the tourism and hospitality industry on a regular basis', and Coles (2004: 178) adds 'when not in crisis, destinations are in an extended programme of the practically pre-event limo, almost waiting for the important trigger event to take place'.

The massive and consistent growth that tourism has experienced over the past 50 years has made the industry an important factor in socioeconomic development in many regions around the world (Pforr, 2006). This growth was partly a consequence of technological advancements in transportation, which brought the world's many destinations, no matter how far from markets, within reach, which has resulted in a much stronger interconnection and complexity within the tourism system. Because tourism is now a big business, any crisis will have a much more substantial global negative impact compared to the past and affect a much larger part of the world's population. Furthermore, the negative consequences of crises in the tourism and hospitality industry are often felt in destinations far from where such crises originated. For example, in the context of SARS, Hall *et al.* (2004: 2) argue that it 'was not only spread internationally through modern aviation services but also resulted in a number of countries issuing travel warnings regarding travel to some destinations in East-Asia and health security measures at their own borders'.

In the tourism research literature on crises, the focus has been primarily on economic rather than health-related crises, and a significant number of these studies investigated crises in developed countries (Jiang *et al.*, 2017). However, the recent economic crises in developed countries have influenced the whole world. For instance, the previous global economic downturn triggered by the subprime mortgage crisis in the second half of 2007 in the United States had a major negative impact on the world economy at large, with effects also being felt as a result in both social and environmental spheres. Both developed and developing economies suffered from either reduced or negative economic growth. Some Asian economies, such as Japan, South Korea, Hong Kong and Singapore, were among the economies worst-hit by this global economic downturn and experienced serious declines in their import and export sectors, the failure of small and medium enterprises, shrinking consumer purchasing power and mounting unemployment. Tourism is often seen as a discretionary consumer good, the demand for which tends to be most affected by adverse economic conditions (Song & Lin, 2010). According to the United Nations World Tourism Organization's World Tourism Barometer (United Nations World Tourism Organization [UNWTO], 2009), international tourism declined by 8% between January and April of 2009 compared with the same period in 2008, and the total tourist flow worldwide dropped to 247 million in those four months from 269 million in 2008. In terms of the tourist arrivals to Asia over the same period, a decline of 6% was witnessed, which is significant compared with the strong growth of tourism in Asia during the previous decade.

International tourism has since been affected by a number of other crises in recent decades (Breitsohl & Garrod, 2016). Several tourism studies investigated the impact of crises on directly related tourism sectors such as airlines (Henderson, 2003), travel agents (Lovelock, 2004), hotels (Chien & Law, 2003) and catering and restaurants (Tse *et al.*, 2006). For instance, the 2010 ash cloud from the Eyjafjallajokull eruption in Iceland had severe impacts on aviation. According to the International Air Transport Association (IATA), the costs of the disruption to the global airline industry caused by the volcanic ash cloud were estimated at US$1.7

billion after just a week of flight restrictions in Europe airspace (Hall, 2010). The European Union transport commissioner stated that the disruption caused by the ash cloud could have cost firms across Europe up to US$2.8 billion (Hall, 2010). As Hall (2010: 401) states:

> the seeming increase in the impacts of economic and financial downturns, political instability or natural disasters on tourism are arguably not a result of any increase in such events but instead illustrate the way in which the world's economies, transport systems, and media and communication networks have now become so integrated that when one destination or region has been affected then the impacts can reverberate through the entire system.

Much of the attention paid to the impact of crises on tourism has been focused on the international side of tourism, despite the fact that what is known as domestic tourism is considered several times greater in terms of numbers of participants. In many cases, potential international tourists have replaced their international travel with domestic tourism to avoid international problems and risks, and as a result, total global tourist numbers may not decline (UNWTO, 2009). The notion of a tourism crisis can consequently be partly understood in the context of the difficulties that tourists face in travelling and also with respect to the problems confronting businesses (Ross, 2005). The term is also widely used in conjunction with the effects of particular events on tourism activities at destinations (Gunlu & Aktas, 2006), on specific sectors (especially aviation) (Niininen & Gatsou, 2007; Noia, 2008), and also more generally on tourism on the global scale (Santana, 1999).

Tourists' travel decisions and destination choices have been affected by their personal and physical security perceptions (Taylor & Toohey, 2007). Hall *et al.* (2003) stressed that the notion of security (as an individual and collective political concept that was primarily concerned with the defence of the nation-state) had expanded considerably to now include socioeconomic and environmental issues (Boulding, 1991). For example, there is an extensive literature on the 2008 crisis at a global scale with respect to the financial system (Crotty, 2009), economies (Stiglitz, 2000), energy (Li, 2007), the environment (Saurin, 2001; Wilshusen *et al.*, 2002), food (Loewenberg, 2008), health (Chen *et al.*, 2004), population and demographics (Sinding, 2000) and water (Duda & El-Ashry, 2000).

Today, tourism destinations are confronted with an increasing degree of risk and an increasing variety of risks on a global scale (Seabra *et al.*, 2013), including terrorism. Terrorism represents a major danger to the success of tourism destinations around the world, precisely because most visitors and tourists are concerned about the risk that terrorism poses to their personal well-being. Unsafe and perceived unsafe destinations face many difficulties in attracting tourists and visitors, and there is considerable research (Coshall, 2003; Isaac, 2019, 2021; Isaac & Van den Bedem, 2021; Pizam & Mansfeld, 1996) demonstrating that safety and security represent one of the most vulnerable areas that influence tourist behaviour and choice of destinations. Other studies have focused on terrorism within specific geographical locations, such as the terrorist attacks on tourists in Egypt (Aziz, 1995; Tomazos, 2017), the 9/11 impact on Washington hotels (Stafford *et al.*, 2002) and the bomb attacks in Bali (Putra & Hitchcock, 2009) among others.

Tourism and Health-related Crises

Unlike political crises, natural disasters and environmental problems cause a severe direct impact on health and climate. Both bring major challenges to tourism given their impacts on travel at various scales as well as their potential to affect the image of destinations. For instance, the Southeast Asian smoke haze (Leiper & Hing, 1998), earthquakes (Huang & Min, 2002), volcanoes (Aguirre, 2007), tsunamis (Calgaro & Lloyd, 2008), cyclones (Prideaux *et al.*, 2007), hurricanes (Baade & Matheson, 2007) and bushfires (Armstrong & Ritchie, 2007) damaged public health and environments and influenced national economies including tourism sectors. However, until the Covid-19 pandemic, only a few studies had focused on such health-related epidemics and crises (Novelli *et al.*, 2018). During the past two decades, a prominent number of health-related crises threatened local communities' daily lives and damaged the tourism sector (Glaesser, 2006). Among these crises were the 2001 UK foot and mouth disease outbreak (Baxter & Bowen, 2004; Frisby, 2002), SARS in South-East Asia (Gu & Wall, 2007; Tew *et al.*, 2008), influenza in Mexico (Page *et al.*, 2006) and bed bug issues at several hotels (Liu *et al.*, 2015). As well, as the development of biosecurity strategies recognised the vulnerability and the potential role of tourism in this area also (Mitchell & Hall, 2006; Trees, 2009). Tourism and travel can accelerate and amplify an epidemic due to greater human mobility primarily driven by air travel. The SARS outbreak spread globally when tourists returned home from the affected areas (Mason *et al.*, 2005). National governments reacted by closing their borders, which led to the loss of 3 million jobs in the tourism sector in South-East Asia (Kuo *et al.*, 2008). In the 2014 Ebola outbreak, foreign tourist arrivals decreased by 5% in the following two years in the affected West-African countries (Novelli *et al.*, 2018).

The aforementioned crises have occurred at different scales and intensities. Many of the crises that can affect tourism are events of a specific duration and occur in an identifiable time and space, although their impacts may be widespread and long-lasting (Ren, 2000). The difference between the current Covid-19 pandemic and other crises is that the complete halt in activity in many sectors across most countries caused by Covid-19 is unprecedented. The closest comparison to the Covid-19 pandemic is that of Spanish Flu, which became a world-wide pandemic following the end of World War I (Butler, 2021). Then, although the disease was faster acting and more fatal than Covid-19, the overall effects on tourism were much less, primarily because of far lower levels of international tourist travel at that time (1918–1919) as a result of very limited international air travel, which meant the disease was not as widespread nor as rapidly spread as a century later. Covid-19 severely impacted both the supply and demand sides of the global economy and, as a result, has driven the global economy into a deep recession. The exact magnitude and length of this recession will depend on a number of factors, including the duration of Covid-19 restrictions, how effective the significant fiscal stimuli being applied by many governments are in enabling economic recovery, and the convincing proof that the pandemic has ended. Covid-19 has highlighted the need for more robust government and business planning for and managing such crises and is likely to leave a lasting impact on global economic structures and consumer behaviour. Global organisations such as the World Health Organization (WHO), United Nations World Tourism Organization (UNWTO), European Centre for Disease Prevention and Control (ECDC) and many national tourism boards have become increasingly interested in the disaster management of such an epidemic and its epidemiology, how to communicate through the media and what precautionary actions could be taken to limit its expansion (Mason *et al.*, 2005; Page *et al.*, 2006). As yet, there is no consensus in the literature on the normalisation process with respect to health epidemics that are infrequent but can spread rapidly across the geographical boundaries in the current era of fast international travel (Novelli *et al.*, 2018).

Changing Practices of Tourism Stakeholders

Few social scientists today would deny that the Covid-19 crisis has affected the social and cultural structures as well as the economies of tourism destinations. Both internal and external tourism stakeholders, including tourists themselves, at tourism destinations are part of these structures, and they all have been affected by the performance of what were everyday practices in pre-pandemic times. In this context, the term 'practice' refers to the everyday real-time doings and sayings of stakeholders involved in tourism (Bourdieu, 1977). It also encompasses the meaning-making, identity-forming of individuals and consequently reshaping their social and cultural structures (Çakmak *et al.*, 2021; Chia & Holt, 2006; Thompson *et al.*, 2020). The practice turn (also known as practice approach) in the social sciences has been influencing several fields of research in recent years, including sustainable development (Shove & Spurling, 2014), strategy (Whittington, 1996), management (Nicolini, 2011), geography (Everts *et al.*, 2011) and tourism studies (Çakmak *et al.*, 2018; Cohen & Cohen, 2019; Lamers *et al.*, 2017) in the past three decades. Using this practice approach, scholars examine the 'practice' of individuals empirically, taking this behaviour as the fundamental unit of analysis and interrogating its role in these fields and how it influences different layers of social structure and, in turn, is influenced by the changes in those structures on both a temporary and permanent basis.

The practices of many, if not virtually all, tourism stakeholders have been rapidly and significantly changed and transformed by the Covid-19 crisis, and tourism destinations have moved in a very short period from hypermobility to stagnation, and from overtourism to the absence of tourism. As a result, many national and local authorities around the world are focused now on thinking about the recovery practices and building resilience to the current and inevitable future disasters. National and local authorities and destination management organisations (DMOs) have adopted different strategies to cope with this crisis (Collins-Kreiner & Ram, 2021). While some authorities in the Western world have focused on disseminating public aid (e.g. tax exemptions, reduction of social security fees, direct financial support), other agencies have focused on reactivating domestic tourism and traditional value chains, but many tourism stakeholders, particularly small enterprises, in developing countries in particular have been left to their fate. The impact of a health crisis (e.g. Covid-19 pandemic) can be devastating in developing countries due to some national economies' overreliance on tourism income and deficiencies in their governance infrastructure (Ritchie, 2009). The fast decline in visitor numbers, increasing unemployment, reduced investments from the private sector and less tourism-related taxes often intensify the state of fragility associated with developing countries (Novelli *et al.*, 2012). Such problems can be aggravated in regions with a traditional heavy reliance on tourism, where it makes up a large percentage of their GDP, such as the Caribbean and South Pacific Islands.

While a vast amount of research has examined the impacts of the Covid-19 pandemic on destinations, tourists and travel (e.g. Higgins-Desbiolles, 2020; Hudson, 2020; Nhamo *et al.*, 2020; Qiu *et al.*, 2020; Sigala, 2020), much less research exists regarding the specific changes in practices of residents, entrepreneurs and migrant workers at tourism destinations in response to the Covid-19 crisis. Many key questions remain both unasked and unanswered. These include what structural tourism field changes have taken place during the Covid-19 pandemic; how were the social fields of power, value and culture affected by the Covid-19 restrictions; what were the struggles/maneuvers of tourism stakeholders concerning their resources, stakes and access; which tourism stakeholders were excluded from the policy actions or denied the freedom to act as they wished; and what were the impacts of changing practices on forms of hospitality and guest-host relations? Many answers to these and similar questions are often context-dependent and require an exploration of practices of local tourism stakeholders at different scales and in different settings and locations. It has become very clear that there has not been a single answer to the many specific problems created by the pandemic and thus a 'one-size-fits-all' approach would be completely inadequate as a solution and might even make situations worse (Baniamin *et al.*, 2020).

This volume explores the changes in practices of tourism stakeholders affected by the Covid-19 crisis in urban and rural tourism contexts using a sociological and anthropological perspective. In examining destinations and their tourism stakeholders, sociological analysis suggests the need for a fluid and interactional perspective (Bauman, 2013). Destinations represent the fields of the complex interplay between social, cultural, political and economic relationships (Allen *et al.*, 1998). The roles and positions of local stakeholders are embedded in their everyday practices that take place in the social and spatial fabrics of destinations (Ateljevic, 2000; Çakmak *et al.*, 2018). In this context, this volume explores the practices of tourism stakeholders in Covid-19 affected destinations by employing epistemological, methodological and discursive approaches in order to understand and explain their everyday real-time doings and sayings. In recent years, practice-based approaches have gained significant attention in tourism studies (Çakmak *et al.*, 2018; Cohen & Cohen, 2019; Lamers *et al.*, 2017) to explain the role of practices in tourism and social structures.

Other recent works that have similarly embraced the impacts of the Covid-19 pandemic include *Counting the Cost of Covid-19 on the Global Tourism Industry*; *COVID-19 and Travel: Impacts, Responses and Outcomes*; *Covid-19 and the Hospitality and Tourism Industry* and *Tourism, Safety and COVID-19, Security, Digitization and Tourist Behaviour*. Some of these, particularly the latter in this list (Monaco, 2021), express changing tourist behaviour reflecting safety and security perceptions. *Counting the Cost of Covid-19 on the Global Tourism Industry* (Nhamo *et al.*, 2020) examines the global issues in general and their impact on tourism sub-sectors. *COVID-19 and Travel: Impacts, Responses and Outcome* (Hudson, 2020) focuses on crisis management and steps that regional and national organisations need to consider for destination marketing. *Covid-19 and the Hospitality and Tourism Industry* (Gursoy *et al.*, 2021) also provides marketing suggestions to the hospitality industry, including destination branding. To this end, the present volume similarly embraces changes in the practices of primarily local tourism stakeholders at Covid-19 affected destinations and aims to enhance scholarship in this field by an understanding of the unfolding of the Covid-19 pandemic impacts on the everyday lives of tourism stakeholders around the globe and their implications.

Structure of the Book

The chapters that follow in this volume are an eclectic collection, representing a variety of viewpoints, scales, geographic locations and cultures. This is not surprising and is perhaps appropriate, given the nature of the Covid-19 pandemic and its effects upon the world's population. It has been an unprecedented medical, economic and social catastrophe for most places and their populations, all the more disconcerting because of its large-scale and rapid spread, and the unpreparedness of almost every country. Shock, surprise and, in some cases, almost panic resulted, and it is not surprising that the actions taken by those facing the ensuing problems were often rushed, often not well thought out in terms of their full effects, and often simply incorrect or inappropriate when viewed with hindsight. Nothing in the past has had such an effect on tourism and travel; not only was foreign travel proving next to impossible, but many countries also imposed domestic lockdowns and restrictions on travel within their own boundaries. While New Zealand and other Pacific islands prevented any visitation from abroad, Australia also saw interstate restrictions, with Western Australia only opening its borders to fellow Australians two years after the beginning of the pandemic. Which actions were successful, and which were not will only be clearly determined some time in the future, and it is not the focus of this volume to evaluate or judge the success or failure of the changes in behaviour discussed in the following chapters, but more to examine the perceptions in play, the motivations of responders and the overall acceptance or rejection of their attempts.

The book is divided into four sections, not including this introductory chapter and the concluding chapter. The sections deal with changes in subfields, transitions of attitudes, perceptions and habitus changes, and emerging perspectives on possible implications for post-Covid-19 tourism. The subsequent chapters cover a wide range of geographical locations, widely varying segments of tourism from individual enterprises to national situations, spiritually driven foci to economic priorities, and changes in the way that residents of tourist areas and operators of tourist enterprises have come to regard their visitors and their operating procedures. The overriding focus, however, is how behaviours and practices have changed in response to the varying impacts of Covid-19. Along with discussion of those changes has been commentary on the development of differing attitudes towards tourism, tourists and priorities related to economic and personal survival as the pandemic has affected the whole fabric of respondents' lives and businesses.

Thus, we see a variety of scales of parties involved, as illustrated in the first section of the book, in which there are examples of small-scale tourism operators modifying their practices in Iran (Ghaderi, Behboodi *et al.* and Seyfi & Hall), in sharp contrast to the massive changes in equipment, timetables and routes made by the global players in the airline industry (Joppe). Despite this range in scale, the responses all reflect the uncertainty of the respondents about effectiveness of their induced changes in operations, the assumption that many of these changes will be temporary rather than permanent, and their concerns about the timescale of the impacts affecting them. The ineffectiveness or absence of government support and the lack of consistency in government actions made some of the changes unavoidable and revealed the lack of preparedness of all sectors for such a disaster.

This section is followed by examples of changes that were driven by both spiritual concerns as well economic necessity, and which were also affected by governmental restrictions on travel and public gatherings in the case of the responses by those involved in religious activities. Olsen and Shinde note some of the responses to restrictions with the increased utilisation of remote and virtual forms of observance to replace physical visitation to churches and related sites, while Sharma revealed how many pilgrims in India ignored the risks of the pandemic, placing greater faith in a higher power than government edicts and continued in traditional patterns of behaviour. In Japan, Progano demonstrated how the stays of visitors at temple sites in Wakayama changed during the course of the pandemic, reflecting the dynamism in economic problems as well as in government restrictions.

A similar theme emerges in the third section, with chapters discussing a single restaurant in Australia and its relations with local residents and its owners/operators described by Gerke, Ooi and Dahles, in comparison to broader reactions by tourism agents in Sri Lanka described by Jayathilaka and Samarathunga. At the other end of the scale are issues such as the changes and responses resulting from the impact of the pandemic on women in tourism in China (Muldoon, Witte and Xu), where it became clear that different populations were affected in different ways by the pandemic, in some case making inequalities greater, but possibly improving appreciation. In the final section, the overall effect of the pandemic on the national and local populations' attitudes and perceptions is further discussed by Korstanje in the context of rising tensions between the visited and the visitors in many countries because of fear of the pandemic. This is an issue also addressed by Wassler in the specific context of Pisa and the way local residents (hosts) there reacted to visitors (guests). Returning to the national scale in conclusion, Everingham reviews the possible rethinking of tourism for the whole of Australia and the likely implications of such actions in broad social, economic and environmental spheres.

Interesting though these changes are in their own right, it is perhaps of greater significance as to whether these changes will become long-lasting or even permanent, or whether they will be abandoned once the pandemic is over, and tourism has resumed its previously little restricted form. In some cases, the use of virtual and remote experiences that Olsen and Shinde discuss is likely to be the precursors of much wider use of this type of experience. Such patterns had been observed before the pandemic when pilgrimage and religious-inspired journeys to shrines and other sites had been prevented or limited because of conflict, religious intolerance and political issues (Collins-Kreiner & Luz, 2018), and the faithful were visiting *in absentia*, and the use of virtual experiences was also becoming more common in other areas of tourism. As electronic capabilities improve inaccessibility, cost and realism, then other problems such as conflict, increased cost of travel and possibly even realistic efforts to reduce over-tourism may cause some potential tourists to choose the virtual visit over the real thing. In the case of Hindu pilgrims, it would appear little change has occurred and the traditional pattern of the Kumlas and other festival events will likely continue unchanged in the future (Kanvinde & Tom, 2018), while some of the changes introduced in the context of temple stays are likely to remain in some form for the medium term at least.

How permanent the shift in attitudes towards women in China (Muldoon *et al.*) is likely to be is more difficult to assess because, as the authors pointed out, while women bore a disproportionate share of the extra workload imposed by the pandemic, sympathies caused by the nega-tive attitudes towards women saw an increase and this may continue although the end of the pandemic is unlikely to be a factor in that. The potential for xenophobia, or tourismophobia (Milano *et al.*, 2019) to remain in the post-pandemic era is a real risk, particularly in those areas that were previously experiencing overtourism and which, given the fail-ure to prevent overtourism in the pre-pandemic period (Butler & Dodds, 2022), are likely to see a resurgence of over-visitation. Wassler noted how attitudes between hosts and guests had already changed as the pandemic began and if the pressures of tourism resume, further negative reactions may occur. The 'wicked (evil)-gaze' of hosts towards guests described by Korstanje is likely to be continued in a number of locations where overde-velopment and excessive visitation continue to take place. In such a sce-nario, the arguments made by Everingham about a rethink of national attitudes towards tourism, including taking a more holistic approach to tourism, integrating it with other issues such as inequality, climate change and increased sustainability, perhaps represent a positive step out of the pandemic situation into a less growth-focused and kinder world and could be one of the few benefits to emerge from the pandemic.

Perhaps, in contrast, some of the changes made by the airline indus-tries are focused on restoring tourism to its former levels, as well as secur-ing the financial viability of the companies involved, and as Joppe points out, some of these changes are in line with other goals, such as reducing carbon emissions, albeit being done for perhaps less selfless reasons. One can hope perhaps that many of these changes do, in fact, become long-term practices, with improvements in fuel consumption, better routings and capacity limits all moving towards greater sustainability. At the other extreme in scale, the changes in offerings at the restaurant in Tasmania (Gerke *et al.*) will only survive if they meet customer preferences, and whether the changes resulting from Covid-19 limitations will be successful is hard to say. The future of changes in behaviour and adjustments to practices noted by Seyfi and Hall and Ghaderi *et al.* in Iran, and by Jayathilaka and Samarathunga, is dependent on what happens at the respective national levels, as the overall level and pattern of tourism in those countries are influenced by a number of exogenous forces such as sanctions and markets, as well as endogenous factors such as religious controls and terrorism.

Inevitably, there have been many other examples and changes that have resulted from the impact of the Covid-19 pandemic, and these chapters represent just a few of the vast array of modifications that have been imposed. Much depends, in all the cases reviewed in this volume and those elsewhere, on how effectively the Covid-19 pandemic can be resolved and eliminated, or at least brought under control to a significant degree. The perceptions and attitudes of the tourists themselves, as well as residents of tourist destinations, will determine whether many, if any, of the changes recorded move from temporary to permanent status, and what effect they continue to have on tourism levels and patterns.

References

Aguirre, J.A. (2007) Tourism, volcanic eruptions and information: Lessons for crisis management in national parks, Costa Rica, 2006. *PASOS. Revista de Turismo y Patrimonio Cultural*, 5, 175–192.

Alan, C.B., So, S. and Sin, L. (2006) Crisis management and recovery: How restaurants in Hong Kong responded to SARS. *International Journal of Hospitality Management*, 25 (1), 3–11.

Armstrong, E.K. and Ritchie, B.W. (2007) The heart recovery marketing campaign: Destination recovery after a major bushfire in Australia's national capital. *Journal of Travel & Tourism Marketing* 23 (2/4), 175–189.

Ateljevic, I. (2000) Circuits of tourism: Stepping beyond the 'production/consumption' dichotomy. *Tourism Geographies* 2 (4), 369–388.

Aziz, H. (1995) Understanding attacks on tourists in Egypt. *Tourism Management* 16 (2), 91–95.

Baade, R.A. and Matheson, V.A. (2007) Professional sports, hurricane Katrina, and the economic redevelopment of New Orleans. *Contemporary Economic Policy* 25, 591–603.

Baniamin, H.M., Rahman, M. and Hasan, M.T. (2020) The Covid-19 pandemic. Why are some countries coping more successfully than others? *Asia Pacific Journal of Public Administration* 42 (3), 153–169.

Bauman, Z. (2013) *Liquid Modernity*. Chichester: John Wiley & Sons.

Baxter, E. and Bowen, D. (2004) Anatomy of tourism crisis: Explaining the effects on tourism of the UK foot and mouth disease epidemics of 1967– 68 and 2001 with special reference to media portrayal. *International Journal of Tourism Research* 6, 263–273.

Boulding, E. (1991) States, boundaries and environmental security in global and regional conflicts. *Interdisciplinary Peace Research* 3 (2), 78–93.

Bourdieu, P. (1977) *Outline of a Theory of Practice* (Vol. 16). Cambridge: Cambridge University Press.

Breitsohl, J. and Garrod, B. (2016) Assessing tourists' cognitive, emotional and behavioural reactions to an unethical destination incident. *Tourism Management* 54, 209–220.

Butler, R.W. (2021) COVID-19 and its potential impact on stages of tourist destination development. *Current Issues in Tourism* 25 (10), 1682–1695.

Butler, R.W. and Dodds, R. (2022) Overcoming overtourism: A review of failure. *Tourism Review,* Vol. ahead-of-print. https://doi.org/10.1108/TR-04-2021-0215

Çakmak, E., Lie, R. and McCabe, S. (2018) Reframing informal tourism entrepreneurial practices: Capital and field relations structuring the informal tourism economy of Chiang Mai. *Annals of Tourism Research* 72, 37–47.

Çakmak, E., Lie, R., Selwyn, T. and Leeuwis, C. (2021) Like a fish in water: Habitus adaptation mechanisms of informal tourism entrepreneurs in Thailand. *Annals of Tourism Research* 90, 103262.

Calgaro, E. and Lloyd, K. (2008) Sun, sea, sand and tsunami: Examining disaster vulnerability in the tourism community of Khao Lak, Thailand. *Singapore Journal of Tropical Geography* 29, 288–306.

Callot, P. (2021) *Tourism Post Covid-19: Coping, Negotiating, Leading Change.* Vienna: Tourism Research Centre.

Chia, R. and Holt, R. (2006) Strategy as practical coping: A Heideggerian perspective. *Organization Studies* 27 (5), 635–655.

Chien, G.C. and Law, R. (2003) The impact of the severe acute respiratory syndrome on hotels: A case study of Hong Kong. *International Journal of Hospitality Management* 22 (3), 327–332.

Cohen, S.A. and Cohen, E. (2019) New directions in the sociology of tourism. *Current Issues in Tourism* 22 (2), 153–172.

Coles, T. (2004) A local reading of a global disaster. Some lessons on tourism management from an Annus Horribilis in South West England. In C.M. Hall, D.J. Timothy and D.T. Duval (eds) *Safety and Security in Tourism. Relationships, Management and Marketing* (pp. 173–198). New York: Haworth Press.

Collins-Kreiner, N. and Luz, N. (2018) Judaism and tourism over the ages: The impacts of technology, geopolitics and the changing political landscape. In R. Butler and W. Suntikul (eds) *Tourism and Religion: Issues and Implications* (pp. 51–67). Bristol: Channel View Publications.

Collins-Kreiner, N. and Ram, V. (2021) National tourism strategies during the Covid-19 pandemic. *Annals of Tourism Research* 89 (1). https://doi.org/10.1016/j.annals.2020.103076

Chen, L., Evans, T., Anand, S., Boufford, J., Brown, H., Chowdhury, M. *et al.* (2004) Human resources for health: Overcoming the crisis. *The Lancet* 364, 1984–1990.

Coshall, J. (2003) The threat of terrorism as intervention on international travel flows. *Journal of Travel Research* 42 (1), 4–12.

Crotty, J. (2009) Structural causes of the global financial crisis: A critical assessment of the 'new financial architecture'. *Cambridge Journal of Economics* 33 (4), 563–580.

Duda, A.M. and El-Ashry, M.T. (2000) Addressing the global water and environment crises through integrated approaches to the management of land, water and ecological resources. *Water International* 25, 115–126.

Everts, J., Lahr-Kurten, M. and Watson, M. (2011) Practice matters! Geographical inquiry and theories of practice. *Erdkunde* 65 (4), 232–334.

Frisby, E. (2002) Communicating in a crisis: The British Tourist Authority's responses to the foot-and-mouth outbreak and 11th September 2001. *Journal of Vacation Marketing* 9, 89–100.

Glaesser, D. (2006) *Crisis Management in the Tourism Industry* (2nd edn). London: Routledge.

Gu, H. and Wall, G. (2007) SARS in China: Tourism impacts and market rejuvenation. *Tourism Analysis* 11, 367–379.

Gunlu, E.A. and Aktas, G. (2006) Vulnerability of coastal resorts to crises: Probable scenarios and recovery strategies. *Tourism in Marine Environments* 3, 3–13.

Gursoy, D., Sarıışık, M., Nunkoo, R. and Boğan, E. (eds) (2021) *Covid-19 and the Hospitality and Tourism Industry: A Research Companion.* Cheltenham: Edward Elgar Publishing.

Hall, C.M. (2010) Crisis events in tourism: Subjects of crisis in tourism. *Current Issues in Tourism* 13 (5), 401–417.

Hall, C.M., Duval, D. and Timothy, D. (eds) (2004) *Safety and Security in Tourism: Relationships, Management and Marketing.* New York: Haworth Press.

Hall, C.M., Timothy, D. and Duval, D. (2003) Security and tourism: Towards a new understanding? *Journal of Travel and Tourism Marketing* 15 (2–3), 1–18.

Henderson, J.C. (2003) Communicating in a crisis: Flight SQ 006. *Tourism Management* 24 (3), 279–287.

Higgins-Desbiolles, F. (2020) Socialising tourism for social and ecological justice after COVID-19. *Tourism Geographies* 22 (3), 610–623.

Huang, J. and Min, C.H.J. (2002) Earthquake devastation and recovery in tourism: The Taiwan case. *Tourism Management* 23 (2), 145–154.

Hudson, S. (2020) *COVID-19 and Travel: Impacts, Responses and Outcomes.* Oxford: Goodfellow Publishers.

Isaac, R.K. (2019) The attitudes of the Dutch market towards safety and security. In R. Isaac, E. Çakmak and R. Butler (eds) *Tourism and Hospitality in Conflict-Ridden Destinations* (pp. 39–55). Abingdon: Routledge.

Isaac, R.K. (2021) An exploratory study: The impact of terrorism on risk perceptions. An analysis of the German market behaviours and attitudes towards Egypt. *Tourism Planning & Development* 18 (1), 25–44.

Isaac, R.K. and Bedem, V.D. (2021) The impacts of terrorism on risk perception and travel behaviour of the Dutch market: Sri Lanka as a case study. *International Journal of Tourism Cities* 7 (1), 63–91.

Jiang, Y., Ritchie, B.W. and Benckendorff, P. (2017) A bibliometric visualization of tourism crisis and disaster research. *Current Issues in Tourism* 22, 1–34.

Kanvinde, P. and Tom, B. (2018) Hinduism and tourism. In R. Butler and W. Suntikul (eds) *Tourism and Religion: Issues and Implications* (pp. 83–98). Bristol: Channel View Publications.

Kuo, H.I., Chen, C.C., Tseng, W.C., Ju, L.F. and Huang, B.W. (2008) Assessing impacts of SARS and Avian Flu on international tourism demand to Asia. *Tourism Management* 29 (5), 917–928.

Lamers, M., Van der Duim, R. and Spaargaren, G. (2017) The relevance of practice theories for tourism research. *Annals of Tourism Research* 62, 54–63.

Leiper, N. and Hing, N. (1998) Trends in Asia-Pacific tourism in 1997–1998: From optimism to uncertainty. *International Journal of Contemporary Hospitality Management* 10 (7), 245–251.

Li, M. (2007) Peak oil, the rise of China and India, and the global energy crisis. *Journal of Contemporary Asia*, 37, 449–471.

Liu, B., Kim, H. and Pennington-Gray, L. (2015) Responding to the bed bug crisis in social media. *International Journal of Hospitality Management* 47, 76–84.

Loewenberg, S. (2008) Global food crisis looks set to continue. *The Lancet* 372, 1209–1210.

Lovelock, B. (2004) New Zealand travel agent practice in the provision of advice for travel to risky destinations. *Journal of Travel & Tourism Marketing* 15 (4), 259–279.

Mason, P., Grabowski, P. and Du, W(2005) Severe acute respiratory syndrome, tourism and the media. *International Journal of Tourism Research* 7, 11–21.

McKercher, B. and Hui, E.L.L. (2004) Terrorism, economic uncertainty and outbound travel from Hong Kong. In C.M. Hall, D.J. Timothy and D.T. Duval (eds) *Safety and Security in Tourism. Relationships, Management and Marketing* (pp. 99–116). New York: Haworth Press.

Milano, C., Novelli, M. and Cheer, J.M. (2019) Overtourism and tourismphobia: A journey through four decades of tourism development, planning and local concerns. *Tourism Planning and Development* 16 (4), 353–357.

Mitchell, R. and Hall, C.M. (2006) Wine tourism research: The state of play. *Tourism Review International* 9, 307–332.

Monaco, S. (2021) *Tourism, Safety and COVID-19: Security, Digitization and Tourist Behaviour.* Abingdon: Routledge.

Nhamo, G., Dube, K. and Chikodzi, D. (2020) *Counting the Cost of COVID-19 on the Global Tourism Industry.* Cham: Springer Nature.

Nicolini, D. (2011) Practice as the site of knowing: Insights from the field of telemedicine. *Organization Science* 22 (3), 602–620.

Niininen, O. and Gatsou, M. (2007) Crisis management – A case study from the Greek passenger shipping industry. *Journal of Travel & Tourism Marketing* 23 (2/4), 191–202.

Noia, A.C. (2008) Managing crises: UK civil aviation, BAA airports and the August 2006 terrorist threat. *Tourism and Hospitality Research* 8, 125–136.

Novelli, M., Morgan, N. and Nibigira, C. (2012) Tourism in a post-conflict situation of fragility. *Annals of Tourism Research* 39 (3), 1446–1469.

Novelli, M., Burgess, L.G., Jones, A. and Ritchie, B.W. (2018) 'No Ebola... still doomed'– The Ebola-induced tourism crisis. *Annals of Tourism Research* 70, 76–87.

Page, S., Yeoman, I., Munro, C., Connell, J. and Walker, L. (2006) A case study of best practice – Visit Scotland's prepared response to an influenza pandemic. *Tourism Management* 27, 361–393.

Pizam, A. and Mansfeld, Y. (1996) *Tourism, Crime and International Security Issues.* Chichester: Wiley.

Pforr, C. (2006) Tourism in post-crisis is tourism in pre-crisis: A review of the literature on crisis management in tourism. Curtin University of Technology School of Management Working Paper Series, 1–11. The Curtin University of Technology.

Prideaux, B., Coghlan, A. and Falco-Mammone, F. (2007) Post-crisis recovery: The case of after cyclone Larry. *Journal of Travel & Tourism Marketing* 23 (2/4), 163–174.

Putra, I.N.D. and Hitchcock, M. (2009) Terrorism and tourism in Bali and Southeast Asia. In M. Hitchcock, V.T. King and M. Parnwell (eds) (2008) *Tourism in Southeast Asia: Challenges and New Directions* (pp. 83–98). NIAS – Nordic Institute of Asian Studies Copenhagen: Denmark.

Qiu, R.T., Park, J., Li, S. and Song, H. (2020) Social costs of tourism during the Covid-19 pandemic. *Annals of Tourism Research* 84, 102994.

Ren, C. (2000) Understanding and managing the dynamics of linked crisis events. *Disaster Prevention and Management* 9 (1), 12–17. https://doi.org/10.1108/09653560010316023

Ross, G.F. (2005) Tourism industry employee work stress—A present and future crisis. *Journal of Travel and Tourism Marketing* 19 (2–3), 133–147.

Ritchie, B.W. (2009) *Crisis and Disaster Management for Tourism.* Bristol: Channel View Publications.

Santana, G. (1999) Tourism: Toward a model for crisis management. *Turizam* 47, 4–12.

Saurin, J. (2001) Global environmental crisis as the 'disaster triumphant': The private capture of public goods. *Environmental Politics* 10 (4), 63–84.

Seabra, C., Dolnicar, S., Abrantes, J.L. and Kastenholz, E. (2013) Heterogeneity in risk and safety perceptions of international tourists. *Tourism Management* 36, 502–510.

Shove, E. and Spurling, N. (2014) *Sustainable Practices: Social Theory and Climate Change.* Abingdon: Routledge.

Sigala, M. (2020) Tourism and COVID-19: Impacts and implications for advancing and resetting industry and research. *Journal of Business Research* 117, 312–321.

Sinding, S.W. (2000) The great population debates: How relevant are they for the 21st century? *American Journal of Public Health* 90, 1841–1845.

Song, H. and Lin, S. (2010) Impacts of the financial and economic crisis on tourism in Asia. *Journal of Travel Research* 49 (1), 16–30.

Stafford, G., Yu, L. and Armoo, A.K. (2002) Crisis management and recovery: How Washington, D.C. hotels responded to terrorism. *Cornell Hotel and Restaurant Administration Quarterly* 43 (5), 27–40. https://doi.org/10.1177/0010880402435003

Stiglitz, J.E. (2000) Capital market liberalization, economic growth, and instability. *World Development* 28, 1075–1086.

Taylor, T. and Toohey, K. (2007) Perceptions of terrorism threats at the 2004 Olympic Games: Implications for sport events. *Journal of Sport & Tourism* 12 (2), 99–114.

Tew, P.J., Lu, Z., Tolomiczenko, G. and Gellatly, J. (2008) SARS: Lessons in strategic planning for hoteliers and destination marketers. *International Journal of Contemporary Hospitality Management* 20, 332–346.

Thompson, N.A., Verduijn, K. and Gartner, W.B. (2020) Entrepreneurship-as-practice: Grounding contemporary theories of practice into entrepreneurship studies. *Entrepreneurship & Regional Development* 32 (3–4), 247–256.

Tomazos, K. (2017) Egypt's tourism industry and the Arab Spring. In R. Butler and W. Suntikul (eds) *Tourism and Political Change* (pp. 214–229). Oxford: Goodfellow Publishers.

Trees, A.J. (2009) Disease threats from travelling pets. *British Veterinary Record* 164 (1), 28–29.

Tse, A.C.B., So, S. and Sin, L. (2006) Crisis management and recovery: How restaurants in Hong Kong responded to SARS. *International Journal of Hospitality Management* 25 (1), 3–11. https://doi.org/10.1016/j.ijhm.2004.12.001

United Nations World Tourism Organization (UNWTO) (2009) *World Tourism Barometer*. Madrid: UNWTO.

Whittington, R. (1996) Strategy as practice. *Long Range Planning* 29 (5), 731–735.

Wilshusen, P.R., Brechin, S.R., Fortwangler, C.L. and West, P.C. (2002) Reinventing a square wheel: Critique of a resurgent 'protection paradigm' in international biodiversity conservation. *Society & Natural Resources* 15, 17–40.

Part 1

Changes in the Subfields of the Tourism Industry

2 The Impacts of Covid-19 on the Airline Industry

Marion Joppe

Since airlines hit the 500 million passengers carried mark in 1973, they have registered a rapid increase with only minor setbacks over the years to reach almost 4.5 billion passengers in 2019. Of these, just over 40% were international passengers contributing substantially to the $575 billion in revenues derived from passengers (ICAO, 2022). In 2020, global seat capacity fell by 44%, from 5.5 billion to 3 billion. The number of passengers carried fell even further, by 60% or 2.7 billion, making it the worst year on record (IATA (2021a). While 2021 saw a slight improvement, seat capacity was still 37% below 2019 and passengers carried -49%, levels last seen in 2009/2010 coming out of the financial crash. The gross passenger operating losses of airlines were staggering at $372 billion in 2020 and $324 billion in 2021 (ICAO, 2022; OAG, 2021, 17 December).

The speed with which the airline market collapsed and the exceedingly slow recovery due to waves of SARS-CoV-2 variants leading governments to repeatedly impose restrictions on potential air travel has forced airlines to change a number of their practices, some likely permanently, and cope with continued uncertainty for the foreseeable future. This chapter will address the major challenges faced by airlines that are transforming their operations in response to the Covid-19 crisis, namely the increased volatility in scheduling, the need for countries to adopt harmonised digital health credentials for testing and vaccination that would be accepted across borders, coping strategies adopted by airlines, and government support extended to airlines. Finally, the chapter will address the urgency imposed by climate change, commitments made by airlines to achieve net-zero carbon by 2050 and proactive measures taken by governments to accelerate the decarbonisation of the airline industry. Interwoven throughout these topics are the changing consumer expectations and trends.

Volatility in Scheduling

Demand for air travel plunged precipitously by 94.3% in April 2020 compared to April 2019, forcing carriers to cut capacity drastically, consolidate flights and reduce schedule frequencies in alignment with lower demand (IATA, 2020c; OAG, 2021, 17 December). Because of many countries closing their borders to all but essential travel or imposing travel regulations to limit the virus spread, the decline was even steeper for the international flights than the domestic ones. After an initial response with a large number of flight cancellations, by the start of summer 2020, airlines were determined to return to the point of schedule stability and predictability, reflecting the industry's optimism that the pandemic would be quickly under control and the demand for air travel would rebound (Grant, 2020). In June 2020, the International Air Transport Association (IATA) estimated losses to reach $84 billion globally (IATA, 2020d, June 9), a far cry from the $372 billion lost by the end of that year. Since then, there have been three different waves of infection fueled by different variants and this global resurgence of the virus and the related shutdowns halted the air travel recovery. Losses from passenger operations were only slightly less in 2021 compared to the preceding year. The latest wave of the highly infective variant Omicron also led to a severe shortage of personnel, forcing carriers to cancel thousands of flights globally.

The uncertainty created by rapidly changing travel restrictions and the concomitant cancellation of flights resulted in deeply shaken consumer confidence. As a result, booking windows decreased globally to less than 30 days (Skyscanner, 2020), and most carriers changed their cancellation and booking modification policies in 2020. While some airlines were obliged to refund tickets for cancelled flights, as is the case under European and UK consumer law, others provided credit only to be used on bookings within one or two years, depending on the carrier. In an effort to boost consumer confidence to book travel further in advance as airlines look beyond the Omicron variant wave into the summer of 2022, some airlines have implemented policies that waive change or cancellation fees, extending ticket validity even further or offering Covid-19 insurance (WTTC & Trip.com Group, 2021).

Health Credentials for Testing and Vaccination

In May 2020, IATA released its biosecurity recommendations (IATA, 2020a) that would allow for air travel to resume while at the same time ensuring that it would not be a vector for the spread of the coronavirus. Although these recommendations addressed changes to be made through the air travel journey – pre-flight; at the departure airport; onboard and post-flight – it recognised that collaboration would be vital among governments 'to implement internationally consistent, mutually accepted measures are essential to restoring air connectivity and passenger confidence in air travel' (2020: 2). It called for contact tracing, temperature screening, physical distancing and the use of face coverings but recognised that while ideal, reliable testing with fast results was not yet a reality. IATA also advocated for touchless and contact-free procedures such as check-in and boarding, baggage handling and security screenings. Although numerous international organisations collaborated on these measures, including the United Nations, the World Health Organization (WHO), the International Civil Aviation Organization (ICAO), IATA, the World Tourism Organization (UNWTO), the World Travel and Tourism Council (WTTC) and the Airports Council International (ACI), they have been unable to convince governments to implement risk-based travel measures that are coordinated across countries.

ICAO's Aviation Recovery Task Force (CART) was established in March 2020 'to provide practical, aligned guidance to world governments and aviation industry operators in order to restart the international air transport sector and recover from COVID-19 on a coordinated, global basis' (ICAO, 2020: §1) in partnership with its Member States, international and regional organisations, and industry, has worked diligently towards managing safety-, security- and health-related risks and ensuring that public health measures work with aviation safety and security systems. In spite of this work, the spread of new and more aggressive variants of the virus in 2020 and 2021 prompted governments to reintroduce strict lockdowns, border closures as well as travel restrictions. This patchwork of measures virtually stalled the recovery of the airline sector. To overcome the haphazard implementation of border risk management, including quarantining, and formalising vaccine approaches, ICAO released a Declaration at the conclusion of its High-level Conference on Covid-19 in October 2021, aspirationally entitled 'One Vision for Aviation Recovery, Resilience and Sustainability beyond the Global Pandemic' (ICAO, 2021). The call to action is for a multilayer risk management strategy for international civil aviation, one that is adaptable, proportionate, non-discriminatory and guided by scientific evidence. However, participating Ministers affirmed that while highly desirable, vaccination would not be a precondition to travel, essentially putting an end to talk about a globally accepted 'vaccine passport'. Numerous countries adopted versions of such a passport or certificate – usually accessed via a mobile phone app or as a paper version – in the summer of 2021 once vaccines had become available and were widely distributed, especially in the wealthier countries around the world. The hope had been that such proof would eliminate the need for testing or quarantining when crossing a border. However, the highly transmissible Omicron variant thwarted that notion as countries banned arrivals from several African countries, contradicting the spirit of solidarity and equality that underpinned the Declaration.

Recent research by Oxera and Edge Health (2022) concluded that travel restrictions do little to control the spread of SARS-CoV-2 and its variants when they are already broadly present in the local population. Only when implemented at a very early stage can they delay the peak of a new wave by a few days and marginally reduce the number of cases.

Hence, it may well be time to remove all travel testing and quarantine requirements, especially in markets with high vaccination and booster dose rates, including children.

Coping Strategies Adopted by Airlines

Faced with a prolonged situation that has no precedent in the history of aviation, carriers needed to quickly adopt a wide range of strategies tailored to their market niche, including dramatic changes in passenger volume and composition, requirements imposed by international agreements and collaboration, country-specific regulations and local practices, and conditions imposed by governments in exchange for aid.

Strategic use of cancellations and refunds

The sharp rise in last-minute cancellations rolled across regions of the globe following the spread of the SARS-CoV-2. Flights to and within China were the first to be hit in late 2019 and early 2020. International airlines stopped operating flights into and out of China in February 2020. This was followed with capacity reductions across the Asia–Pacific region and Europe where 18 airlines had suspended all of their passenger services by the end of March. Of the European carriers that remained operational, up to 99% capacity reductions compared with equivalent weeks in 2019 and mass aircraft groundings were recorded (Budd *et al.*, 2020; Eurocontrol, 2020). Even more worrisome, by the end of May 2020, a large majority of European-registered airlines had suspended operations (Budd *et al.*, 2020). Although the US had declared a public health emergency on 31 January 2020 (Cohen *et al.*, 2020), incoming flights from Europe (Schengen Area) were not suspended until 14 March (NYTimes, 2020, 11 March), and the border between the US and Canada was closed on 18 March (Oliver *et al.*, 2020, 18 March). By the end of 2020, at least 40 airlines had gone under (Kimani, 2021).

The sudden drop in demand and revenue-stifling crisis forced airlines to minimise cash burn. Refunding the cost of cancelled flights, whether at the instigation of passengers or the airline itself, became a major headache for carriers trying to preserve cash. Forced to cut capacity on a scale that had never been seen before, airline operators grounded aircraft, rationalised their network by withdrawing operations from certain airports and cut routes (Vinod, 2020). Nevertheless, unless forced to refund tickets due to consumer protection laws, as was the case in Europe and the UK, airlines often opted for vouchers and credits for future flights instead of full refunds. Although airlines in the US received over $25 billion in government aid early in the pandemic to support operating expenses (Horton, 2020) and the US Department of Transportation clarified that both US and foreign airlines are obligated 'to provide a prompt refund to passengers for flights to, within, or from the United States when the carrier cancels the passenger's scheduled flight or makes a significant schedule change and the passenger chooses not to accept the alternative offered by the carrier' (US Department of Transportation, 2020: §1) even when the flight disruptions are outside of the carrier's control, airlines made it very difficult to for passengers to receive refunds, especially if the flight was cancelled at the passenger's request and due to Covid restrictions.

British Airways opted for a somewhat different strategy to preserve liquidity: they did not change their schedule and cancelled flights as late as possible. This allowed them to boost their cash position but risked exacerbating consumer confidence in the longer-term (Rowland, 2020).

Over time, airlines in countries with vast domestic markets such as China, the US, Brazil, Japan, Russia and India were able to stabilise their schedules and grow back the number of passengers carried. This was mainly due to vaccination rates above 70% and no or limited domestic travel restrictions (Cirium, 2021). Indeed, between March and July 2021, China's air capacity exceeded its 2019 performance by about 10% (OAG, 2021, 17 December), almost exclusively due to its domestic market since international borders remained closed. Domestic traffic in Russia has already surpassed 2019, and predictions are that domestic traffic in North America, Europe and Latin America will end 2022 at 2019 levels (Cirium, 2021, OAG, 2021, 17 December). With the start of the winter holiday season in Europe and North America, predictions had been for solid growth in both domestic and international passenger numbers. Instead, the arrival of the Omicron variant led to another round of large numbers of last-minute cancellations.

Reconfiguring fleets and cabins

Pre-Covid-19, an average of 2000 aircraft were in storage. By April 2020, more than 16,000 planes were grounded worldwide, representing 62% of the world's total (Cirium, 2021). This represented not only a very significant strain on airline finances, but also represented a major problem as space on the ground at airports is limited, and longer-term storage requires arid places and constant maintenance 'that includes running engines and powering up aircraft, checking flight controls, and covering sensors and engines to protect inner workings from sand and dust' (Kotoky *et al.*, 2020: §6). By late 2021, 5000 aircraft remained in storage, but Cirium (2021) forecast that most of the single-aisle surplus fleet will have returned to service by the end of 2022, with 2023 seeing the twin-aisle follow suit.

One bright spot for the aviation industry was the boom in e-commerce that fueled a continued growth in air cargo (Cirium, 2021). As a result, several passenger planes – especially wide-bodied ones whose value has fallen precipitously because of the massive grounding of planes – were converted to freighters. Another strategy implemented by airlines was to re-think or accelerate the reconfiguration of their fleet. Carriers either retired older generation planes such as the A320ceos or current engine option, down 22% since early 2020 and wide-bodied planes such as the B777, also down 22%, to improve fuel efficiency as well as reduce the maintenance and training costs by focusing on fewer aircraft types and reducing first and business class seats. Aircraft leasing came into its own after the financial crisis of 2008–2009 and has seen rapid growth since then (Bjelicic, 2012). The pandemic has accelerated the growth of the leased fleet, and the lessor market share now accounts for about 50%, with estimates that it could well reach 60% in the near future (KPMG in Ireland, 2022). Lessors' support of the aviation industry has been critical throughout the pandemic period, by 'providing aircraft from their order-books, enabling airlines to defer their own orders to free, as well as combinations of sale-leasebacks and renegotiated leases to assist airline cashflow' (KPMG in Ireland, 2022: §3).

Business travel expenses peaked at $1.29 trillion in 2019, dropping by 53.8% in 2020 (Statista, 2022, with North America the hardest-hit region, followed by Western Europe (GBTA, 2021). Historically, full-service airlines in particular have been very dependent structurally on the revenue earned from business travellers. Most carriers derive profits from a small group of high-yielding passengers on long-haul flights. 'While these travellers made up on average 12% of an airlines' passenger count, they would normally be twice as profitable. For some flights, business passengers accounted for 75% of an airline's profits' (Skyscanner, 2020: 11). These high-yield passengers travel in first and business class, but also book economy-class seats close to departure when prices tend to be highest (Bouwer et al., 2021). Since remote work and other flexible working arrangements, as well as travel restrictions, have been implemented by businesses to curb the spread of SARS-CoV-2, the drop off in business travel expenses alone saved a company like Amazon close to $1 billion in the first six months of the pandemic (Palmer, 2020, 29 October).

Leisure trips have always rebounded first after past crises, with business trips taking on average four years to reach pre-crisis levels. The extent to which business travel will recover post-Covid-19 is much contested. While the Global Business Travel Association (GBTA) forecasts a full recovery of global business travel by 2024 (GBTA, 2021), others are less optimistic. Reed (2021, 14 September) suggested that the Delta variant undermined the business travel recovery in the summer and fall of 2020, and the Omicron variant is having a similar impact on the winter season of 2022. Citing the American Hotel & Lodging Association's survey of corporations and individual business travellers around the US undertaken in August 2021, he states that over two-thirds of respondents expect to take fewer trips going forward. This reduction in business-class demand is forcing some airlines to reconfigure the layout of their cabins, shifting to better cater to premium-leisure passengers (Bouwer *et al.*, 2021; Skift, 2021, 18 October). Skyscanner (2020) goes even further in their predictions:

> We can see a premium economy 'plus' option giving travellers who are willing to pay more an experience between business class and premium economy. It might recall the glamourous air travel days of old, with a cocktail bar, more gourmet dining options and additional space that's traditionally associated with business class. (2020: 12)

This trend is in part driven by the growth of bleisure travel – where a leisure component is added to a predominantly work-related trip – that allows for much of the trip cost to be charged to the business.

Preserving Airport Slots and Routes

According to IATA (2021b, 15 December), the airport slot system has been the backbone of building global air connectivity. Prior to the pandemic, this system served 4.5 billion passengers across a route network that over 20 years had doubled while fares had halved in price. A slot is an authorisation to either take-off or land at a particular airport on a particular day during a specified time period. All airports worldwide are categorised into three levels based on their capacity constraints. In 2019, 1.5 billion passengers – 43% of global traffic – departed from over 200 slot coordinated airports. This number is expected to increase substantially due to a lack of expansion in airport infrastructure to cope with increasing demand post-pandemic (IATA, 2019). The slot real estate is therefore extremely valuable, especially for highly competitive long-haul routes at the most congested airports. If an airline does not use an allocation of slots (typically 80% usage over six months), it can lose the rights to them.

> While airport slot rules were suspended fairly quickly for affected flights to and from mainland China and Hong Kong following the viral outbreak, in many other regions the rules remained in force through February and early March, leading to the rise of 'ghost flights' – empty or nearly empty flights that continued to operate simply to ensure that the corresponding airport slot is used. (Lo, 2020)

By mid-to-late March 2020, most aviation regulators worldwide had introduced waivers for airport slot allocation systems, allowing airlines to cancel unnecessary flights to cover the summer season.

While the American Federal Aviation Administration waived its slot requirements through March 2022 for international flights, the European Union (EU) set them at 50% until March 2022 increasing to 64% thereafter for the summer season. Stein (2022) cites Lufthansa anticipating flying 18,000 'poorly booked' flights to secure its slots. Both the pollution caused by these 'ghost flights' and the financial losses for airlines have generated much criticism. However, EU officials say 'they need to strike a balance between protecting consumers and boosting a hampered airline industry' (Stein, 2022, §7).

Rationalising networks by withdrawing operations from certain airports and cutting routes was another immediate response by those airlines that continued operating after March 2020. However, few carriers saw the closure of bases or a reduction in the geographic scope of their network as a permanent solution post-Covid, preferring reductions in their flying schedules to improve load factors. A gradual and phased return, starting with domestic and intra-continental services plus a limited number of flights to strategically important long-haul destinations, is the preferred approach (Budd *et al.*, 2020). Only low-cost carriers such as Ryanair in Europe (Budd *et al.*, 2020) and Southwest Airlines in the US (Cirium, 2021) had any intention to significant expand their route network, hoping to capitalise on a growing leisure market. The deregulation and liberalisation of worldwide air transport markets have made airline route networks increasingly dynamic structures that frequently show discontinuous changes. While airlines added many flights over the past few years between hubs and smaller cities (Bouwer *et al.*, 2021) to cater to business demand, they are also able to reconfigure their network offer by dropping cities as Delta and United Airlines did in late 2021(Kiersz *et al.*, 2021).

Government Support

While most airlines have struggled with the impact of the pandemic, there have been relatively few outright failures, although numerous carriers find themselves in some sort of bankruptcy protection. Some high-profile cases include Avianca, LATAM, SAA, Thai Airways and Virgin Atlantic (OAG, 2001, 17 March). Some mergers have also occurred, such as Cathay Dragon being absorbed by Cathay Pacific and Korean Air acquiring Asiana (OAG, 2001, 17 March). However, airlines have also been quite successful in raising liquidity, in part due to the low cost of borrowing but also by accessing significant government aid.

As of September 2021, airlines around the world had received almost $38 billion in direct aid from the government to avoid bankruptcy (Mazareanu, 2022). Nevertheless, they also received an additional $205 billion in various other aids. The nature of the financial intervention varied from renationalisation (e.g. Alitalia), to equity investment in airlines (France, Germany, the Netherlands, Canada), to loans and guarantees, to wage subsidies and cost reductions (e.g. tax reductions on fuel and tickets, fee reductions) (Budd *et al.*, 2020; Mazareanu, 2022; OECD, 2021).

The US Congress approved $54 billion in three rounds, covering much of US airline payroll costs for 18 months. Out of $54 billion, airlines must repay $14 billion, or 26.2%. Treasury also extended $25 billion in low-cost government loans to carriers (Shepardson, 2021). Although airlines that accepted government assistance to funded payroll costs through 30 September were prohibited from furloughs or firing workers and faced limits on executive compensation and bans on stock buybacks and dividends, by the end of 2020, it was estimated that airline jobs would fall by about 90,000 full-time equivalent positions (Josephs, 2020) through furloughs, buyouts and retirements. Globally, it was estimated that 400,000 jobs would be lost, with the most significant losses occurring in North America and Europe (Kotoky *et al.*, 2020).

Canada was the only G7 country to steer clear of a sector-specific bailout for the aviation industry, preferring to negotiate with each airline separately. Unlike most other countries that provided aid to hard-hit airlines, Canada chose not to do so until early 2021. The biggest deal was with Air Canada. Relief granted was $4.7 billion in loans plus a 6% equity stake in exchange for pledges to restore regional routes, ban share buybacks and dividends, cap executive compensation at $1 million and maintain current job levels. That job level was at just under 15,000, while the carrier had already shed 20,000 or over half of its workforce. Crucially, it also compelled Air Canada to refund customers whose flights were cancelled due to Covid-19. (Reuters *et al.*, 2021; Reynolds, 2021).

A different approach was taken by the governments providing the two largest airline packages in Europe, Germany for Lufthansa and the governments of France and the Netherlands for Air France/KLM. Conditions required the aid recipients to take steps towards 'greening' their operations in the future (OECD, 2021) and committing to significant decarbonisation initiatives. (Dunn, 2020). Details are discussed below.

Addressing Climate Change

While the SARS-CoV-2 pandemic has undoubtedly hit the airline industry extremely hard, the amount of government aid provided and the speed with which many governments responded to the industry requests for assistance has ensured that there were surprisingly few bankruptcies. The more or less high vaccination rates in key markets in North America, Europe, Asia and the Middle East also contribute to a return to profitability, although 2019 levels of passengers transported are not expected to be reached until 2024 or 2025, depending on the mutations of the coronavirus. However, climate change and the need to decarbonise has presented a more long-standing challenge to the airline industry and will continue to do so as the volume of flights increases once again.

While CO_2 emissions of domestic flights fall under the purview of the United Nations Framework Convention on Climate Change and are covered by the 2015 Paris Agreement, emissions of international flights are addressed by ICAO. Although much technological progress has been made over the years, with a flight today producing only half the CO_2 it did in 1990 (Air Transport Action Group, n.d.), the growth of the number of flights and Revenue Passenger Kilometers (RPK) has increased far more rapidly, outstripping any efficiency improvements made. In 2016, in partnership with industry, ICAO adopted a historic global market-based measure for aviation emissions called the Carbon Offsetting and Reduction Scheme for International Aviation (CORSIA). Under this scheme, airlines and other aircraft operators offset any growth in CO_2 emissions above 2020 levels. This means that aviation's net CO_2 emissions will be stabilised, while other emissions reduction measures, such as technology, sustainable aviation fuel (SAF), operations and infrastructure options, are pursued. At their Annual General Meeting in 2021, IATA went a step further when member airlines committed to achieving net-zero carbon emissions from their operations by 2050.

The pandemic provided an opportunity for many airlines to restructure their fleet and bring more efficient aircraft into service, expecting their fleets to deliver average per-seat efficiency gains of several percentage points compared with pre-pandemic levels (Cirium, 2021). A few countries, most notably France and the Netherlands, also attached environmental conditions to their aid. For instance, Air France must set the goal of becoming the most environmentally friendly carrier in the world by cutting its carbon emissions by half per passenger and per kilometre by 2030, from 2005 levels; deriving 2% of the fuel used by its planes from alternative, sustainable sources by 2025; directing investments in the coming years to renewing the fleet to more effectively fight emissions; and ending short-haul internal flights where train alternatives exist (Anonymous, 2021; Cirium, 2020). Although Germany's conditions were formulated rather generally, Lufthansa has now committed to halving its carbon emissions from 2019 levels by 2030, in part by buying newer, more efficient planes, purchasing about 1% of its fuel consumption in SAF, and utilising offsets (Wilkes, 2021). The carrier is also considering a new rewards plan that would tap into customers' desire to be seen as environmentally conscious. Travellers would pay not just for offsetting their flight but to visually demonstrate their support for alternative jet fuels or carbon-offset purchases, perhaps by creating digital badges that can be shown on a phone. IATA has been estimated that it will cost about $2 trillion to reach carbon neutrality by 2050, and airlines face the challenge of shifting some of this cost onto passengers (Philip & Schlangenstein, 2021).

To achieve IATA's 'Fly Net Zero' 2050 targets set, the industry will increasingly look at understanding the actual fuel burn of flights, and to SAF and offsets (Cirium, 2021). However, Becken (2019: 419) believes that 'only systemic changes at a large scale will be sufficient to break or disrupt existing arrangements and routines'. She blames tourism's embeddedness in the prevailing growth paradigm and the institutionalisation of interests, among other reasons. The lack of political will to be serious about climate action can be seen in the fact that so few governments attached any environmental conditions to the aid they provided their aviation industry or continue to exonerate aviation fuel from taxes.

Technology will also help consumers distinguish between flights based on their CO_2 emissions. For example, Skyscanner's 'Greener choice' feature highlights flights that emit less CO_2 than average for a particular route and found that in 2019, 10 million travellers using Skyscanner selected a 'Greener choice' option (Skyscanner, 2020).

Conclusion

In October 2021, at ICAO's High-level Conference on Covid-19, a new ministerial Declaration was adopted in the presence of over 50 Ministers and Deputy Ministers that 'recognizes the severity of the COVID-19 crisis for civil aviation, and its cascading impacts on global supply chains and the many national economies which rely so significantly on international flights for tourism and trade' (ICAO, 2021: §3).

Considering the staggering debt levels, airlines have had to assume to cope with high daily cash burn rates, recouping these costs will undoubtedly lead to higher ticket prices over time. As we have seen, carriers adopted a variety of strategies to address the rapid drop in demand, cancellation of flights and volatility of schedules. However, they also tapped into 'state-provided aid, credit lines, and bond issuances, [amassing] more than $180 billion worth of debt in 2020, a figure equivalent to more than half of total annual revenues that year' (Bouwer *et al.*, 2021: 3–4). Bouwer *et al.* (2021) also note:

> a glut of latent demand of people eager to travel. It will take time for airlines to restore capacity, and bottlenecks such as delays in bringing aircraft back to service and crew retraining could lead to a supply–demand gap, resulting in higher short-term prices. (2021: 4)

By taking or increasing equity positions in carriers, the government will also play a more prominent role in the sector, at least near- to medium-term. Those airlines that were proactive in restructuring for greater efficiency, such as by reconfiguring their fleet, their route network and their cabins, will find themselves in a good position to face the many headwinds they will be facing. Those that resisted cost, organisational or operational restructuring may yet see failure in their future.

> With airline balance sheets expected to remain under strain for the next year or two, and with airlines under pressure to operate more fuel-efficient fleets, the expectation is for leasing to continue to gain market share as leasing provides much needed flexibility and capital in an uncertain market. (KPMG in Ireland, 2022; §12)

The liquidity issue and passenger claims caused by the severe reduction in flights and ongoing volatility as SARS-CoV-2 variants of concern make their appearance are aggravated by other factors not within complete control of carriers, such as fuel prices and staffing shortages. Airlines hedge fuel costs, that is, agree to purchase a certain amount of oil in the future at a predetermined price to protect themselves against market fluctuations. The pandemic caused a sudden and massive oil price slump, but since many carriers had locked in oil prices at far higher fuel prices, they had to take billions of dollars in charges mainly due to overhedging (Kimani, 2021). With major economies returning to growth, oil prices are spiking again, increasing oil procurement costs for airlines. Many of the airlines that had used hedging strategies gave these up after the heavy losses suffered when crude prices plummeted, leaving them more exposed to the subsequent sharp rise in prices. 'Airlines would typically try to pass rising costs on to passengers by raising ticket prices, but the industry is still operating in a highly uncertain environment, with passenger numbers well below normal levels' (Georgiadis, 2021: §6). In addition, SAF use targets will contribute to ticket price increases. According to IATA (2020b), SAF is currently on average between 2 and 4 times more expensive than fossil fuels.

The layoffs and furloughs employed by airlines at the onset of the pandemic to control cash burn led to crew shortages in the summer of 2021, when air travel demand began picking up again. The persistence of flight cancellations into the fall and winter seasons of 2021 and 2022 has been mainly due to the emergence of the highly infectious Omicron variant and widespread sick calls. Although airlines are busily training for some positions, such as flight attendants, the training of pilots takes years. With furloughs, defections, an ageing pilot population in some countries like the US and the heavy use of early retirements, a pilot shortage will become a major headache for many carriers. According to Murray (2022), the global gap between supply and demand for pilots is estimated to be at least 34,000 by 2025, with shortages being most severe in North America, Asia Pacific and the Middle East.

The challenges presented by the Covid-19 pandemic are particularly difficult to whether by more traditional full-service carriers, but in some ways have conferred real opportunities to low-cost (LCC) and ultra-low-cost airlines (ULCC), an airline business model pioneered by Ryanair. More nimble and with aggressive growth strategies, these airlines have recovered well and in some instances are growing their network pairs and frequencies (Grant, 2022). There are even several newcomers in this category, such as Jetliner and Lynx Air in Canada, Avelo, Breeze Airways and Aha in the US and Play in Europe. We can only hope that no new variants of concern will emerge to yet again halt this industry's recovery.

References

Air Transport Action Group (n.d.) Corsia Explained, *Aviation Benefits Beyond Borders*. See https://aviationbenefits.org (accessed January 2022).

Anonymous (2021) France moves to ban short-haul domestic flights. *BBC*. See https://www.bbc.com/news/world-europe-56716708 (accessed April 2021).

Becken, S. (2019) Decarbonising tourism: Mission impossible? *Tourism Recreation Research* 44 (4), 419–433.

Bjelicic, B. (2012) Financing airlines in the wake of the financial markets crisis. *Journal of Air Transport Management* 21, 10–16.

Bouwer, J., Saxon, S. and Wittkamp, N. (2021) Back to the Future? Airline Sector Poised for Change Post-COVID-19. See https://www.mckinsey.com.

Budd, L., Ison, S. and Adrienne, N. (2020) European airline response to the COVID-19 pandemic – Contraction, consolidation and future considerations for airline business and management. *Research in Transportation Business & Management* 37, 100578.

Cirium (2020) French government sets green conditions for Air France bailout. *Flight Global*. See https://flightglobal.com (accessed April 2020).

Cirium (2021) *The Airlines Insights Review 2021*. See https://resources.cirium.com/cirium-airline-insights-review-2021 (accessed January 2022).

Cohen, E., Andone, D. and Tinker, B. (2020) U S government declares the novel coronavirus a public health emergency and suspends entry for foreign nationals who visited China. *CNN*. See https://www.cnn.com/2020/01/31/health/us-coronavirus-friday/index.html (accessed January 2020).

Dunn, K. (2020) Climate conditions on airline government bailouts are rare—and the coronavirus likely won't be an exception. *Fortune*. See https//fortune.com (accessed October 2022).

Eurocontrol (2020) *ANS Performance Dashboard*. See www.ansperformance.eu (accessed June 2020).

GBTA (2021) *From Setback to Surge: Business Travel Expected to Fully Recover by 2024*. See https://www.gbta.org/blog/from-setback-to-surge-business-travel-expected-to-fully-recover-by-2024/ (accessed January 2022).

Georgiadis, P. (2021) Fuel price increase threatens airlines' recovery from pandemic. *Financial Times*. See https://www.ft.com/content/cb53e204-362d-4dd1-b84d-9e697b92e692 (accessed February 2022).

Grant, J. (2020) The Fastest Week of Recovery as Airlines Prepare for Summer, OAG Coronavirus Update – Week 24. See www.oag.org (accessed June 2021).

Grant, J. (2022) Ryanair and EasyJet bring back significant capacity in Europe. See www.oag.org (accessed February 2022).

Horton, W. (2020, 15 April) How the U.S. is distributing airline bailout funds in Covid-19 relief deal. *Forbes*. See www.forbes.com (accessed June 2020).

IATA (2019) *Worldwide Airport Slot Guidelines*. See https://www.iata.org/en/policy/slots/slot-guidelines/ (accessed January 2022).

IATA (2020a) *Biosecurity for Air Transport: A Roadmap for Restarting Aviation, V. 2*. See www.iata.org (accessed January 2022).

IATA (2020b) IATA calls on governments to support industry move to SAF. *Press Release No: 100*. See https://www.iata.org/ (accessed February 2022).

IATA (2020c) Ready for takeoff. *Airlines*, 2. See https://www.airlines.iata.org/news/aviation-ready-for-takeoff (accessed June 2020).

IATA (2020d, June 9) Industry losses to top $84 billion in 2020. *Press Release No: 50*. See https://www.iata.org/ (accessed 9 June 2020).

IATA (2021a, 21 August) Airline industry statistics confirm 2020 was worst year on record. *Press Release No: 54*. See https://www.iata.org/ (accessed August 2021).

IATA (2021b, 15 December) Statement on the announcement of new EU slot use rules for summer 2022. *Pressrelease*. See https://www.iata.org/en/pressroom/2021-releases/2021-21-15-01/ (accessed January 2022).

ICAO (2020) Reconnecting the world. Aviation Recovery Task Force (CART). See https://www.icao.int/covid/cart/Pages/default.aspx (accessed January 2022).

ICAO (2021) Ministers adopt important commitments to help restore international travel and trade. See https://www.icao.int/ (accessed January 2022).

ICAO (2022) *Effects of Novel Coronavirus (COVID-19) on Civil Aviation: Economic Impact Analysis*. Economic Development – Air Transport Bureau, Montreal, Canada.

Josephs, L. (2020) U.S. airline employment to reach lowest levels in decades after pandemic cuts 90,000 jobs. *CNBC*. See www.cnbc.com (accessed January 2020).

Kiersz, A., Lichtenberg, N. and Rains, T. (2021) It used to be illegal for an airline to cancel routes the way Delta just took 3 cities off its flight list. *Business Insider*. See www.businessinsider.com (accessed January 2022).

Kimani, A. (2021) Airlines pull back from oil hedging after losing billions. See Oilprice.com (accessed February 2022).

Kotoky, A., Modi, M. and Turner, M. (2020) Jobs are being wiped out at airlines, and there's worse to come. *Bloomberg Quint*. See https://www.bloombergquint.com/business/400-000-jobs-lost-at-airlines-during-coronavirus-pandemic (accessed January 2022).

Kotoky, A., Stringer, D. and Saxena, R. (2020) Two-thirds of the world's passengers jets are grounded amid covid-19 pandemic. Here's what that means. *Bloomberg*. See https://time.com/5823395/grounded-planes-coronavirus-storage/ (accessed January 2022).

KPMG in Ireland (2022) *Aviation Industry Leaders Report 2022*. See https://home.kpmg/ie/en/home/ insights/2022/01/aviation-industry-leaders-report-2022/airline-leasing-proven-resilience.html (accessed January 2022).

Lo, C. (2020) Airport slot suspensions: Easing the pressure for ailing airlines amid Covid-19. *Airport Technology*. See https://www.airport-technology.com/features/covid-19-airport-slot-rules/ (accessed January 2022).

Mazareanu, E. (2022) Types of government aid to airlines due to Covid-19 as of September 2021. *Statista*. See www.statista.com (accessed January 2022).

Murray, G. (2022) After Covid-19, aviation faces a pilot shortage. *OliverWyman*. See https://www.oliverwyman.com (accessed February 2022).

NYTimes (2020, 11 March) U.S. to suspend most travel From Europe. See https://www.nytimes.com/2020/03/11/world/coronavirus-news.html (accessed March 2022).

OAG (2001, 17 March) *What Are Airlines Doing to be Ready for Recovery?* See www.oag.org (accessed March 2022).

OAG (2021, 17 December) *Aviation Turbulence: Reviewing 2021 and Taking Stock for 2022 and Beyond*. See www.oag.org (accessed December 2021).

OECD (2021) *State Support to the Air Transport Sector: Monitoring Developments Related to the Covid-19 Crisis*. Paris: OECD.

Oliver, D., Ellis, N.T. and Tate, C. (2020, 18 March) US-Canada border to close Saturday: What it means for travelers. *USA Today*. See https://www.usatoday.com/story/travel/news/2020/03/18/coronavirus-united-states-canada-border-shut-down-trump-says/2863086001/ (accessed March 2022).

Oxera and Edge Health (2022) *Impact of Travel Restrictions on Omicron in Italy and Finland*. Brussels, Belgium and Montréal, Canada: ACI Europe and IATA.

Palmer, A. (2020, 29 October) Amazon says the coronavirus pandemic saved it $1 billion in travel expenses. *CNBC*. See https://www.cnbc.com/2020/10/29/amazon-saved-1-billion-in-travel-expenses-due-to-the-pandemic.html (accessed November 2020).

Philip, S. and Schlangenstein, M. (2021) Airline industry targets net-zero carbon emissions by 2020. *BNN Bloomberg*. See http://www.bnnbloomberg.ca/airline-industry-targets-net-zero-carbon-emissions-by-2050-1.1661409 (accessed January 2022).

Reed, D. (2021, 14 September) All those business travel chickens that airlines were counting? They aren't hatching, undercutting forecasts. *Forbes*. See www.forbes.com (accessed January 2022).

Reuters, Ljunggren, D. and Lampert, A. (2021) Air Canada signs C\$5.9 bln government aid package, agrees to buy Airbus, Boeing jets. *Reuters*. See www.reuters.com (accessed January 2022).

Reynolds, C. (2021) WestJet CEO Ed Sims finds Air Canada aid package 'bittersweet' as talks drag on. *CP24*. See www.cp24.com (accessed January 2022).

Rowland, B. (2020, 28 July) *The Strategic Use of Cancellations: How Airlines Managed Schedules During Covid*. See www.oag.org (accessed July 2020).

Shepardson, D. (2021) U.S. airlines to defend \$54 billion COVID-19 government lifeline. *Reuters*. See www.reuters.com (accessed January 2022).

Skift (2021, 18 October) Is premium leisure the next big thing? *Airline Weekly, 835*, See https://airlineweekly.com/issues/2021/10/is-premium-leisure-the-next-big-thing/ (accessed January 2022).

Skyscanner (2020) *New World of Travel Report*. See www.partners.skyscanner.net/insights/new-world-of-travel (accessed September 2020).

Statista (2022) Percentage change in expenditure of business tourists worldwide from 2001 to 2022, with forecast until 2026. See https://www-statista-com.subzero.lib.uoguelph.ca/statistics/324786/global-business-travel-spending-growth-forecast/ (accessed October 2022).

Stein, P. (2022) Airlines in Europe say they are flying near-empty planes as omicron derails travel. They say E.U. rules mean they can't stop. *The Washington Post*. See https://www.washingtonpost.com/world/2022/01/22/omicron-airlines-europe/ (accessed January 2022).

US Department of Transportation (2020) *U.S. Department of Transportation Issues Enforcement Notice Clarifying Air Carrier Refund Requirements, Given the Impact of COVID-19*. See https://www.transportation.gov/briefing-room/us-department-transportation-issues-enforcement-notice-clarifying-air-carrier-refund (accessed January 2022).

Vinod, B. (2020) The COVID-19 pandemic and airline cash flow. *Journal of Revenue and Pricing Management* 19 (4), 228–229.

Wenzel, M., Stanske S. and Lieberman M.B. (2020) Strategic responses to crises. *Strategic Management Journal* 41 (7/18), 231–232.

Wilkes, W. (2021) Lufthansa to charge customers to flaunt green credentials. *Bloomberg*. See https://www.bloomberg.com/news/articles/2021-11-13/lufthansa-to-charge-customers-to-flaunt-their-green-credentials (accessed January 2022).

WTTC and Trip.com Group (2021) *Trending in Travel: Emerging Consumer Trends in Travel & Tourism in 2021 and beyond*. See https://pages.trip.com/images/group-home/2021_Trending_in_Travel_EN.pdf (accessed January 2022).

3 The Impacts of the Covid-19 Pandemic on Tour Operators' Business in Iran: The Role of Organisational Learning and Resiliency

Zahed Ghaderi, Zahra Behboodi,
Faraz Sadeghvaziri and Ian Patterson

Introduction

Today, the significance of the economic impact of tourism on destinations and individual organisations is evident, and tourism can be considered an economic driving force for many countries/destinations. However, small- and large-scale crises in the tourism industry often led to the loss of business, either temporarily or permanently, creating serious challenges for the public and private sectors (Ghaderi *et al.*, 2021; Paraskevas & Quek, 2019); and raising the issue of their capability to manage crises, and making them better prepared for future events. Tour operators are one of the most critical intermediaries among the tourism businesses, which are fragile to external shocks due to their activities (because they mainly rely on international collaboration and communications). Experience has shown that the impact of domestic and international crises on this type of tourism activity is considerable and often causes irreparable damage (Ritchie & Jiang, 2019). Therefore, to survive and continue the business, it is necessary for successful tour operators to be resilient, practise organisational learning and apply coping strategies in their businesses.

The Covid-19 pandemic is considered the most potent crisis of the century (UNWTO, 2020) and has profoundly affected all tourism activities and stakeholders, including travel and tourism companies. According to the Iranian Ministry of Culture, Tourism and Handicrafts, more than half of Iran's tour operators have been completely locked down or have had their activities suspended due to the closure of borders to all source markets (Ministry of Culture, Tourism and Handicrafts, 2021). This meant that the crisis had added a significant number to the country's unemployment market. Much research has been undertaken in the past to examine the effects of various crises on the tourism and hospitality industry (Filimonau & De Coteau, 2020; Israeli *et al.*, 2011) and how the Covid-19 pandemic has affected the economics and reduction in the number of tourists arrivals (Bakar & Rosbi, 2020; Gössling *et al.*, 2020; Hoque *et al.*, 2020). Nevertheless, only limited research has been conducted specifically on tour operators, how they manage different crises and the impact of various crises on the activity of tour operators (Ritchie & Jiang, 2019).

Tour operators play a significant role in distributing trips and the tourism benefits across tourist destinations (Do *et al.*, 2021), and any disruption in their business affects the entire tourism industry. Nonetheless, considering the vital role of these travel intermediaries, minimal information is available about how the Covid-19 crisis has affected these companies. How resilient are they to the crisis, and what lessons have they learned in the past from managing other previous crises? A literature review shows a significant gap in the research that examines the impact of the Covid-19 crisis on this business sector. Therefore, this chapter seeks to fill this research gap and provide insightful managerial implications for tourism industry stakeholders. As the practice of individual stakeholders in managing the Covid-19 crisis is vital in realising the actions, impacts and resilience to the pandemic, this chapter can shed light on the practice of tour operators as one of the most affected tourism sectors.

Literature Review

Corporate crisis management

A literature review indicates that crisis management in tourism is still a relatively new field of academic research. For the business world in general, crisis management is 'the art of eliminating much of the risk and uncertainty to allow you to have more control over your own destiny' (Fink, 1986: 15). Managers need to envisage the evolution of a crisis as a series of steps covering signal action, prevention, preparation, containment, damage limitation and recovery (Pauchant & Mitroff, 1992). According to Spillan and Hough (2003), crisis management requires minimising the impact of an unexpected event on an organisation's life (Anderson, 2006). Since crises are events that threaten organisational compatibility (Pearson & Mitroff, 1993), immediate management decisions must always be made, which most often are not part of the organisation's standard practice. Pearson and Mitroff (1993) noted that crisis management aims not to produce a set of programmes but to prepare the organisation to think creatively about the unthinkable so that the best possible decisions can be made in times of crisis. While there has been an increasing research stream on tourism and hospitality crisis management in recent years, it has mainly focused on the destinations' crisis management, impact assessment and recovery strategies (Ritchie & Jiang, 2019).

Surprisingly, limited attention has been paid to corporate crisis management, particularly tour operators susceptible to external uncertainties. For instance, Ritchie and Jiang (2019) and Ghaderi *et al.* (2014) noted that future research should consider crisis planning and practice for travel agents and tour operator companies in different localities to help them understand their crisis management intentions. Furthermore, current research on the Covid-19 pandemic impacts on the tourism sector has primarily ignored tour operators as one of the most affected sectors of the pandemic (Do *et al.*, 2021). This chapter sheds light on this issue within the context of Iran.

Organisational resilience to crises

The term resilience was first coined in the field of ecology by Holling, who defined *resilience* as the ability of a system to maintain its identity and adapt its basic structure and function in the face of turbulence (Holling, 1973). The concept has received significant attention in various disciplines, including psychology, management and tourism (Prayag *et al.*, 2020). For example, Meyer (1982) was the first scholar who used the term resilience in the management literature, and his research reveals how organisations respond to external threats. The second stream of research emerged in the 1980s and 1990s following large-scale disasters such as Chernobyl, Exxon Valdez and the Challenger Space Shuttle, focusing on the resilience of organisations to unexpected disasters (Linnenluecke, 2017). In line with these investigations, Dalziell and McManus (2004) applied the term to the business world and described it as the overall goal of a system to continue its activities and tasks in the face of disruptive conditions and changes to achieve its functions. In this case, resilience is considered a function of the system's vulnerability and capacity to adapt to new conditions. The vulnerability of a system is measured by the ease and speed that organisational members move from a fixed to an unstable condition, while the degree to which the company copes with this change is referred to as the capacity for adaptation (Dalziell & McManus, 2004). Erol *et al.* (2010) also defined *business resilience* as the ability of a business to reduce its degree of vulnerability to predictable and unpredictable threats, its ability to change and adapt to a turbulent environment and its rapid recovery from this change (Erol *et al.*, 2010).

Organisational resilience has been a growing research interest among tourism scholars. In the past decade, several research studies have been conducted on the resilience of tourism and hospitality organisations to different disasters and crises (see Butler, 2017; Cheer & Lew, 2017; Fountain

& Cradock-Henry, 2020; Hallak *et al.*, 2018; Jiang *et al.*, 2019; Orchiston *et al.*, 2016; Prayag *et al.*, 2020). For example, Orchiston *et al.* (2016) identified the dimensions of resilience for tourism organisations in a post-disaster context in New Zealand. They found that organisational planning, culture, collaboration and innovation are key attributes of resilience (Chowdhury *et al.*, 2019). In another study, Jiang *et al.* (2019) highlighted the significance of resilience for travel and tourism organisations facing various crises. They proposed a dynamic capabilities model which provides a mechanism that allows tourism organisations to respond to disruptive changes '…through a process of routine transformation, resource allocation, and utilisation' (Jiang *et al.*, 2019: 882). Hall *et al.* (2018) noted that achieving organisational resilience is essential when a sudden crisis/disaster occurs to sustain the growth of these tourism organisations.

Moreover, in other studies, Butler (2017) and Cheer and Lew (2017) have discussed the concept of reliance and its application to the sustainable development of tourism. Resilience from crises and disasters is the subject of several collections that make timely contributions to understanding this concept within the tourism and hospitality context. Nevertheless, the organisational resilience of tour operators to crises and disasters was not the focus of those studies in the literature. Thus, a knowledge gap still exists about the extent to which tour operators are resilient to the impacts of the Covid-19 pandemic and what resilient strategies they have applied to sustain their businesses.

Organisational learning among tour operators

The phrase 'organisational learning' was first used in 1963 by Cyert and March (1963) during their initial research on the behavioural aspects of organisational decision making. Although organisational learning is a relatively well-established concept, it received little attention until the late 1970s (Argyris & Schön, 1997). Between the 1970s and 1990s, it received significant attention from academics and practitioners because of increasing pressure from external events and organisation change (e.g. Ali *et al.*, 2020; Lemmetyinen & Go, 2009). Thus, a scattered but constant flow of research emerged in the late 1970s in the extant literature. Since this time, substantial studies have helped to strengthen its foundation, creating increased interest in the topic of organisational learning (Easterby-Smith & Araujo, 1999; Ghaderi *et al.*, 2014).

Different definitions have been proposed for the concept of organisational learning. However, Argyris and Schön's (1978) definition is regarded as one of the oldest ones in which organisational learning is understood to be 'the process by which organisational members detect errors or anomalies and correct them by restructuring organisational "theory-in-use"' (1978: 313). They believed that organisations learn like individuals, detect their errors and correct them by constant learning efforts. They further argued that organisations fail to learn unless they can revise their theories of action (Argyris & Schon, 1978). Similarly, Huber (1991) noted that learning occurs in an organisation when the organisation's behaviour also changes over time. In this way, a learning organisation is ideal for purposefully establishing structures and strategies that promote organisational learning to the highest possible level. Most researchers believe that organisational learning should lead to changes in the performance and behaviour of members of the organisation concerned (Blackman & Ritchie, 2008; Ghaderi et al., 2014; Paraskevas et al., 2013), and organisational change is often seen as an advanced outcome of organisational learning (Huysman, 1999). Few studies have been conducted on organisational learning in tourism crisis management (Ghaderi & Paraskevas, 2021). Ample evidence shows that despite the significant role of learning and knowledge management in managing crises and disasters, tourism organisations are reluctant to apply learning practices, making them vulnerable to future crises (Blackman & Ritchie, 2008).

After analysing the literature, this suggests that travel and tourism organisations should apply knowledge management strategies and learn from their crisis management exercises for future crisis planning (Paraskevas et al., 2013). Surprisingly, few research studies have focused on the concept of organisational learning in tourism crisis management (Ghaderi et al., 2021), with scant research focusing on tour operators.

Methodology

Sample and data

The present study uses in-depth semi-structured interviews to analyse tour operator managers' perspectives and examine how the Covid-19 pandemic has affected their businesses, how they responded to the crisis by applying different recovery and resiliency strategies, and if they have learned any lessons for handling future crisis management. The population of the present study consisted of managers of inbound and outbound tour operator companies in Tehran, Iran. According to the Ministry of Culture, Tourism, and Handicrafts, there are about 3000 active and semi-active travel agents and tour operators in Tehran, but among them, only 200 companies are considered to be tour operators; the rest are travel retailers (MCTH, 2020). Applying a qualitative research design, the sample size for this study was determined by using the criterion of 'saturation', as defined by Patten (2007: 152) as, 'at the point at which several additional participants fail to respond with new information that leads to the identification of additional themes, the researcher might conclude that the data collection process has become saturated'.

In the present study, a snowball sampling technique was used to find the most knowledgeable and appropriate respondents who could produce reliable and in-depth information about the issue in question (Browne, 2005). The process began by interviewing the President of the Iranian Travel Agents and Tour Operators Association in Tehran. Then, the data collection process continued through a referral chain until the required information for this study was collected. A total of 18 senior managers and department heads were interviewed until the saturation point was reached, and no new information was raised by the respondents (Patten, 2007). The profile of respondents is presented in Table 3.1.

Interviews were conducted in multiple ways through face-to-face (seven), online (three) and by phone (eight). The original interviews were conducted in Persian and were then translated into English for analysis. The average duration of each interview was 60 to 80 minutes, depending on the depth of explanations provided by the interviewees. An interview guide was prepared based on the previous literature (Filimonau & De Coteau, 2020; Ghaderi *et al.*, 2014; Jiang *et al.*, 2019; Prayag *et al.*, 2020), and the questions focused on the effects of the pandemic on the business of tour operators, their resiliency to the crisis, their crisis management approach and the lessons they had learned from their crisis management practices.

Data analysis

All interviews were transcribed verbatim for analysis, and transcripts were then sent back to respondents for further review of the content, interpretation precision and accuracy. Any modifications made in the materials were considered primary data for the analysis, and the formerly recorded data were discarded. This process is called 'member checking', which adds both internal and external validity to the overall study (Guba & Lincoln, 1985). Thematic analysis and coding techniques derived from data were applied to identify and categorise the main themes across all the interview transcripts. Braun and Clarke (2006) stated that thematic analysis offers an accessible and theoretically flexible approach to analysing qualitative data. According to this method, transcribed materials are read several times by the researchers to become immersed in the depth and breadth of the content, and then the exciting features of the data (Braun & Clarke, 2006) were coded systematically across the entire data set. Extensive probing for potential themes was started, and then all data relevant to each potential theme were gathered. The result of the thematic analysis is presented in the following sections.

Results and Discussion

The effects of the Covid-19 pandemic on tour operators' business

In analysing the respondents' opinion on the topic 'Impacts of the Covid-19 crisis on the tour operators' business', several sub-themes were identified: (a) '*A tsunami of job redundancy among employees*', which led to the loss of

Table 3.1 Respondent profiles

Row	Code	Company name	Gender	Experience (Years)	Area of activity
1	A	Pardisan Gasht	Male	28	Inbound and outbound (Cultural and nature-based tours, historical, etc.)
2	B	Iran Sabt Tour	Male	24	Inbound and outbound (Cultural and nature-based tours, historical, MICE, etc.)
3	C	Ariya Ponel Ghasht	Male	20	Inbound and outbound (Offering a variety of cultural and classic tours, nature tours, sports, business, health, etc.).
4	D	Persian Gulf	Male	5	Inbound and outbound (cultural and classic tours, nature tours, sports, business, educational, etc.).
5	E	Pasargadae Tour	Male	32	Only inbound (offering different types of nature tours, sports, and specialised tours, etc.).
6	F	Iran Doustan	Male	20	Inbound and outbound. Travelling from individual to group requests, cultural, historical, student, nature, business tours.
7	G	Arge Jadid	Male	20	Inbound and outbound. Providing all tourism services such as cultural, business tours, conferences, nature tours, etc.
8	H	Maral	Male	10	Inbound and outbound. Offering a variety of tours, train ticket sales, car rental in Iran and car rental abroad.
9	I	Iranian Ziggurat	Male	15	Inbound and outbound (Nature tours, domestic and international plane ticket sales).
10	J	Aftab Kalout	Male	20	Inbound and outbound (Nature tours, creative tours, etc.).
11	K	Roz Abi	Male	16	Inbound and outbound (Categorisation of different tours according to customers' interests Land tastes, cultural tours, nature and ecotourism, medical and post-treatment tours, etc.)
12	M	Sourinet Parvaz (a)	Female	10	Inbound and outbound (Customised multi-purpose programmes).
13	N	2001	Female	22	Inbound and outbound (Business tours, MICE, etc.).
14	O	Marco Polo	Male	30	Inbound and outbound (Historical, cultural and nature tours).
15	P	Split Albuorz	Male	15	Inbound and outbound (Mountain nature tours, tickets, same-day tours, etc.)
16	Q	Sourinet parvaz (b)	Male	25	Inbound and outbound (Pilgrimages, ecotourism, ticket, hotel reservation, visa issuance, etc.)
17	R	Aras	Male	21	Inbound and outbound (Organising classic tours, ticket sales and accommodation reservations, cultural and health tours, etc.).
18	S	Arfa	Male	25	Inbound and outbound (Cultural, pilgrimage, medical tour, ticket sales, etc.).

trained experts, (b) *'Temporary business closure'* refers to the closure of countries' borders and the closure of outbound and inbound trips, (c) *'Losing image and credit'*, (d) *'Psychological and social impacts'*, which refers to the feeling of stress and anxiety due to uncertainty about the future, (e) *'Immigration of elites in the business sector'*, (f) *'Financial losses'* refers to losing revenue and profits that could be used to pay staff salaries and other operational costs to maintain their businesses. The following comment confirms this claim:

> When we talk about losses, we do not mean just money. This is a credit loss, it is psychological, and it is even a time that we have already spent at relatively high costs. For example, marketing, this is an important part of our work. Therefore, when it comes to losses, we can really say that Covid-19 was a massive storm for us. It destroyed all connections, and if we want to reconnect with them and come back and be like the pre-crisis, I think it will be expensive for us. But it will take a long time just to go back to the pre-Covid-19 era. So, even if it goes back to normal, it certainly requires more energy, it will take a long time for all people who have worked in it [business] to start again…all activities such as promotion, advertising, branding, etc. to be reset due to the disappearance of many markets. (Respondent B, Male)

As the above finding indicates, Covid-19 disturbed the economic capital and the social capital of tour operators, which they had been attempting to establish over the years, and resilient disaster strategies are needed to remedy the disruptions (Do *et al.*, 2021).

When comparing the effects of the Covid-19 crisis with previous crises, all interviewees believed that the pandemic crisis was an unprecedented and universal shock for the travel and tourism industry. They also pointed out that Covid-19 is the most significant and most prolonged crisis of the past century. All respondents further believed that alternative pathways were used to mitigate its negative effects when a crisis had occurred previously. For example, when there was an economic crisis and instability in the national currency, people turned to domestic travel instead of abroad. Previously, there was a way to deal with all kinds of crises, but the Covid-19 crisis blocked all pathways and operational channels; therefore, previous solutions did not work well in managing this crisis. One of our respondents (Respondent S) compared the Covid-19 crisis to *'an iceberg, which only the tip is visible'*. This result has been widely supported in the literature, namely, that Covid-19 has been an unprecedented crisis and probably the most severe one in the past century (Gössling *et al.*, 2020; UNWTO, 2020; Yeh, 2021).

Resilience to the crisis

The majority (almost 70%) of the study respondents explained that they had no option other than to develop a resilient organisational culture. They asserted that they had experienced such resiliency in managing previous crises. Therefore, their experience in managing previous crises has already helped them prepare to be resilient. In the analyses, two main themes were extracted related to crisis resiliency: (a) *'The financial approach'*, which refers to the methods used to reduce expenses. (b) *'Creating diversity in the product portfolio'*, which refers to the development of various domestic packages when the international borders were closed. The study respondents further explained that they have previously applied the same strategy in other crises such as economic and political crises. Nevertheless, Covid-19 was not comparable with other crises in terms of the scale, the scope of impacts and the duration of involvement. Financial control and cost reduction were exercised through employee redundancy and discontinuation of costly promotional and advertisement activities in international markets. In this case, Respondent A said:

> When our incoming and outgoing tours almost stopped, we tried to expand our activities with domestic tours. In principle, we tried to adjust our income and expenses. If you do not have income, then you spend it more slowly. We tried to adjust our costs and avoid additional costs.

Respondents further explained how they diversified their product portfolio amid the pandemic crisis. Product diversification has been experienced in previous crises such as political upheavals, economic crises and nuclear-related sanctions to maintain competitiveness and remain abreast of contemporary trends. An interviewee (Respondent O) explained:

> We moved to offer more nature-based packages as we could conform health protocols compared to other cultural and MICE packages. Now we also offer nature-based tours to attract different markets and stay competitive.

It is worth noting that Vietnam's tour operators have practised these strategies (i.e. cost reduction and product diversification) during the pandemic crisis, where product and market diversifications helped them find the path towards recovery (Do *et al.*, 2021).

Applied resilient strategies

In the analysis of the theme *'Strategies used for resiliency during the pandemic crisis'*, the answers led to the extraction of several sub-themes such as (a) *'Maintaining mutual communication with partners in different markets'*; (b) *'using collective wisdom'*, which refers to collective thinking and creating regular contact with other agents and partners; (c) *'encouraging innovation and creativity at the work environment'* that represents the provision of new services and products offered for the first time by an agency. Other strategies included (d) *'diversifying the products and services considering health protocols and social distancing'*. One particular example was organising responsible tour packages in the form of small groups such as ecotourism and nature-based tours. (e) *'Financial control'* indicates ways to reduce costs and expenses or perform low-profit activities. (f) *'Travel aligned with health protocols'*, which means setting up and running tours in full compliance with health protocols. (g) *'Creating an alternative source of income'* is related to using other available specialities and facilities to create income. (h) *'Technology improvement'*, which refers to the improvement of software infrastructure and activation of the IT department in the company to provide digital communication mechanisms and other activities. One respondent explained his resilience strategy in the form of organising domestic tours:

> With the closure of the borders, we did not have any entry and exit tours in 2020. Due to the fact that we have nature tours, and our tours are run outdoors, and the risk of getting the virus is low or non-existent, we were able to have normal outdoor tours. We were lucky that we could still work compared to other companies which they were solely relying on a single market. Nonetheless, the fact is that the domestic tour market is not something that can very well cover the costs of an agency, and more income should come from inbound and outbound markets. So even we, who had domestic tours, still had a year of losses. (Respondent Q)

Organisational resilience in times of crisis is one of the essential strategies for survival and recovery (Fang *et al.*, 2020; Mat Som *et al.*, 2013). As was apparent, tour operators applied various strategies to adapt to this new situation, which is called the 'new normal' (Gössling *et al.*, 2020). While Covid-19 is assumed to be a unique occurrence that created the most devastating tourism crisis of the past century (UNWTO, 2020), travel companies practised various resilient strategies to show that the industry has a high degree of resiliency and adaptability. This indicates the dynamic nature of travel and tourism to severe external shocks and the hope for a business recovery (Israeli *et al.*, 2011; Ritchie & Jiang, 2019).

Perception of organisational learning

Organisational learning is a vital but neglected issue in crisis management (Ghaderi *et al.*, 2014). The study respondents were asked to discuss their lessons in managing the crisis. Their answers led to the extraction of several themes and sub-themes such as (a) *'understanding the importance of organisational learning in managing the Covid-19 crisis'*, (b) *'Learning from different crises in the form of either single-loop or double-loop learning'.* For instance, one informant (Respondent F) noted:

> The pandemic crisis and also previous crises have reminded us of the significance of organisational learning and how past lessons helped us manage the uncertainties.

Another respondent asserted:

> any crisis sends out signals of deep or superficial learning. In the new pandemic crisis, we have deeply learned to not put all our eggs in one basket, and we should change our organisational strategies, and restructure everything from scratch. (Respondent A)

While single-loop learning refers to superficial learning, which does not question the organisational core values, structure and norms (Ghaderi *et al.*, 2014), double-loop learning denotes a type of learning that leads to a change in mechanism, a review of systems and methods and the application of change strategies (Argyris & Schön, 1997; Blackman & Ritchie, 2008). The findings indicate that in the studied companies, discussion of organisational learning has remained at a single-loop level, and only a very limited number of companies (3 out of 18) practised double-loop learning and the lessons that they had learned led to a change in mechanism and a review of their organisational structure.

The majority of surveyed companies were not in a position to learn critically or even change their organisational behaviour to identify errors and practice proactively. Respondents confessed that these fundamental changes had not occurred within their organisations, but they pointed out that they have seen some positive modifications, though not to that extent which triggered in-depth learning, as supported by a comment given by one of the pioneers in the field:

> Some changes happened in our company; like for example, employees' need to learn how to deal with different markets, learn new skills, knowledge and to practice risk management scenarios. (Respondent A)

Therefore, it can be stated that the level of understanding of organisational learning by Iranian tour operators during the Covid-19 crisis and concerning other past crises (such as political and economic crises) did not extend much beyond the single-loop level, except in very limited cases, and the majority did not enter into double or triple-loop learning. This result is similar to Ghaderi *et al.* (2014), who stated that most tourism organisations in Malaysia were interested in a single-loop rather than double-loop learning. Reluctance to critically learn and an unwillingness to change their organisational core structure were the main challenges of crisis management that needed to be faced by senior managers of travel organisations (Ghaderi et al., 2014). Learning is a fundamental process for achieving an appropriate response to a crisis, returning to normalcy, and averting future losses (Blackman & Ritchie, 2008), or in other words, building a 'resilient organisation'. Indeed, the single-loop perspective on organisational learning exposes tour operators to various external risks and crises and prolongs their business recovery.

Conclusion

The purpose of this research was to explore how the Covid-19 pandemic affected tour operators' businesses, how resilient they have been to the crisis and if they had learned any lessons in managing this crisis. This study was conducted because, unlike the predominant research on the impacts of the Covid-19 pandemic on tourism destinations and travel in general, much less research is available on specific business sectors such as tour operators, and there was a need to explore the practice of individual operators in managing the crisis. It was commonly believed that crises are negative events that have devastating effects on organisations, but from the other side, they also provide unique opportunities for change. The Covid-19 pandemic had an overwhelming impact on the businesses of different sectors, including most tour operator companies.

However, as many researchers have argued, although crises have adverse effects, they may also drive positive change and learning (see Faulkner, 2001; Ritchie, 2004; Simon & Pauchant, 2000; Wang, 2008). While a crisis or disaster is often accompanied by feelings of extreme anxiety, tension, doubt, as well as loss and confusion that may lead to resistance to change, it paradoxically can also bring about positive changes to the organisation (Bartunek & Moch, 1994; Becken & Khazai, 2017; Ghaderi *et al.*, 2021; Schein, 1993; Wang, 2008). For example, Laws *et al.* (2007) noted that although the 2004 Indian Ocean tsunami created terrible damage and anxiety in affected areas, it offered an opportunity for industry players to create positive modifications to their organisational culture. Therefore, effective crisis management focusing on organisational learning becomes an essential factor for the organisation's long-term survival. This process is embedded with a continuous assessment and learning about the current situation, redefining the vision and planning to achieve these goals by implementing fully developed crisis management and knowledge management plans (Ghaderi *et al.*, 2014). Interviews with managers of tour operators in Iran showed that change, either positive or negative, is inevitable after each crisis. Positive change provides an opportunity for organisations to re-evaluate and reorganise their organisational culture, structure, mission, values and beliefs. Therefore, it is recommended that both medium-sized and small-scale tour operators take the opportunity to obtain what benefits they can from the crisis.

This study has also highlighted the role of organisational learning as an important concern when managing future crises. Nevertheless, our respondents were not involved in either in-depth or double-loop learning, where they could critically reflect on their performances. The discrepancies between the espoused theory of action and the actual theory-in-use are important in double-loop learning. Argyris (1976) posited that sometimes leaders obtain little genuine feedback, while others tend not to violate their values and disturb the accepted structure. Therefore, what these managers created would be accepted as minimum opposition. In this research, reflection did not generate a significant learning outcome. Critical reflection involves challenging the established and habitual patterns of organisational culture. It is highly recommended that tour operators apply in-depth critical double-loop learning rather than single-loop learning to plan for future uncertainties proactively. Enhancing organisational resilience is an essential strategy in crisis recovery (Prayag et al., 2019), applying and promoting a resilient culture focusing on effective crisis management strategies. The travel and tourism industries are dynamic and prone to different externalities, and adapting a dynamic organisational culture helps them enhance their flexibility to new changes that are always on the way.

Finally, as the results of this study confirmed, the pandemic crisis has disrupted almost all types of links and connections that the tour operators had with their international counterparts. Thus, massive efforts should be invested to revive and restructure these connections. Losing these links and connections will cause significant losses for the whole tourism system as tour operators are major travel intermediaries and distributors (Do et al., 2021). In light of this finding, improving organisational memory and knowledge management systems at different corporate, business and industry levels are important practices (Paraskevas et al., 2013).

References

Ali, S., Peters, L.D., Khan, I.U., Ali, W. and Saif, N. (2020) Organisational learning and hotel performance: The role of capabilities' hierarchy. *International Journal of Hospitality Management* 85, 102349. https://doi.org/10.1016/j.ijhm.2019.102349

Anderson, B.A. (2006) Crisis management in the Australian tourism industry: Preparedness, personnel and postscript. *Tourism Management* 27 (6), 1290–1297.

Argyris, C. (1976) Single-loop and double-loop models in research on decision making. *Administrative Science Quarterly* 21 (3), 363–375. https://doi.org/10.2307/2391848

Argyris, C. and Schön, D.A. (1997) Organisational learning: A theory of action perspective. *Reis* (77/78), 345–348.

Argyris, C. and Schon, D. (1978) *Organisational Learning: A Theory of Action Perspective*. Reading, MA: Addison-Wesley.

Bartunek, J.M. and Moch, M.K. (1994) Third-order organisational change and the Western mystical tradition. *Journal of Organisational Change Management* 7 (1), 24- 41. https://doi.org/10.1108/09534819410050795

Bakar, N.A. and Rosbi, S. (2020) Effect of Coronavirus disease (COVID-19) to tourism industry. *International Journal of Advanced Engineering Research and Science* 7 (4), 189–193. https://doi.org/10.22161/ijaers.74.23

Becken, S. and Khazai, B. (2017) Resilience, tourism and disasters. In R.W. Butler (ed.) *Tourism and Resilience* (pp. 96–104). Wallingford: CABI.

Blackman, D. and Ritchie, B.W. (2008) Tourism crisis management and organisational learning: The role of reflection in developing effective DMO crisis strategies. *Journal of Travel & Tourism Marketing* 23 (2–4), 45–57.

Braun, V. and Clarke, V. (2006) Using thematic analysis in psychology. *Qualitative Research in Psychology* 3 (2), 77–101.

Browne, K. (2005) Snowball sampling: Using social networks to research non-heterosexual women. *International Journal of Social Research Methodology* 8 (1), 47–60.

Butler, R.W. (2017) *Tourism and Resilience*. Wallingford: CABI.

Cheer, J.M. and Lew, A.A. (eds) (2017) *Tourism, Resilience, and Sustainability: Adapting to Social, Political and Economic Change*. Abingdon: Routledge.

Chowdhury, M., Prayag, G., Orchiston, C. and Spector, S. (2019) Post-disaster social capital, adaptive resilience and business performance of tourism organisations in Christchurch, New Zealand. *Journal of Travel Research* 58 (7), 1209–1226.

Cyert, R.M. and March, J.G. (1963) *A Behavioral Theory of the Firm*. Englewood Cliffs, NJ: Prentice Hall.

Dalziell, E.P. and McManus, S.T. (2004) Resilience, vulnerability, and adaptive capacity: Implications for system performance. International Forum for Engineering Decision Making (IFED), University of Canterbury, Christchurch.

Do, B., Nguyen, N., D'Souza, C., Bui, H.D. and Nguyen, T.N.H. (2021) Strategic responses to COVID-19: The case of tour operators in Vietnam. *Tourism and Hospitality Research*, 22 (1), 5–17. https://doi.org/10.1177/1467358421993902

Easterby-Smith, M. and Araujo, L. (1999) Organisational learning: Current debates and opportunities. In M. Easterby-Smith, J. Burgoyne and L. Araujo (eds) *Organisational Learning and the Learning Organisation* (pp. 1–21). London: SAGE.

Erol, O., Sauser, B.J. and Mansouri, M. (2010) A framework for investigation into extended enterprise resilience. *Enterprise Information Systems* 4 (2), 111–136.

Faulkner, B. and Vikulov, S. (2001) Katherine, washed out one day, back on track the next: A post-mortem of a tourism disaster. *Tourism Management* 22 (4), 331–344. https://doi.org/10.1016/S0261-5177(00)00069-8

Fang, S. (Echo), Prayag, G., Ozanne, L.K. and de Vries, H. (2020) Psychological capital, coping mechanisms and organisational resilience: Insights from the 2016 Kaikoura earthquake, New Zealand. *Tourism Management Perspectives*, 34 (January), 100637. https://doi.org/10.1016/j.tmp.2020.100637

Filimonau, V. and De Coteau, D. (2020) Tourism resilience in the context of integrated destination and disaster management (DM2). *International Journal of Tourism Research* 22 (2), 202–222. https://doi.org/10.1002/jtr.2329

Fountain, J. and Cradock-Henry, N.A. (2020) Recovery, risk and resilience: Post-disaster tourism experiences in Kaikōura, New Zealand. *Tourism Management Perspectives* 35, 100695. https://doi.org/10.1016/j.tmp.2020.100695

Fink, S. and American Management Association (1986) *Crisis Management: Planning for the Inevitable*. New York: Amacom.

Ghaderi, Z., Mat Som, A.P. and Wang, J. (2014) Organisational learning in tourism crisis management: An experience from Malaysia. *Journal of Travel and Tourism Marketing* 31 (5), 627–648.

Ghaderi, Z., King, B. and Hall, C.M. (2021) Crisis preparedness of hospitality managers: Evidence from Malaysia. *Journal of Hospitality and Tourism Insights*. https://doi.org/10.1108/JHTI-10-2020-0199

Ghaderi, Z. and Paraskevas, A. (2021) *Organisational Learning in Tourism and Hospitality Crisis Management*. Berlin: Walter de Gruyter.

Gössling, S., Scott, D. and Hall, C.M. (2020) Pandemics, tourism and global change: A rapid assessment of COVID-19. *Journal of Sustainable Tourism* 29 (1), 1–20. https://doi.org/10.1080/09669582.2020.1758708

Guba, E.G. and Lincoln, Y.S. (1985) *Naturalistic Inquiry*. Vol. 75. Beverly Hills, CA: Sage Publications Inc.

Hall, C.M., Prayag, G. and Amore, A. (2018) *Tourism and Resilience: Individual, Organisational and Destination Perspectives*. Bristol: Channel View Publications.

Hallak, R., Assaker, G., O'Connor, P. and Lee, C. (2018) Firm performance in the upscale restaurant sector: The effects of resilience, creative self-efficacy, innovation and industry experience. *Journal of Retailing and Consumer Services* 40, 229–240.

Holling, C.S. (1973) Resilience and stability of ecological systems. *Annual Review of Ecology and Systematics* 4 (1), 1–23.

Hoque, A., Shikha, F.A., Hasanat, M.W., Arif, I. and Hamid, A.B.A. (2020) The effect of Coronavirus (COVID-19) in the tourism industry in China. *Asian Journal of Multidisciplinary Studies* 3 (1), 52–58.

Huber, G.P. (1991) Organisational learning: The contributing processes and the literatures. *Organization Science* 2 (1), 88–115.

Huysman, M. (1999) Balancing biases: A critical review of the literature on organisational learning. In M. Easterby-Smith, J. Burgoyne and L. Araujo (eds) *Organisational Learning and the Learning Organisation* (pp. 59–74). London: SAGE.

Israeli, A.A., Mohsin, A. and Kumar, B. (2011) Hospitality crisis management practices: The case of Indian luxury hotels. *International Journal of Hospitality Management* 30 (2), 367–374.

Jiang, Y., Ritchie, B.W. and Verreynne, M.L. (2019) Building tourism organisational resilience to crises and disasters: A dynamic capabilities view. *International Journal of Tourism Research* 21 (6), 882–900.

Laws, E., Prideaux, B. and Chon, K.S. (eds) (2007) *Crisis Management in Tourism*. Wallingford: CABI.

Lemmetyinen, A. and Go, F.M. (2009) The key capabilities required for managing tourism business networks. *Tourism Management* 30 (1), 31–40.

Linnenluecke, M.K. (2017) Resilience in business and management research: A review of influential publications and a research agenda. *International Journal of Management Reviews* 19 (1), 4–30.

McManus, S., Seville, E., Vargo, J. and Brunsdon, D. (2008) Facilitated process for improving organisational resilience. *Natural Hazards Review* 9 (2), 81–90.

Mat Som, A.P.M., Ghaderi, Z. and Aguenza, B. (2013) Tourism crises and regionalisation in Southeast Asia. *BIMP-EAGA Journal for Sustainable Tourism Development* 2 (1), 1–9.

Meyer, A.D. (1982) Adapting to environmental jolts. *Administrative Science Quarterly* 27 (4), 515–537.

Ministry of Culture, Tourism, and Handicrafts (2020) The effects of the Covid-19 pandemic on the tourism industry in Iran. Unpublished Report. Tehran, Iran.

Orchiston, C., Prayag, G. and Brown, C. (2016) Organisational resilience in the tourism sector. *Annals of Tourism Research* 56, 145–148.

Pauchant, T.C. and Mitroff, I. (1992) *Transforming the Crisis-Prone Organisation: Preventing Individual, Organisational and Environmental Tragedies*. San Francisco: Jossey-Bass.

Paraskevas, A., Altinay, L., McLean, J. and Cooper, C. (2013) Crisis knowledge in tourism: Types, flows and governance. *Annals of Tourism Research* 41, 130–152.

Paraskevas, A. and Quek, M. (2019) When Castro seized the Hilton: Risk and crisis management lessons from the past. *Tourism Management* 70, 419–429.

Patten, M.L. (2007) *Understanding Research Methods: An Overview of the Essentials*. Glendale, CA: Pyrczak Pub.

Pearson, C.M. and Mitroff, L.I. (1993) From crisis prone to crisis prepared: A framework for crisis management. *Academy of Management Executives* 7 (1), 48–59.

Prayag, G., Ozanne, L.K. and de Vries, H. (2020) Psychological capital, coping mechanisms and organisational resilience: Insights from the 2016 Kaikoura earthquake, New Zealand. *Tourism Management Perspectives* 34, 100637. https://doi.org/10.1016/j.tmp.2020.100637

Ritchie, B.W. and Jiang, Y. (2019) A review of research on tourism risk, crisis and disaster management: Launching the annals of tourism research curated collection on tourism risk, crisis and disaster management. *Annals of Tourism Research* 79 (September), 102812. https://doi.org/10.1016/j.annals.2019.102812

Ritchie, B.W. (2004) Chaos, crises and disasters: A strategic approach to crisis management in the tourism industry. *Tourism Management* 25 (6), 669–683. https://doi.org/10.1016/j.tourman.2003.09.004

Simon, L. and Pauchant, T.C. (2000) Developing the three levels of learning in crisis management: A case study of the Hagersville tire fire. *Review of business-Saint Johns University* 21 (3), 6–11.

Schein, E.H. (1993) On dialogue, culture, and organisational learning. *Organisational Dynamics* 22 (2), 40–52.

Spillan, J. and Hough, M. (2003) Crisis planning in small businesses: Importance, impetus and indifference. *European Management Journal* 21 (3), 398–407.

Wang, J. (2008) Developing organizational learning capacity in crisis management. Advances in Developing Human Resources, 10 (3), 425–445. https://doi.org/10.1177/1523422308316464

UNWTO (2020) Tourism back to 1990 levels as arrivals fall by more than 70%. See https://www.unwto.org/news/tourism-back-to-1990-levels-as-arrivals-fall-by-

Yeh, S.S. (2021) Tourism recovery strategy against COVID-19 pandemic. *Tourism Recreation Research* 46 (2), 188–194.

4 The Covid-19 Pandemic and Tourism Small- and Medium-sized Enterprises (SMEs): Insights From a Developing Country Perspective

Siamak Seyfi and C. Michael Hall

Introduction

Tourism has been one of the industries most severely and widely impacted by the Covid-19 pandemic as global and local travel declined amid mandated border closures, mobility lockdowns and imposition of biosecurity measures (Kim *et al.*, 2021; Seyfi *et al.*, 2020a). Small- and medium-sized enterprises (SMEs) were severely impacted by the outbreak and are at much higher risk from prolonged Covid-19 lockdown measures given their size, scarce resources and limited cash flows, as well as the more limited range of risk-management mechanisms they can access (Haqbin *et al.*, 2021; Kukanja *et al.*, 2020; Vargas-Sánchez, 2021). This is particularly important as SMEs represent 80% of the tourism sector in some destinations and also account for many self-employed micro-SMEs, as well as the employment of women and youth (UNWTO, 2020). The employment of women by tourism SMEs is especially important because in some countries, which have cultural or other limitations on the capacity of women to be engaged in employment, hospitality services in particular offer otherwise scarce employment opportunities (Hall *et al.*, in press; Seyfi *et al.*, 2020b).

Given that SMEs are critical to destination offerings, it is important that an improved understanding is gained of the survival mechanisms they adopt during and after a crisis (Prayag & Hall, 2021). While the disaster preparedness and resilience of large businesses in the tourism supply chain system has often been prioritised (Mandal & Saravanan, 2019), the resilience of SMEs has largely been neglected, and there is only limited knowledge as to how such SMEs continue to operate in times of crisis and afterwards (Biggs *et al.*, 2012, 2015).

Research has shown that a 'one-size-fits-all' approach to understanding resilience and managing the impacts of triggering events is futile (Hall *et al.*, 2018; Prayag, 2020). This is particularly so given that resilience is a multi-scaled concept and that external actors can greatly influence destination and SME resilience strategies (Gibson *et al.*, 2016). However, insufficient research has been conducted to identify the factors that make SMEs resilient enough to cope with operating in the risky and unpredictable business environments that often occur within a crisis (Hall *et al.*, 2021). Importantly, there is a need to understand how SME survival is ensured in times of crisis, especially given their contribution to the sustainable development and recovery of destinations.

This chapter examines these issues with a particular focus on SMEs in a developing country context. SMEs are often regarded as the engine of economic growth in developing countries, and their success directly impacts the economic development of these countries. Like many other destinations, Iran has experienced severe economic impacts from far-reaching consequences of the Covid-19 pandemic (Abdoli, 2020; Gonzalez-Perez *et al.*, 2021), which was particularly significant given that the country was one of the outbreak's earliest and most severe epicentres. The estimate indicates that Iran's tourism industry has lost around 7.6 billion dollars in revenue since the Covid-19 outbreak (Tehran Times, 2022), and over 44,000 jobs in the country's once-burgeoning travel sector. Additionally, because of unemployment and financial losses, the accommodation sector has suffered the most. The pandemic has cost the accommodation sector around $6.6 billion, while over 21,000 people in the lodging and accommodations sector have lost their jobs (Tehran Times, 2022). Adding to this are travel agencies and tour operators which faced over $238 million of damage and more than 6000 people unemployed (Tehran Times, 2022). Moreover, tourism complexes, eco-lodges and tour guides are also among the most affected groups in the Iranian tourism industry.

Additionally, the country was already struggling with long-running sanctions that have negatively affected the country's tourism industry (Seyfi & Hall, 2019b, 2020). The Covid-19 outbreak subsequent restrictions on travels and lockdowns intensify the economic problems in Iran as tourism was one of the major sources of employment and growth during the sanctions period (Cafiero, 2020; Seyfi & Hall, 2018). Furthermore, the Iranian labor market was already suffering from a higher rate of unemployment due to structural problems of the economy and imposed sanctions. Overall, this chapter therefore examines how Covid-19 affected tourism-related SMEs in Iran and sheds light on the policy responses and resilience measures necessary to tackle this crisis for SMEs.

SMEs in Crisis-Affected Tourism Destinations

SMEs play a significant role in the growth of tourism (UNWTO, 2020) and account for a significant share of private sector economic activity and employment generation in both developed and developing countries (OECD, 2019). Tourism SMEs are increasingly recognised as important to the competitiveness of the economies of countries in which international tourism is significant (Vargas-Sánchez, 2021). Even though SMEs contribute significantly to economic development, they are often the businesses that are most fragile and prone to crisis situations (Carruthers, 2020; Hall *et al.*, 2021) because of lack of preparedness, short-term and restricted cash flows, lack of business continuation insurance and an inability to properly deploy resources (Hall *et al.*, 2016; Lu *et al.*, 2020). The study of Lu *et al.* (2020) on the perceived impact of the pandemic on SMEs in China showed that the primary issues facing Chinese SMEs during pandemics are a lack of cash flow, supply chain disruption and poor market demand. Such factors may significantly restrict the period over which SMEs can survive a crisis as well as sustaining the business operations compared to larger firms (Carruthers, 2020; Lu *et al.*, 2020). However, it is significant to note that in their study of small tourism operators in Queensland, Australia and Thailand, Biggs *et al.* (2012, 2015) found that SMEs that had a strong sense of attachment to their destinations and local networks were much more likely to survive than those with weak place attachment. The capacity of SMEs to survive crises, such as the Covid-19 pandemic, is regarded as important for a destination's ability to contribute to the achievement of the Sustainable Development Goals (SDGs) by their 2030 target (Gregurec *et al.*, 2021). Given the important role of SMEs in economic activity through job creation, particularly for the poor and marginalised groups, the development of these businesses is critical for achieving the SDGs, and SMEs are largely viewed as crucial to the *Leaving No One Behind principle* that is central to the 2030 Agenda (OECD, 2019).

Enhancing Tourism SMEs' Resilience in Times of Crisis

As noted above, SMEs often do not have adequate resources to respond to crisis situations. The extant literature has heightened the need for broader integration of crisis and disaster management principles in destination management plans for enhancing the resilience of tourist destinations and businesses (Amore *et al.*, 2018; Hall *et al.*, 2018; Prayag, 2018, 2020). The growing resilience discourse in tourism studies has divided into three major strands of the application of resilience thinking at the macro (e.g. tourism system, destinations and community level) (Amore *et al.*, 2018; Bui *et al.*, 2020; Hall *et al.*, 2020), meso (e.g. organisations) (Jiang *et al.*, 2019; Prayag *et al.*, 2020) and micro levels (e.g.

individuals and micro-SMEs) (Hall *et al.*, 2018). Nonetheless, research on resilience at the micro level (which includes micro entrepreneurs and businesses) is scarce.

As noted above, research has shown that a 'one-size-fits-all' approach to understanding resilience and managing crisis consequences is ineffective (Prayag, 2018), particularly given the multi-scaled nature of the tourism system. This demonstrates the need for a more comprehensive examination of the resilience mechanisms used by these micro-operators in sustaining their businesses in times of crisis. Additionally, the existing literature focuses primarily on the recovery mechanisms following natural disasters such as floods, tsunami and earthquakes (Amore & Hall, 2021; Hall & Prayag, 2021; Hall *et al.*, 2016; Lu *et al.*, 2020). There is relatively little focus on resilience to more longer-term health crisis events such as epidemics or pandemics, which are distinct from environmental hazards in terms of impact on business continuity and human mobility, and which can potentially have more severe and longer-lasting effects on both populations and economies at a national scale. This points to the main focus of this chapter.

Tourism SMEs in Iran

Iran's historic strategic position at the crossroads of major civilisations and trade routes (e.g. the Silk Road), along with its varied climate and landscape, has created an abundance of opportunities for tourist development (Seyfi & Hall, 2018). While the country had traditionally been a destination for cultural tourists before the Islamic revolution of 1979, the country still attracts many religious tourists and pilgrims from the surrounding countries in the aftermath of the Islamic revolution and the subsequent replacement of monarchy with an Islamic theocracy (Mozaffari *et al.*, 2017; Seyfi & Hall, 2019a). The country has abundant and varied tourism resources and internationally is positioned primarily in terms of cultural and heritage related tourism as well as the substantial Persian diaspora. As of February 2022, 24 historical sites and 2 natural sites are listed under the UNESCO World Heritage List, while 61 more sites are tentatively listed (United Nations Educational and Scientific and Cultural Organization [UNESCO], 2022). Significantly, the tourism industry plays an increasingly important role in the country's economy. Based on the World Travel and Tourism Council (WTTC) report, the total contribution of travel and tourism to Iran's GDP was 6.5% of the total GDP and 5.4% of total employment (1.344 million jobs) in 2019 (WTTC, 2020).

Despite these enormous resources and potential, the Iranian tourist has suffered substantially since the late 1970s, due to a negative image in key tourism markets, the government's anti-Western stance and Middle East political instability and war (Morakabati, 2011; Mozaffari *et al.*, 2017; Seyfi & Hall, 2018). Iran's economy has been harmed by decades of sanctions, which have hindered important commercial operations, including tourism. Iran's access to the global financial system has also been restricted by successive rounds of financial sanctions, limiting foreign investment and preventing Iran from acquiring new aircraft and improving its tourism and transport infrastructure (Seyfi & Hall, 2019b, 2020).

Iran is the Middle East's second-largest country with a population of over 85 million and has one of the largest economies in the MENA area in terms of GDP (World Bank, 2021). Iran's economy is heavily based on oil revenues and is characterised by massive state and quasi-public businesses that control around 80% of the economy (UNIDO, 2003). Iranian authorities, on the other hand, have sought to progressively shift towards a market-oriented economy and the growth of the private sector under many administrations. According to the Government's 20-year Vision document and Iran's fifth Five-Year Development Plan, it aims to privatise around 20% of state-owned firms each year (World Bank, 2021).

Definitions of SMEs are different country by country. There is no official account of the number of tourism SMEs in Iran. This is mostly owing to the absence of a unified and consistent definition for SMEs in Iran, with various ministries, institutions and organisations assigning SMEs to different categories and classifications. For instance, Iran's Small Industries and Industrial Parks Organization defines SMEs as businesses with less than 100 employees. Firms with less than nine workers are estimated to comprise most businesses (about 96.1%) (Yadollahi Farsi & Toghraee, 2014), while a different estimate suggests that SMEs account for 52% of all industrial units and 45% of industrial employment in Iran (Financial Tribune, 2020). Prior to the Covid-19 pandemic, a report from Iran's Small Industries and Industrial Parks Organization indicated that over 33,000 SMEs were operating in the country, with 1100 exporting their products and services to foreign markets, highlighting the critical role of SMEs in the Iranian economy, particularly given the length of the sanctions imposed (Zamani, 2022).

In Iran, the tourism sector is comprised of a variety of SMEs including travel agencies, tour operator agencies, small-scale accommodations, handicraft and souvenir businesses, and car rental companies (Khoshkhoo & Nadalipour, 2016; Shafiei & Karoubi, 2018). The study of Khoshkhoo and Nadalipour (2016) indicated that travel and tourism agencies are the most important of Iran tourism SMEs due to their numerous functions including selling tickets and tours, guiding travellers, and assisting them with organising their vacations, bookings, visa and passport arrangements, and insurance. Despite uncertainty about their number, it is clear is that SMEs play a significant role in Iranian tourism.

Method

The study discussed in this chapter was undertaken during the early stage of the Covid-19 pandemic in July to August 2020. Given the unavailability of data on tourism SMEs in Iran, a purposeful snowball sampling technique was therefore adopted in line with the study research questions. Snowball sampling was used to find participants when those first contacted were invited to indicate others who would be eligible and interested in doing an interview. This sampling technique was deemed most appropriate to attain a purposive sample suitable for this study (Flick, 2018). The target participants were approached by email and LinkedIn messages, and the study's goal were explained to them. Those who were available and answered positively were given more details on the interview process and scheduling a telephone, WhatsApp or Skype interview. It has been recognised that using developing internet technologies as a research medium in qualitative studies is more conducive for difficult-to-reach and geographically scattered populations (Hanna, 2012) and was regarded as especially in the Covid-19 context given the role of lockdowns and biosecurity protocols in limiting face-to-face interviews.

Qualitative research tends to target a relatively small and focused sample to understand the individuality of the phenomenon being explored and the uniqueness of its circumstances (Creswell & Poth, 2018). Overall, 15 interviews were carried out. Owners/staff of travel agencies, tour operators, small-scale lodgings sector, souvenir stores, restaurant and car rental companies were included in the sample (Table 4.1).

Additional data were gathered via the analysis of policy documents and secondary sources such as newspaper articles and online forums. The semi-structured interviews lasted for 45 minutes on average and were done in Persian. Given the small number of interviews, the data were manually

Table 4.1 Profile of interviewees

Participant	Gender	City	Sector
1	Male	Tehran	Travel agency
2	Female	Tehran	Travel agency
3	Male	Isfahan	Travel agency
4	Male	Mashhad	Travel agency
5	Male	Tehran	Tour operator
6	Male	Tehran	Car rental
7	Female	Mashhad	Restaurant
8	Male	Shiraz	Traditional guesthouse
9	Male	Isfahan	Traditional guesthouse
10	Male	Isfahan	Souvenirs and handicrafts store
11	Female	Isfahan	Souvenirs and handicrafts store
12	Female	Shiraz	Traditional guesthouse
13	Male	Tehran	Car rental
14	Male	Mashhad	Entertainment park
15	Female	Tehran	Apartment hotel

coded as this form of coding provides more control and ownership over data analysis and keeps the data within the context (Saldaña, 2021). Qualitative thematic analysis was adopted for data analysis. Thematic analysis is a 'method for identifying, analysing and reporting patterns (themes) within data' (Braun & Clarke, 2006: 6). The interviews were initially reviewed and then read and re-read numerous times to reduce the number of codes. They were then grouped into discernible themes. Three main themes were formed that are reflected in the next section.

Impacts of Covid-19 on Tourism SMEs in Iran

This section offers an overview of the different impacts perceived by SMEs within Iranian tourism sector during the Covid-19 pandemic. Three main themes identified included risk perception and uncertainty, economic impacts and coping strategies.

Risks perception and uncertainty

For many interviewees, the Covid-19 outbreak has challenged their financial risk perception. One of the respondents who runs a small apartment hotel noted that:

> I had many ideas for expanding my business and building more boutique hotels in touristic villages in the country ... but I'm unsure whether to pursue these plans or not, since we have no clue when the trip will resume normally or when our return on investment would occur.

This was echoed by a handicraft store owner:

> ... It is now hard for us to expand our operations, and the new branch that we hoped to create has been halted for the time being. There is a very significant financial risk if we want to create a new branch with the spread of COVID-19 around the world and in our country.

For many respondents, the high levels of uncertainty surrounding the pandemic pose risks to the SMEs. A tour operator noted that:

> One of the things we worry about is that we do not know how we should develop the business in the future and what changes we will face. There is an uncertainty and ambiguity about changing the trends of service businesses, and that definitely affects the inbound travel market.

A similar observation was made by a traditional hotel owner:

> It is now impossible to foresee what tourists' preferences will be when it comes to selecting a location and lodging. Trips rise or decrease in

number. It is not at all clear what the future of tourism is going to be like and what challenges the accommodation sector will face.

Economic impacts

Nearly all the respondents noted that sustaining business operations has been very difficult for SMEs in the Iranian tourism sector. Many of the small businesses that were highly dependent on tourism suffered significant losses. While they had been able to adapt and respond to the limitations on tourism that had occurred because of sanctions, it was much harder to cope with the dramatic cut in people's mobility as a result of Covid-19 restrictions and the associated economic consequences. Given the prolonged economic crisis due to the Covid-19, SMEs have suffered disproportionately from economic downturns, because of their limited financial resources (Kim *et al.*, 2021).

The owner of a gift shop in Isfahan, which is major tourism destination in Iran, noted that:

> Tourism has created many jobs for local people in my city. My income was directly related to the tourism. Since the closure of my shop following the lockdowns, I have no other source of income for my family.

A director of a travel agency also mentioned that:

> I had to lay off several employees at my travel agency. I could only pay their salary for a few months and without the government support, I was unable to keep my business running. I have only kept my accountant and all the other employees were laid off.

Other interviewees also mentioned that as Covid-19 had resulted in a significant decline in their income, they were no longer able to pay back the mortgage. One of the respondents running a travel agency mentioned that:

> *I obtained a large loan from a bank in order to expand my business in the capital. had hoped to cover this mortgage. But, as a result of the pandemic and lockdowns, we became bankrupt and I am no longer able to repay the mortgage with a high interest rate.*

This was echoed by another travel agency director:

> *Our revenue largely depends on ticket sales and domestic and foreign tours. But all this has been affected and we have a lot of administrative, office and personnel expenses that have all been accumulated for us.*

A car rental company noted that

> *We fired several of our employees. The staff we trained and invested in. It will be very difficult for them to get back to work.*

Coping Strategies

Embracing digital marketing

Although SMEs are the first and the most important victims of a prolonged Covid-19 crisis, the interviews with the SMEs revealed some coping strategies adopted to survive in times of crisis. A tour operator mentioned that:

> We have been working hard to reassure our past customers. We increased our Instagram engagement and created new Twitter and Facebook profiles to be visible in major social media platforms. Because individuals are mostly at home during the lockdowns, we generated marketing campaigns and hashtags. For example, we invited people to tag their favourite places with our agency's name so they may go there in future.

A handicrafts shop owner noted that:

> Before the coronavirus, visitors could come to our workshop and purchase products. Then we thought of establishing an online business, we created an Instagram page and sending goods to our consumers by post.

Shifting towards the domestic tourism market

Some of the respondents believed that domestic tourism has the potential to revive the country's tourism industry. Many SMEs in the country's tourism sector have focused on domestic tourists as the travel restrictions on foreign tourists halted any inbound tourism market. A travel agency manager noted that:

> People now prefer visiting rural and less congested destinations. We have designed several attractive nature-based tour packages that we will offers to domestic visitors once travel restrictions ease.

> We have now introduced our cheaper packages to attract more domestic tourists. We have also developed some all-inclusive packages targeting family with kids.

Tourism Policy Responses to the Covid-19 Crisis in Iran

While the Covid-19 pandemic has struck various countries with differing degrees of severity, dealing with this crisis has presented most governments with an unprecedented challenge (Hall *et al.*, 2021). Different countries responded differently to the Covid-19 pandemic to mitigate the crisis's impact on the travel and tourism sector, restart tourism and accelerate recovery (UNWTO, 2022). Iran introduced policies to address the economic consequences of pandemic mitigation measures shortly after the crisis began, including the reopening of businesses, relaxation of quarantine laws and declaration of normalcy. This policy approach was founded on a strategy of reorienting short-term threats, exchanging epidemic mitigation for economic stability. Iran's fragile economic situation caused the government to change its focus from pandemic management to economic repercussions management. Adding to this, Iran was already vulnerable and already economically weakened by international sanctions (Seyfi *et al.*, 2020). Iran's government was forced to consider short-term trade-offs between public health and social stability in pandemic response, with imminent unemployment and food insecurity used to justify a policy pivot from mitigation to economic continuity. This illustrates how countries with pre-existing challenges manage acute crises. In their study on Iran's policy response to the Covid-19 pandemic, Sajadi and Hartley (2021) argue that weakness in economic policy, failure to coordinate public health initiatives, priority of treatment over prevention, insufficient public engagement and insufficient healthcare infrastructure were the primary factors contributing to Iran's initially ineffective pandemic response.

To support many SMEs in the country's tourism industry that were severely impacted by Covid-19 and to mitigate its negative effects, a committee was formed in the Ministry of Cultural Heritage, Tourism, and Handicrafts (MCTH) shortly after the pandemic began in Iran to advise health officials on how to limit damage and support a rapid recovery. To assist SMEs and stakeholders in times of crisis, plans are being made to create a fund for tourism development and compensation via public-private collaboration. To tackle the effects of the Covid-19 pandemic, MCTH took a range of fiscal policy and other measures in three phases (UNWTO, 2022).

Phase one: Planning to manage the crisis

- Creating a special national committee to collect data on the loss of tourism-related jobs and establishments.
- Cooperating with health system authorities and other stakeholders.
- Promoting domestic travel (a virtual campaign similar to the UNWTO's food campaign).
- Promoting the country's off-the-beaten-track tourist potentials.

Phase two: Supporting country tourism stakeholders in some steps:

- Ratifying income tax.
- Added value tax exemption.
- Deferring repayment of insurance installments (e.g. the insurance premium for employers and staff).
- Postponing of the deadline for utilities (paying charges in smaller installments).

- Government's bailout of tourism companies through saving bonds and other banking facilities with low interest rate.
- Utilising best practices as a guideline for business.

Phase three: Pronouncement of directives and executive orders

- Closure of all accommodation and tourism service providers.
- Paying back all cancelled bookings.
- Extending all government certifications granted to people and properties.
- Utilising some tourism related establishments as camps for Covid patients.
- Holding online training courses providing information on how to deal with the crisis.

Nevertheless, as commented by the interviewees, most of the tourism SMEs are restricted in liquidity and access to finance, and they believe that the government-funded bailout for businesses is not enough to cover the financial compensation for employees. Additionally, the Iranian labour market was already experiencing a high rate of unemployment because of the economy's pre-existing problems and sanctions. Therefore, the Covid-19 pandemic only exacerbated the already existing issues that tourism SMEs faced.

Conclusion

Covid-19 has been a major crisis for the global tourism industry, not least because of its dramatic curtailment of international tourism. Its affects have been felt at all levels of the industry. Much of the attention has been given to the airlines and other large tourism-related organisations that have received government assistance (Khalid *et al.*, 2021). However, relatively little attention has been given to smaller and micro-SMEs that make up the bulk of the tourism sector and are essential for the creation of employment opportunities. These business organisations are significant in understanding tourism resilience at different scales because they are often ignored in post-disaster or crisis assistance, especially because they are often highly informal in nature (Biggs *et al.*, 2012, 2015).

The Iranian tourism SME context is interesting in several different ways, particularly when considered from a resilience perspective. First, it highlights the role of external actors in influencing tourism SME strategies and survival outside of the immediate destination context. Foremost among these is the actions of central government with respect to Covid-19 related policy responses. What is notable is that the Iranian government policy response, on paper at least, shares much in common with many other countries, particularly Phases one and two (UNWTO, 2021).

However, judging from the interviewee responses the policy action gap is substantial and is seen as insufficient to meet the economic and fiscal pressures faced by tourism SMEs. Furthermore, some of these measures with respect to marketing can arguably be regarded as business as usual in the Iranian context. Second, the sanctions context of Iranian SMEs highlights that 'learning' gained from a previous crisis (sanctions) may not be sufficient to respond to a new one (Covid-19). This may be because, in part, the sanctions have different effects on the tourism system than Covid-19. Instead, Covid-19 only served to further impact an already weakened tourism system and the capacity of businesses to respond, and prior learning from one crisis did not readily translate into learning for another, different, type of crisis.

This chapter has highlighted three main themes in understanding Iranian SME response to Covid-19: risk perception and uncertainty, economic impacts and coping strategies. The first two themes highlight the unusual nature of the pandemic and how it is different from many other crisis or disaster events that require resilient responses. Within a tourism systems framework, disasters at a destination such as floods or earthquakes clearly affect business capacity at the destination scale, but they do not impact tourist-generating areas, apart from potential short-term shifts in destination perception (Hall & Prayag, 2021). In contrast, the Covid-19 pandemic is so widespread that it affects both destinations and generating regions. Moreover, unlike a more conventional economic crisis which may reduce people's propensity to travel (Hall, 2010), government responses to Covid-19 meant fundamental restrictions on tourist-related mobility. This is something that Iranian SMEs were fundamentally unprepared for and did not enter their risk perceptions. In addition, while the experience of sanctions may have provided some level of capacity to develop coping strategies, the loss of the domestic tourism market was extremely hard to prepare for or respond to.

Interestingly, responses to the pandemic saw an intensification of some previously existing strategies, including even greater dependence on the already highly competitive domestic market as well as further embrace of digital marketing strategies. The latter being a response shared with many other countries as businesses sought to build relationships with customers, often in the absence of, or at least restricted, face-to-face contact when lockdowns occurred. The Iranian context also highlights that experience of previous crises or disasters (e.g. sanctions) does not necessarily make micro-SMEs any more nimble or adaptable than their larger counterparts (Ghaderi *et al.*, 2021). Organisational learning gained from previous disasters does not seem to have incurred or be relevant. This is possibly because they were a different type of crisis to respond to, and previous crises may also have, in some cases, only served to weaken the capacity of micro-SMEs to adapt and respond quickly to another new crisis event. Therefore, a more sophisticated understanding of the inter-relationships between tourism-related resilience and disaster is needed, one that acknowledges that disasters and crises may have cumulative effects on the capacity of micro-SMEs to respond. As such, the reasons for the longer-term resilience of tourism businesses may rely more on social capital and place attachment than the more simplistic economic metrics often used in the assessment of the impacts of crises on tourism.

References

Abdoli, A. (2020) Iran, sanctions, and the COVID-19 crisis. *Journal of Medical Economics* 23 (12), 1461–1465.
Amore, A. and Hall, C.M. (2021) Elite interview, urban tourism governance and post-disaster recovery: Evidence from post-earthquake Christchurch, New Zealand. *Current Issues in Tourism.* https://doi.org/10.1080/13683500.2021.1952940.
Amore, A., Prayag, G. and Hall, C.M. (2018) Conceptualizing destination resilience from a multilevel perspective. *Tourism Review International* 22 (3–4), 235–250.
Biggs, D., Hall, C.M. and Stoeckl, N. (2012) The resilience of formal and informal tourism enterprises to disasters: Reef tourism in Phuket, Thailand. *Journal of Sustainable Tourism* 20 (5), 645–665.
Biggs, D., Hicks, C.C., Cinner, J.E. and Hall, C.M. (2015) Marine tourism in the face of global change: The resilience of enterprises to crises in Thailand and Australia. *Ocean & Coastal Management* 105, 65–74.
Braun, V. and Clarke, V. (2006) Using thematic analysis in psychology. *Qualitative Research in Psychology* 3 (2), 77–101.
Bui, H.T., Jones, T.E., Weaver, D.B. and Le, A. (2020) The adaptive resilience of living cultural heritage in a tourism destination. *Journal of Sustainable Tourism* 28 (7), 1022–1040.
Cafiero, G. (2020) COVID-19: The last nail in the coffin of Iran's tourism industry? See https://www.atlanticcouncil.org/blogs/iransource/covid-19-the-last-nail-in-the-coffin-of-irans-tourism-industry/ (accessed October 2022).
Carruthers, P. (2020) How coronavirus can kill small businesses. *Personal Finance* 2020 (471), 8–10.
Creswell, J.W. and Poth, C.N. (2018) *Qualitative Inquiry and Research Design: Choosing Among Five Approaches.* Thousand Oaks, CA: Sage.
Financial Tribune (2020) Small enterprises account for 45% of Iran's industrial jobs. See https://financialtribune.com/articles/domestic-economy/104668/small-enterprises-account-for-45-of-iran-s-industrial-jobs (accessed October 2022).
Flick, U. (2018) *Designing Qualitative Research.* London: Sage.
Ghaderi, Z., King, B. and Hall, C.M. (2021) Crisis preparedness of hospitality managers: Evidence from Malaysia. *Journal of Hospitality and Tourism Insights.* https://doi.org/10.1108/JHTI-10-2020-0199.
Gibson, T.D., Pelling, M., Ghosh, A., Matyas, D., Siddiqi, A., Solecki, W., Johnson, L., Kenney, C., Johnston, D. and Du Plessis, R. (2016) Pathways for transformation: Disaster risk management to enhance resilience to extreme events. *Journal of Extreme Events* 3 (1), 1671002.
Gonzalez-Perez, M.A., Mohieldin, M., Hult, G.T.M. and Velez-Ocampo, J. (2021) COVID-19, sustainable development challenges of Latin America and the Caribbean, and the potential engines for an SDGs-based recovery. *Management Research* 19 (1), 22–37.
Gregurec, I., Tomičić Furjan, M. and Tomičić-Pupek, K. (2021) The impact of COVID-19 on sustainable business models in SMEs. *Sustainability* 13 (3), 1098.
Hall, C.M. (2010) Crisis events in tourism: Subjects of crisis in tourism. *Current Issues in Tourism* 13 (5), 401–417.

Hall, C.M., Mahdavi, M.A., Oh, Y. and Seyfi, S. (in press) Contemporary Muslim travel and tourism: Cultures and consumption. In C.M. Hall, S. Seyfi and S.M. Rasoolimanesh (eds) *Contemporary Muslim Travel Cultures: Practices, Complexities and Emerging Issues* (14–46). Abingdon: Routledge.

Hall, C.M., Malinen, S., Vosslamber, R. and Wordsworth, R. (eds) (2016) *Business and Post-disaster Management: Business, Organisational and Consumer Resilience and the Christchurch Earthquakes*. Abingdon: Routledge.

Hall, C.M. and Prayag, G. (eds) (2021) *Tourism and Earthquakes*. Bristol: Channel View Publications.

Hall, C.M., Prayag, G. and Amore, A. (2018) *Tourism and Resilience: Individual, Organisational and Destination Perspectives*. Bristol: Channel View Publications.

Hall, C.M., Prayag, G., Fieger, P. and Dyason, D. (2021) Beyond panic buying: Consumption displacement and COVID-19. *Journal of Service Management* 32 (1), 113–128.

Hall, C.M., Scott, D. and Gössling, S. (2020) Pandemics, transformations and tourism: Be careful what you wish for. *Tourism Geographies* 22 (3), 577–598.

Hanna, P. (2012) Using internet technologies (such as Skype) as a research medium: A research note. *Qualitative Research* 12 (2), 239–242.

Haqbin, A., Shojaei, P. and Radmanesh, S. (2021) Prioritising COVID-19 recovery solutions for tourism small and medium-sized enterprises: A rough best-worst method approach. *Journal of Decision Systems*. https://doi.org/10.1080/12460125.2021.192 7487.

Jiang, Y., Ritchie, B.W. and Verreynne, M.L. (2019) Building tourism organizational resilience to crises and disasters: A dynamic capabilities view. *International Journal of Tourism Research* 21 (6), 882–900.

Khalid, U., Okafor, L.E. and Burzynska, K. (2021) Does the size of the tourism sector influence the economic policy response to the COVID-19 pandemic? *Current Issues in Tourism* 24 (19), 2801–2820.

Khoshkhoo, M.H.I. and Nadalipour, Z. (2016) Tourism SMEs and organizational learning in a competitive environment: A longitudinal research on organizational learning in travel and tourism agencies located in the city of Ahvaz, Iran. *The Learning Organization* 23 (2/3), 184–200.

Kim, M.J., Bonn, M. and Hall, C.M. (2021) What influences COVID-19 biosecurity behaviour for tourism? *Current Issues in Tourism* 25 (1), 21–27.

Kukanja, M., Planinc, T. and Sikošek, M. (2020) Crisis management practices in tourism SMEs during the COVID-19 pandemic. *Organizacija* 53 (4), 346–361.

Lu, Y., Wu, J., Peng, J. and Lu, L. (2020) The perceived impact of the Covid-19 epidemic: Evidence from a sample of 4807 SMEs in Sichuan Province, China. *Environmental Hazards* 19 (4), 323–340.

Mandal, S. and Saravanan, D. (2019) Exploring the influence of strategic orientations on tourism supply chain agility and resilience: An empirical investigation. *Tourism Planning & Development* 16 (6), 612–636.

Morakabati, Y. (2011) Deterrents to tourism development in Iran. *International Journal of Tourism Research* 13 (2), 103–123.

Mozaffari, A., Karimian, R. and Mousavi, S. (2017) The return of the 'Idea of Iran' (2005–2015). In R. Butler and W. Suntikul (eds) *Tourism and Political Change* (pp. 186–199). Oxford: Goodfellow Publishers.

OECD (2019) OECD SME and entrepreneurship outlook 2019. See https://www.oecd.org/industry/oecd-sme-and-entrepreneurship-outlook-2019-34907e9c-en.htm (accessed October 2022).

Prayag, G. (2018) Symbiotic relationship or not? Understanding resilience and crisis management in tourism. *Tourism Management Perspectives* 25, 133–135.

Prayag, G. (2020) Time for reset? COVID-19 and tourism resilience. *Tourism Review International* 24 (2–3), 179–184.

Prayag, G. and Hall, C.M. (2021) Conclusion: Earthquakes and tourism – An emerging research agenda. In C.M. Hall and G. Prayag (eds) *Tourism and Earthquakes* (pp. 193–202). Bristol: Channel View Publications.

Prayag, G., Ozanne, L.K. and de Vries, H. (2020) Psychological capital, coping mechanisms and organizational resilience: Insights from the 2016 Kaikoura earthquake, New Zealand. *Tourism Management Perspectives* 34, 100637.

Sajadi, H. and Hartley, K. (2021) COVID-19 pandemic response in Iran: A dynamic perspective on policy capacity. *Journal of Asian Public Policy.* https://doi.org/10.1080/17516234.2021.1930682.

Saldaña, J. (2021) *The Coding Manual for Qualitative Researchers* (4th edn). London: Sage.

Seyfi, S. and Hall, C.M. (eds) (2018) *Tourism in Iran: Challenges, Development and Issues.* Abingdon: Routledge.

Seyfi, S. and Hall, C.M. (2019a) Deciphering Islamic theocracy and tourism: Conceptualization, context, and complexities. *International Journal of Tourism Research* 21 (6), 735–746.

Seyfi, S. and Hall, C.M. (2019b) International sanctions, tourism destinations and resistive economy. *Journal of Policy Research in Tourism, Leisure and Events* 11 (1), 159–169.

Seyfi, S. and Hall, C.M. (2020) Sanctions and tourism: Effects, complexities and research. *Tourism Geographies* 22 (4–5), 749–767.

Seyfi, S., Hall, C.M. and Shabani, B. (2020a) COVID-19 and international travel restrictions: The geopolitics of health and tourism. *Tourism Geographies.* https://doi.org/10.1080/14616688.2020.1833972.

Seyfi, S., Hall, C.M. and Vo-Thanh, T. (2020b) The gendered effects of statecraft on women in tourism: Economic sanctions, women's disempowerment and sustainability? *Journal of Sustainable Tourism.* https://doi.org/10.1080/09669582.2020.1850749.

Shafiei, Z. and Karoubi, M. (2018) E-business adoption in small and medium sized tourism firms in Iran: Challenges and prospects. *Tourismos* 13 (1), 54–75.

Tehran Times (2022) COVID-19 causes $7.6b damage to Iran tourism. See https://www.tehrantimes.com/news/463458/COVID-19-causes-7-6b-damage-to-Iran-tourism

UNIDO (2003) Strategy document to enhance the contribution of an efficient and competitive small and medium-sized enterprise sector to industrial and economic development in the Islamic republic of Iran. See https://open.unido.org/ (accessed October 2022).

United Nations Educational and Scientific and Cultural Organization (UNESCO) (2022) Iran (Islamic Republic of). See https://whc.unesco.org/en/statesparties/ir (accessed October 2022).

UNWTO (2020) Tourism and COVID-19 – Unprecedented economic impacts. See https://www.unwto.org/tourism-and-covid-19-unprecedented-economic-impacts (accessed October 2022).

UNWTO (2022) COVID-19: Measures to support travel and tourism. See https://www.unwto.org/covid-19-measures-to-support-travel-tourism (accessed October 2022).

Vargas-Sánchez, A. (2021) Strategic management of the COVID-19 crisis in rural tourism settings: Lessons learned from SMEs. In D. Troubes and N. Araújo-Vila (eds) *Risk, Crisis, and Disaster Management in Small and Medium-sized Tourism Enterprises* (pp. 1–26). Hershey: IGI Global.

World Bank (2021) Islamic Republic of Iran. See https://www.worldbank.org/en/country/iran/overview#1 (accessed October 2022).

WTTC (2020) Iran. 2021 annual research: Key highlights. See https://wttc.org/Research/Economic-Impact (accessed October 2022).

Yadollahi Farsi, J. and Toghraee, M.T. (2014) Identification the main challenges of small and medium sized enterprises in exploiting of innovative opportunities (Case study: Iran SMEs). *Journal of Global Entrepreneurship Research* 4 (1), 1–15.

Zamani, Z. (2022) The impact of COVID-19 on Iran's SMEs: Policy implications for current and post pandemic. See https://www.kiep.go.kr/galleryExtraDownload.es?bid=0026&list_no=9312&seq=5 (accessed October 2022).

Part 2

Transition of Attitudes in Spiritual Tourism

5 The Impact of Covid-19 on Japanese Temple Stays: The 2021 Situation

Ricardo Nicolas Progano

Introduction

The emergence of Covid-19 and the subsequent restrictions imposed by governmental bodies across the globe have had an immense impact on the tourism industry. According to the UNWTO (2021), the January–May 2021 period experienced an 85% decline in international arrivals when compared to 2019. Tourism in Asia and the Pacific, a fast-growth region in pre-pandemic 2019, was particularly affected, undergoing a 95% decline in international arrivals in the first five months of 2021 over the same period in 2019. Also, this region has the highest number of destinations that completely closed their borders. Still, other regions fared little differently, with Europe (-85%), the Middle East (-83%), Africa (-81%) and the Americas (-72%) seeing sharp declines as well. Despite the grim situation of the tourism industry, a slight recovery is noticeable, with domestic tourism playing a large role. International tourism, while still in an uncertain and ever-changing situation, has also shown a small recovery of -82% in May from -86% in April 2021 (UNWTO, 2021). In this context, religious travel, gatherings and activities were put under restrictions as new public health policies were established. This chapter aims to assess the impact on temple stays through the case study of the Buddhist temple complex Kōyasan (Wakayama prefecture, Japan) during 2021 in order to contribute to the study of Covid-19 impacts and the practices of relevant religious stakeholders involved in tourism. The chapter builds upon previous research done about the impacts on Kōyasan's temple stays during the January–September 2020 period (Progano, 2021).

Religious travel was deeply affected by this situation, with examples from various creeds and locations. For example, the South Korean Shincheonji Church of Jesus ignored preventive measures and continued to gather during the early months of 2020, resulting in an increase in cases during February 2020. Similar cases were reported in the UK, Iran, India,

Brazil, the US and Pakistan, among others (Ebrahim & Memish, 2020; Olsen & Timothy, 2020; Quadri, 2020). The pandemic led to restrictions and cancellations of religious travel and gatherings. Perhaps one of the more known cases was the heavy restrictions that the Saudi Arabian government placed for the 2020 *hajj*, including the exclusion of all international pilgrims (Olsen & Timothy, 2020). Also, there were calls for voluntary restrictions and cancellations during the Holy Week 2020 in Latin America (Rodriguez-Morales *et al*., 2020). In such a context, alternatives were explored. For example, certain religious institutions encouraged their followers to conduct virtual gatherings or send online prayers. Other institutions kept in contact with their congregations through television, radio and social media (McLaughlin, 2020; Raj & Griffin, 2020; Sulkowski & Ignatowski, 2020). This is of importance for religiously inclined populations, as studies show that people tend to turn to religious performances such as prayers to cope with uncertain environments (Bentzen, 2020; Dein *et al*., 2020). However, the absence of visitors had a negative economic impact on religious destinations, which often depended financially on them (Olsen & Timothy, 2020; Raj & Griffin, 2020). Similarly, religious professionals who relied on income and donations to support themselves and their institutions also endured negative economic consequences (McLaughlin, 2020). Virtual alternatives also transformed religious performances, which used to be an opportunity for devotees to gather and manifest their beliefs together (Olsen & Timothy, 2020).

One sector that was affected by the complex situation described above was temple stays, a well-established accommodation service available to both Buddhist believers and the public. Temple stays comprise accommodation services provided by religious organisations on their temple grounds, providing visitors with a unique experience. Aside from staying overnight, visitors can sample Buddhism traditions such as meditation, Buddhist cuisine, observing ceremonies and sutra copying. Finally, visitors also interact with authentic Buddhist monks and get a glimpse of their religious lifestyle. As such, temple stays are a well-established accommodation service. For example, the South Korean government has promoted stay programmes since 2002 to experience Buddhism and display its national culture to visitors (Kaplan, 2010). This development, however, was affected by the Covid-19 pandemic. In South Korea's case, temple stays and religious gatherings were suspended in March 2020, and later in April 2020 individual visitors were began to be accepted (Ross *et al*., 2021).

Case Study: Kōyasan

Outline of Kōyasan and its tourism development

Kōyasan is well-known as an important Shingon Buddhism temple complex in Kōya town, Wakayama prefecture (Japan), and serves as the seat of the headquarters temple of Kōyasan Shingon Buddhism, called Kongōbu-ji. The site was established by the famed monk Kūkai (空海), also known as Kōbō Daishi (弘法大師), in 819 CE after being initiated in esoteric Shingon teachings during his study journey to the Chinese imperial capital of Chang'an (Nicoloff, 2008). While Kōyasan enjoyed patronage from the nobility since the Heian period (794–1185 CE), temple stays (*shukubō* – 宿坊) have their origin later, in the 14th century, when different monasteries in Kōyasan built protective affiliations with influential warrior clans, in which the temples obtained political and financial support while providing religious and accommodation services. Gradually, nearly all the temples at Kōyasan realised the benefits of such associations and obtained patronage from powerful families (Matsunaga, 2014; Nicoloff, 2008). The traditional term for Buddhist patrons is *dan'otsu* (檀越) and is derived from the Sanskrit language (Sōkka Gakkai, 2017). While Kōyasan continued to be a centre of pilgrimage and Buddhist scholarship, reforms during the Meiji period (1868–1912 CE) opened the site to a wider public with the proclamation of an 1872 edict ending the traditional ban on women from the mountain, with Kongōbu-ji officially admitting women to enter in 1906. The gradual opening of Kōyasan eventually led to the establishment of schools and businesses. In this sense, while the site continued to be a temple town populated by ancient Buddhist institutions, the lay population could carry out their economic activities and lifestyles.

Among other reforms, the Meiji government also ordered the discontinuance of the patronage affiliation between powerful families and temples, as well as severing the relationship between Kōyasan and the imperial family. In 1889, the Japanese government merged Kōyasan and nearby villages into Kōya-village; and later in 1925, further merging finally created the current Kōya-town. The construction of transport infrastructure was an important factor in the subsequent tourism development of Kōyasan. The Nankai railroad and cable cart construction completed in 1934 provided easy access to visitors from the bustling city of Osaka. The end of automobile circulation restrictions inside Kōyasan in 1952 allowed the introduction of tour buses to easily carry visitors to different well-known sites. These improvements in transport infrastructure also transformed travel patterns, as visitors directly travelled to Kōyasan and detoured from the surrounding temples and pilgrimage trails. Some service providers, such as *jinrikisha*, also disappeared due to these transport innovations (Reader, 2020). With increasing numbers of domestic visitors arriving and the end of clan patronage, the *shukubō* temples started to lend their accommodation services to the public. This provided the temples with an additional income source to address their income difficulties (Yanata & Sharpley, 2022), reflecting the overall financial challenges that Japanese Buddhism faces due to falling numbers of donators, depopulation of rural temples and loss of traditional land-holdings (Covell, 2005).

The profile of these visitors also changed over time, with religious travel groups affiliated to a Buddhist temple in Kōyasan gradually giving place to small non-affiliated groups who had varied motivations such as relaxation (Yanata & Sharpley, 2022).

In 2004, original properties in Kōyasan were designated as part of the 'Sacred Sites and Pilgrimage Routes in the Kii Mountain Range' UNESCO World Heritage Site (Matsunaga, 2014). Some of Kōyasan's main tourism attractions include the Okunoin (奥の院) cemetery, where Kūkai's mausoleum is located as well as tombs of famous figures, and the Danjō Garan (壇上伽藍), a complex of religious buildings that includes the iconic 49-meter tall Great Stupa. Due to its importance as the headquarters of Shingon Buddhism and its collection of historic artifacts, Kongōbu-ji is also one of the highlights for visitors. Access by the 23-kilometer long Kōyasan Chōishi Michi (the mountain trail that has historically led pilgrims to Kōyasan) is no longer a requirement due to the development of the modern transport infrastructure but remains as an attractive hiking option. Apart from its rich tangible cultural heritage, Kōyasan also attracts visitors seeking its intangible heritage, including meditation experiences, sutra copying sessions, religious festivals and Buddhist cuisine.

In recent times, the economy of Kōyasan has become more and more connected to tourism, while traditional industries such as forestry and agriculture have declined. As such, the town's economic sector is largely dominated by the service sector such as tourism, with 84.4% of the workforce employed in it during 2015 (Kōya Town, 2019). According to official statistics, during 2019, a total of 1,481,788 people visited the town, and 224,393 of them stayed the night (Wakayama Tourism Agency, 2020). Before 2020, inbound tourism played an important role, as the 2004 UNESCO World Heritage Site inscription increased the destination's popularity overseas (Matsunaga, 2014). In 2019, 48.57% of all overnight visitors were foreigners. Regarding nationality, most inbound visitors come from Western countries such as France (22,834), the US (12,174), Germany (8884) and the UK (6923), although Chinese visitors were also a growing presence (6975) (Wakayama Tourism Agency, 2020). Kōyasan's popularity among Western visitors is attributed to their general interest in Buddhism, as well as the opportunity of experiencing shukubō lodgings and Buddhist cuisine (shōjin ryōri -精進料理) (Jimura, 2016; Matsunaga, 2014). As can be observed, Buddhist temples play a central role in tourism development. First, the intangible and tangible heritage of Buddhism is the main travel motivation for visitors (Wakayama Tourism Agency, 2020). Recent research also shows that both Japanese and international visitors place importance on the religious aspects of Kōyasan (Yanata, 2021). Second, the shukubō temples provide 6185 out of a total of 6242 beds, covering almost all of Kōyasan's accommodation capacity. They also provide attractive experience services such as sutra copying, mediation, ritual observation and Buddhist cuisine as well. These temples operate independently but recognise the religious authority of Kongōbu-ji. They are also members of the local Kōyasan Shukubō Association, a private organisation that offers an online reservation system for *shukubō*, advice to its members and visitor assistance. In contrast to South Korea's case (Kaplan, 2010; Song *et al.*, 2015), the Japanese government does not have a direct influence on the temple management and activities.

Impact of Covid-19 during 2020

According to previous research by the author between July and September 2020 (Progano, 2021), Covid-19 and its related travel restrictions have had a deep impact on Kōyasan's temple stays since March 2020. During March and June 2020, reservation numbers dramatically decreased by -95% compared to 2019. April was perhaps the most negative month as most *shukubō* temples decided to temporally close, following the state of emergency declared by the national government. Inbound tourists practically disappeared because of Japan's entry restrictions and had not recovered at the time of the study, although some stakeholders mentioned that they expected international visitors to come again from March 2021 (Progano, 2021). Since July 2020, stakeholders reported that, while the situation of temple stays was far from normal, reservation numbers showed a slight recovery as some *shukubō* reported a 50% occupation during weekdays. However, the absence of inbound tourists meant that tourism demand was concentrated on weekends when domestic tourists also tend to travel. To stimulate domestic demand, local stakeholders engaged in different tourism campaigns, as well as participating in the 'Go To' national campaign. These efforts showed the importance of pre-established collaborative networks among stakeholders in order to articulate responses during disasters. In this scenario, the emergence of new wellness-related services in Ekō-in and Fukuchi-in temples, which started to offer teleworking stations and oxygen capsules respectively, was a remarkable finding that reflected the importance of wellness products in the post-Covid-19 tourism scenario anticipated by researchers (Ma *et al.*, 2020). This wellness trend had existed at Kōyasan previously, as wellness programmes were present before 2020, such as forest-bathing (*shinrin'yoku* – 森林浴), similar to other religious destinations in Japan (Mori, 2005; Progano & Kato, 2018) and elsewhere (Stausberg, 2011).

During the 2020 fieldwork, the researcher argued that Kōyasan reached an intermediate phase between June and September 2020, as the national state of emergency was ended, while national and local tourism campaigns aimed to stimulate a slow recovery in domestic demand. Events and festivals remained largely cancelled, with a few local events taking place only, such as food fairs. However, Buddhist monks continued performing their obligatory religious ceremonies (*hōe* – 法会) while following health protocols and discouraging the general public from assisting (Progano, 2021).

Methods

This study re-evaluates the results of previous fieldwork done between July and September 2020 in Kōyasan (Progano, 2021) to observe how impacts on temple stays have changed over approximately one year. Therefore, fieldwork was carried out in Kōyasan from September–October 2021 (see Figure 5.1). First, the same key stakeholders were contacted in order to inquire about this topic: the Kōyasan Town Tourism Association (hereafter, the Tourism Association), the Kōyasan Shukubō Association (hereafter, the Shukubō Association), the Kōyasan Tourism Information Center (hereafter, the Center), which acts as the local Destination

Figure 5.1 Kōyasan on September 2021 (source: author)

Management Organization, and Kongōbu-ji itself. The Tourism Association and the Center are both involved in the tourism promotion and development of Kōyasan, with the Center being more involved in PR campaigns. The Shukubō Association is a private organisation that provides visitors with services related to temple stays, including an online reservation system. It also provides assistance to its shukubō members on tourism matters. Finally, Kongōbu-ji is included due to its religious importance as well as being a central tourism attraction for visitors, although it does not provide accommodation. These stakeholders were interviewed in Japanese, following a semi-structured questionnaire containing seven questions related to visitor number and profile, tourism initiatives, *shukubō* activities, events, impact on restaurants and souvenir stores, stakeholder collaboration and their perspective on the current situation. Next, representatives of the five *shukubō* temples who were previously interviewed were contacted again: Ekō-in, Sōji-in, Fukuchi-in, Fudō-in and Ichijō-in. They were also interviewed in Japanese through a semi-structured questionnaire containing nine questions related to visitor numbers, access to *shukubō* management, financial support, stakeholder collaboration, health-related measures, ritual performance, donations, tourism initiatives and their thoughts on the overall situation. As can be observed, this study used purposive sampling, as only the stakeholders and *shukubō* temples interviewed in 2020 were contacted again. However, for this study, Fukuchi-in and the Center could not be reached for participation, and thus were not included in the current fieldwork. All interviews were done in Japanese and recorded, except in Ichijō-in's case, which requested to answer the interview by email. Excerpts from the interviewees, translated by the author, are included in the Findings and Discussion section to further illustrate the research findings.

For analysing the findings, this chapter utilises the tourism disaster management framework created by Faulkner (2001), which describes six phases in the process of tourism disaster management as shown in Table 5.1.

Table 5.1 Six phases in tourism disaster management (Source: Faulkner, 2001)

Phase	Description
1) Pre-event	Managerial action can be taken to prevent or mitigate the disaster.
2) Prodromal	In this phase, the disaster becomes inevitable.
3) Emergency	The effects of the disaster are felt, and it is necessary to protect both the people and property.
4) Intermediate	The short-term needs of the people are secured, so efforts can be mobilised towards the restoration of services and the daily route of the community if this is desirable or possible.
5) Long term	As a continuation of the fifth phase, other items that could not be attended to quickly are put in focus.
6) Resolution	Either routine is restored, or a new improved state is established.

This model was originally applied to disaster management of floods (Faulkner & Vikulov, 2001) and was later applied to pandemics as well (Henderson, 2003; Miller & Ritchie, 2003). Faulkner's tourism disaster management framework was selected as this is the same framework utilised in the author's previous study about Covid-19 impacts on Kōyasan's temple stays (Progano, 2021), thus providing a shared theoretical framework between the two studies.

Findings

Findings show that the overall tourism situation had almost no noticeable variations since the 2020 fieldwork, with the presence of slight recoveries that were later interrupted by declarations of states of emergency issued by the government, which urged the public to refrain from leisure travels. However, these states of emergency did not constitute mandatory lockdown measures, as observed elsewhere. Regardless, the Japanese government heavily restricted inbound flights and, as in 2020, the absence of inbound visitors transformed domestic visitors into the only viable tourism market. Due to the disappearance of inbound tourism, visitation patterns became uneven, as Japanese visitors concentrate on weekends and be mostly absent on weekdays. This point was mentioned during the 2020 fieldwork, showing that it has become an established travel pattern. Long weekends and holidays also attract larger numbers of visitors.

> (Inbound visitors) don't come. They don't come but sometimes there are foreign visitors here. I believe the reason is that these visitors are already living in Japan. (Kongōbu-ji)

> Last year (2020) was like this, and this year (2021) is the same. There was an incredibly great impact. Due to that impact, the number of visitors who came from overseas was reduced to almost 100%. Also, domestic visitors were around 80% reduced. (Sōji-in)

> This year (2021) visitors are less but they come. When compared to 2020 it is better, but certainly, it is still less than half of 2019, when inbound visitors came. (Ekō-in)

> During the spring of last year (2020), around April and May, at the time of the first state of emergency, every day there were clusters of hundreds of people all across the country, right? Hundreds of them. At that time, everyone stayed inside and almost nobody came. Now, in the state of emergency of the fifth wave, it is not zero. Some people still come. Especially many people from Tokyo and the capital's metropolitan area. Now, more than half of the visitors are from Tokyo, Kanagawa and Saitama. (Fudō-in)

Events, both religious and non-religious, remain largely cancelled for the short and medium term with a few exceptions. The Kōyasan Fire Festival was carried out during both March 2020 and 2021, as its purpose is related to the miraculous prevention of illnesses. Other important events, such as the Birthday of Kōbō Daishi (June 15) and the Candle Festival (August 13), were cancelled. Also, similar to 2020, the Buddhist monks continued to carry out their obligatory religious ceremonies while performing prevention measures and asking the public to not participate in person. Other events celebrated at the temples, such as weddings, were partially cancelled as well. Regarding the adoption of online tools, it was observed to a certain degree. For example, Kongōbu-ji switched certain experiential activities aimed at visitors to online, such as sutra copying. Still, the adoption of online tools is limited. Going back to Kongōbu-ji's example, only specific activities went online, while others did not, such as the Ajikan meditation as they were judged to not be viable online. The *shukubō* (see Figure 5.2) themselves did not mention the adoption of innovative online tools. Instead of new tools, they continued to rely on the same health-related measures from 2020, including the use of masks, hand sanitation, air ventilation, disinfection of surfaces and limiting the number of visitors per room. Both prefectural and national government health authorities guide the *shukubō* on these issues. Additionally, the Wakayama Ryokan & Hotel Hygiene Association, which functions under the national Ministry of Health, Labour and Welfare, extends certifications to accommodations that comply with prevention measures, including *shukubō*. The Wakayama prefecture is also extending certificates to *shukubō* that adhere to a list of health prevention guidelines. However, the acquisition of neither certification is obligatory for operation. Finally, due to the increasing availability of Covid-19 vaccines produced by different pharmaceutical companies, vaccination of the *shukubō* staff was noted as another measure to alleviate visitor anxiety. Still, as in the case of certification, vaccination is not mandatory.

> *(Prevention measures) have not changed much. Last year (2020), we received plenty of guidance from the national government. 'Please put partitions and plates', 'please disinfect', 'please wear masks'. It is the same as last year.* (Ekō-in)

> *This is the main temple (honzan - 本山) so during the year we conduct many research meetings and classes, but most of them are canceled. Also, during sutra copying sessions the number of people who can enter is capped.* (Kongōbu-ji)

> *The first Sunday of March is the Kōyasan Fire Festival and we managed to celebrate it (in 2021). We prayed for the dispel of the plague. Around 1,000 people came.* (Kōyasan Tourism Association)

> *We received much guidance from the prefectural government to obtain this certification. From our side, we asked many questions and collaborated with them.* (Sōji-in)

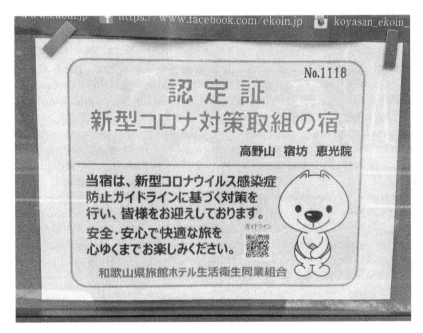

Figure 5.2 Certification of the Wakayama Ryokan & Hotel Hygiene Association, posted outside a *shukubō* temple (source: author)

Anxiety related to Covid-19 has also altered visitor behaviour. Stakeholders mentioned visitors avoid public transport and use their automobiles as a prevention measure. They also avoid staying the night in *shukubō* or other accommodation types. According to stakeholders, crowd avoidance has also led to a decrease in bus tours, in contrast to observations during the 2020 fieldwork. For these reasons, stakeholders mentioned how visitors now tend to visit Kōyasan on a day trip to the key sites such as Kongōbu-ji and the Okunoin cemetery, avoiding staying the night. Stakeholders also indicated that some tourists do not want to let others know that they are currently travelling, as they fear being accused of negligence or egotism by their peers. Because of this, they also refrain from long stays and even from buying souvenirs in tourist shops. The *shukubō* themselves are also anxious about receiving large groups, due to the fear of infection. The lack of a hospital for Covid-19 patients inside Kōyasan further increases these worries. In consequence, large tour groups have been replaced by smaller groups such as families. Stakeholders mentioned that *shukubō* occupation gravitated between 30% and 50%, showing that domestic tourism, while the only viable market in the current situation, has not been able to satisfactorily replace the international markets. This number is similar to the official 2020 statistics, which state that only 51,052 visitors stayed the night in Kōyasan, showing a 78% interannual decrease from 2019 (Wakayama Tourism Agency, 2021).

Still, the absence of tour buses and loud tourist crowds had a positive effect on visitor experience, as a quiet atmosphere now prevailed at the destination.

> *Definitely, the state of emergency is very related to accommodation. In Kōyasan, during summer (of 2021) visitors came for day trips on Saturdays, but while many cars came, lodging numbers did not increase.* (Shukubō Association)

> *Normally, (visitors) would come to Kōyasan, buy a souvenir and go back, but now everyone is coming in secret so they do not buy them anymore (...) I heard about it many times from the shopkeepers.* (Kōyasan Tourism Association)

> *I think that Kōyasan's souvenir shops have been in a dire situation. During the fall colors season (kōyō – 紅葉) and the Goldenweek some visitors came, but certainly there are few on weekdays. Also, buses do not come and there are no more day tours. The visitors who walk around only go a bit inside the shops.* (Kongōbu-ji)

Finally, signs of efforts towards tourism revitalisation have been mostly absent during 2021 fieldwork. The different tourism campaigns mentioned in 2020, such as the national Go To Travel, were cancelled as the government aimed to restrain population movement due to a new surge of cases during the late fall of 2020. The general uncertainty of the situation, with no clear end in sight, further contributed to this absence. Still, some stakeholders mentioned the preparation for campaigns in 2022. For example, the Shukubō Association mentioned the creation of a new PR video in Japanese with subtitles in multiple languages to be shot in October 2021. The *shukubō* mentioned that they were refurbishing their rooms as well, expecting more visitors in the future.

> *We are collaborating in the creation of a PR video with the (Wakayama) prefecture.* (Ichijō-in)

> *Financial support was released to the shukubō to make them of higher quality, to make even better rooms. Now we passed the application so, in winter of this year (2021), we will make a single large suite room from four common guest rooms.* (Ekō-in)

> *(With the prefectural government) we have been actively collaborating. We obtained financial aid and have maintained close communications.* (Fudō-in)

While the 2020 fieldwork showed that religious organisations such as the *shukubō* were having problems obtaining public financial aid, the 2021 fieldwork showed that the *shukubō* have been able to attain it. For example, the temples reported that they obtained financial support for their employees. This financial aid was also utilised for refurbishing rooms in different ways, such as the improvement of toilet facilities and automatic doors in order to improve accommodation quality during an expected post-pandemic tourism.

Finally, referring to Faulkner's framework, during September 2021, the general situation in Kōyasan can be placed in the Emergency phase, showing a regression from the Intermediate phase during September 2020, as the tourism revitalisation initiatives from 2020, both national and local, were interrupted and, instead, efforts had to be directed towards protecting the population. The regression to the Emergency phase shows the non-linear nature of certain disaster types, such as pandemics. This possibility was mentioned during the 2020 fieldwork (Progano, 2021) and confirmed in the 2021 fieldwork. The non-linearity of the Covid-19 pandemic has led to uncertainty among stakeholders because the pandemic has become longer than originally expected and tourism revitalisation remains unclear.

Discussion

Findings showed that the Covid-19 pandemic and its associated public health policies had a profound impact on the tourism practice of *shukubō* temples in Kōyasan. Following the previous fieldwork done on 2020 (Progano, 2021), it can be observed that certain practices of religious stakeholders have become firmly established over time. Health measures such as temperature checks, masks, hand hygiene, social distance and air ventilation have become a common and relevant issue in the provision of hospitality services in the *shukubō*. Such practices have also expanded to include new certification schemes, as the fieldwork showed. These trends show the further 'medicalization' of religious travel, as previous researchers pointed out (Olsen & Timothy, 2020). Additionally, these new health practices have altered host–guest relationships, as well as the guest–guest relationship. Anxiety is an important factor for the application of these practices, as the *shukubō* and other stakeholders mentioned.

Regarding the utilisation of technology, a staple of pandemic-related countermeasures in religious circles has been implemented (McLaughlin, 2020; Sulkowski & Ignatowski, 2020); this practice continues to be limited in Kōyasan, as observed during 2020. There may be multiple reasons for this. First, the monks may not be familiar with their utilisation for complex tasks such as online activities. Second, virtual technologies may be seen as inadequate for translating the experience that participants undergo in real settings. For example, Kongōbu-ji mentioned that certain activities could not be properly translated to online, such as Ajikan meditation. Translating the experience of staying in an authentic Buddhist temple located in a holy mountain through virtual devices is a complex task, as the overall sensitive experience and sense of place is lost (Progano,

2021; Sigala, 2020). However, attempts at virtual temple stays elsewhere were reported by other researchers (Ross *et al.*, 2021).

Stakeholder collaboration is widely recognised in Kōyasan as vital implementing both public health measures and tourism revitalisation promotion, as the 2020 fieldwork demonstrated as well (Progano, 2021). Temples implemented public health measures in collaboration with the local government and the other tourism-related stakeholders, such as the Shukubō Association, who provided assistance and advice. Tourism revitalisation campaigns also involved the collaboration of the *shukubō* temples with the other stakeholders, as during the 2020 fieldwork. The importance of stakeholder collaboration for the effective involvement of religious stakeholders is an important point, as religious organisations may lack formal tourism-related skills and know-how (Shackley, 2001). However, it is essential that collaboration schemes are voluntarily agreed between parties and not unilaterally imposed by public authorities, in order to avoid conflicts. In Kōyasan's example, the authorities did not impose policies or restrictions upon the *shukubō*, but instead provided advice and health provisions. Previous studies provide evidence of conflict between tourism policies and local communities in sacred sites (McGuire, 2013; Yasuda, 2010), and a complex situation such as the Covid-19 pandemic may be no exception. Other researchers, such as Olsen and Timothy (2020), mention that, in the current context, public officials may impose health policies on religious institutions and their faith communities to prevent them from conducting their usual activities. In this sense, new tourism practices should be carried out on collaborative terms to be sustainable and conflict-free.

Conclusions

The 2021 fieldwork showed that, after approximately one year, the practice of religious stakeholders in Kōyasan, specifically temple stays, has not changed substantially, reflecting the overall impact of the Covid-19 pandemic on religious tourism mentioned by previous research (Olsen & Timothy, 2020; Raj & Griffin, 2020). Domestic tourism continued to be the sole market in Kōyasan, as inbound tourism virtually disappeared since Spring 2020. The situation of the *shukubō* temples remained largely the same as in 2020, with low levels of visitation concentrated on weekends. Preventive measures continued to be in place with little variance, while authorities collaborated by providing prevention guidelines and certifications. The adoption of new technological tools was not noticeable, although cases existed, as Kongōbu-ji mentioned the existence of activities done online. The reason for this limited adoption of technological tools by religious institutions, such as the *shukubō*, is outside the chapter's scope, but may be an area worth exploring in future research. Next, the impact of fears and anxiety caused by Covid-19 is an area of importance for future research because of its impact on travel patterns and tourism practices, as the present fieldwork in Kōyasan demonstrated. The anxiety of the community itself, which believes that the arrival of large groups may become a potential health threat, is another area of interest. The *shukubō* themselves are anxious about accommodating large groups, not only because of the health threat, but the negative image it may draw to them by the public. This issue echoes back to the mentioned incidents before, where the activities of religious groups allegedly led to an increase in infections and a consequent criticism from society (Ebrahim & Memish, 2020; Olsen & Timothy, 2020; Quadri, 2020). In this sense, the new health-related practices, such as certification schemes found during field-work, can be understood not only as a health prevention measure but also as a way to present *shukubō* activities as safe and protect their image. The eventual reintroduction of inbound tourists, while desirable to tourism stakeholders, may create tensions and fears among the community, thus being an area worth exploring in future studies.

Regarding practical implications, tourism operators and policymakers should notice the new travel patterns of visitors that COVID-related anxiety and restrictions have brought about. In particular, visitor reluctance to stay overnight may further complicate *shukubō* operations, which are already under strain due to the loss of inbound markets. These difficulties are particularly relevant for destinations in the rural periphery that have become reliant on tourism, such as Kōyasan. Indeed, if visitors stay less time, their spending also reduces and a hypothetical post-COVID tourism recovery involving rural communities may not have the expected benefits. The question of economic impacts of pilgrimage sites such as Kōyasan has been debated by previous studies. In their study about Santiago de Compostela, Lois-Gonzalez and Santos (2015) noticed that, while visitor spending was limited on pilgrimage trails, upon reaching their destination, consumption tended to normalise again as they spent more time in the location. Other studies showed similar findings, as visitor spending is usually scarce in communities alongside pilgrimage trails (Fernandes *et al.*, 2012; Progano, 2018). However, this study showed that, due to COVID-induced anxiety, visitors are spending less time at the pilgrimage goal too. In particular, reluctance towards using accommodations is of particular concern for temple stays. The *shukubō* mentioned different health-related measures in their accommodations, including limiting the number of people per room. However, at the time of this study, the said measures appear to be ineffective in curbing anxiety. This point also casts doubts over the actual importance of domestic tourism during travel restrictions, at least in certain destinations that partially relied on inbound visitors such as Kōyasan. Even in September–October 2021, the *shukubō* stated occupation levels between 30 and 50%, while souvenir shops and restaurants were reported to have low activity levels. Still, as the study showed, the pandemic is a non-linear and dynamic event and thus future increases and decreases of Covid-19 are expected to continue influencing visitor behaviour and stakeholder responses. Finally, stakeholder collaboration emerged as a central point for both public health measures and tourism revitalisation campaigns, in particular for religious stakeholders that may not have formal tourism skills or know-how. Policymakers should seek to build these networks and seek collaboration while aiming to not impose practices unilaterally that may cause conflict later on.

References

Bentzen, J.S. (2020) In crisis, we pray: Religiosity and the Covid-19 pandemic. See https://cepr.org/active/publications/discussion_papers/dp.php?dpno=14824 (accessed November 2020).

Covell, S.G. (2005) *Japanese Temple Buddhism: Worldliness in a Religion of Renunciation*. Honolulu: University of Hawai'i Press.

Dein, S., Loewenthal, K., Lewis, C.A. and Pargament, K.I. (2020) COVID-19, mental health and religion: An agenda for future research. *Mental Health, Religion and Culture* 23 (1), 1–9.

Ebrahim, S.H. and Memish, Z.A. (2020) COVID-19: The role of mass gatherings. *Travel Medicine and Infectious Disease* 34, 1–3.

Faulkner, B. (2001) Towards a framework for tourism disaster management. *Tourism Management* 22, 135–147.

Faulkner, B. and Vikulov, S. (2001) Katherine, washed out one day, back on the track the next: A post-mortem of a tourism disaster. *Tourism Management* 22, 331–344.

Fernandes, C., Pimenta, E., Goncalves, F. and Rachao, S. (2012) A new research approach for religious tourism: The case study of the Portuguese route to Santiago. *International Journal of Tourism Policy* 4 (2), 83–94. https://doi.org/10.1504/IJTP.2012.048996

Henderson, J.C. (2003) Managing a health-related crisis: SARS in Singapore. *Journal of Vacation Marketing* 10 (1), 67–77.

Jimura, T. (2016) World Heritage Site management: A case study of sacred sites and pilgrimage routes in the Kii mountain range, Japan. *Journal of Heritage Tourism* 11 (4), 1–13.

Kaplan, U. (2010) Images of monasticism: The Temple Stay Program and the re-branding of Korean Buddhist temples. *Korean Studies* 34, 127–146.

Kōya Town (2019) *Kōya Town Fourth Long-term General Plan*. Kōya Town: Kōya Town (in Japanese).

Lois-Gonzalez, R.C. and Santos, X.M. (2015) Tourists and pilgrims on their way to Santiago. Motives, Caminos and final destinations. *Journal of Tourism and Cultural Change* 13 (2), 149–164. https://doi.org/10.1080/14766825.2014.918985

Ma, S., Zhao X., Gong Y. and Wengel, Y. (2020) Proposing "healing tourism" as a post-COVID-19 tourism product. *Anatolia*. https://doi.org/10.1080/13032917.2020.1808490

Matsunaga, Y. (2014) *Kōyasan*. Tokyo: Iwanami Shoten (in Japanese).

McGuire, M.P. (2013) What's at stake in designating Japan's sacred mountains as UNESCO World Heritage Sites? Shugendo Practices in the Kii Peninsula. *Japanese Journal of Religious Studies* 40 (2), 323–354.

McLaughlin, L. (2020) Japanese religious responses to COVID-19: A preliminary report. *The Asia-Pacific Journal: Japan Focus* 18 (9), 1–23.

Miller, G.A. and Ritchie, B.W. (2003) A farming crisis or a tourism disaster? An analysis of the foot and mouth disease in the UK. *Current Issues in Tourism* 6 (2), 150–171.

Mori, M. (2005) *The Modernization of Shikoku Henro: From a 'Modern Pilgrimage' to a 'Healing Journey'*. Tokyo: Sogensha (in Japanese).

Nicoloff, P.L. (2008) *Sacred Kōyasan: A Pilgrimage to the Mountain Temple of Saint Kōbō Daishi and the Great Sun Buddha*. New York: State University of New York Press.

Olsen, D.H. and Timothy, D.A. (2020) The COVID-19 pandemic and religious travel: Present and future trends. *International Journal of Religious Tourism and Pilgrimage* 8, 170–188.

Progano, R.N. and Kato, K. (2018) Spirituality and tourism in Japanese pilgrimage sites: Exploring the intersection through the case of Kumano Kodo. *Fieldwork in Religion* 13 (1), 23–43.

Progano, R.N. (2018) Residents' perceptions of socio-economic impacts on pilgrimage trails: How does the community perceive pilgrimage tourism? *Asian Journal of Tourism Research* 3 (2), 148–178.

Progano, R.N. (2021) The impact of COVID-19 on temple stays: A case study from Koyasan, Japan. *International Journal of Religious Tourism and Pilgrimage* 9 (5), 116–127.

Quadri, S.A. (2020) COVID-19 and religious congregations: Implications for spread of novel pathogens. *International Journal of Infectious Diseases* 96, 219–221.

Raj, R. and Griffin, K.A. (2020) Reflecting on the impact of COVID-19 on religious tourism and pilgrimage. *International Journal of Religious Tourism and Pilgrimage* 8 (7), 1–8.

Reader, I. (2020) Turning to tourism in a time of crisis? Buddhist temples and pilgrimage promotion in secular(ized) Japan. In C. Bruntz and B. Schedneck (eds) *Buddhist Tourism in Asia* (pp. 161–179). Honolulu: University of Hawai'i Press.

Rodriguez-Morales, A.J., Sah, R. and Paniz-Mondolfi, A. (2020) Should the Holy Week 2020 be cancelled in Latin America due to the COVID-19 pandemic? *Travel Medicine and Infectious Disease* 36, 1–2. doi: 10.1016/j.tmaid.2020.101633

Ross, S.L., Hur, J.Y.C. and Hoffman, J. (2021) Temple stay-cation opportunities during and beyond pandemic conditions. *Journal of Tourism & Sports Management* 4 (1), 357–364.

Shackley, M. (2001) *Managing Sacred Sites*. London: Continuum.

Sigala, M. (2020) Tourism and COVID-19: Impacts and implications for advancing and resetting industry and research. *Journal of Tourism Business* 117, 312–321.

Sōkka Gakkai (2017) *Buddhist Studies: Terminology Collection*. Tokyo: Seikyō Shinbunsha (in Japanese).

Song, H.K., Lee, C.L., Park, J.A., Hwang, Y.H. and Reisinger, Y. (2015) The influence of tourist experience on perceived value and satisfaction with temple stays: The experience economy theory. *Journal of Travel & Tourism Marketing* 32 (4), 401–415.

Stausberg, M. (2011) *Religion and Tourism: Crossroads, Destinations and Encounters*. New York: Routledge.

Sulkowski, L. and Ignatowski, G. (2020) Impacts of COVID-19 pandemic on organization of religious behavior in different Christian denominations in Poland. *Religions* 11, 254. https://doi.org/10.3390/rel11050254

UNWTO (2021) *UNWTO World Tourism Barometer*. https://doi.org/10.18111/wtobarometereng

Wakayama Tourism Agency (2020) *Reiwa 1 Tourist Motivation Research Report*. Wakayama: Wakayama Tourism Agency (in Japanese).

Wakayama Tourism Agency (2021) *Reiwa 2 Tourist Motivation Research Report*. Wakayama: Wakayama Tourism Agency (in Japanese).

Yanata, K. (2021) What makes tourists' experience spiritual?: A case study of a Buddhist sacred site in Koyasan, Japan. *International Journal of Religious Tourism and Pilgrimage* 9 (3), 5–21.

Yanata, K. and Sharpley, R. (2022) Coexistence between tourists and monks: Managing temple-stay tourism in Koyasan, Japan. In D.H. Olsen and D.J. Timothy (eds) *The Routledge Handbook of Religious and Spiritual Tourism* (pp. 398–410). Abingdon: Routledge.

Yasuda, H. (2010) World heritage and cultural tourism in Japan. *International Journal of Culture, Tourism and Hospitality Research* 4 (4), 366–375.

6 Practising Faith From Afar: The Impact of the Covid-19 Pandemic on Pilgrim Behaviour

Daniel H. Olsen and Kiran A. Shinde

Introduction

The 1951/2008 film *The Day the Earth Stood Still* depicts a fictional story of an alien visitor who visits Earth. Landing, as most aliens do in the movies, in the US, the extraterrestrial announces that because of the proliferation of cold-war era nuclear weapons, the Earth had become a threat to other planets. As such, the conflicts between the Earth's governments needed to end or the inhabitants of the earth would be destroyed. The title of the film derives from the fact that in a demonstration of power, the robot companion of the alien visitor stopped all forms of power around the world for the space of half an hour. In addition, the presence of this alien visitor drew the attention of the entire world, and the earth 'stood still' as people waited nervously to know if the alien visitor would follow through on his threat.

While several world events, such as 9/11, have caught the attention of the world's population and slowed down time and human mobility, the ongoing Covid-19 pandemic led to the majority of the world's inhabitants 'standing still'. Countries quickly enacted almost draconian strategies and measures to limit the mobilities of its citizens at various scales, including the closing of international borders, restaurants and large- and small-scale public and private gatherings, in the name of public safety and 'flattening the curve' (Thunström *et al.*, 2020) However, this limit on people's mobility led to the world's economy effectively shutting down. Certain industries, such as airlines, were suspended; global supply chains were disrupted, leading to store shelves being emptied of essential food storage items; workplace and leisure patterns were confined to telework and virtual experiences in people's homes; and hospitals were over-run with infected patients. As discussed *ad nauseam* by tourism academics (e.g. Gössling *et al.*, 2021; Seyfi *et al.*, 2020; Sigala, 2020), the impacts of the pandemic on tourism and tourists were devastating. In 2020, international tourism numbers declined by almost 74% (1 billion fewer international travellers), leading to a 1.3 trillion USD decline in export revenues (Khalid *et al.*, 2021; Shih-Shuo, 2021; UNWTO, 2021).

However, research showed that this immobility enforcement led to a reduction of transportation and industrial activities, which further led to reduced fossil fuel consumption, a decrease in greenhouse gas emissions, and therefore better air and water quality (Rume & Islam, 2020). As well, reduced tourist presence at destinations led to both reduced tourism-generated pollution and natural ecological restoration (e.g. Crossley, 2020; Rume & Islam, 2020; Spalding *et al.*, 2021). Some commentators also suggested that a critical analysis of the effects of the pandemic on tourism should highlight 'the ways in which tourism has supported neo-liberal injustices and exploitation' (Higgins-Desbiolles, 2020: 620), which, in turn, could lead to the development of less-exploitative tourism strategies (e.g. Carr, 2020; Rastegar *et al.*, 2021). Indeed, much of the research on the impact of the pandemic on tourism development has been couched in what some scholars referred to as development of a 'new normal'. This 'new normal' is predicated on tourism industry stakeholders rejecting a business-as-usual economic model to implement developmental strategies that would create a more resilient tourism industry focused on environmental and social justice – a human-centred tourism at the expense of the economic benefits of tourism (e.g. Ateljevic, 2020; Benjamin *et al.*, 2020; Cave & Dredge, 2020; Khmara & Kronenberg, 2020; Niewiadomski, 2020; Stankov *et al.*, 2020).

While much of the research and discussion regarding tourism and the pandemic has focused on institutional and macro-scale issues, such as sustainability, political economy, social and environmental justice, and the medicalisation of tourism, what has gone missing from much of this dialogue is how the pandemic affected tourists (for exceptions, see Benoit *et al.*, in press; Yousaf, 2021). Most of the aligned literature in this area is on tourist travel intentions post-Covid-19 (e.g. Peco-Torres *et al.*, 2021; Polyzos *et al.*, 2020) or on tourist's perceptions of risk (e.g. Li *et al.*, 2020; Sánchez-Cañizares *et al.*, 2021) rather than how actual and potential tourists attempted to overcome this restricted mobility. In this vein, using secondary sources, the focus of this chapter is on how the inability to visit sacred sites during the Covid-19 pandemic impacted pilgrims and religious tourists. To begin, this chapter focuses on the effects of the Covid-19 global lockdown on pilgrimage, including how these limits on pilgrim mobility influenced religious institutions and their sacred sites. Then, attention is turned to examine two ways in which pilgrims coped with or adapted to the inability to participate in pilgrimages, which include *physical pilgrimage* and *stay-at-home-pilgrimages*, before discussing whether these adaptive strategies and practices may constitute a 'new normal' post-Covid-19.

Pilgrimage and the Covid-19 Pandemic

The impact of the Covid-19 pandemic on pilgrimage travel and practices was in many ways intertwined with the tourism industry. As Bremer (2005: 9260) noted, 'tourism and its associated practices interact with religious life and the institutions of religion in virtually every corner of the world'. Indeed, the movement of pilgrims towards sacred sites is in many cases structurally tied to tourism infrastructure and amenity availability (see Chapter 5, this volume, Progano). This is particularly the case at an international scale, where tourism transportation and telecommunication infrastructure facilitate the movement of both tourists and pilgrims from around the world to places such as Mecca, Lourdes, Mount Sinai, Jerusalem, Vatican City, the Notre-Dame Cathedral, the Basilica of Our Lady of Guadalupe, the Ise Grand Shrine and the Kashi Vishwanath Temple, among others. As such, at all scales, when the tourism industry struggles due to economic recessions, conflict and climate change, so does long- and short-haul pilgrimage. At the same time, pilgrimage tends to be relatively 'recession-proof' (Singh, 1998), as not only does travel to sacred sites help people who seek solace and comfort during troubled times, but pilgrims also tend to be less risk-averse due to 'redemptive suffering' – where pilgrimage during difficult times can lead to salvific rewards (Nikjoo et al., 2021). Indeed, standing in holy places is one way in which religious believers cope with life events that create uncertainty and 'deeply rooted existential anxiety' (Peteet, 2020: 2203).

However, what made pilgrimage less recession-proof during the Covid-19 pandemic was that government and medical quarantining mandated affected travel at international, regional and local scales. As a result, people were unable to leave their homes to visit their local mosque, shrine, synagogue or church, let alone travel to distant sacred locations. Complicating this lack of mobility was the closure of religious sites, the banning of religious events and the restriction of pilgrim mobilities by government and health officials, in some cases following the recommendations of academics (e.g. Ahmed & Memish, 2020; Al-Rousan & Al-Najjar, 2020; Crubézy & Telmon, 2020; Ebrahim & Memish, 2020; Kang, 2020; Lee et al., 2021; Mat et al., 2020; Yezli & Khan, 2021). This was in part because attendees at religious shrines and events did not adhere to physical distancing and masking mandates (Lee et al., 2021). A prime example of religious gatherings acting as super-spreader events was when a person known as 'Patient 31' was responsible for spreading the Covid-19 virus to 5000 individuals who attended a worship service at the Shincheonji Church of Jesus in Daegu, South Korea (Kim et al., 2020).

Lee et al. (2021: 2) argue that traditionally, 'religious communities have played an intimate role in shaping collective beliefs or theological systems which inform responses to health crises'. Olsen and Timothy (2020) note that there are two main ways in which religious leaders and organisations have responded to calls by government and medical officials to close pilgrimage sites and stop other religious practices at the beginning of the Covid-19 pandemic. The first response was to contest these efforts. Several religious leaders came out condemning the banning of large religious events, with many lamenting that the harsh medicalisation of pilgrimage was leading to 'even the gods [being] out of bounds' (Chaturvedi, 2020: n.p.). Other religious leaders refused to close their religious sites or cancel religious gatherings. This was the case in the cities of Qom and Mashad in Iran, where site managers would not close their shrines even when it was discovered that pilgrims who visited these sites were spreading the Covid-19 virus (OpIndia, 2020). In Brazil, evangelical leaders refused to suspend religious worship services, telling their congregants 'not to fear the virus, as God would protect those of faith...as closing churches down...would mean a lack of confidence in the divine power' (Capponi, in press: n.p.). In Gowa, Indonesia, organisers of an evangelical Muslim conference were reluctant to cancel the conference because 'they were more afraid of God than COVID-19' (Muhtada, 2020, n.p.). In Israel, ultra-Orthodox leaders resisted government efforts to curb religious customs and rites, including ritual bathing and Sabbath Day observance (Tarnopolsky, 2020), while in Trinidad, health officials pled with the managers of places of worship to close their doors until further notice (Wildman *et al.*, 2020).

At issue was the long-term tension between religion versus medicine, where religion as both the explanatory and healing factor in people's lives has been overtaken by scientific medical practices (see Amundsen, 1996; Ferngren, 2014). Or, as Lee *et al.* (2022: 1) suggest, the tension was between whether science or faith and trust in God would 'protect (or spiritually vaccinate) true believers'. This was evidenced in the case of Orthodox Christian leaders being told to suspend the practice of using a single spoon to distribute Communion to pilgrims. Church leaders took this as an affront to the long-established doctrine of transubstantiation, where the elements used in the Eucharist are converted to the blood and body of Christ, and as such it was blasphemy to suggest that partaking of this sacrament would pose any Covid-19 risk to the faithful (Papazoglou *et al.*, 2021).

However, most religious leaders and organisations cooperated with government and medical mandates and encouraged compliance among believers to stop the transmission of the Covid-19 virus. This was particularly effective where religious leaders were involved in policymaking regarding how to mitigate the spread of the virus (Olsen & Timothy, 2020). Examples of such cooperation included Saudi officials restricting pilgrim participation in the Umrah and Hajj pilgrimages (Ebrahim & Memish, 2020), the closing of the Church of the Nativity by Palestinian officials (CGTN, 2020) and the healing pools at the Shrine of Our Lady of Lourdes in France (Wooden, 2020), and the cancellation of Holy Week celebrations at St. Peter's Square by Vatican officials (Burke, 2020).

This cooperation, however, led to religious organisations and site managers scrambling to develop strategies to manage this sudden lack of pilgrim mobility both economically and in terms of pastoral outreach. Indeed, this was a time of anxiety for many religious site managers. As Msgr. John Armitage, shrine rector at The Catholic National Shrine of Our Lady of Walsingham, noted:

> *Normal pilgrimages aren't going to resume for at least 18 months to two years, which puts us in a very challenging financial situation, but along with the rest of the world. It's not just that we don't know where our next penny is coming from, many people don't. We are sharing that anxiety.* (cited in Dunn-Hensley, 2020: 124)

Most of these strategies revolved around using existing communication technologies to engage with the faithful through techno-religious practices (El-Sayed *et al.*, 2010). Many religious organisations were able to create virtual reality apps, some of which had already been in production before the pandemic, that allowed people to visit sites such as the Great Mosque in Mecca, the Sistine Chapel in Rome and Christian sites in Jerusalem from the safety of their home (Cheng, 2017; Miller, 2020; Tercatin, 2020). Other organisations livestreamed religious ceremonies and rituals, led virtual tours of pilgrimage sites, created online discussion groups, offered adherents online one-on-one meetings with religious leaders and made contact with the faithful through social media posts (Mróz, 2021; Olsen & Timothy, 2020; Séraphin & Jarraud, in press).

Pilgrimage Travel During the Covid-19 Pandemic

> *COVID-19 is not such a big tragedy and this country has overcome graver ones. The prayers of the pure youth and pious are very effective in repelling major tragedies* – Iranian leader Ayatollah Ali Khamenei, on 3 March 2020 (cited in Ahmed, 2021: n.p.)

> *Jesus is my protection… He is my sanitizer* – Rev. Majdi Allawi of the Maronite Catholic Church (cited in Yee, 2020: n.p.).

> *It's not a concern....The virus, we believe, is politically motivated. We hold our religious rights dear and we are going to assemble no matter what someone says* – Rev. Tony Spell is pastor of Life Tabernacle Church, Baton Rouge, USA (cited in Wildman *et al.*, 2020: 115).

When religious leaders made appeals such as the ones quoted above for keeping faith in the divine even in wake of the Covid-19 pandemic, it is natural that ordinary worshippers and devotees would follow these religious directions and maintain, as much as possible, regular religious behaviours. Indeed, the pandemic seemed to strengthen their belief in God (divine powers) and in the efficacy of God's holy places or the earthly abodes of the gods – even if these sites were potential super-spreaders for the Covid-19 virus. This is clear from the sentiments expressed by churchgoers in Manila when the pandemic had just begun:

> *The virus can't dampen my faith… "God is always there and won't aban-don us"* – 55-year-old male at the Binondo Church in Manila (cited in AP, 2020: n.p.)

> *We will not get the virus because God exists here* – 60-year-old housewife at the Batu Caves temple in Malaysia (cited in AP, 2020: n.p.).

A similar commitment was on display when organisers of the annual Palkhi pilgrimage in India – where thousands of devotees walk the 210-km long pilgrimage – claimed, 'we should not break the centuries-old tradition of carrying the "padukas" of Sant Dnyaneshwar Maharaj to Pandharpur….One thing is certain that the "padukas" will reach Pandharpur' (cited in More, 2020: n.p.).

As noted above, while the focus of much on the research on pilgrimage and Covid-19 has been on religious organisations and site managers, not as much has been written on the effects of the pandemic on pilgrims. This is surprising, as 'faith may promote resilience especially during crisis' (Pirutinsky *et al.*, 2020: 2288), and standing in holy places is an important part of creating this resilience within both individuals and communities. Indeed, in the context of pandemics, many people travel to sites related to 'pandemic saints', such as Padre Pio in Italy, and 'disease divinities' (*ekjin*) in Japan (McLaughlin, 2020), 'to whom the faithful pray specifically to alleviate their suffering and that of the community, and who serves as a model for moral behaviour, during a pandemic' (Di Giovine, 2020: 131). This section focuses on peoples' responses to the deeper needs of expressing faith through religious and pilgrimage travel in the middle of a pandemic, including the continuation of physical pilgrimages and participating in pilgrimages while staying at home.

The continuation of physical pilgrimages

Even though government and medical mandates necessitated the enforced immobility of pilgrims around the world and the cancellation of large religious events, many religious site managers still welcomed pilgrims. As noted above, many religious leaders encouraged as many people as possible to come to their pilgrimage sites without enforcing distancing or other sanitary mandates. Pilgrimage to their sites, they argued, was an act of faith and demonstrated a commitment to the view that God would bless and protect them from the Covid-19 virus. In the case of pilgrimage to Qom's Masumeh pilgrimage site in Iran, two male pilgrims licked parts of the holy shrine to demonstrate this conviction. As one of the pilgrims stated before licking the door of the shrine, 'I'm not scared of coronavirus' (Sini & Shahbazian, 2020: n.p.). Pilgrims continued to the shrine until government officials forced its closure. Other pilgrims sought to travel to religious sites even when authorities shut down sacred sites and international borders. For example, in September 2020, 2000 Hasidic pilgrims attempted to cross the Belarus-Ukraine border as a part of their yearly pilgrimage to the grave of the movement's founder Reb Nachman.

However, Ukraine authorities blocked their crossing and forced the pilgrims to return home (Sherwood, 2020; Varenikova, 2020).

However, in cases where religious leaders cooperated with government and medical mandates after the initial Covid-19 shutdown in March 2020, pilgrims were eventually allowed to visit, albeit in very limited numbers. For example, as described by Papazoglou *et al.* (2021), Mount Athos reopened in June 2020 but limited the number of COVID-tested pilgrims that could enter the site to 15 at each monastery. In July 2020, the Cathedral of St. James in Santiago, Spain, was allowed to open with only 20 people inside at one time, and around the same time, limited numbers of pilgrims (50) were allowed back to Lourdes after religious authorities worked with government and health officials to develop health protocols that pilgrims had to follow (Mróz, 2021). Since February 2021, only 20 pilgrims at a time have been allowed into Jerusalem's holy sites in Jerusalem (Papazoglou *et al.*, 2021), and in the case of the Shrine of Our Lady of Jasna Góra in Częstochowa, Poland, not only were the number of pilgrims limited in the shrine, but the age of pilgrims was also restricted (14-65) due to the Covid-19 virus more seriously affecting the elderly (Mróz, 2021).

In the case of yearly or important mass religious rituals and events, it was harder for religious leaders to follow health protocols. This was the case at the iconic annual pilgrimage events in India, where devotees with firm beliefs in the auspicious timing of religious rituals and preservation of traditions found ways of participating in pilgrimage travel during festivals. Because pilgrims chose to participate in these events regardless of Covid-19 mandates being in place, religious officials attempted to downscale these events considerably, which led to 'an unprecedented challenge for the authorities – that of striking a balance between *"aastha"* (religious faith) and COVID-19 protocols' (Verma, 2021b: n.p).

A prime example of this was the Kumbh Mela pilgrimage, the largest gathering of humans on earth that takes place every 12 years. This pilgrimage was scheduled to be celebrated in 2021 in Haridwar, North India. To discourage pilgrim attendance, the four-month celebration (January to April) was curtailed to just one month in length. However, despite the implemented standard operating procedures (SOPs) and restrictions put in place to deter pilgrims from attending (see Box 6.1), more than 200,000 pilgrims and saints (*sadhus* or holy men who belong to a religious order) came to bathe in the sacred river Ganga on the 12th and 14th of April that marked Makar Sankranti and Maha Shivratri – two important Hindu festivals. While the number of pilgrims who participated in the Kumbh Mela was minuscule compared to the millions of devotees that would attend during normal times, by mid-April, 'at least 59 saints [had] tested positive... apart from more than 200 pilgrims (of the 154,000 tested)'. After the death of a few noted saints or holy men, the Indian Prime Minister appealed to the religious authorities to, where possible, participate in 'symbolic' pilgrimages, where a small group of pilgrims comprised of *sadhus* would serve as 'proxy' and pilgrimage to a sacred destination on behalf of a pilgrim community (Verma, 2021a: n.p.).

Box 1: Pilgrimage at Kumbha Mela

Mandatory conditions to visit Kumbh Mela in Hardwar

– As per the SOP, only those devotees who have a negative RT-PCR test report (done 72 hours prior to the date of visit) will be allowed to enter the Kumbh Mela area. They will have to produce negative RT-PCR reports at the entry points and checkposts established at the district border.

– Prior to their travel, all devotees will have to mandatorily register on the Kumbh Mela web portal. Only after validation of uploaded documents that they will be issued an e-pass to enter the mela area. The e-pass and the RT-PCR negative test report can be randomly verified at the border checkpost/railway station/airport, in hotel/dharmashala or while boarding trains, buses and in commercial vehicles.

– Devotees without e-pass and medical certificate will be denied entry in the mela area

Covid-appropriate behaviour

– At the Kumbh Mela, the use of face cover/masks will be mandatory. There will be arrangements for mask dispensing kiosks at entry points and parking lots, and masks will also be distributed free of cost.

– Levying fines/penalties on defaulters for not wearing mask/face cover or for not following social safety and distancing norms should be done by the enforcement agencies.

– Any persons/officers involved in the Haridwar Kumbh Mela 2021 found violating these SOPs will be liable to be proceeded against as per the provisions of the Disaster Management Act, 2005 besides legal action under section 188 of IPC and other legal provisions as applicable.

– Ashram and dharmashala have been asked to allow entry to devotees only after checking e-pass, RT-PCR report and checked-mark on the wrist. If there will be any symptom of Covid-19 in any visitor, that person will be isolated and covid control room has to be informed. Similar guidelines stand for restaurants and guest houses.

– Organising group bhajans, recitations and bhandare (community kitchen) will remain prohibited in the entire mela area.

– At ghats, devotees will be allowed to take bath for maximum 20 minutes only. Vulnerable age groups and pregnant women will be discouraged from entering ghat and taking a dip.

Source: Verma, 2021, n.p.

This idea of symbolic or proxy pilgrimages played out well with the Indian public. For example, one Temple Trust tried to convince the regional government that the traditional yearly Palkhi pilgrimage to the Vitthal Temple in Pandharpur, in which hundreds of thousands of people participate, should be undertaken by a handful of pilgrims in quite an unusual manner:

> We are prepared to spend Rs 8 lakh [800,000 India Rupee = $10,770 USD] on this symbolic pilgrimage of Sant Janabai's [a 13th century religious poet] padukas. We have booked a helicopter, we want permission to land at the Pandharpur helipad, drive to the Chandrabhaga river and complete the holy dip as per tradition. (President of a temple trust, cited in Iyer, 2020: n.p.)

However, the regional government rejected this idea for health-related reasons (Verma, 2021a). Symbolic pilgrimages were also a part of the 2020 Hajj. While international pilgrims were not allowed to take part in Hajj, the Hajj was still held with 1000 local residents representing the over 2 million Muslims who would usually participate in the pilgrimage ritual. These participants had to undergo strict testing requirements and had to wear an electronic bracelet that monitored their movements so health officials could do contact tracing in the event of an outbreak (AP, 2021; Gautret *et al.*, 2020).

The desire to be faithful and to serve deity over medical experts through engaging in pilgrimage travel, however, seemed to affect the collective behaviour of pilgrims. Or, as Singh (2020: 306) suggests, 'people are capable of suspending reason and behaving with a motive inspired by faith'. For example, a volunteer at Kumbha Mela who 'deployed to hand out sanitisers to pilgrims' complained that 'Only 50% accept it… Many say sanitisers make them impure after the dip' (Verma, 2021a: n.p.). Such an attitude resonates with other aspects of this gathering, particularly when one examines whether or not pilgrims gave evidence of Covid-19 negative tests that allowed them to attend the Mela or followed the SOPs of the event. One Kumbh Mela official said that 'managing social distancing was a joke on any ordinary day of the Mela', let alone during the 2020 Kumbh Mela, while another official pointed out that 'We have our limitations. If we try to challan [give tickets to] people in a crowd [for not wearing masks or social distancing] in a gathering of Naga sadhus [Naked Yogis or holy men], or try to stop people, it can have serious consequences in the form of a stampede' (Verma, 2021a: n.p.). Similar apprehensions were expressed at the Golden Temple in Amritsar, a popular Sikh pilgrimage site. As one trustee of the temple management committee commented:

> When devotees are inside the Golden Temple premises, you cannot force them to do something that is not related to devotion. We can only make requests. For most devotees, it is a matter of faith and they believe that

they cannot get infected inside the Golden Temple. It is here that they want to believe more in God and their faith than the instructions... The devotees know what is best for them. (cited in Brar, 2020: n.p.)

The opportunity for more devotees to participate in pilgrimage travel and rites was better once vaccinations were developed. For example, while reopening the famous Char Dham Yatra to four Hindu sacred places in the state of Uttarakhand in North India, the state government made it 'mandatory for pilgrims to either have a certificate of both doses of the Covid vaccine or a negative Covid test report to obtain the e-pass for the yatra'. The government declared that 'On a daily basis, 1000 pilgrims will be allowed to visit Badrinath, 800 in Kedarnath, 600 in Gangotri and 400 in Yamunotri' (Verma, 2021c: n.p.). Similarly, limits were imposed in other popular pilgrimage places such as Sabrimala (5000 pilgrims a day), Vaishno Devi (2000 pilgrims a day) and Tirupati (7000 pilgrims a day) to facilitate *darshan* or viewing deities at religious sites for vaccinated pilgrims.

Stay-at-home pilgrimages

Because of the immobility that came with the Covid-19 mandates, people who would have participated in pilgrimage were left to search for alternative pilgrimage outlets. While virtual forms of pilgrimage have generally been seen as poor substitute for physical pilgrimage, technology-assisted pilgrimages have been a part of online religion and religious practice for decades in western societies (e.g. Dawson & Cowan, 2004; Hill-Smith, 2011; MacWilliams, 2002). Undertaken from the comfort of a home, these cyber-pilgrimages, or online pilgrimages, virtual pilgrimages or digital pilgrimages as they are often referred to by academics, to which they are sometimes referred, are 'contemporary expression of the pilgrimage tradition' in which people seek to participate in forms of pilgrimage that do not require physical movement (Hill-Smith, 2011: 236). However, this form of online pilgrimage does not involve just sitting in front of a screen and watch pilgrimage take place. As Hill-Smith (2011: 236) argues, online pilgrimage is 'hugely diverse in scale, complexity, content, design and purpose, ranging from technologically "simple" web pages displaying photographic galleries and explanatory text, to more sophisticated websites that attempt to reconstruct and repackage iconographic, structural and sensed aspects of the experience of "real-life" pilgrimage'.

As noted above, the Covid-19 pandemic provided the right impetus for available information and communication and web-based virtual reality technologies to be used to create a diverse range of virtual experiences related to real sacred places. For example, over 700,000 people downloaded the Muslim 3D app that allows users to make a virtual Hajj trip to Mecca on various devices. According to the app designer, people have since asked for the app to include the ways in which users can perform acts of worship, listen to excerpts from the Quran and interact with other pilgrim users (Miller, 2020). Many people who would have walked the Camino de Santiago de Compostela had to opt for virtually walking the Camino. One example of this was the *Camino de Santiago Virtual Challenge*, which involved people exercising at home, and for every mile they ran, walked, biked or swam, they could track how far they had travelled along the Camino (see https://www.theconqueror.events/camino/). Another app, the *Camino For Good*, was also designed for a similar experience, where people would not only be able to track their movement along the Camino but also see photographs of the stage of the Camino where they would be on the actual pilgrimage route (see https://caminoforgood.com/).

Another type of experience that drew pilgrims to online forms of pilgrimage included slideshow-based talks about sacred journeys. On 31 May 2021, the second author participated in a virtual event where, in celebration of the Buddhist festival of Vesak, the Friends of the Museums in Singapore invited a noted speaker and teacher of Buddhism to talk about her experiences organising tours to Buddhist pilgrimage places in India and Nepal. Via Zoom, she delivered a one-hour talk titled 'Remembering the Enlightened One', which was attended by over 250 participants. As the speaker gave her presentation, online participants who had taken one of her previous pilgrimage tours used the chat function to express gratitude for their previous experiences with the speaker, to connect with other online participants and to reminisce about their own pilgrimage experiences. For many of the online attendees, nostalgia had taken over, and this event was a time for them to relive their pilgrimage journeys. At the end of the presentation, many of the attendees expressed how special it was to have participated in such a peaceful and pacifying experience in the middle of the challenges of the pandemic. Many of the attendees also expressed a desire to engage in post-pandemic travel to many of the places mentioned in the presentation. As such, this event created post-pandemic demand for pilgrimage.

A further example of an alternative pilgrimage outlet during the pandemic was another event attended by the second author. *Vyatra* (https://vyatra.online) is an online portal that started to offer virtual journeys when the pandemic began. One of their popular offerings is *Mystical Ganga*, which they promote as follows:

> *Watch the Ganga flow by in real time, with a soul stirring vocal Kabir bhajan, or a lilting Santoor, or Flute. All this delivered live via Zoom into your phone or laptop (ideally hooked up to your TV screen), in the comfort of your own home. With up 20 local people involved in delivering*

each vyatra Mystical Ganga session, this endeavour is pumping money back into these tourism-dependent economies that have been otherwise devastated by the lockdowns (https://vyatra.online).

This idea of virtual pilgrimage as satisfying a pilgrim's short-term need to travel was also evident in an e-pilgrimage developed by religious authorities at the Lourdes pilgrimage shrine in France. Eighty million viewers attended what was called the 'Lourdes United' virtual pilgrimage, which was held on 16 July 2020. According to a content analysis of Facebook posts by participants in this virtual pilgrimage, Séraphin and Jarraud (in press) argue that most of the participants were quite satisfied with their virtual online pilgrimage experience. However, many of them noted that they missed being at Lourdes in person for this event and that virtual pilgrimage events should be an addition to, not a substitute for, in person pilgrimage.

Conclusion

Yee (2020: n.p.) suggests that '[I]n a world where so many routines have been obliterated, it is the rites themselves that many cherish'. Indeed, pilgrimage can have a great effect on not just the emotional and mental health of people, but also on their spiritual health and religious coping and resilience (Benoit *et al.*, in press; Warfield *et al.*, 2014). As such, when various mandates limited the mobility of pilgrims, many people desperately sought for viable alternative practices to maintain solidarity with their faith communities as well as to sacred spaces that helped them sustain their religious and/or spiritual identities. These alternatives included active (e.g. continuing to participate in in-person pilgrimages) and passive (e.g. virtual pilgrimage) forms of pilgrimage activity. In most of these cases, religious authorities helped facilitate these active and passive forms of pilgrimage through negotiating with government and medical officials to allow some pilgrims to visit sacred sites as well as creating the online environment within which virtual pilgrimage participation could take place.

Lee *et al.* (2020) argue that the virtual adaptions made by religious organisations and site managers to limit the transmission of disease at religious events and sites should now become the 'new normal' – that pilgrimage should continue to be limited in scale to mitigate potential future pandemics outbreaks due to mass religious gatherings (see Olsen, 2020). Technology did allow more people to access religious sites as well as help religious leaders increase their outreach and pastoral care missions, while also providing pilgrims satisfactory virtual spiritual experience (Séraphin & Jarraud, in press); there is no replacing being 'in place'. As such, virtual forms of pilgrimage should continue to be used to facilitate pilgrimage travel for those that may not have the financial means or physical ability to visit sacred sites but must remain an add-on to physical pilgrimages.

References

Amundsen, D.W. (1996) *Medicine, Society, and Faith in the Ancient and Medieval Worlds*. Baltimore, MD: John Hopkins University Press.

Ahmed, K. (2021) Religious congregations and beliefs need a relook in times of coronavirus. *The Indian Express*. See https://indianexpress.com/article/opinion/columns/coronavirus-pakistan-iran-religion-tablighi-jamaat-infection-lockdown-6353784/ (accessed 1 November 2021).

Ahmed, Q.A. and Memish, Z.A. (2020) The cancellation of mass gatherings (MGs)? Decision making in the time of COVID-19. *Travel Medicine and Infectious Disease* 34, 1–4.

Al-Rousan, N. and Al-Najjar, H. (2020) Is visiting Qom spread CoVID-19 epidemic in the Middle East? *European Review for Medical and Pharmacological Sciences* 24 (10), 5813–5818.

AP (2020) No handshakes: Coronavirus outbreak spooks Asian places of worship. *The Indian Express*. See https://indianexpress.com/article/world/coronavirus-outbreak-philippines-china-asia-6269960/ (accessed 1 November 2021).

AP (2021) Virus transforms hajj in Mecca and future of the pilgrimage. *The Indian Express*. See https://indianexpress.com/article/world/virus-transforms-hajj-in-mecca-and-future-of-the-pilgrimage-7410879/ (accessed 1 November 2021).

Ateljevic, I. (2020) Transforming the (tourism) world for good and (re)generating the potential 'new normal'. *Tourism Geographies* 22 (3), 467–475.

Benjamin, S., Dillette, A. and Alderman, D.H. (2020) "We can't return to normal": Committing to tourism equity in the post-pandemic age. *Tourism Geographies* 22 (3), 476–483.

Benoit, C.T., Thomas, P.A. and Remley Jr., T.P. (in press) Tibetan Buddhist pilgrims and the Covid-19 pandemic. *Mental Health, Religion & Culture*. https://doi.org/10.1080/13674676.2021.1953454.

Brar, K.S. (2020) At Golden Temple, devotees, sewadars flout mask guideline, SGPC 'helpless'. *The Indian Express*. See https://indianexpress.com/article/cities/chandigarh/at-golden-temple-devotees-sewadars-flout-mask-guideline-sgpc-helpless-6517669/ (accessed 1 November 2021).

Bremer, T.S. (2005) Tourism and religion. In L. Jones (ed.) *Encyclopedia of Religion* (pp. 9260–9264). Detroit, MI: MacMillan Reference USA/Thomas Gale.

Burke, D. (2020) The great shutdown 2020: What churches, mosques and temples are doing to fight the spread of coronavirus. *CNN*. See https://www.cnn.com/2020/03/14/world/churches-mosques-templescoronavirus-spread/index.html (accessed 15 June 2020).

Capponi, G. (in press) Overlapping values: Religious and scientific conflicts during the COVID-19 crisis in Brazil. *Social Anthropology*. https://doi.org/10.1111/1469-8676.12795.

Carr, A. (2020) COVID-19, indigenous peoples and tourism: A view from New Zealand. *Tourism Geographies* 22 (3), 491–502.

Cave, J. and Dredge, D. (2020) Regenerative tourism needs diverse economic practices. *Tourism Geographies* 22 (3), 503–513.

CGTN (2020) COVID-19 global roundup: Coronavirus impact on religious activities. See https://news.cgtn.com/news/2020-03-07/COVID-19-Global-RoundupCoronavirus-impact-on-religious-activities-OF6ny0X3zi/index.html (accessed 21 June 2020).

Chaturvedi, A. (2020) COVID-19 puts curbs on religious travel. *India Times*. See https://economictimes.indiatimes.com/news/politics-and-nation/covid-19-putscurbs-on-religious-travel/articleshow/74742051.cms (accessed 1 June 2020).

Cheng, S. (2017) The first Oculus developer from the Middle East is inviting people to visit Mecca in VR. *QZ.com*. See https://qz.com/980821/mecca-in-vr-the-first-oculus-developer-from-the-middle-east-is-inviting-people-to-the-hajj/ (accessed 12 November 2021).

Crossley, É. (2020) Ecological grief generates desire for environmental healing in tourism after COVID-19. *Tourism Geographies* 22 (3), 536–546.

Crubézy, E. and Telmon, N. (2020) Pandemic-related excess mortality (COVID-19), public health measures and funerary rituals. *EClinicalMedicine* 22, 100358.

Dawson, L.L. and Cowan, D.E. (2004) *Religion Online: Finding Faith on the Internet.* New York: Routledge.

Di Giovine, M.A. (2020) Padre Pio, pandemic saint: The effects of the Spanish flu and COVID-19 on pilgrimage and devotion to the world's most popular saint. *The International Journal of Religious Tourism and Pilgrimage* 8 (7), 130–154.

Dunn-Hensley, S. (2020) Virtual pilgrimage in a time of pandemic: Lessons from the Shrine of Our Lady of Walsingham. *The International Journal of Religious Tourism and Pilgrimage* 8 (7), 121–129.

Ebrahim, S.H. and Memish, Z.A. (2020) Saudi Arabia's drastic measures to curb the COVID-19 outbreak: Temporary suspension of the Umrah pilgrimage. *Journal of Travel Medicine* 27 (3), 1–2.

El-Sayed, H., Greenhill, A. and Westrup, C. (2010) On the emergence of techno-religious spaces: Implications for design and end users. In H. Isomäki and S. Pekkola (eds) *Reframing Humans in Information Systems Development* (pp. 17–29). London: Springer.

Ferngren, G.B. (2014) *Medicine & Religion: A Historical Introduction.* Baltimore: John Hopkins University Press.

Gautret, P., Goumballa, N. and Sokhna, C. (2020) The 2020 Grand Magal of Touba, Senegal in the time of the COVID-19 pandemic. *Travel Medicine and Infectious Disease* 38, 101880.

Gössling, S., Scott, D. and Hall, C.M. (2021) Pandemics, tourism and global change: A rapid assessment of COVID-19. *Journal of Sustainable Tourism* 29 (1), 1–20.

Higgins-Desbiolles, F. (2020) Socialising tourism for social and ecological justice after COVID-19. *Tourism Geographies* 22 (3), 610–623.

Hill-Smith, C. (2011) Cyberpilgrimage: The (virtual) reality of online pilgrimage experience. *Religion Compass* 5 (6), 236–246.

Iyer, K. (2020) Maharashtra: Religious institutions, politicians seek govt nod to participate in Ashadhi Ekadashi event. *The Indian Express.* See https://indianexpress.com/article/india/maharashtra-religious-institutions-politicians-seek-govt-nod-to-participate-in-ashadhi-ekadashi-event-6476690/ (accessed on 1 November 2021).

Kang, Y.J. (2020) Characteristics of the COVID-19 outbreak in Korea from the mass infection perspective. *Journal of Preventive Medicine and Public Health* 53 (3), 168–170.

Khalid, U., Okafor, L.E. and Burzynska, K. (2021) Does the size of the tourism sector influence the economic policy response to the COVID-19 pandemic? *Current Issues in Tourism* 24 (19), 2801–2820.

Khmara, Y. and Kronenberg, J. (2020) Degrowth in the context of sustainability transitions: In search of a common ground. *Journal of Cleaner Production* 267, 122072.

Kim, H.J., Hwang, H.S., Choi, Y.H., Song, H.Y., Park, J.S., Yun, C.Y. and Ryu, S. (2020) The delay in confirming COVID-19 cases linked to a religious group in Korea. *Journal of Preventive Medicine and Public Health* 53 (3), 164–167.

Lee, M., Lim, H., Xavier, M.S. and Lee, E.Y. (2022) "A divine infection": A systematic review on the roles of religious communities during the early stage of COVID-19. *Journal of Religion and Health* 61, 866–919.

Li, Z., Zhang, S., Liu, X., Kozak, M. and Wen, J. (2020) Seeing the invisible hand: Underlying effects of COVID-19 on tourists' behavioral patterns. *Journal of Destination Marketing & Management* 18, 100502.

MacWilliams, M.W. (2002) Virtual pilgrimages on the internet. *Religion* 32 (4), 315–335.

Mat, N.F.C., Edinur, H.A., Razab, M.K.A.A. and Safuan, S. (2020) A single mass gathering resulted in massive transmission of COVID-19 infections in Malaysia with further international spread. *Journal of Travel Medicine* 27 (3), 1–4.

McLaughlin, L. (2020) Japanese religious responses to COVID-19: A preliminary report. *The Asia-Pacific Journal* 18 (9), 1–23.

Miller, E.M. (2020) Digital pilgrimages allow the faithful to travel the world from their couches. *National Catholic Reporter*. See https://www.ncronline.org/news/people/digital-pilgrimages-allow-faithful-travel-world-their-couches (accessed 12 November 2021).

More, M.D. (2020) Coronavirus puts fate of annual palkhi processions in limbo. *The Indian Express*. See https://indianexpress.com/article/cities/pune/lockdown-puts-fate-of-annual-palkhi-processions-in-limbo-6397503/ (accessed 1 November 2021).

Mróz, F. (2021) The impact of COVID-19 on pilgrimages and religious tourism in Europe during the first six months of the pandemic. *Journal of Religion and Health* 60 (2), 625–645.

Muhtada, D. (2020) Religion and COVID-19 mitigation. *The Jakarta Post*. See https://www.thejakartapost.com/academia/2020/03/26/religion-and-covid-19-mitigation.html (accessed 26 June 2020).

Niewiadomski, P. (2020) COVID-19: From temporary de-globalisation to a re-discovery of tourism? *Tourism Geographies* 22 (3), 651–656.

Nikjoo, A., Razavizadeh, N. and Di Giovine, M.A. (2021) What draws Shia Muslims to an insecure pilgrimage? The Iranian journey to Arbaeen, Iraq during the presence of ISIS. *Journal of Tourism and Cultural Change* 19 (5), 606–627.

Olsen, D.H. (2020) Disease and health risks at mass religious gatherings. In K.A. Shinde and D.H. Olsen (eds) *Religious Tourism and the Environment* (pp. 116–132). Wallingford: CABI.

Olsen, D.H. and Timothy, D.J. (2020) COVID-19 and religious travel: Present and future directions. *International Journal of Religious Tourism and Pilgrimage* 8 (7), 170–188.

OpIndia (2020) Watch: Iranians lick and kiss shrines amidst coronavirus outbreak, say they are not scared of the deadly virus. *OpIndia.com*. See https://www.opindia.com/2020/03/iran-coronavirus-shrine-qomfatima-masumeh-lick/ (accessed 1 July 2020).

Papazoglou, A.S., Moysidis, D.V., Tsagkaris, C., Dorosh, M., Karagiannidis, E. and Mazin, R. (2021) Spiritual health and the COVID-19 pandemic: Impacts on Orthodox Christianity devotion practices, rituals, and religious pilgrimages. *Journal of Religion and Health* 60 (5), 3217–3229.

Peco-Torres, F., Polo-Peña, A.I. and Frías-Jamilena, D.M. (2021) The effect of COVID-19 on tourists' intention to resume hotel consumption: The role of resilience. *International Journal of Hospitality Management* 99, 103075.

Peteet, J.R. (2020) COVID-19 anxiety. *Journal of Religion and Health* 59, 2203–2204.

Pirutinsky, S., Cherniak, A.D. and Rosmarin, D.H. (2020) COVID-19, mental health, and religious coping among American Orthodox Jews. *Journal of Religion and Health* 59 (5), 2288–2301.

Polyzos, S., Samitas, A. and Spyridou, A.E. (2020) Tourism demand and the COVID-19 pandemic: An LSTM approach. *Tourism Recreation Research* 46 (2), 1–13.

Rastegar, R., Higgins-Desbiolles, F. and Ruhanen, L. (2021) COVID-19 and a justice framework to guide tourism recovery. *Annals of Tourism Research* 91, 103161.

Rume, T. and Islam, S.D.U. (2020) Environmental effects of COVID-19 pandemic and potential strategies of sustainability. *Heliyon* 6 (9), e04965.

Sánchez-Cañizares, S.M., Cabeza-Ramírez, L.J., Muñoz-Fernández, G. and Fuentes-García, F.J. (2021) Impact of the perceived risk from Covid-19 on intention to travel. *Current Issues in Tourism* 24 (7), 970–984.

Séraphin, H. and Jarraud, N. (in press) COVID-19: Impacts and perspectives for religious tourism events. The case of Lourdes pilgrimages. *Journal of Convention & Event Tourism.* https://doi.org/10.1080/15470148.2021.1906810.

Seyfi, S., Hall, C.M. and Shabani, B. (2020) COVID-19 and international travel restrictions: The geopolitics of health and tourism. *Tourism Geographies.* https://doi.org/10.1080/14616688.2020.1833972.

Sherwood, H. (2020) Jewish pilgrims blocked from entering Ukraine over Covid fears. *The Guardian.* See https://www.theguardian.com/world/2020/sep/18/jewish-pilgrims-blocked-entering-ukraine-covid-fears (accessed 22 September 2021).

Shih-Shuo, Y. (2021) Tourism recovery strategy against COVID-19 pandemic. *Tourism Recreation Research* 46 (2), 188–194.

Sigala, M. (2020) Tourism and COVID-19: Impacts and implications for advancing and resetting industry and research. *Journal of Business Research* 117, 312–321.

Singh, D.E. (2020) Practice of faith under COVID-19: Exceptional cases. *Transformation* 37 (4), 306–316.

Singh, S. (1998) Probing the product life cycle further. *Tourism Recreation Research* 23 (2), 61–63.

Sini, R. and Shahbazian, A. (2020) Coronavirus: Iran holy-shrine-lickers face prison. *BBC.* See https://www.bbc.com/news/blogs-trending-51706021 (accessed 15 November 2021).

Spalding, M., Burke, L. and Fyall, A. (2021) Covid-19: Implications for nature and tourism. *Anatolia* 32 (1), 126–127.

Stankov, U., Filimonau, V. and Vujičić, M.D. (2020) A mindful shift: An opportunity for mindfulness-driven tourism in a post-pandemic world. *Tourism Geographies* 22 (3), 703–712.

Tarnopolsky, N. (2020) Ultra-Orthodox Jews hit disproportionately hard by Israel's coronavirus outbreak. *Los Angeles Times.* See https://www.latimes.com/world-nation/story/2020-04-07/ultra-orthodox-jews-hitdisproportionately-hard-in-israels-coronavirus-outbreak (accessed 1 July 2020).

Tercatin, R. (2020) At the time of coronavirus, Jerusalem comes to pilgrims in VR. *Jerusalem Post.* See https://www.jpost.com/Israel-News/At-the-time-ofcoronavirus-Jerusalem-comes-to-pilgrims-in-VR-621919 (accessed 18 June 2020).

Thunström, L., Newbold, S.C., Finnoff, D., Ashworth, M. and Shogren, J F. (2020) The benefits and costs of using social distancing to flatten the curve for COVID-19. *Journal of Benefit-Cost Analysis* 11 (2), 179–195.

UNWTO (2021) 2002: Worst year in tourism history with 1 billion fewer international arrivals. See https://www.unwto.org/news/2020-worst-year-in-tourism-history-with-1-billion-fewer-international-arrivals (accessed 2 November 2021).

Varenikova, M. (2020) On Ukraine's border, the coronavirus ends a Hasidic pilgrimage. *The New York Times.* See https://www.nytimes.com/2020/09/18/world/europe/ukraine-border-belarus-pilgrims-coronavirus.html (accessed 22 September 2021).

Verma, L. (2021a) Covid SOP crumbles before Kumbh numbers, Akhadas take own steps. *The Indian Express.* See https://indianexpress.com/article/india/kumbh-mela-akhadas-covid-death-coronavirus-7277145/ (accessed 1 November 2021).

Verma, L. (2021b) How Covid protocols may reduce crowd at Kumbh Mela in Hardwar. *The Indian Express.* See https://indianexpress.com/article/explained/explained-how-covid-protocols-may-reduce-crowd-at-kumbh-mela-in-haridwar-7215612/ (accessed 1 November 2021).

Verma, L. (2021c) Uttarakhand issues SOP for Char Dham Yatra. *The Indian Express.* See https://indianexpress.com/article/india/uttarakhand-issues-sop-for-char-dham-yatra-7516726/ (accessed 1 November 2021).

Warfield, H.A., Baker, S.B. and Parikh Foxx, S.B. (2014) The therapeutic value of pilgrimage: A grounded theory study. *Mental Health, Religion & Culture* 17 (8), 860–875.

Wildman, W.J., Bulbulia, J., Sosis, R. and Schjoedt, U. (2020) Religion and the COVID-19 pandemic. *Religion, Brain & Behavior* 10 (2), 115–117.

Wooden, C. (2020) Lourdes shrine closes healing pools as precaution against coronavirus. *Catholic Philly*. See https://catholicphilly.com/2020/03/news/world-news/lourdes-shrine-closes-healing-pools-asprecaution-against-coronavirus/ (accessed 7 July 2020).

Yee, V. (2020) In a pandemic, religion can be a balm and a risk. *The New York Times*. See https://indianexpress.com/article/coronavirus/in-a-pandemic-religion-can-be-a-balm-and-a-risk-6330609/ (accessed 1 November 2021).

Yezli, S. and Khan, A. (2021) COVID-19 pandemic: It is time to temporarily close places of worship and to suspend religious gatherings. *Journal of Travel Medicine* 28 (2), taaa065.

Yousaf, S. (2021) Travel burnout: Exploring the return journeys of pilgrim-tourists amidst the COVID-19 pandemic. *Tourism Management* 84, 104285.

7 When Faith and Fear Intersect: Pilgrimage During the Covid-19 Pandemic

Nitasha Sharma

Introduction

It is wonderful, the power of faith like that, that can make multitudes upon multitudes of the old and weak and the young and the frail enter without hesitation or complaint upon such incredible journeys and endure the resultant miseries without repining. It is done in love, or it is done in fear, I do not know which it is. No matter what the impulse is, the act borne of it is beyond imagination, marvelous to our kind of people, the cold white.

– Mark Twain, in the book *Following the Equator* (1895)
about the Kumbh Mela in India.

Religion and spirituality have always been a source of resilience and personal comfort in times of crises and disaster recovery. The Covid-19 pandemic not only had an enormous impact on pilgrimage and religious tourism due to restrictions on mass gatherings, international travel bans, lockdowns and shutdown of religious places but also had an impact on related industries such as hotels, transport, food and service. Following the advisory of public health experts and pandemic-related guidelines, the early part of the year 2020 witnessed several country-wide and local lockdowns all over the world that restricted mobility and led to the closure of religious buildings, institutions and sacred heritage sites (Gettleman & Schultz, 2020), resulting in the emergence of new digital forms of social engagement and worship. Religious events and festivals form an integral component of religious tourism and suffered a huge blow during the pandemic either due to cancellations, scaling down, adjustments in worshipping style or crowding. There have been several studies over the past few months that have investigated the resilience of the event industry (Shipway & Miles, 2020) demonstrating how religious 'faith may promote resilience especially during a crisis' (Pirutinsky *et al.*, 2020: 2288). However, the relationship between faith and tourism is not so simple especially when religious events, festivals and public gatherings are restricted or not encouraged in the interest of public health. Since the academic boundaries between pilgrimage, religious tourism and spiritual tourism are often blurred, the study uses the term 'pilgrim' instead of tourist since religion is the primary reason for choosing the destination in this context.

The Covid-19 pandemic revealed the complexities associated with pilgrimage and religious tourism in India as collective forms of worship and religious mass gatherings were believed to increase the transmission of the virus. Quadri (2020) mentions how a Christian congregation in South Korea and a Baptist congregation in Germany turned out to be responsible for a substantial number of Covid-19 infections among its attendees. In India, there was massive outrage over a Muslim congregation called Tablighi Jamaat held in Delhi in March 2020, which not only led to Covid-19 cases across the country (Jha & Dixit, 2020) but also caused socioreligious discord and polarisation among communities and a rise in Islamophobia. This was followed by a Covid-19 outbreak in Punjab, the source of which was traced to a religious preacher who had ignored advice to self-quarantine after returning from a trip to Europe (Frias, 2020). Similarly, a major Hindu religious event and the world's largest religious congregation called the Kumbh Mela, which is held every 12 years on the banks of the Ganga river (Singh & Haigh, 2015) was held according to its schedule despite severe criticism. The festival drew millions of Hindu devotees from all parts of the country. As organisers of these religious events haplessly tried to discourage large crowds from attending and enforce guidelines and social distancing measures among the pilgrims, no precautions were followed. While officially there were no reports of infection clusters at the event, the health officials claimed a definite spike in Covid-19 cases in the whole country after the event as pilgrims returned to their home towns (Pandey, 2021). Critics in India referred to these as 'super-spreader events' as India battled against a devastating second wave of the coronavirus.

Although researchers have recently attempted to understand the impacts of Covid-19 on religious tourism and pilgrimage around the world (Manhas & Nair, 2020; Mróz, 2021; Nhamo *et al.*, 2020; Raj & Griffin, 2020; Yasin *et al.*, 2020) from a managerial perspective with suggestions for marketing, coping and recovery strategies, there is a need to examine the nexus between religion and tourism from a critical sociopsychological perspective. There have been several studies on travel behaviour during the pandemic. Yang and Wong (2021) reported that the positive outcomes of travel have been replaced by anxiety, insecurity and psychological distress and fear of contagion has led to increased tourist discrimination. Another study mentions that seeing foreign tourists can cause fear due to the pandemic (Hosseini *et al.*, 2020). However, in the context of religious tourism where faith and religion are involved, travel behaviour, risk perception, decision-making and judgement can be different. Therefore, drawing upon a mix of sociopsychological theories and geographical theory of space, this study attempts to understand how religious belief and fear of death intersect, how it impacts travel decision-making, how pilgrims create new subjectivities in the process and how the perception of religious spaces has been transformed during the pandemic. Within the context of the Covid-19 pandemic, the objectives of this study are twofold: (a) to explore the underlying psychological factors associated with perceptions and decision-making among pilgrims to religious events and spaces; (b) to analyse the adaptive transformation of religious spaces. As Zeller and Kessler (2021: 3) noted, 'COVID-19 is a fertile case study to examine how religion is both challenged and rejuvenated at a particularly painful moment in time'. The study attests to this paradox using the context of pilgrimage adding an interesting and challenging perspective to the goals of this edited volume. In doing so, this chapter reveals that despite an overall structural and transformational change in the mode and practice of religious worship during the Covid-19 pandemic in India, there were few outlier events, such as the Kumbh Mela, which challenged the conventional and expected attitudes, perceptions and behaviours among pilgrims. Although a commentary on the ethical and rational aspects of such behaviour and perceptions is beyond the scope of this chapter, it nevertheless demonstrates the sociopsychological underpinnings of non-conformist behaviour and decision-making in pilgrimage during the pandemic.

The Kumbh Mela

The Kumbh Mela (mela=fair) is the largest religious event or festival in India. Celebrated in a cycle of approximately 12 years, it attracts millions of pilgrims from within the country and outside to four major sacred sites in northern India, situated on the banks of the sacred river Ganga. The Kumbh Mela, rooted in Hindu mythology, has been recognised by UNESCO as an intangible cultural heritage. According to Hindu religious significance, bathing during the auspicious dates during the event helps attain salvation from the cycle of rebirths. Lamba *et al.* (2022) have reported that the motivations for attending the Kumbh Mela are due to a religious calling, karmic cleansing, seeking forgiveness for sins, for knowledge and love of the Sanskrit language, or to find inspiration and peace. Although these motivations appear straightforward, the sociopsychological factors associated with them are quite complex. Most pilgrims known as *kalpvasis* stay at the event sites and participate in different prayer sessions, spiritual activities and purificatory rituals including the holy dip in the Ganga. The 2021 Kumbh Mela started in January and the Mahakumbh Mela in Haridwar began on the 1st of April and ended on the 30th of April. It was held in the state of Uttarakhand and was attended by several million people as the second wave of Covid-19 raged across India, and it became the second most affected country in the world. The situation became worse as several cases were reported following the event (Slater & Masih, 2021). This study is based on the perceptions of the pilgrims at the Kumbh Mela to understand the psychological factors associated with their attendance.

Theoretical Context

To position the findings on a valid theoretical foundation, the study particularly focuses on two concepts: death anxiety and psychological distance. The biggest fear associated with the Covid-19 virus infection is mortality. Hence, these two themes were used to understand the pilgrims' fear of mortality and their perceptions of how the pandemic affects them.

Death anxiety

One of the key concepts that this study focuses upon is death anxiety, which can be understood through an empirical analysis of death anxiety levels among pilgrims who decided to travel during the pandemic. The psychological encounter with death and associated death anxiety has been the subject of inquiry for sociologists, psychologists, philosophers and healthcare practitioners for many decades (Kastenbaum, 2000; Neimeyer, 1988; Solomon *et al.*, 1991). The concept of death anxiety is borrowed from thanatology (death studies) which is a subdiscipline of sociology. Death anxiety has been defined as 'the state in which an individual experiences apprehension, worry, or fear related to death and dying' (Carpenito-Moyet, 2008: 39) or a 'vague uneasy feeling of discomfort or dread generated by perceptions of a real or imagined threat to one's existence' (Moorhead *et al.*, 2008: 761). Individuals' death anxiety and experience of grief are strongly structured by their social environment and personal life-worlds (Tercier, 2005). Institutional orders such as religion, politics and mass media, indirectly or directly filter and mould our mortality experiences and actions and influence the individual order. According to Freud (1992), people have defense mechanisms, such as denial, to fight against the threat of death. Anxiety results when these defense mechanisms are dismantled. For Freud, death fears are a product of unresolved psychological conflicts.

Death anxiety is universal, present in all societies; however, the experience of death anxiety may vary depending on religiosity, gender, psychological state and age (Dadfar &Lester, 2020; Lehto & Stein, 2009). There have been multiple efforts to develop and validate scales and questionnaires that can be useful in assessing the various aspects of the concept. The use of measuring instruments for death anxiety such as the Death Anxiety Scale (Templer, 1970) and Multidimensional Fear of

Death Scale (Hoelter, 1979) have been prevalent in different clinical and occupational settings. In the context of Covid-19, Silva *et al.* (2021) investigated the conditions under which concerns about death itself and anxiety are related to psychological well-being. While discussing coping conditions during the pandemic, Liu *et al.* (2021) stated that people's mental health concerns have been severely affected as a consequence of social distancing measures since involuntary isolation frustrates the social nature of people leading to increased anxiety and depression (Pietrabissa & Simpson, 2020).

Fear among people during the pandemic has mostly been related to adherence to social isolation and distancing measures, the fear of being infected with the virus or dying as a result of Covid-19. Using the Terror Management Theory rooted in social psychology, Pyszczynski *et al.* (2015) argued that 'regardless of whether one consciously believes that the virus is a major threat to life or only a minor inconvenience, fear of death plays an important role in driving one's attitudes and behaviour related to the virus'. For this study, a measurement of the fear of death among pilgrims who visited the Kumbh Mela indicates their travel behaviour. It can be hypothesised that those with higher fear of death choose to be more careful in terms of their travel behaviour while those with lower fear of death choose to be less careful in travel-related decisions.

Psychological distance

Another sociopsychological theory applied in this study is psychological distance. This theory seemed to fit best in terms of understanding how the pilgrims viewed the pandemic and its impact on themselves. According to Liberman and Trope (2008), psychological distance refers to the human evaluation of distance to specific objects in four dimensions – geographical, social, temporal and hypothetical. It is based on the construal level theory, according to which humans use mental constructs of different abstraction levels to represent objects or events (Trope & Liberman, 2010). These construals, mental representations or perceptions made by human beings are either high level (more abstract and referring to distant objects and events) and events or low level (more concrete and detailed referring to close objects and events). The construal level theory asserts that mental representations are based on psychological distance – the subjective distance of an object, action or event from an individual's direct immediate reality of the here and now (Liberman & Trope, 2008; Trope & Liberman, 2010). It means that when an object or an event is perceived as psychologically distant, the representation or construal formed is at a high level. It is abstract and decontextualised in nature. On the other hand, when an object or an event is perceived as psychologically proximal, the representation or construal formed is of a low level. It is more concrete and contextual in nature with incidental features. The level of construal and psychological distance is reciprocal; that is, 'more distant objects will be construed at a higher level, and high-level construal will bring to mind more distant objects' (Trope & Liberman, 2010: 444).

The concept of psychological distance has been used in various health-related studies such as those related to the Ebola virus or Zika disease (Johnson, 2018). White *et al.* (2014) demonstrated that low psychological distance towards viral diseases meant that people perceived them as more dangerous and were willing to conform to protective measures. Blauza *et al.* (2021) demonstrated the role of geographical and hypothetical distance for health-related behaviours and education. In the context of tourism, it can be hypothesised that higher psychological distance is associated with increased motivation for travel and less conformity to precautions or health-related regulations. While individual psychological distances are different, the concept provides a rigorous theoretical basis to understand human behaviour in general, and therefore, the study uses it as a supplementary theory to investigate the perceptions about Covid-19 among pilgrims to understand why they chose to travel during the pandemic.

Geographical psychological distance is applicable when the mental representations are spatially far from where the individual is positioned (Fujita *et al.*, 2006). Temporal distance is applicable when the representation is further away in time from the present, for example, a thing or an event that the individual believes is not relevant to the present and is situated in the past or the future (Wakslak *et al.*, 2006). In both these cases, the mental representation is abstract in nature resulting from a high construal. Social distance is related to the level of personal closeness to a thing or an event (Liviatan *et al.*, 2008) and hypothetical distance refers to the likelihood of occurrence or probability that a thing, event, or action will happen (Wakslak *et al.*, 2006).

Methodology

Due to the Covid-19 crisis in India and associated restrictions, a qualitative method combining deductive and inductive approaches comprising thematic analysis and an online questionnaire have been used. From a deductive standpoint, the analysis is anchored in two themes (death anxiety and psychological distance) generated deductively from theory and prior research. From an inductive standpoint, a thematic analysis has been used to analyse the data and draw out further themes to generate an understanding of the pilgrims' experiences. A purposive sampling method was followed due to the difficulties associated with recruiting respondents in the field. The first respondents for the study were chosen among the researcher's circle of acquaintances and contacted online within a month of their return from the event. It was not possible to be physically present at the event and be able to randomly select pilgrims for the study due to the pandemic-induced travel restrictions to India. Therefore, the pilgrims based in India were selected from the researcher's circle of acquaintances. This was followed by a snowball technique where the first respondents were asked to assist in identifying other potential respondents. A survey containing questions in English and Hindi related to the pilgrims' perceptions of death anxiety and the impact of the pandemic was shared with the participants. The questionnaire was slightly adapted from the well-established Revised Collett-Lester Fear of Death Scale (Collett & Lester, 1969; Lester *et al.*, 2007) with a reduction in the number of original questions and some modifications. The scale has acceptable reliability and validity and has been widely used across multiple disciplines. The purpose of using the scale was to measure the level of death anxiety and perception of mortality among the pilgrims and to provide a context when examining travel decision-making during the pandemic. The questionnaire utilises the Likert scale of measurement, which allows for a pre-coding of responses ranging from 1 (not anxious at all) to 5 (very anxious) against different questions on mortality of self and others. Twenty male subjects participated in the survey.

Due to logistical barriers caused by the pandemic, recruiting a diverse sample was difficult. Further, gender equality among attendees at the Kumbh Mela has always been a contentious issue. The target population consisted of Hindu pilgrims from India who had visited the Kumbh Mela between January and April 2021, with ages ranging from 30 to 60 years. The questionnaire contained questions related to the pilgrims' views on mortality, the pandemic, travelling and the Kumbh Mela. The questionnaire included open-ended questions such as: What are your views about the Covid-19 pandemic? How do you think that the pandemic can affect you now or in the future? What motivated you to attend the Kumbh Mela during a pandemic? What changes in religious practice and rituals have you observed in your daily life during the lockdown? Besides these, the questionnaire contained statements (e.g. I am afraid of dying due to Covid-19, I am afraid of the shortness of life, etc.) that assess attitudes towards death, and the process of dying with a 5-point Likert-type scale (1 = not anxious to 5 = very anxious). All ethical and data privacy procedures were followed during the study, and informed consent on conditions of anonymity and confidentiality was obtained from the participants before filling up the questionnaires. The secondary data sources comprised academic articles and publicly available media reports that provided a contextual understanding of the event and effects of the pandemic. A thematic analysis was further carried to identify overarching and recurrent themes and their meanings in the open-ended responses and comments collected from the questionnaire and the internet. The data were organised and categorised under the themes identified and subsequently, compared to academic literature. The following section presents the findings of the study.

Findings

The following broad themes emerged from the results of the death anxiety scale combined with the thematic analysis of pilgrim responses to the open-ended questions.

Fear of death associated with Covid-19

Figure 7.1 illustrates the aggregate results from the Revised Collett-Lester Fear of Death Scale, whereby responses from a series of questions on mortality provide a measure of death anxiety of the pilgrims.

Despite limitations and concerns, the scale provides a general indication of respondent perceptions on fear of death. Additional analysis and correlations could reveal how they negotiate it with factors such as personal experiences and religiosity. It was observed that the majority of the respondents (80%) were either less anxious or not anxious at all about death, about 20% were somewhat anxious about death, and none of the respondents were anxious or very anxious over their mortality. It has to be noted that while a majority of the respondents in the survey research suggested they were not anxious about death, the results may be situational and not generalisable. Further, the low death anxiety values may also vary and fluctuate due to temporal, spatial, cultural and personal reasons.

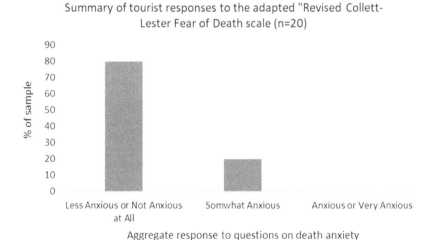

Figure 7.1 Overall response of pilgrims (*n* = 20) to questions on death anxiety as adapted from the Revised Collett-Lester Fear of Death scale

'The virus won't affect me': Psychological distance to the pandemic

A question was provided to the pilgrims to assess their general views on the pandemic and how it affected them. Similarly, opinions and views of pilgrims on Covid-19 in online media reports were analysed for themes that pointed towards a psychological distance towards the pandemic. This was based on the assumption that any experience associated with the pandemic affecting the pilgrims or anyone in their social circle is bound to affect their perception of events, outlook towards life and travel behaviour. The text from the data was analysed for words or references that indicated (a) geographical distance, (b) a reference to something situated in the past or future (e.g. 'when I grow old'), (c) proximity or distance to social relations and (d) the probability or likelihood of occurrence of an event based on some assumption. The responses collected pointed towards the four dimensions of psychological distance and indicated a high-level construal. The pandemic was found to be psychologically distant from pilgrims' minds, especially when travel

Table 7.1 Selected pilgrim narratives related to the Covid-19 pandemic categorised under the four dimensions of psychological distance with the subsequent level of construal

Dimension	Continuum of construal	
	Low-level construal (concrete)	High-level construal (abstract)
Geographical distance		'India is not like Europe... when it comes to immunity, we are better. It's really sad to see people not gathering at Kumbh in the same numbers as they would earlier ... The greatest truth on Earth is death. What's the point of living with fear?' – (Sherwood & Agence France-Presse, 2021) 'The pandemic might be severe in other countries, but not in India. I have full faith in the government and we shall overcome whatever we are facing'. – (Male, 43 years old)
Temporal distance		'Young people have the strength to endure COVID. I am not worried. I will worry about it when I grow old' – (Male, 25 years old)
Social distance	'I know people who have died of COVID in my town but thankfully, no one in my family has been affected' – (Male, 47 years old)	'COVID affects only those with comorbidities'. – (Male, 38 years old) 'I don't have any people on my social media friend list who have been infected. Sometimes media tends to blow news out of proportion' – (Male, 39 years old)
Hypothetical distance		'I take a lot of Ayurvedic medicines and do a lot of Yoga. I don't think I will get COVID'. – (Male, 54 years old)

decisions are made. The following narratives obtained from the questionnaire survey and secondary media reports corroborate the hypothesis. Table 7.1 provides an overview of how the pilgrim narratives can be classified under the dimensions of psychological distance with the respective construal level.

The above narratives can be categorised under abstract, high-level construals except one that has been categorised as concrete and low level. The first two responses indicate a spatial psychological distance where the pilgrims still chose to believe that the Covid-19 mortality in India is lower compared to other countries that are geographically further away, which in reality, was not true as India was the second worst-infected country after the USA during that period. In reality, these perceptions are inaccurate and likely to be influenced by several factors such as the level of awareness, scepticism towards international media reports, and dismissing them as fear-mongering or leftist propaganda, etc. According to Fujita *et al.* (2006), mental representations of the same phenomenon formed are more abstract in nature when the spatial distance is increased. The third response indicates a temporal distance where the pilgrim considers Covid-19 as something that will affect him only in the future and not in the present. The fourth and fifth responses indicate that the pilgrims consider COVID-related infections and deaths to be distant from their physical world, personal experiences and from those who fall in their immediate social circle. This is further augmented by the disconnection in the virtual online environment and social media platforms. It also illustrates that the reverse, that is, a personal experience of the pandemic (i.e. knowing someone infected or dead within one's social circle) would have entailed a more concrete representation. The sixth response indicates that the pilgrim considers the likelihood of getting infected to be low. The occurrence of an event or disease as unlikely or uncertain implies that the pilgrim perceives Covid-19 as hypothetically distant from his mind.

Although the pilgrims are aware of the pandemic, their concern values appear to be psychologically distant and are undermined by the immediate religious event which they want to attend, thereby affecting their travel decisions. Most of the responses confirm the assumptions of construal-level theory on how a large psychological distance entails more abstract representations about the respective issue, event or action (Trope & Liberman, 2010). Therefore, the likelihood of Covid-19 infecting someone in the past or the future, in a geographically distant place, related to other people not within one's social circle, and that appears to be less likely to happen, results in higher construal with abstract mental representations among the pilgrims. This abstract mental representation has a major bearing on travel decision-making as the pilgrim is less likely to be bothered or scared about getting affected by the pandemic.

'God will protect me': Religion as a buffer against death anxiety

An obvious and recurrent theme that emerged in the responses of the pilgrims was the concept of religiosity. Religiosity or a person's active commitment to religious beliefs and practice is an important cultural factor that has the potential to influence fear of death. Religiosity may act as a symbolic shield that protects people from the consequences of death particularly while encountering life-threatening events and crises. A strong religious belief system may promote a perception of increased control and predictability, which may lessen the fear of death. Florian *et al.* (1984) claimed that religions that emphasise ideas of divine purpose and reincarnation can inhibit the recognition that death is an inevitable, universal and irreversible phenomenon. A few studies also indicate that a belief in religion represents the denial of death (Kastenbaum, 2000). Research using unidimensional measures of fear of death showed that it is inversely associated with religiosity (Feifel & Nagy, 1981; Templer, 1972). Other studies (Florian & Kravetz, 1983; Florian *et al.*, 1984; Florian & Mikulincer, 1997) reported that commitment to religious beliefs and practice protects people from worries concerning the consequences of death to the body and the self. Lamba *et al.* (2022) identified that in a population, pilgrims with a higher level of religiosity have significantly lower death anxiety than pilgrims with a lower level of religiosity. According to Alvarado *et al.* (1995), a strong religious belief in life after death can reduce death anxiety (which applies to Hinduism). However, the relationship between religiosity and fear of death is a contentious topic (Pollak, 1979), and some studies show no correlation between the two (Abdel-Khalek & Lester, 2009). While there are several psychological instruments and scales to measure religiosity level, doing so is beyond the scope of the study. However, the narratives reveal that the mention of religiosity was linked to the idea that religion acts as a shield for them against any fear of death related to Covid-19.

> *It's the voice of God, who says nothing will happen. God won't let anything happen to us. I have full faith, said Baba Prakash Puri Maharaj, a 48-year-old seer from West Bengal, dripping wet from the dip he had just taken in the Ganga.* (Sirur, 2021)

> *I'm sure Maa Ganga will take care of their safety.* (PTI, 2021)

> *This religious event has the blessing of God. When God is near, what do I have to fear?* – (Male, 42 years old)

> *I knew that I was travelling for an auspicious cause. Even if I get infected, God will take care of me.* – (Male, 37 years old)

This is in line with several empirical studies that have assessed the relationship between death anxiety and religiosity. The pilgrims believed that the sacred Ganga River symbolises the presence of God or mother (referring to the river as 'Maa' which means mother) and is the epitome of purity. The consideration of the River Ganga as sacred is derived from writings in the Hindu religious texts which state that if one were to bathe in the Ganga even after sinning, the water of the river will cleanse him/her. The river water is considered sacred and used in all ceremonial and religious activities. The level of symbolic sanctity accorded to the river is so high that irrespective of the water being polluted and unpotable, the river still stands as one of the highest symbols of religion, faith and purity. Therefore, a dip in the river during the Kumbh Mela is an important ritual.

'We Shall Overcome': Religious Space, Resilience and Communitas

The journey and the religious event altogether provided the pilgrims solace from any existing pandemic-related concerns. Studies have shown that many individuals regard religion as a source of coping with the difficult moments of their lives (Mohammadzadeh & Najafi, 2020; Willis *et al.*, 2019). While religious faith and spiritual belief are believed to reduce death anxiety and act as a preventive mechanism against feelings of existential despair (Lewis, 2014; Mohammadzadeh & Najafi, 2020), it also holds the potential of acting as a source of community resilience and a medium through which a community can overcome collective and individual trauma, experience belongingness and shared identities.

> *The fact that so many people came together for this religious event shows that no virus can beat us or dampen our spirit. I travelled with my friends in a group as well.* – (Male, 41 years old)

> *COVID cannot defeat us if we are united and we believe in God* – (Male, 39 years old)

> *I am tired of reading and hearing all the COVID-related news. Attending this event and seeing so many devoted Hindu people around me gave me peace, hope and courage. The place energizes you.* – (Male, 42 years old)

> *I felt like taking a dubki (dip) in the river has washed away all my sins. I feel blessed. I don't regret attending the event at all* – (Male, 48 years old)

> *The Kumbh Mela is a place for cosmic energy healing. You have to be there to feel that vibe. You cannot feel it through your computer screens or live streaming.* – (Male, 55 years old)

> *So many people were there from all parts of the country. Many were in groups. It felt good and lively. There was a strong vibe and camaraderie'* – (Male, 50 years old)

> *I invite all devotees across the world to come to Haridwar and take a holy dip in the Ganga during Mahakumbh. Nobody will be stopped in*

the name of COVID-19 as we are sure the faith in God will overcome the fear of the virus – Tirath Singh Rawat (former Chief Minister of the state Uttarakhand where the event was organised)

Despite religion being blamed for spiking the incidence of Covid-19 cases and making the situation worse, the first six pilgrim responses reveal that religion and the Kumbh Mela during Covid-19 was regarded by the pilgrims as a source of community resilience, healing, salvation, peace, hope, coping against the pandemic and a ritualistic place where they experienced a sense of togetherness, a shared identity or *communitas*. This was supported by the political leaders as evident from the last response where they refused to impede the right to worship and hold a public gathering. These factors symbolising community resilience may have indirectly contributed towards assuaging any fear of death associated with Covid-19.

The Virtual Sacred Space: Adaptive Transformation of Spaces for Religious Rituals and Worship

Drawing upon Bourdieu's work on field and habitus, Bryson *et al.* (2020) noted the emergence of a new, third, 'infra-secular' space due to the pandemic as the lines between sacred and secular spaces were blurred and homes and spaces within homes were transformed into temporary sacred spaces. According to him, an inter-sacred space is created virtually in 'which different places, generally homes, are transformed into inter-linked "fields" through the application of "habitus" based on rules, conventions, and expectations linked to worship' (2020: 364). This is also built on the notion of 'infra-secular' geography (della Dora, 2018), an interstitial and fluid dimension, that concerns the transformation of 'sacred space' to 'incorporate both religious and secular functions'. Rountree (2021) also notes that when virtual sacred space and sacred places 'in the world' interweave, physical/material and imagined places connect, and all these places merge into a single place in a sacred collective consciousness or a sense of shared connection to a sacred place, called a 'timescape'.

A similar emergence of infra-secular space was observed in India as some of the major religious sites started virtual prayer services and webcasting live *aarti* (a Hindu ritual ceremony in which lamps are lit and prayers are offered to one or more deities) and *darshan* (ritual of viewing the deity's idol at a temple) sessions on official temple websites, private apps, social media and other digital platforms such as Zoom. Some of these digital platforms even allowed pilgrims to book prayer slots. These practical and virtual activities were adopted by religious communities including Hindus, Muslims, Sikhs and Christians (Kumar, 2020).

In India, the pandemic caused a nationwide lockdown restricting travel leading to an adaptive transformation of spaces for rituals and worship and the emergence of new worshipping practices and restrictions. Notwithstanding their attendance at the Kumbh Mela, the pilgrims were asked about the different adaptive practices they were aware of. All the pilgrims were aware of digital sacred spaces and virtual prayer sessions with 40% of them having attended them online. For example, the famous Jagannath Yatra in Puri (Odisha state), another major Hindu religious event was available to devotees worldwide through a live streaming app and YouTube. The ritual performers at the site were only allowed after a negative Covid-19 test. These virtual services provided an opportunity for devotees to participate in groups and engage in shared worship rituals and community prayer sessions from their homes amidst the lockdowns and mobility restrictions. Zeller and Kessler (2021) observed that 24/7 virtual access to sacred places not only provided comfort and sustenance to the devotees but also attracted a global audience 'creating new forms of religious competition as well as glocal forms of prayer and connection'. Manhas and Nair (2020) observed that religious sites could play a substantial role in reviving the Indian tourism sector by promoting staycations and micro-holidays, by reforming existing projects such as the Swadesh Darshan and the Pilgrimage Rejuvenation and Spiritual Augmentation Drive (PRASAD), and fostering collaboration with practices such as Yoga, Wellness and Ayurveda, which have deep-seated relationships with Hinduism.

While most large-scale religious gatherings were reduced, the organisation of Kumbh Mela was an exception that was influenced by the scale of the event, the religious significance of the event for Hindus, the ontological significance of the religious site and political support. The organisation of the Kumbh Mela amidst the pandemic was labelled as a political and economic decision by the critics. Besides expected financial losses for not holding the event, it was still allowed to happen because the state elections polls were due in the next eight months, and being a Hindu majority country, the government of India didn't want to alienate its voter base. Despite these influencing factors, the pilgrims stressed the significance of physical emplacement for the rituals in the context of Kumbh Mela. Emplacement not only recognises the significance and intensity of the place event and its contingencies, but also the historicity of processes associated with the place. This is also in line with Moser and Feldman's (2014: 1) argument that a 'ritual must be examined in its specific material and the topographical context in which ritual action impacts its physical setting while, simultaneously, the location in which the ritual is enacted informs and guides the religious practice'. Radermacher (2016: 304) noted that the 'materiality of space influenced sensory perception, communication, and embodiment, and also relates to imaginations about space as well as social norms'. Although Rountree (2021) states that physical emplacement is not essential to generate a sense of shared connection to a sacred place, the case of Kumbh Mela proves it otherwise.

Conclusion

Using the case of an outlier religious event, the study challenges the conventional and expected behaviour among tourism stakeholders in response to the pandemic by exploring the sociopsychological underpinnings of non-conformist behaviour among pilgrims. It reveals a paradoxical situation where on one hand, religious practices underwent an adaptive transformation in the country, and on the other hand, a major religious event such as the Kumbh Mela was held sidelining this adaptive transformation and actively supported by Hindu pilgrims and political leaders with vested interests. It demonstrates that while the organisation of a major religious event in India was criticised for transmission of the Covid-19 virus (Pandey, 2021), it was significant for the pilgrims as it symbolised community resilience, healing, salvation, peace, hope, coping against the pandemic and a ritualistic place where they experienced *communitas*. The Kumbh Mela further highlights the importance of material interconnection between religious rituals and place. While this interconnection got sidelined due to the pandemic and the emergence of virtual spaces that provided a secure environment for performing religious rituals, it was observed that the idea of emplacement took precedence over virtual presence in the case of Kumbh Mela. This shows that certain religious rituals of significance cannot be understood as a disembodied event or series of events – removed from their locations and separate from the physicality of their performance. Although online forms of worship or rituals might allow individuals to be more embodied within the communities in which they already exist, there are exceptions like the Kumbh Mela. The findings reveal that the Kumbh Mela pilgrims prioritised the materiality of space and emplacement of their religious belief over pandemic-related concerns. The underlying psychological factors observed in this prioritisation process were low death anxiety, higher psychological distances and religiosity as a source of comfort and community resilience. It must be noted that these psychological factors are not causal and generalisable. Nevertheless, the study highlights the importance of place-based and community-based experiences in religious pilgrimage during the pandemic. As Radermacher (2016: 307) noted, 'spatiality becomes "real," i.e., tangible and sensory experience, only through and in the body of the emplaced individual'. In terms of limitations, the study could have benefited from a larger and more representative sample size. While results reveal that pilgrims at the Kumbh Mela prioritised emplacement of religious practice over a virtual experience, this study by no means intends to encourage low proximity, large-scale gatherings during a pandemic and recognises that virtual religious experiences were the need of the hour. The Kumbh Mela is an exemplar of the perils of political power structures risking public health to appease a section of the majoritarian religion of the country for electoral gains.

Considering future implications, the study suggests that during a crisis, there will always be anti-utilitarian instances, actions and events when religious faith trumps fear, and therefore, associated contingencies need to be taken into account during crisis planning and management in tourism. Although it is difficult to account for contingencies and eliminate the threat of infections at large religious gatherings, there is room for preventive efforts that focus on better risk evaluation and risk communication among tourism stakeholders, government officials, healthcare professionals and religious leaders who can influence the public. For example, the World Health Organization provides a Risk Assessment tool and a Decision Tree that reflects health-related guidance and new evidence on both Covid-19 and religious mass gatherings. Before the event, Quadri and Padala (2021) had suggested measures like restricting the number of attendees, introducing an online pilgrim registration system, GPS tracking of pilgrims, employing drones to monitor public movement, having a robust screening in place at various entrance points, scaling up the healthcare and quarantine infrastructure and resources to meet any large-scale outbreaks. Despite multiple suggestions and measures, religious events have demonstrated that large congregations could turn out to be dispersal hubs of Covid-19 (Quadri, 2020). The Tablighi Jamat and Kumbh Mela in India were no exception. Therefore, following WHO (2020)'s view, countries like India with a large population and with heightened community transmission risks should seriously consider postponing or reducing large religious gatherings in the interest of public health during a pandemic.

References

Abdel-Khalek, A.M. and Lester, D. (2009) Death anxiety as related to somatic symptoms in two cultures. *Psychological Reports* 105 (2), 409–410.

Alvarado, K.A., Templer, D.I., Bresler, C. and Thomas-Dobson, S. (1995) The relationship of religious variables to death depression and death anxiety. *Journal of Clinical Psychology* 51 (2), 202–204.

Bajpai, S. (2021, 15 April) 'Corona jihad' to 'holy dip' – India's TV channels shocked at Kumbh but it's no 'human bomb'. *The Print*. See https://theprint.in/opinion/telescope/corona-jihad-to-holy-dip-indias-tv-channels-shocked-at-kumbh-but-its-no-human-bomb/640034/ (accessed 5 March 2021).

Basu, A., Roy, A., Hazra, A.K. and Pramanick, K. (2020) Analysis of youths' perspective in India on and during the pandemic of COVID-19. *Social Science Quarterly* 101 (5), 1969–1978.

Bhambhra, M. and Tiffany A. (2021) From the sanctuary to the sofa: What COVID-19 has taught us about sacred spaces. See https://blogs.lse.ac.uk/covid19/2021/04/30/from-the-sanctuary-to-the-sofa-what-covid-19-has-taught-us-about-sacred-spaces/ (accessed 6 August 2021).

Blauza, S., Heuckmann, B., Kremer, K. and Büssing, A.G. (2021) Psychological distance towards COVID-19: Geographical and hypothetical distance predict attitudes and mediate knowledge. *Current Psychology* 1–12.

Bryson, J.R., Andres, L. and Davies, A. (2020) COVID-19, virtual church services and a new temporary geography of home. *Tijdschrift voor economische en sociale geografie* 111 (3), 360–372.

Carpenito-Moyet, L.J. (2008) *Handbook of Nursing Diagnosis*. Philadelphia: Lippincott, Williams and Wilkins.

Collett, L.J. and Lester, D. (1969) The fear of death and the fear of dying. *The Journal of Psychology* 72 (2), 179–181.

Dadfar, M. and Lester, D. (2020) Death distress constructs: A preliminary empirical examination of the Farsi form in nurses: A brief note. *Nursing Open* 7 (4), 1026–1031.

della Dora, V.D. (2018) Infrasecular geographies: Making, unmaking and remaking sacred spaces. *Progress in Human Geography* 42 (1), 44–71.

Feifel, H. and Nagy, V.T. (1981) Another look at fear of death. *Journal of Consulting and Clinical Psychology* 49 (2), 278.

Florian, V. and Kravetz, S. (1983) Fear of personal death: Attribution, structure, and relation to religious belief. *Journal of Personality and Social Psychology* 44 (3), 600.

Florian, V. and Mikulincer, M. (1997) Fear of death and the judgment of social transgressions: A multidimensional test of terror management theory. *Journal of Personality and Social Psychology* 73 (2), 369.

Florian, V., Kravetz, S. and Frankel, J. (1984) Aspects of fear of personal death, levels of awareness, and religious commitment. *Journal of Research in Personality* 18, 289–304.

Freud, A. (1992) *The Ego and the Mechanisms of Defense*. London: Karnac Books.

Frias, L. (2020) Officials say a Covid positive Indian who refused to isolate left 40,000 in quarantine. *Business Insider South Africa*. See https://www.businessinsider.com/coronavirus-super-spreader-linked-to-quarantine-of-40000-in-india-2020-3 (accessed 10 March 2021).

Fujita, K., Henderson, M.D., Eng, J., Trope, Y. and Liberman, N. (2006) Spatial distance and mental construal of social events. *Psychological Science* 17 (4), 278–282.

Gettleman, J. and Schultz, K. (2020) Modi orders 3-week total lockdown for all 1.3 billion Indians. *The New York Times*. See https://www.nytimes.com/2020/03/24/world/asia/india-coronavirus-lockdown.html (accessed 11 November 2021).

Hoelter, J.W. (1979) Multidimensional treatment of fear of death. *Journal of Consulting and Clinical Psychology*, 47, 996–999.

Hosseini, S., Bahrevar, V. and Rahmanian, V. (2020) Fear of COVID 19 pandemic: A case study in Iran. *Pakistan Journal of Medical and Health Sciences* 14 (2), 484–487.

Jha, N. and Dixit, P. (2020) A cluster of coronavirus cases can be traced back to a single mosque and now 200 million Muslims are being vilified. *BuzFeed News*. See www.buzzfeednews.com/amphtml/nishitajha/coronavirus-india-muslims-tablighi-jamaat (accessed 31 March 2021).

Johnson, B.B. (2018) Residential location and psychological distance in Americans' risk views and behavioral intentions regarding Zika virus. *Risk Analysis* 38 (12), 2561–2579.

Kastenbaum, R. (ed) (2000) *The Psychology of Death*. New York: Springer.

Kumar, R. (2020, 21 September). Religious festivals in India adapt to pandemic 'new normal' as followers and businesses miss out on celebrations. *South China Morning Post*. See https://www.scmp.com/lifestyle/travel-leisure/article/3102093/religious-festivals-india-adapt-pandemic-new-normal?module=perpetual_scroll_0&pgtype=article&campaign=3102093 (accessed 12 March 2021).

Lamba, N., Bhatia, A., Shrivastava, A. and Raghavan, A. (2022) Religious factors affecting death anxiety in older adults practicing Hinduism. *Death Studies* 46 (8), 1973–1981.

Lehto, R. and Stein, K. (2009) *Death Anxiety: An Analysis of an Evolving Concept*. New York: Springer.

Lester, D., Templer, D.I. and Abdel-Khalek, A. (2007) A cross-cultural comparison of death anxiety: A brief note. *OMEGA-Journal of Death and Dying* 54 (3), 255–260.

Lewis, A.M. (2014) Terror management theory applied clinically: Implications for existential-integrative psychotherapy. *Death Studies* 38 (6), 412–417.

Liberman, N. and Trope, Y. (2008) The psychology of transcending the here and now. *Science* 322 (5905), 1201–1205.

Liu, X., Zhu, M., Zhang, R., Zhang, J., Zhang, C., Liu, P, Zhengzi, F. and Chen, Z. (2021) Public mental health problems during COVID-19 pandemic: A large-scale meta-analysis of the evidence. *Translational Psychiatry* 11 (1), 1–10.

Manhas, P.S. and Nair, B.B. (2020) Strategic role of religious tourism in recuperating the Indian Tourism sector post-COVID-19. *The International Journal of Religious Tourism and Pilgrimage* 8 (7), 52–66.

Mohammadzadeh, A. and Najafi, M. (2020) The comparison of death anxiety, obsession, and depression between Muslim population with positive and negative religious coping. *Journal of Religion and Health* 59 (2), 1055–1064.

Moorhead, S., Johnson, M., Maas, M.L. and Swanson, E. (2008) *Nursing Outcomes Classification (NOC)*. St. Louis: Mosby Elsevier.

Moser, C. and Feldman, C. (2014) Introduction. In C. Moser and C. Feldman (eds) *Locating the Sacred: Theoretical Approaches to the Emplacement of Religion* (pp. 1–12). Oxford: Oxbow Books.

Mróz, F. (2021) The impact of COVID-19 on pilgrimages and religious tourism in Europe during the first six months of the pandemic. *Journal of Religion and Health* 60 (2), 625–645.

Nhamo, G., Dube, K. and Chikodzi, D. (2020) Impact of COVID-19 on global religious tourism and pilgrimages. In G. Nhamo, K. Dube and D. Chikodzi (eds) *Counting the Cost of COVID-19 on the Global Tourism Industry* (pp. 251–272). Cham: Springer.

Neimeyer, R.A. (1988) Death anxiety. In H. Wass, F.M. Berardo and R.A. Neimeyer (eds) *Dying: Facing the Facts* (2nd edn, pp. 97–136). Washington, DC: Hemisphere Publishing Corporation.

Pandey, G. (2021) India Covid: Kumbh Mela pilgrims turn into super-spreaders. *BBC News*. See https://www.bbc.com/news/world-asia-india-57005563 (accessed 25 May 2021).

Pietrabissa, G. and Simpson, S.G. (2020) Psychological consequences of social isolation during COVID-19 outbreak. *Frontiers in Psychology* 11, 2201.

Pirutinsky, S., Cherniak, A.D. and Rosmarin, D.H. (2020) COVID-19, mental health, and religious coping among American Orthodox Jews. *Journal of Religion and Health* 59 (5), 2288–2301.

Pollak, J.M. (1979) Correlates of death anxiety: A review of empirical studies. Omega: *Journal of Death and Dying* 10 (2), 97–121. https://doi.org/10.2190/4KG5-HBH0-NNME-DM58

PTI (Press Trust of India, 14th January 2021). Maa Ganga will take care of us: Coronavirus fails to deter Kumbh Mela in Haridwar. *New Indian Express*. See https://www.newindianexpress.com/nation/2021/jan/14/maa-ganga-will-take-care-of-us-corona-virus-fails-to-deterkumbh-mela-in-haridwar-2250084.html (accessed 10 May 2021).

Pyszczynski, T., Solomon, S. and Greenberg, J. (2015) Thirty years of terror management theory: From genesis to revelation. *Advances in Experimental Social Psychology* 52, 1–70.

Quadri, S.A. (2020) COVID-19 and religious congregations: Implications for spread of novel pathogens. *International Journal of Infectious Diseases* 96, 219–221.

Quadri, S.A. and Padala, P.R. (2021) An aspect of Kumbh Mela massive gathering and COVID-19. *Current Tropical Medicine Reports* 8, 1–6.

Radermacher, M. (2016) Space, religion, and bodies: Aspects of concrete emplacements of religious practice. *Journal of Religion in Europe* 9 (4), 304–323.

Raj, R. and Griffin, K. (2020) Reflecting on the impact of COVID-19 on religious tourism and pilgrimage. *The International Journal of Religious Tourism and Pilgrimage* 8 (7), 1–8.

Rountree, K. (2021) Transcending time and place in the context of Covid-19: Imagination and ritual in modern pagans' and shamans' creation of sacred space. *Ciencias Sociales y Religión/Ciências Sociais e Religião* 23, 021014-021014.

Séraphin, H. and Jarraud, N. (2021) COVID-19: Impacts and perspectives for religious tourism events. The case of Lourdes Pilgrimages. *Journal of Convention & Event Tourism* 23 (1), 1–20.

Sherwood, H. and Agence France-Presse (2021, 14 January) Up to 1m Hindus gather in India as festival goes ahead amid Covid fears. *The Guardian*. See https://www.theguardian.com/world/2021/jan/14/hindus-gather-india-kumbh-mela-festival-covid-fears (accessed 12 February 2021).

Shinde, K.A. (2015) Religious tourism and religious tolerance: Insights from pilgrimage sites in India. *Tourism Review* 70 (3), 179–196.

Shipway, R. and Miles, L. (2020) Bouncing back and jumping forward: Scoping the resilience landscape of international sports events and implications for events and festivals. *Event Management* 24 (1), 185–196.

Silva, W.A.D., de Sampaio Brito, T.R. and Pereira, C.R. (2021) Anxiety associated with COVID-19 and concerns about death: Impacts on psychological well-being. *Personality and Individual Differences* 176, 110772.

Singh, R.P. and Haigh, M.J. (2015) Hindu pilgrimages: The contemporary scene. In Brunn, S.D. (ed.) *The Changing World Religion Map* (pp. 783–801). Dordrecht: Springer.

Sirur, S. (2021, 15 April) 'Covid won't affect sadhus': At Kumbh, many shun masks & distancing, say faith will save them'. *The Print*. See https://theprint.in/india/covid-wont-affect-sadhus-at-kumbh-mela-devotees-shun-masks-say-faith-will-save-them/640339/spreader-linked-to-quarantine-of-40000-india-2020-3 (accessed 26 May 2021).

Slater, J. and Masih, N. (2021, 8 May) In India's surge, a religious gathering attended by millions helped the virus spread. *The Washington Post*. See https://www.washington-post.com/world/2021/05/08/india-coronavirus-kumbh-mela/ (accessed 11 November 2021).

Solomon, S., Greenberg, J. and Pyszczynski, T. (1991) A terror management theory of social behavior: The psychological functions of self-esteem and cultural worldviews. In M.P. Zanna (ed.) *Advances in Experimental Social Psychology* (Vol. 24, pp. 93–159). New York: Academic Press.

Templer, D.I. (1970) The construction and validation of a death anxiety scale. *Journal of General Psychology* 82, 165–177.

Tercier, J. (2005) *The Contemporary Deathbed: The Ultimate Rush*. Basingstoke: Palgrave Macmillian.

Trope, Y. and Liberman, N. (2010) Construal-level theory of psychological distance. *Psychological Review* 117 (2), 440–463.

Wakslak, C.J., Trope, Y., Liberman, N. and Alony, R. (2006) Seeing the forest when entry is unlikely: Probability and the mental representation of events. *Journal of Experimental Psychology: General* 135 (4), 641–653.

White, A.E., Johnson, K.A. and Kwan, V.S.Y. (2014) Four ways to infect me: Spatial, temporal, social, and probability distance influence evaluations of disease threat. *Social Cognition* 32, 3, 239–255.

WHO (2020) *WHO mass gathering COVID-19 risk assessment tool – Religious events. Guidance for authorities and event organizers planning mass gatherings during the current COVID-19 pandemic.* WHO/2019-nCoV/Religious_Leaders_RAtool/2020.2. World Health Organization. See https://www.who.int/publications/i/item/10665-333186 (accessed October 2022).

Willis, K.D., Nelson, T. and Moreno, O. (2019) Death anxiety, religious doubt, and depressive symptoms across race in older adults. *International Journal of Environmental Research and Public Health* 16 (19), 3645.

Yang, F.X. and Wong, I.A. (2020) The social crisis aftermath: Tourist well-being during the COVID-19 outbreak. *Journal of Sustainable Tourism* 29 (6), 859–878.

Yasin, R., Jauhar, J., Rahim, N.F.A., Namoco, S. and Bataineh, M.S.E. (2020) COVID-19 and religious tourism: An overview of impacts and implications. *International Journal of Religious Tourism and Pilgrimage* 8, 155–162.

Zeller, T.L. and Kessler, E. (2021) "It's not doctrine, this is just how it is happening!": Religious creativity in the time of COVID-19. *Religions* 12 (9), 747.

Part 3

Perceptions and Habitus Changes of Tourism Stakeholders

8 Bourdieu on Tasmania: How Theory of Practice Makes Sense of the Emergence of Regenerative Tourism in Times of Covid-19

Maree Gerke, Can-Seng Ooi and Heidi Dahles

Introduction

Over the past two decades, tourism scholarship, critical of the increasingly eroding impact of tourism on social justice and environmental preservation (Cave & Dredge, 2020; Higgins-Desbiolles, 2020), has generated an impressive body of knowledge advancing alternative forms of tourism. Among such alternative tourisms, 'regenerative tourism' is a recent addition. Like so many types in this genre, regenerative tourism gives equal consideration to the social and natural environment as it does to economic outcomes (Pollock, 2016). Yet, in contrast to other approaches that have accomplished very few changes so far (Sharpley, 2020), regenerative tourism advocates practices that claim to be transformational (Ateljevic, 2020).

Regenerative approaches are unique to place, engaging with the community and natural boundaries (Gössling & Hall, 2016). However, involving the community is not without its problems. Local communities are also replete with agendas and inequalities that can be further perpetuated through collaborative processes (Ooi, 2019). Nevertheless, there are examples of niche community solutions that deliver tourism which is more broadly beneficial and limits negative impacts (Cave & Dredge, 2020). So far, research in this area rarely occurs in agricultural regions and ignores the perspective of local stakeholders, such as small business, their employees and patrons.

Brimming with small businesses, Tasmania, well known for its natural beauty, premium produce and friendly people, is an ideal context for adopting regenerative tourism practices. *Timbre Kitchen* (hereafter referred to as Timbre), the business at the centre of this study, is nestled in Tasmania's Tamar Valley, one of the oldest wine regions in Australia. This local restaurant is venturing into regenerative practices at a time when a global pandemic has brought international travel to a standstill. The temporary pause in tourist arrivals has created space for local entrepreneurs and researchers alike to consider the vulnerability of the industry and spawned a renewed interest in more sustainable tourism.

Taking a Bourdieuan perspective, this study seeks to understand the challenges and tensions emerging in the transition to a more regenerative approach to tourism, in particular in times of a pandemic crisis. Bourdieu's theory of practice (Bourdieu, 1977) provides the conceptual lens for the analysis of how established patterns of doing things both enhance and inhibit progress towards adopting alternative practices. Many scholars have identified the relevance of Bourdieu's work for the tourism sector (e.g. Çakmak *et al.*, 2018; Czernek-Marszałek, 2020; Ferguson *et al.*, 2017), but none could be found applying his work to studies on regenerative tourism. In that vein, this study raises the question as to the ways in which deviating food habits and conflicting expectations divide local patrons and tourist customers and create challenges for the budding enterprise on its pathway to regenerative practices. Based on qualitative research featuring ethnographic fieldwork, it is argued that social, cultural and symbolic capital affects the ability of the business to overcome simmering tensions and unsettling dilemmas and turn them into opportunities.

This chapter is structured as follows: The next section offers a review of relevant literature from a Bourdieuan perspective. In the subsequent sections, the study will be situated in its geographic setting, followed by a brief description of the research methodology. Then, revolving around tensions between local and tourist stakeholders, the research findings will be presented and discussed against the backdrop of the key concepts. The concluding section will highlight the contribution of this study to the growing body of knowledge about ways in which tourism stakeholders adapt to structural changes spawned by the unfolding climate crisis and the global pandemic. In addition, the research findings, combined with the local response to the sudden and complete collapse of the tourism industry, provide rich context-specific insights that, on a practical level, may support Timbre to identify further opportunities to progress their regenerative agenda.

Literature Review: Regenerative Tourism in a Bourdieuan Perspective

Regenerative (food-)tourism

The concept of regenerative tourism has emerged in the critical literature emphasising the social issues created or exacerbated by tourism. It advances an approach that values and celebrates people, place and diversity, aiming for quality over quantity (Higgins-Desbiolles, 2020). For the purposes of this study, regenerative tourism is understood in terms of a positive, transformative and collaborative mindset underpinning practices designed to enhance the social and natural environments that are impacted by tourism activities (Hussain, 2021). The implementation of regenerative practices requires the collaboration of multiple stakeholders, which commonly meets with obstacles and challenges (Higgins-Desbiolles, 2020). Consequently, change is more likely to occur if multiple stakeholder assumptions and perceptions are closely aligned with a shared commitment to regenerative practices.

Food is an increasingly significant dimension of tourism while also being a popular leisure pursuit more generally (Bertella, 2020; Cleave, 2020). Hall (2020) suggests that food tourism is a key area for further research given its current and projected growth and its potential impact on the development of more sustainable forms of tourism, a view that finds broad support among tourism scholars (Gössling & Hall, 2016; Sharpley, 2020). Yet, many food businesses rely heavily on industrialised food production and supply chains to manage the price and consistency of produce (Ateljevic, 2020). Furthermore, restaurants are more likely to plan menus reliant on high-order proteins, such as beef and dairy products (Gössling & Hall, 2016). In high demand among middle-class patrons, or 'cultural intermediaries', whose identities and tastes are aligned to such foods – these products exert more negative impacts on the planet than plant-based foods (Ahmad, 2013; Gössling & Hall, 2016). Consequently, food and, particularly, food consumed at restaurants has far-reaching implications, often further intensified by popular and social media, which push food trends that shape and legitimise the production and consumption of certain foods (Ahmad, 2013; Cleave, 2020; Hall, 2020). While food businesses cannot create sweeping changes to consumer behaviours, they can contribute to changing consumer habits by presenting them with more sustainable food options (Bertella, 2020).

Bourdieu's field theory

In providing a comprehensive theory of social practice, Bourdieu's field theory offers an understanding as to how individual actors create the social structures (fields) that come to shape their assumptions and behaviours (habitus), and that is simultaneously reinforced and transformed through the strategic investment of competitive resources (capitals) within groups and society (Bourdieu, 1977, 1989). In so doing, Bourdieu's field theory provides a heuristic framework through which regenerative tourism can be understood as a contextually embedded and dynamic social phenomenon, as will be argued below.

Fields are dynamic structures with malleable boundaries. Where boundaries between fields overlap, spaces of fluidity and contestation emerge,

actors leverage capitals to gain an advantage, assumptions become challenged, behaviours adjusted, rules redefined, boundaries reshaped and structures transformed. The socially ingrained habits, skills and dispositions
– habitus in Bourdieu's theory of practice – are the lens through which individuals perceive and symbolically construct the world around them
(Bourdieu, 1989). Consequently, habitus influences how people see themselves within specific contexts and transforms with the accumulation of capital such as wealth, qualifications and membership in specific social groups.

The theory of practice identifies a number of different forms of 'capital'
that serve both as material and tacit resources in human exchanges, among
which economic, cultural, social and symbolic capital (Bourdieu, 1984).
Bourdieu's concept of economic capital refers to wealth in the narrow
sense, represented in monetary value. Cultural capital denotes certified
knowledge and expertise accumulated through (formal) education and
comprises cultural competence, represented in the form of diplomas or
(academic) titles. The concept of social capital is defined in terms of durable network relations, trust and credentials. Symbolic capital, in Bourdieu's
thinking, is 'the form that the various species of capital assume when they
are perceived and recognised as legitimate' (1989: 17). The above forms of
capital are interrelated, in the sense that social, cultural and symbolic capital can generate economic capital, but economic capital does not buy
social, symbolic or cultural capital in a simple, direct way (Bourdieu, 1984:
252). As the dynamic field of gastronomy becomes entwined with the transition from conventional to regenerative tourism, culinary standards (habitus) are reshaped by strategically employing a range of resources such as
gastronomic competencies (cultural capital), recognised reputations (symbolic capital) and social capital in the form of multi-layered networks. As
our study shows, this transition is wrought with tensions caused by deviating food habits and different appreciation of economic capital.

Tourism in a Bourdieuan perspective

Tourism establishes a field in the Bourdieuan sense in that it exists
within social structures and groups espousing specialised knowledge,
practices and rules that both advance and constrain the thinking and
behaviour of actors, including their ability to change or question accepted
norms (Bourdieu, 1989). The field theory provides a framework for understanding the perspectives held by tourism stakeholders, including partially
converging and partially conflicting values and assumptions that inform
their behaviours and choices.

People who travel and engage in leisure are more likely to have access to
resources (or 'capitals' in Bourdieuan terms), enabling them to consume in
ways that align with their tastes and strengthen their identities through symbolic lifestyle consumption practices (Ahmad, 2013). Bourdieu (1984) referred
to these agents as 'cultural intermediaries' as they influence the tastes,

artefacts and behaviours to be considered legitimate among varying social categories (Ahmad, 2013; Higgins-Desbiolles, 2020). They may do so, for example, by enjoying buffet-style food offerings during all-inclusive package holidays, while others by engaging in a premium food and wine tour. Tourists spend more (in terms of economic capital) than locals, especially foodie tourists, who are often identified as high-yield customers (Cleave, 2020; Gössling & Hall, 2016). They are seen as more discerning (investing cultural capital), looking for special food with connections to place and people while aligning with their tastes and identity (Cleave, 2020; Stringfellow *et al.*, 2013).

Tourist destinations present themselves as 'authentic' and 'traditional', inviting visitors to experience the local culture and heritage. These factors combined make restaurants offering local food particularly attractive to tourists while also making tourists attractive to the business. As restaurants in regional areas can also be attractive to urbanites seeking a regional experience, they cater largely for their local communities (Gössling & Hall, 2016). For locals, eating out is a leisure pursuit of food but equally about seeking out places where they have a social connection (Cleave, 2020). As food is highly symbolic, it reinforces a sense of identity and belonging (Cleave, 2020), making it a medium for conveying an ideological position (Bourdieu, 1989). This position is not fixed but rather malleable dynamic, and highly dependent on context (Bennett *et al.*, 2020). More recently, the global pandemic has highlighted the importance of trusting relationships between businesses and their communities as consumers shift further towards prioritising local and sustainable options (Cornejo-Ortega & Dagostino, 2020).

Regenerative tourism emerges as a sub-field (in Bourdieuan terms) where individual actors travel to gain new perspectives and take responsible action (Cave & Dredge, 2020). Networks of change-makers are well connected via social media and various events where they congregate to advance their shared interest in social transformation (Lee *et al.*, 2014). In a study on the impact of attracting tourists for supporting business innovation, Hall and Baird found that wine businesses in New Zealand that attracted tourists were more innovative than those that mainly attracted locals (cited in Gössling & Hall, 2016: 19). Conversely, while cultural capital is the key mechanism through which social and economic capital is reproduced, not all valued cultural capital aligns with the middle classes (Bennett *et al.*, 2020). Therefore, both locals and tourists can help regenerative progress goals through new transformative experiences and events that trigger personal change.

As Jean Anthelme Brillat-Savarin, a famous 19th-century gastronome, once wrote: 'Tell me what you eat, and I will tell you who you are' (cited in Stringfellow *et al.*, 2013: 6). This is highly relevant to this study, as a solid alignment to a socially and environmentally responsible business can positively shape consumption practices and identities (Stringfellow *et al.*, 2013), which, in turn, may motivate businesses to pursue regenerative practices. Yet, adopting regenerative tourism practices poses challenges to tourism businesses. As suggested by the literature reviewed in this section, there are two particular areas where such challenges occur. First, tensions arise around identity matters. Tourists are attracted to experiences that provide insights into place and heritage. Their definition of an authentic experience, as mediated by tour operators, may diverge from the ideas that community members may hold regarding their local identity. Second, tensions arise at the intersection of commercial viability and the local community. While attracting tourists to regional areas is an economic imperative for local operators, they also need to maintain community as their key priority and give residents a say in how tourists are accommodated in their shared space. Therefore, where new tourisms enter established fields, tourism stakeholders have to navigate rising tensions, leveraging their habitus and a range of capitals to broker agreement or initiate change. How this unfolds will be discussed in this chapter.

Setting

Tasmania is a small island state situated to the south of mainland Australia, with a distinct rural character. In recent years, Tasmania has become a popular tourist destination. In the north of the state, just a short drive from the regional town of Launceston amid much agricultural foods and tourism businesses, Timbre is situated at the gateway to the Tamar Valley wine region, in an area branded the *Northern Forage Drive* (see Figure 8.1). The West Tamar region is one of the fastest-growing residential areas in Tasmania.

In the past 20 years, Tasmania has experienced significant tourism growth, from approximately 897,000 arrivals in 2008 to 1.32 million in 2019, the vast majority (over 1 million) being domestic arrivals (Denny *et al.*, 2020; Tourism Tasmania, 2021). Tourism is Tasmania's second industry after mining and is one of the promising sectors in the state's economic strategy. Tourism contributes about 10.3% (AU$3.2 billion) to the Gross State Product, the highest proportion across Australia (Tourism Tasmania, 2021). Tasmania's tourism strategy, known as the *T21 Visitor Economy Strategy,* aims to increase visitor arrivals and constrain demand in more popular destinations such as the capital city of Hobart and Cradle Mountain (Tourism Tasmania, 2021). The *West Tamar Destination Action Plan* for the West Tamar region (West Tamar Council, 2018) designates 'putting out the welcome mat' as a key role for the local community to diffuse some perceived community resistance to growing tourism within the region.

The global pandemic severely impacted Tasmania's tourism economy throughout 2020 and 2021, with border restrictions in place for several months, affecting international arrivals (down by 98% in the year ending in June 2021) and domestic arrivals (down 35% in the same period). As international tourism spending was reduced to virtual nil, domestic

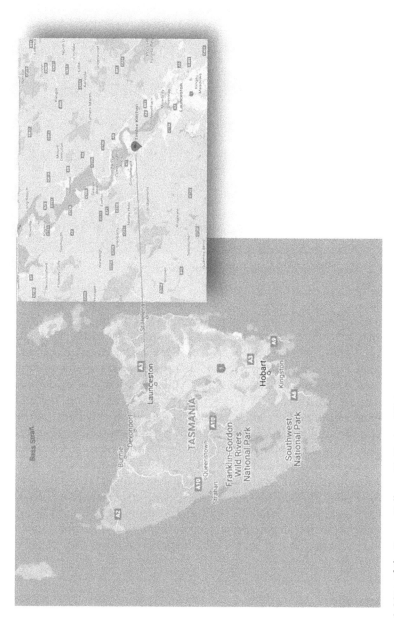

Figure 8.1 Map of the Tamar Valley with Timbre Kitchen

Source: https://www.google.com/maps/@-41.3703352,147.0466076,11z (accessed on 03/08/2021)

Figure 8.2 Aerial photo of Timbre and Vélo on site
Courtesy Vélo

tourism spending, on the other hand, suffered a loss of only 12% (Tourism Tasmania, 2021). Timbre is embedded within one of the leading vineyards in Tamar Valley, offering a place to eat, drink and appreciate the rural setting (see Figure 8.2). Timbre leases the restaurant at the vineyard and operates as a separate business but often collaborates with local producers, artists and performers. The owner of Timbre, Matt Adams, is a well-known and respected Tasmanian chef with significant experience within the hospitality industry. A small group of permanent, full-time staff is employed at Timbre, supported by casual front-of-house staff. Often featured in travel magazines and other media, Timbre is a destination eating spot. Opening, prior to Covid-19, on Wednesday to Sunday for lunch, and dinner on Friday and Saturday, it offers a sharing-style menu, chefs design that every week to use available produce. The atmosphere is friendly and unpretentious, with staff who present as quirky, cool and genuine, aiming to provide an enjoyable and accessible experience for a wide range of people.

Methodology

Focused ethnography (Fusch *et al.*, 2017), the methodology underlying this study, is well-suited to research that builds on existing connections between researcher and stakeholders and is particularly relevant for exploring new and emerging subcultures as it enables the collection of multiple perceptions within a context. At the beginning of this research, ethics approval was sought and obtained at the institutional level. While Timbre's owner and their staff members have elected to remain identifiable, other participants have been anonymised. Stakeholders were initially approached by Timbre based on stakeholder categories discussed and agreed with the key participant, as suggested by Adams (2015).

A total of 13 participants, all stakeholders of Timbre, were interviewed, including staff members, suppliers and customers. Stakeholder participation was voluntary, and no personal or work performance information was collected. An information sheet and a short video outlining the study rationale and process were provided. Timbre staff were interviewed during paid work hours. Semi-structured interviews lasted between 30 and 60 minutes, supported by pre-planned questions and topics that served as prompts. Implementing this flexible approach maximised the sharing of relevant narratives without unnecessary interruptions (Adams, 2015). Interviews were recorded using a mobile phone application and then fully transcribed manually. The onsite observation was conducted at Timbre on three occasions and focused mainly on customer arrival times and their initial engagement with Timbre staff. Observation notes included researcher reflections on observable behaviours and the process of observation.

Data storage planning occurred upfront to ensure that any ethical issues related to data management were minimised. A process of sorting and eliminating was undertaken as part of initial data analysis, with irrelevant data being discarded. The remaining data were analysed in two ways. First, it was mapped out into themes by identifying words and phrases that were significant to stakeholder perceptions, but also to determine if there were any unexpected tensions evident. Comments that provided some insights into stakeholder perceptions about regenerative tourism were arranged into categories. Second, data were mapped out and analysed according to Bourdieu's field theory to identify key fields identified, habitus apparent within those fields, and how stakeholders were exerting capitals to influence and push the field boundaries. Quotes from stakeholder interviews were chosen to represent stakeholders' varying perspectives and positions appear within these fields. Observations were reviewed for evidence of conflicts in data and to validate interview data. This approach provided in-depth data on the varying perceptions of stakeholders within the areas of tension being explored.

'Tell Me What You Eat': Empirical Findings

The owner of Timbre, Matt, identifies being sustainable as core to his identity saying: 'it's about who we are as people touching the earth gently and being respectful'.

Tourists versus guests

Members of the local community are a priority for Timbre. While Timbre is well supported by locals, with regular customers confirming that they eat there often, Timbre also attracts visitors touring the region. Some tourists are part of organised group wine tours, visiting the cellar door and then eating a set banquet lunch at Timbre. Others are self-drive tourists, who stop for a light lunch or mid-afternoon drinks and snacks on their way back to Launceston. On warmer days, sitting on the deck overlooking the vines (see Figure 8.3) is popular with locals and tourists alike.

Tourists rarely visit the restaurant for dinner and, those who do so appear to be restaurant destination tourists rather than visitors exploring the region. During an observation of a typical Friday night dinner service, most diners were local couples, aged 30–50 years old, comfortable with dining out etiquette, inferred by the ease with which they conversed with staff upon arrival, passing their coats to be hung up without invitation and ordering pre-dinner drinks. Then, the following scene unfolded:

Vignette 1: Tourists from country Victoria

As most diners studied the menu to select a banquet and order a bottle of wine while conversing with staff, a young, casually dressed couple entered Timbre without a reservation. As they looked around the restaurant, they appeared extremely uncomfortable and hesitant, scanning the

Figure 8.3 View from Timbre sun deck looking towards the Tamar River
Copyright: Maree Gerke

room and then looking at each other. A front of house staff member welcomed them and led them to a table where they were seated and provided with menus. The couple spent a few minutes intermittently looking around the room, then talking to each other and using their phones while looking at the menu. When a front of house staff member came over to talk about the menu, they asked many questions about the dishes and how the menu worked. At last, they left the restaurant.

The front of house staff described the situation as really awkward as walk-ins for dinner are rare. She assumed that the couple were from regional Victoria (mainland Australia), probably staying at the nearby caravan park and likely looking for a pub meal. This encounter shows that, while Timbre is attractive to tourists, it is not attractive to all tourists. After all, expectations of an authentic Tasmanian culinary experience differ widely, as was illustrated by a comment made by a wine tour operator: '... the local experience is an $18 parmigiana and a pot at the local hotel...cheapskate central'.

In contrast to the opinion of the same tour operator who defined the average patron of Timbre as 'tourist', local community residents are attracted to this restaurant for its spacious setting and location and invited by the staff, who they often refer to as friends. The social connections regular customers have with Timbre staff, and the atmosphere created through interactions, music and the general *vibe*, are important pull factors, and so is the pricing, which is compared favourably with other restaurants in the area (see Table 8.1).

While the wine tour operator highlighted the importance of produce provenance for tourists, saying 'the more Tasmanian it [the food] is the better', a key factor mentioned by local diners was the changing menu that was described as generous, varied and different to what most restaurants offer. A shared and constantly varying menu, arranged around banquet options, allows Timbre to use what they have at hand and only order in what they need from a diversity of local suppliers, the underlying philosophy being 'keep it simple and accessible' (see Figure 8.4 for the Timbre menu).

The artist versus the merchant

There is a distinct difference in philosophies related to business purpose and how these translate into experiences offered. Matt aims to provide all customers with a good experience through good food and good service. However, the wine tour operator aims to create a memorable tour experience for tourists, and consequently values owners who 'put themselves forward', stating that 'anytime you get less than generous, people feel that on the tour. You look for the wow factor'. As Timbre prioritises local customers, a significant tension has built between the restaurant management and tour operators. Entertaining different priorities and

Table 8.1 Comparison of dining costs in Launceston

Item	Similar food experience			Fine dining
	Timbre (old/new price)	Restaurant X	Restaurant Y	Restaurant Z
Single small dish	$9–18	$50pp	$12–20	$70pp
Smaller banquet	$44/$55pp	$70pp	$65pp	$95pp
Larger banquet	$66/$75pp	$85pp		$110pp
Dessert	$12 (included in banquet)	$10–15 (not included)	$12–16 (not included)	Not sold separately
Wine	$52–70 average per bottle. Vélo wines in lower price bracket.	No details available, but typically higher range.	$55–75 average per bottle	Higher range

values that inform their business approach, the wine tour operator described Matt as 'a bit like a Van Gogh, an artist with food, but a difficult character'. Tour operators contend that Timbre should offer tourists a more traditional vineyard menu. Matt is aware of the discontent simmering among the tour operators: '... they [wine tour groups] used to get platters, but I rudely stopped platters when I came here. That was a massive conundrum'. The tension between Timbre and this wine tour operator was so significant that it resulted in a cessation of the business relationship for several months. While Timbre and the wine tour operator reconciliated and work together again, tensions often surface during peak periods.

Vignette 2: Mismatch in customer focus

Both stakeholders described a situation involving the inclusion of additional wine tour guests from two quite different perspectives. The wine tour operator elaborated how he went out of his way to accommodate two extra people in a tour, even though the tour was underway. He was of the view that this was 'a good thing' to do because he had provided them with a service and increased the number of participants on tour. However, the front of the house staff member at Timbre identified the same situation as a problem because the two unannounced additional eaters caused Timbre staff to make some last-minute changes to the tables and settings. The front of house staff felt that this gave tour guests a negative impression of Timbre.

Wine tour operators are highly reliant on businesses such as Timbre and must carefully manage relationships to ensure the ongoing success of their business. Tours are pre-booked with Timbre for a specific number of guests, and it is not unusual for them to be fully booked. Timbre is set up for guests on that basis. For a relatively small restaurant, accommodating two extra guests can be difficult, and it may cause guests to have to

food

banquets - shared table
40pp/50pp/65pp
see waitstaff for details

or

small..
devilled eggs, Korean chilli, sesame 12
grilled cheese, granny Jean's mustard pickle (g) 10
quail, zucchini, hazelnut, 'nduja 16
broad bean, beans, tongola zoe, ham 18
raw beef, bagna cauda, anchovy, fresh peas, flax cracker 18

big..
chicken, almond, salsa verde 34
smoked pork, raisins, cabbage, miso butter 34
lamb, beet, onion, honey, mint 34

side..
cos, mustard, cheese 9
kohlrabi, kimchi, fennel, yoghurt 9
vinegar potatoes 9
fries 9

sweet..
miso semifreddo, honeycomb, peanut butter, brown butter 10
buttermilk pannacotta, cherries, raspberries
, seeds 10

cheese..
coal river brie, fruit paste, toast (g) 14

dietary requirements are no problem at all, let us know
we love creating vegetarian / vegan dishes and are done on the fly
YES to split bills - 4 splits and above per bill will incur a $1 surcharge per split
10% surcharge on public holidays. no amex
(g) = contains gluten

Menu

food

LUNCH 75pp
bread, tongola curd
brisket, cheddar custard
potato hummus, broad beans
blue eye trevalla, gribiche

potato, 'nduja
iceberg, caeser, pecorino
chicken, almond, salsa verde
lamb rump, kale, onion

miso caramel mousse, honeycomb

55pp LUNCH
bread, tongola curd
brisket, cheddar custard
potato hummus, broad beans

potato, 'nduja
iceberg, caeser, pecorino
chicken, almond, salsa verde

miso caramel mousse, honeycomb

plates etc
grilled cheese 12
bread, tongola curd 12
potato hummus, broad beans 16
brisket, cheddar custard 18
chicken, almond, salsa verde 35
lamb rump, kale, onion 35
potato, 'nduja 9
iceberg, caeser, pecorino 9
coal river brie, toast 15
miso caramel mousse, honeycomb 12
strawberry pavlova 12

dietary requirements are no problem at all,
let us know
we love creating vegetarian / vegan dishes and
are done on the fly
YES to split bills - 4 splits and above per
bill will incur a $1 surcharge per split
10% surcharge on public holidays. no amex

please check-in using the QR
code with
the Check in Tas app

Figure 8.4 Timbre Menu and Wine List, July 2020

Wine List

SPARKLING / PET NAT

2016 velo sparkling rosé TAS	15 / 72
NV house of arras brut elite TAS	120
2021 latta 'essential crisis' pet nat VIC	65
2020 mallaluka sauvignon blanc NSW	70

WHITE

2019 velo riesling TAS	12 / 52
2021 velo pinot gris TAS	12 / 52
2020 velo sauvignon blanc TAS	12 / 52
2018 velo chardonnay TAS	12 / 52
2020 utzinger riesling TAS	70
2020 mac forbes 'RS22' riesling VIC	70
2021 stargazer 'tupelo' TAS	75
2019 utzinger fumé blanc TAS	65
2021 alkina semillon SA	70
2021 stoney rise sauvignon TAS	75
2020 mallaluka vermentino NSW	70
2021 koerner 'pigato' vermentino SA	70
2020 latta 'jurassique' chardonnay VIC	76
2020 two tonne TMV chardonnay TAS	75
2009 three wishes chardonnay TAS	115
2020 holyman chardonnay TAS	115

ROSE / CHILLED REDS / IN-BETWEENS

2020 velo rosé TAS	12 / 52
2020 mac forbes EB&G 'aromanticism' VIC	68
2021 year wines 'noodle juice' grillo/riesling SA	65
2021 dr edge 'gold' chardy blend TAS	75
2021 express winemakers 1' orange WA	62
2021 dr edge 'amber' gris + schonburger TAS	75
2021 Hughes Hughes 'equinox TAS	70
2019 luna wines pinot gris TAS	70
2021 stoney rise no clothes pinot gris TAS	70
2021 charlotte dalton rosé SA	68

ROSE / CHILLED REDS / IN-BETWEENS CONTINUED.

2021 rory's clive rosé TAS	60
2021 stoney rise no clothes pinot noir TAS	70
2020 express winemakers drinking red WA	65
2020 utzinger roter satz TAS	82
2018 domaine de la loue labrute pinot FRA	95
2020 herve villemade bovin rouge (1 litre) FRA	85
2020 mosse 'bangarang' FRA	85
2019 sextant pinot/gamay FRA	110

RED

2019 velo pinot noir TAS	12 / 52
2018 velo cabernet sauvignon TAS	12 / 52
2019 velo shiraz TAS	15 / 72
2021 ochota barrels pinot meunier SA	78
2020 wolfe at the door pinot meiunier TAS	65
2018 velo old vine pinot noir TAS	62
2020 utzinger pinot noir TAS	75
2020 two tonne TMV pinot noir TAS	75
2019 sailer seeks horse 'one monkey' noir TAS	90
2020 marco lubiana pinot noir TAS	82
2021 stoney rise trousseau TAS	75
2020 hughes&hughes dornfelder TAS	80
2020 ochota barrels gamay SA	85
2021 latta 'presence' grenache VIC	76
2018 mesta grenache SPA	52
2021 ochota barrels 'fugazi' grenache SA	70
2020 koerner 'nielluccio' sangiovese SA	70
2019 koerner 'vivian' SA	75
2020 havilah shiraz + malbec TAS	70

STICKY

2018 moores hill late harvest riesling TAS	10 / 48
2012 nigl gruner veltliner eiswein AT	110

CARAFES (375ml) - see blackboard/staff for daily bottles

Figure 8.4 (continued)

wait for tables to be adjusted, which is deemed unprofessional by Timbre staff. This is frequently tested as tour operators deviating from pre-booked arrangements 'often get bumped' as Timbre may be booked out with locals, which commonly happens for special events, such as a Mother's Day lunch. However, it also appears to be related to financial consider-ations, as the wine tour guests are provided with lunch at a lower set price, and as such, accommodating them on busy days has a negative financial impact on Timbre. Paradoxically, the success of wine tour businesses also ensures a continued flow of tourists to businesses in the Tamar Valley and, therefore, Timbre, vineyards and tour operators are all mutually depen-dent upon each other for their financial viability.

Similar tensions are simmering between Timbre and the vineyard cellar door, the bone of contention being the opening hours of the restau-rant. The opening hours are aligned with customer demand. As visitors tend to come to Tasmania for short breaks, largely from mainland Australia, operating from Wednesdays to Sundays, both capture these visitors and accommodate locals. This enables Matt to employ permanent full-time staff who are the core of the business. Opening longer would likely lead to smaller numbers of guests spread across more days, neces-sitating Matt to take on additional staff, which is less financially viable. As Matt argues:

> I think we are more viable now because we have got better balance and the staff are happier. We would only make the same amount of money over five days instead of four days and the staff are happier doing four days.

While the reduced opening hours make sense for the restaurant, the cellar door is open every day. Tensions flare when visitors to the cellar door express disappointment that lunch at the restaurant is not an option. Matt indicated that he 'got a bit of pressure from next door', but also pointed out that 'they're [the vineyard] still getting their rent'. Matt referred to the vineyard owners as a 'demographic that thinks if you're open, you gotta be open', also suggesting that they may not understand or appreciate that Timbre's business model is working well for Matt and his employees. While both parties seem to accept the status quo, it was clear that there was still some background tension regarding this matter.

When the pandemic came to Tasmania

Notwithstanding the hardship the pandemic crisis has brought to the tourism sector, it also offers an exceptional opportunity to pause and rethink future strategies for tourism development. As the first analyses of the impacts of the pandemic crisis emerge (see, e.g. Adams *et al.*, 2021), among the coping strategies adopted by host societies we find a shift to

Table 8.2 Tasmanian Covid-19 timeline and Timbre response

Date	Covid Event	Date	Timbre's response
02-03-20	First case of Covid in Tasmania confirmed		
17/19-03-20	Public Health Emergency declared for Tasmania; border closure.		Timbre closed for an indefinite period.
		22-03-20	Timbre offers pizza and wine takeaway or eat on the deck/ lawn.
23-03-20	Restaurants, entertainment venues, businesses and public services closed. Takeaway or home delivery only.	27-03-20	Timbre announces 'A Pizza Project': takeaway or eat on the lawn pizzas every Friday and Saturday night.
18-05-20	10 people allowed in restaurants	23/24-05-20	Timbre announces 'Timbre Table': purchase a table for a max of 10 of your friends and family for shared plates, multi-course menu. The 'Pizza Project' continues.
26-06-20	Restrictions significantly eased to allow up to 250 people inside venues and 500 outside	3-07-20	Timbre opens for 'usual style of service' but reduced to Friday/ Saturday lunch and dinner, Sunday lunch only.
9-07-20	Melbourne commences second lockdown (of 111 days)		Timbre launches new menu (see Figure 8.4). Prices for the banquets have been raised by about 25% (see table 1)..
		20-07-20	Minor adjustments to menu.
6-07-20	Tasmanian Government offeres travel vouchers for Tasmanians to encourage travel intrastate		While vouchers cannot be used to pay restaurant bills, more Tasmanians booked wine tours including pre-booked lunches. Timbre benefits from an increase in lunch bookings.
5-08/30-09-21	Second and third round of travel vouchers offered		No change
29-10-21	Travel vouchers open to residents of Queensland, South Australian and Western Australia for travel in Tasmania		No change
15-12-21	Tasmania opens its border		

domestic markets. This resonates with the Tasmanian experience. As the owner of the neighbouring vineyard reports:

We had a fair few internationals until COVID-19, but our sales at the moment, in the last month or so, would be better than pre-pandemic and so they are locals. We've had more people visiting than last year, or two years ago. Well, they are all Tasmanians.

This story is backed by other stakeholders in the industry mentioning the surge in visits by local people to local attractions. As Tasmanians massively descended upon local vineyards, soaring visitor numbers put the relationship between the vineyard owner and Timbre-owner Matt on edge. Instead of dining the expanding vineyard clientele, Timbre puts in place reduced opening hours soon after the outbreak of Covid-19 as part of a package of adjustments introduced in response to government measures (for a timeline of events see Table 8.2). With more time at hand, Matt reconsidered his approach to food and the preparation process, deciding that prices had to be raised to ensure the financial viability of the business as the number of patrons was fluctuating due to changing Covid-restrictions. The menu was also changed to mitigate the risk of possible shutdowns and to achieve sustainable food usage. Moreover, he and his team started to value time in a different way: 'COVID-19 changed us, like we worked our asses off for like 20 years being chefs, and like we don't want to work like that anymore'.

' … and I Will Tell You Who You Are': Discussion

Undeniably, tourists are essential for the viability (or economic capital) of local businesses in regional areas, as they constitute a significant share of their total number of customers. However, at Timbre, in contrast to widely held assumptions (see, e.g. Gössling & Hall, 2016; Hussain, 2021), not all tourists are a higher yield than locals. Those who have planned to dine there, such as restaurant destination visitors, book in for dinner in advance. On the other hand, tourists who stop at Timbre during the day, for a quick lunch or snack, or groups on wine tours, are lower yield customers.

Timbre stays true to its stated purpose by offering special events and service periods that are designed to be attractive to locals (see Vignette 2), prioritising their access over tourist groups. Conversely, locals are attracted by the changing menu, the perceived affordability and the social connections with Timbre staff. Having established Timbre's standing among Tasmania's restaurants, representing its symbolic capital, its signature narrative of how they source food and minimise their environmental footprint is highly appealing to their local clientele. Importantly, the set menu style at Timbre, combined with removing field rules regarding the selection of a suitable matching wine, reduces the need for customers to have specialised knowledge, or cultural capital, of the gastronomic field required to confidently select dishes from an à la carte menu. However, offering a different type and style of food experience does create some challenges for Timbre and their stakeholders.

At the individual customer level, Timbre offers an experience that is attractive to some locals and some tourists rather than to either category in particular. As Ooi and Pedersen (2017) have pointed out, the local, seasonal and fresh food brand has global appeal. From a Bourdieuan perspective, eating out at restaurants requires a certain level of financial resources (or economic capital), but also access to the right kinds of social and cultural capital to participate with confidence (Bennett *et al.*, 2020; Stringfellow *et al.*, 2013). Tastes are strongly linked to social backgrounds and formative experiences, causing people to seek practices that align with their palate and contribute to their chosen identity (Bennett *et al.*, 2020; Bourdieu, 1989; Ferguson *et al.*, 2017; Lee *et al.*, 2014). The young Victorian couple in the above example (see Vignette 1) did not espouse the cultural capital and habitus relevant to the context, causing them to feel uncomfortable at Timbre. They seemed unfamiliar with the dishes listed on the menu (for want of cultural capital) and felt uncomfortable in this setting (because of an incompatible habitus).

As fine dining restaurants may come across as intimidating, all stakeholders interviewed identified the social and cultural context of Timbre as comfortable, primarily due to the social connections that they had with Timbre staff (see also Cleave, 2020). Timbre appears to leverage a significant amount of social capital to establish rapport and build enduring connections with regular customers, and those customers have been willing to try new food within Timbre's casual and friendly ambience. Tastes are malleable and change over time, as do the capitals that are mobilised to transform them, and it appears that the tastes of some Timbre customers have changed to accommodate new food and experiences (see also Bennett *et al.*, 2020; Stringfellow *et al.*, 2013).

Tensions between Timbre and tourism operators are mainly due to stakeholders having different perceptions and assumptions regarding the fields of enterprise and tourism. Tourism-focused businesses prioritise financial goals and business growth, which is entirely consistent with literature highlighting the alignment of tourism with market systems more broadly (Sharpley, 2020). For the wine tour operator in our case, increasing tourist numbers is synonymous with business success which enhances both their economic capital (income) and symbolic capital – the latter being tied up with their standing as one of the leading wineries in Tamar Valley. Hence his preoccupation with ways to help Timbre grow the number of tourist diners to attract. He recognised and valued Timbre's aim to develop a more regenerative approach because this strategy generates economic capital in that it is appealing to tourists as a brand and a critical component of what makes Timbre successful.

Tensions between the vineyard owner and Matt – among other things about opening hours and business branding – are somewhat different, as above and beyond their business relationship they are also friends. This creates an opportunity for power to be exerted through friendship (as social capital), without acknowledging the imbalance of power created by the formal contractual agreement between landlord and tenant. These tensions may be mitigated because of their close personal relationship and the positive impact friendships have on building professional and business networks (Czernek-Marszałek, 2020). Yet, prioritising friendship may also prevent the open and honest discussion from occurring, which has been found to limit business partnerships (D'hont *et al.*, 2016). Consequently, while social capital mitigates the impact of tensions, simmering discontent can affect operations.

Traditionally, food and food service that are aligned to classic European tastes are held in high regard and provide symbolic capital within the field of gastronomy (Cleave, 2020; Ooi & Pedersen, 2017). While doing things differently and moving towards regenerative practices at the same time, Timbre succeeds in meeting customer expectations largely by maintaining strong connections with all patrons both in person and through their publicity. Symbolic capital such as fame and public accolades can elevate the status of restaurants (Ooi & Pedersen, 2017). As Timbre has been featured on television and in popular magazines, customers attach symbolic value to it and, consequently, place a higher value on their dining experience (Stringfellow *et al.*, 2013).

Conclusions

This study addresses the challenges and dilemmas a Tasmanian local restaurant faces on its pathway to more regenerative practices. Diverging and conflicting expectations split local patrons and tourist customers and drive a wedge between local stakeholders in their attempt to cater to the partially incompatible demands, as the ongoing friction between Timbre-owner Matt and the vineyard owner vividly exemplifies. After all, local communities have their own politics and agendas that mirror the broader society and, consequently, community involvement may just perpetuate established social hierarchies and ways of doing things (Ooi, 2019). With a nod to Bourdieu's theory of practice (1977), it is shown that social, cultural and symbolic capital affects the ability of the business under study to overcome simmering tensions and unsettling dilemmas, and turn them into opportunities.

As this study exemplifies, stakeholders hold different views about food experiences. Food, and the way it is prepared and presented, is rife with symbolic capital. Commonly, people prefer foods that are familiar to them, contributing to their idea of what is legitimate (Bourdieu, 1989). Conversely, there is a persistent view that consumers do not recognise or value unfamiliar food experiences and are not willing to pay more for food that is grown, sourced and prepared using regenerative practices. Timbre seems to balance this by engaging with customers in ways that leverage their social capital. In so doing, Timbre creates social connections that are deeper and more enduring, building a new kind of cultural capital that is non-traditional but valued by supporters. In a recent Australian study, Bennett *et al.* (2020) found a similar shift away from cherishing more traditional cultural activities to engaging in new culturally valued activities and pursuits.

Implementing regenerative practices requires Timbre to break field rules and do things differently. What seems to be the personal project of a rather ego-driven chef running a restaurant for his own pleasure is, however, an ethos-focused innovation in the restaurant business. Timbre's approach is regenerative first and foremost in terms of regenerating the engagement with the local community. Being socially embedded helps Timbre to mobilise their networks in ways that support them and their stakeholders to be innovative and push boundaries. However, social embeddedness also creates challenges, as friendship and social connections are sometimes prioritised above genuine business needs, and so there is a constant need for Timbre to balance relationships with operational imperatives to remain commercially viable.

More recently, the global pandemic has highlighted the importance of domestic tourism embedded in trusting relationships between businesses and their communities, as consumers shift further towards prioritising local and sustainable options (Cornejo-Ortega & Dagostino, 2020). Communities want to support local enterprises and local products, when they have positive social connections with them. Higgins-Desbiolles (2020) has proposed a local community-centred tourism model in which communities are involved in decision-making and planning to create social contracts between tourism operators and community members. Such a model defines tourists as guests rather than customers and seeks to include diverse views and perspectives in decision-making.

References

Adams, W.C. (2015) Conducting semi-structured interviews. In K.E. Newcomer, H.P. Hatry and J.S. Wholey (eds) *Handbook of Practical Program Evaluation* (4th edn, pp. 492–505). San Francisco: Jossey-Bass. https://doi.org/10.1002/9781119171386.ch19

Adams, K.M., Choe, J., Mostafanezhad, M. and Phi, G.T. (2021) (Post-) pandemic tourism resiliency: Southeast Asian lives and livelihoods in limbo. *Tourism Geographies* 23 (4), 915–936.

Ahmad, R. (2013) Working with Pierre Bourdieu in the tourism field making a case for 'third world tourism'. *Cultural Studies* 27 (4), 519–539.

Ateljevic, I. (2020) Transforming the (tourism) world for good and (re) generating the potential 'new normal'. *Tourism Geographies* 22 (3), 467–475.

Bennett, T., Carter, D., Gayo, M., Kelly, M. and Noble, G. (2020) *Fields, Capitals, Habitus: Australian Culture, Inequalities and Social Divisions*. Abingdon: Routledge.

Bertella, G. (2020) Re-thinking sustainability and food in tourism. *Annals of Tourism Research* 84, 2014–2016.

Bourdieu, P. (1977) *Outline of a Theory of Practice*. Cambridge: Cambridge University Press.

Bourdieu, P. (1984) *Distinction: A Social Critique of the Judgment of Taste*. (Trans. Richard Nice). Cambridge, MA: Harvard University Press.

Bourdieu, P. (1989) Social space and symbolic power. *Sociological Theory* 7 (1), 14–25.

Çakmak, E., Lie R. and McCabe, S. (2018) Reframing informal tourism entrepreneurial practices: Capital and field relations structuring the informal tourism economy of Chiang Mai. *Annals of Tourism Research* 78, 37–47.

Cave, J. and Dredge, D. (2020) Regenerative tourism needs diverse economic practices. *Tourism Geographies* 22 (3), 503–513.

Cleave, P. (2020) Food as a leisure pursuit, a United Kingdom perspective. *Annals of Leisure Research* 23 (4), 474–491.

Cornejo-Ortega, J.L. and Dagostino, R.M.C. (2020) The tourism sector in Puerto Vallarta: An approximation from the circular economy. *Sustainability* 12 (11), 4442. https://doi.org/10.3390/su12114442.

Czernek-Marszałek, K. (2020) Social embeddedness and its benefits for cooperation in a tourism destination. *Journal of Destination Marketing and Management* 15, 100401.

Denny, L., Shelley, B. and Ooi, C.S. (2020) State of the tourism workforce in Tasmania. In A. Hardy and C.S. Ooi (eds) *Tourism in Tasmania* (pp. 209–219). Lindisfarne: Forty South Publishing.

D'hont, L., Doern, R. and Delgado Garcia, J. (2016) The role of friendship in the formation and development of entrepreneurial teams and ventures. *Journal of Small Business and Enterprise Development* 23 (2), 528–561.

Ferguson, J.E., Dahles, H. and Prabawa, T.S. (2017) The Indonesian tourism industry under crisis: A Bourdieuan perspective on social boundaries among small-scale business owners. *Asia Pacific Business Review* 23 (2), 171–191.

Fusch, P.I., Fusch G.E. and Ness, L.R. (2017) How to conduct a mini-ethnographic case study: A guide for novice researchers. *The Qualitative Report* 22 (3), 923–941.

Gössling, S. and Hall, C.M. (2016) From food tourism and regional development to food, tourism and regional development. Themes and issues in contemporary foodscapes. In C.M. Hall and S. Gössling (eds) *Food Tourism and Regional Development: Networks, Products and Trajectories* (pp. 197–223). Abingdon: Routledge.

Hall, C.M. (2020) Improving the recipe for culinary and food tourism? The need for a new menu. *Tourism Recreation Research* 45 (2), 284–287.

Higgins-Desbiolles, F. (2020) Socialising tourism for social and ecological justice after COVID-19. *Tourism Geographies* 22 (3), 610–623.

Hussain, A. (2021) A future of tourism industry: Conscious travel, destination recovery and regenerative tourism. *Journal of Sustainability and Resilience* 1 (1), 1–10.

Lee, K.H., Scott N. and Parker, J. (2014) Habitus and food lifestyle: In-destination activity participation of slow food members. *Annals of Tourism Research* 48, 207–220.

Ooi, C.S. (2019) Asian tourists and cultural complexity: Implications for practice and the Asianisation of tourism scholarship. *Tourism Management Perspectives* 31 (July), 14–23.

Ooi, C.S. and Pedersen, J.S. (2017) In search of nordicity: How new nordic cuisine shaped destination branding in Copenhagen. *Journal of Gastronomy and Tourism* 2 (4), 217–231.

Pollock, A. (2016) Social entrepreneurship in tourism: The conscious travel approach. *Tourism Innovation Partnership for Social Entrepreneurship* 7, 38–46.

Sharpley, R. (2020) Tourism, sustainable development and the theoretical divide: 20 years on. *Journal of Sustainable Tourism* 28 (11), 1932–1946.

Stringfellow, L., Maclaren, A., Maclaren, M. and O'Gorman, K. (2013) Conceptualizing taste: Food, culture and celebrities. *Tourism Management* 37, 77–85.

Tourism Tasmania (2021) *Tourism Snapshot*. Year ending June 2021. See https://www.tourismtasmania.com.au/__data/assets/pdf_file/0019/103807/Tasmanian-Tourism-Snapshot-YE-March-2021-TVS,-NVS,-IVS.PDF (accessed October 2022).

West Tamar Council (2018) *West Tamar Council Strategic Plan 2018-2028*. See https://www.wtc.tas.gov.au/Your-Council/Governance-Law-and-Publications/Strategic-Plan (accessed October 2022).

9 Covid-19, Tourism Structural Changes and the Habitus Adaptations at Tourist Destinations: Perspectives of Tourism Agents

G.K. Jayathilaka and W.H.M.S. Samarathunga

Introduction

The coronavirus disease (Covid-19), which escalated into a pandemic within months, devastated the entire globe through an unprecedented socioeconomic cataclysm. Since early 2020, fear and precaution have left entire countries and regions under lockdown and whole cities and streets deserted. Incomparable with other natural disasters such as floods, fires or earthquakes, pandemics can adversely affect societies long-term with a tendency for recurrence. More importantly, whereas other disasters primarily cause material damage, pandemics have the propensity to cause diverse impacts such as unemployment, economic crisis and inherent psychological volatility (Jiang *et al.*, 2021; Xiong *et al.*, 2020). The pandemic's current state of myriad social-, economic- and health-related dilemmas has led the world into unprecedented transformations in almost all sectors, not least travel and tourism (Jiang *et al.*, 2021).

The present chapter employs a Bourdieusian conceptual framework for scrutiny of the structural changes to tourism and hospitality in the face of the Covid-19 pandemic. We do so in perspective and in examining some of the agents of developing tourist destinations of Sri Lanka. We utilise the concept of 'agents' as social actors that can reason and make decisions on specific actions through micro-level processes of interaction and meaning-making. Specifically, the study engages an in-depth qualitative inquiry to understand perceptions, attitudes and expectations of selected tourism agents and their resilience towards distinctively transforming deep-seated industry practices embedded within the fabric of Sri Lankan society and culture spanning centuries.

Employing the Bourdieusian concepts field, doxa and habitus, we explore the deep-seated pre-pandemic assumptions about and within the field of tourism and hospitality as commonly held and inculcated by tourism agents. As such, we closely scrutinise the way in which long-standing tourism-related doxa have begun to gradually shift under the working of tourism agents amidst uncertainties and new realities surrounding the Covid-19 virus. Finally, factoring in transformations such as changes to host–guest relations, traditional modes of expressing hospitality, discontinuation of certain tourism services, changes to government policy and shifting types of tourism and tourists, we conclude how these agents endeavour not only to understand and internalise the changes to this field but achieve resilience and readiness to welcome some of the more impending permanent structural changes to the field of tourism and hospitality.

Literature Review

Travel has been acknowledged as a universal need amongst modern individuals, and it is recognised as one of the 'necessary structured breaks from ordinary life' (Graburn, 1983: 11). It is a feature of all human societies and the tourist, embracing potentials for freedom, autonomy and, most importantly, the choice has been identified as the epitome of contemporary life (Bauman, 1993). As noted by World Travel and Tourism Council, the tourism sector contributes to 10% of the world GDP leading to the generation of 1 in 10 jobs with its business volume equalling or exceeding that of other major sectors such as exports of oil, food products or automobiles (Castanho *et al.*, 2020). Nonetheless, when considered a field, tourism is also exceedingly vulnerable, yet at the same time resilient to various external occurrences (Choe *et al.*, 2021). Risk factors such as serious diseases may greatly influence travel decision-making and lead to the transformation in the broader dynamics of tourists, tourist destinations and locals living in tourism areas (Chew & Jahari, 2014). The Covid-19 pandemic affected the entire globe made this evident.

The rapid global spread of a contagion attests to the increasingly mobile pre-pandemic world with the ability to transmit a deadly virus irrespective of geographical boundaries affecting people across all countries and cultures (Jamal & Budke, 2020). Governments, in response, imposed laws and regulations in an attempt to contain physical mobilities; restrictions that would have in pre-pandemic times been unthinkable. Concurrently, the phrase 'social distancing' became a prevalent worldwide notion (Baum & Hai, 2020), which soon gave rise to the antithesis of accepted tourism-related doxa (Long, 2020). Thus, in the field of tourism, this led not only to the decreases in tourist numbers, loss of employment, plummeting of hotel occupancies but also, more importantly, to a total number of tourists who feared to travel or changed plans to reduce their risks and host destinations that resented the arrival of tourists. These disruptions have caused severe and overwhelming effects on various tourism behaviours, supply chain tourism and the economy, which received attention from scholars recently (Foo *et al.*, 2020; Jaipuria *et al.*, 2021; Yeh, 2021).

However, while tourism researchers in tourism studies have called for more scrutiny and engagement with practice-based approaches to tourism, there have been very few such efforts (Çakmak *et al.*, 2018; de Souza Bispo, 2016; Lamers *et al.*, 2017). The Bourdieusian framework has rarely been employed in investigating this sphere, particularly in consideration of the tourism Covid-19 nexus, with Negacz's (2021) study of 'distinction through ecotourism' a noteworthy exception.

Utilising the Bourdieusian conceptual framework in the study of crosscultural contextualisation in international tourism, Platenkamp (2007) posits that when those participating in international tourism derive from diverse cultural backgrounds, a cross-cultural understanding is vital to consider the various cultural background assumptions (Platenkamp, 2007). Negacz (2021) explores types of capital that influence sustainable consumer choices amidst a context of progressing climate change and the crisis of Covid-19, which have both called for a transition to more sustainable behaviour (Negacz, 2021). Sustainable consumption and ecotourism are used as 'fields' or social arenas within which struggles often occur or networks, or configurations, of objective relations between positions (Bourdieu & Wacquant, 1992: 97). Recent studies scrutinise the relationship of conditioning between the habitus and field, where the field shapes a habitus, and habitus contributes to shaping a field (Çakmak *et al.*, 2021; Negacz, 2021). Further, Negacz (2021) argues that even though various forms of capital impact the sustainable habitus behaviour of ecotourists, education, knowledge and awareness-related cultural capital plays a vital function that considerably influences sustainable consumption. Bourdieu's concepts field, habitus, capital and doxa offer the prominent potential for tourism research, particularly in the study of doxa and habitus within the field of tourism amidst the Covid-19 pandemic on which we focus attention in the subsequent subsection.

The context of this study is Sri Lanka. The country is famous for its natural and cultural attractions and is one of the key tourist destinations in South Asia. Despite its attraction, Sri Lanka suffers from a dearth of foreign currency, thus heavily dependent on foreign loans and donations (Var & Po, 2017). In Sri Lanka, the primary source of foreign exchange earnings is workers' remittances, followed by textiles, garments and tourism (Central Bank of Sri Lanka, 2021). Sri Lankan tourism industry suffered a severe hit from the Covid-19 pandemic, and as a result, the foreign exchange earning plummeted from US\$ 3.6 billion in 2019 to US\$ 0.7 billion in 2020 (Sri Lanka Tourism Development Authority, 2020b). The number of direct and indirect employees associated with the Sri Lanka tourism industry was well 500,000 out of the country's 8.5 million labour force (Central Bank of Sri Lanka, 2021; Sri Lanka Tourism Development Authority, 2020b). Due to the international travel restrictions, many tourism employees lost their jobs, making around 2.5 million people vulnerable to poverty (Weerathunga & Samarathunga, 2020). Almost all Sri Lanka hotels and travel agencies experienced a zero income period from April 2020 to July 2021 (COVID19 Emergency Response Center for Sri Lanka Tourism, 2020; W. Samarathunga, 2020, 2021).

Methodology

From an epistemological standpoint, this study employs a constructivist framework, in which the authors strive to generate meanings through interactions with others and society (Neuman, 2014). The primary data have been collected through semi-structured interviews, focus groups and participant observations. Purposive sampling based on respondents' professional and academic credentials was used to capture a variety of perspectives on the impacts of Covid-19 on tourism stakeholders in Sri Lanka. A total of nine interviews were conducted with selected tourism agents in Sri Lanka. All the interviews were held in English. The duration of each interview ranged from 23 minutes to 72 minutes. The researchers employed pseudonyms to maintain the anonymity of the respondents. A profile of the respondents who participated in the interviews is exhibited in Table 9.1.

In order to circumvent the risk of being biased due to the limited sample size, the study also adopted a method of triangulation (Easterby-Smith *et al.*, 1991). It espoused investigator triangulation, a collaborative strategy whereby different investigators operated independently on data

Table 9.1 Sri Lanka tourism stakeholders interviewed

Pseudonyms	Education	Profession	Professional experience (in years)	Age (in years)	Gender
RES1	Bachelor degree	General Manager/Hotel	38	56	Male
RES2	Masters degree	Tourism Authority (SLTDA)	18	42	Female
RES3	Advanced level	Tourist Shop Owner	26	46	Male
RES4	Ordinary level	Community Member	–	53	Male
RES5	Masters degree	Tourism Consultant	36	57	Male
RES6	Diploma	Tourist Driver	08	32	Male
RES7	Masters degree	Tour Consultant	15	44	Male
RES8	Diploma	Tourist Guide	18	39	Male
RES9	PhD	Tourism Academic	13	38	Female

collection. Additionally, five participatory observations were performed to identify the current level of tourism operations at key tourist destinations, including Colombo, Kandy, Galle, Anuradhapura and Habarana. The critical observable content was the host–guest interactions, public response and attitude towards the tourists, and tourism operations at the destinations. Finally, four focus-group discussions were held with key tourism stakeholders residing within selected key tourist destinations: the locals, restaurant workers, tuk-tuk drivers and beach facilitators. The duration of the focus group discussions varied from 30 to 45 minutes, and the two main discussion topics were tourism before and after the Covid-19. The focus-group discussions were conducted in the Sinhalese language and later translated to English. The data gathering was carried out between July and August of 2021 when Sri Lankan tourism began to show indications of recovery, and the country continued to receive travellers due to the Sri Lanka Tourism Development Authority's 'Travel Bubble' concept. All collected data through interviews and focus group conversations were audiotaped and verbatim transcribed. This resulted in generating 13 source files consisting of 33 A4 size pages, which were forwarded for the data analysis. The source files, audio recordings and image files were uploaded to the NVivo (v.12) software analysing the content. A content analysis method has been employed to allow in-depth examination of the phenomena, to recognise themes, explanations and propositions generated through the data analysis process (Krippendorff, 2004). Additionally, the researchers used the data immersion technique (Green *et al.*, 2007) to ensure significant facts emerged from the transcriptions. Table 9.2 shows the coding spectrum.

Table 9.2 Coding spectrum

Main codes	Subcodes
Pre-pandemic and new-normal tourism	Pre-pandemic tourism
	New-normal tourism
Host–guest relationships	Interactions between hosts and guests
	Fear towards each other
	Change of behaviour
Relationships with the agents of authority	Pre-pandemic relationship
	Training and development
	Interactions between the hosts and the agents of authority
Perspectives on tourism resilience and readiness	Absence of tourism
	Importance of tourism resilience
	Emergency relief fund
	Alternative income sources

Findings

Pre-pandemic and new-normal tourism

With understanding the Bourdieusian notion of 'doxa' as a sense of reality (Bourdieu, 1977: 156), we consider the presence of tourists and the associated political economy within the selected major tourist destinations as the first deep-seated pre-pandemic doxa. Accordingly, the respondents perceived tourism within the selected destinations as vibrant and growing before the pandemic since the destinations were popular among domestic and foreign tourists. Thus, the circulation of tourism-related capital within these destinations has been felt; the logic orders each struggle within a specific field (Harker *et al.*, 1990). For instance, these destinations' economies are dependent mainly on foreign tourists. On one hand, diversified tourism services and facilities available at the destinations allowed many local people to engage with the industry. On the other hand, the availability of numerous tourism services, facilities and activities expanded the length of stay of tourists at these destinations. According to an officer attached to the National Tourism Organization:

> *A vast majority of the people in Galle area were engaged in tourism as service providers. The tourists used to book safari tours, elephant back rides and village safaris through the villagers.* (RES02)

Before the pandemic, the developing destinations in Sri Lanka were attracting foreign investors that injected foreign currency into the economy. Such investors persistently partnered with local investors, resource owners and authorities to implement their projects effectively. However, the provision of different types of tourism investments was insufficient during the peak periods due to the excessive number of tourists visited. A tourism consultant expressed his opinion as follows:

> *Not only the people from Habarana, but also investors from other areas came to Habarana to set up hotels, restaurants, spa centres, tourist shops etc. Still, considering the volume of tourists we got, they supply was not sufficient.* (RES7)

The responses were not homogeneous when inquiring about the type of tourists received before the pandemic. While the types of tourists varied significantly across these tourism destinations, the number of backpackers had got the limelight. Backpackers depend on subsidised public services, including public transportation, public sanitary facilities, public cafeterias and staying at local guest houses. Although the economic impact of backpackers at the destinations is relatively lower compared to the mass tourists, there is always a set of local stakeholders relying on the backpackers. According to a host community member:

> *We, in Anuradhapura, mostly received the backpackers to Galle who used public transportation and stayed at local guest houses.* (RES4)

The tourism agents never anticipated a pandemic threat or any other type of calamity prior to this incident. Even the Easter Sunday attack in Sri Lanka on 21st April 2019 (Gunasingham, 2019) was perceived as a stand-alone incident, and the tourism agents still had hoped over the tourists. Against this backdrop, the tourism agents depended on the tourism sector without involving any alternative income source. This shows tourism agents' doxa internalisation and high dependency on tourism. A tourist driver expressed his idea as follows:

> *Why would anyone think the bad side of it as long as the tourists come. We never anticipated a pandemic situation, and now we understand that we were wrong.* (RES6)

Undoubtedly, the pandemic has had a most significant impact on the tourism sector, and the Sri Lankan context has been no different. Irrespective of the level and type of destinations distinguished according to diverse tourist destination development models, visitation to all heretofore popular destinations reached a sudden halt with the Covid-19 pandemic. A tourism academic excessively compared the tourist arrivals before and during the pandemic. He posited that the prime concern currently of tourists is 'health and safety' rather than leisure and recreation. He further expressed:

> *The tourist arrivals went from hundreds per day to zero in no time.... we are wrong in our predictions on tourist arrivals since tourists' safety has not been prioritised in our conventional operational model.* (RES9)

Tourism is a field that promotes both forward linkages and backward linkages. Therefore, a broad cross-section of the society participates in tourism service supplies, product development, event planning knowingly or unknowingly. Consequently, changes in the tourism demand equation equally affect all agents directly or indirectly associated with the tourism business.

> *It is not only the hoteliers but also the guides, chauffeurs, salespeople, tuk-tuk drivers, mahouts etc. etc. etc. It is undoubtedly the biggest hit to all the stakeholders in the industry.* (RES5)

In order to bring the crippled tourism industry back to normal, the national tourism organisation has launched different initiatives to secure the industry and the tourists. Sri Lanka Tourism Development Authority (SLTDA) is the National Tourism Organization (NTO) committed to establishing a conducive environment for all tourism stakeholders. Before the pandemic, the authority's duties were mainly restricted to business registration, renewal of the license, inspections, promoting tourism investments and so on. The Covid-19 pandemic has imposed a whole new line of responsibilities in their administrative functions. They include setting-up guidelines on the tourism and hospitality-related operations during a pandemic, conducting awareness programmes and workshops, facilitating the stakeholders to follow the standards and certifying hotels. According to a senior officer at the SLTDA:

> *SLTDA organised many training programs on post-COVID-19 hotel operational procedures, and some hotels were able to obtain certificates on best practices.* (RES2)

A tour guide appreciated the initiatives of the SLTDA to standardise the tourism and hospitality services adhering to the new normal guidelines. He said:

> *Now that we see 1 - 2 tourists walking along the road. However, it is not sufficient to open the closed hotels and to hire more staff. Also, we cannot provide the services to the tourists as we did before due to the health and safety concerns.* (RES8)

It is also interesting to note the change of tourism concepts and typologies during the new normal situation as the tourists largely ignore the famous and crowded destinations in fear of Covid-19. Samarathunga (2020) identified the emergence of alternative tourism during the post-pandemic era; many other scholars also attested this. This is mainly due to the health concerns of the tourists. However, mass tourism is still practised in Sri Lanka under the 'travel bubble' concept. In addition to that, large-scale hotels are now less demanded, and the stand-alone hotels seem to be doing well despite the pandemic. The foreign tourists mainly demand the beach hotels under the travel bubble concept and have patronised the countryside boutiques and other up-class hotels. Therefore, the countryside large-scale hotels, without being able to operate even at the break-even point, have launched large-scale promotional campaigns, especially with the credit card companies, to attract the local crowd.

In a similar context, certain tourism services involved with contact-based professions have been either banned or discouraged by the authority to prevent the spread of the virus. The alternative tourism products, including bird watching, tracking and trekking, community-based tourism, yoga, Ayurveda tourism and spiritual tourism, have received increased demand as they cater to individuals or small groups of travellers. A tourism consultant and a hotelier who participated in the interview expressed their opinions as follows:

> *The type of the tourists visiting are changing, and the type of tourism products demanded have been changed. The tourists want to get away from the mass and the crowded places to ensure their safety.* (RES7)

Now we can welcome the tourists, but the number of the bookings we receive are low compared to the tourists that visit this area. We happened to close our spa section due to government regulations. (RES1)

These examples attest to the structural transformations that have taken place within the field of tourism in Sri Lanka and shed light on how these have influenced the habitus behaviours of agents within. Habitus is the partially unconscious 'internalisation' of rules, values and dispositions that social actors inculcate from their cultural history that become durable and transposable across contexts or fields (Harker *et al.*, 1990). In its deeply embodied form, habitus is shaped by being within specific contexts and situations long-term regularly. Accordingly, it comprises cultural discourses, perceptions, attitudes, past experiences, skills and gestures (Çakmak *et al.*, 2021). Tourism is fluid and dynamic and constitutes a range of institutions, rituals, conventions, categories, designations, appointments or titles (Jayathilaka, 2019) that interact with each other, generating an objective hierarchy authorising certain discourses and activities (Webb *et al.*, 2002: 21). The SLTDA, as described above, represents such authority within the field capable of shifting tourism-related discourse and the habitus behaviours of agents (Bourdieu, 1977).

Thus, the rules and regulations within the field are adopted by new norms such as social distancing and safety internalised by social agents. The participants have had the time to process these changes as unavoidable, imminent and therefore believe that they must adapt to new and changing contexts. For instance, one of the participants, a chauffeur, explained how he knows many places and routes off-the-beaten-track, which he firmly believed he would use post-pandemic. He believed that his clients would not prefer previously popular mass tourist destinations. This attests that social agents unconsciously absorb discourses, traditions and regularities of fields manifested through their conduct. They shift their practical intuition required for the field and act through improvisation (Çakmak *et al.*, 2021).

Host–Guest Relationships

According to many scholars (Kenway & Fahey, 2009; Samarathunga, 2018; Zhang *et al.*, 2006), the success of any destination largely depends on positive interactions between the hosts and the guests. Interactions between visitor and host through social contact is critical in economically disadvantaged areas (Sinkovics & Penz, 2009), not only to raise the standard of life but also to increase the likelihood that the guest will return, to the satisfaction of both parties (Zhang *et al.*, 2006). In the context of Sri Lanka, possibly influenced by the traditional Sri Lankan hospitality, both hosts and guests had a very positive and friendly relationship that benefited both hosts and guests. One community member and a tourist guide expressed their ideas as follows:

> *The interactions between the local residents and the tourists were very friendly. The tourists reached the locals mainly to get the information and the locals, especially the kids, reached the tourists out of curiosity.* (RES4)

> *The tourists and residents enjoyed each other's company a lot. The residents support the tourists and tourists also support back to the community in their different capacities.* (RES8)

Under such circumstances and within a trendy tourist destination for decades, many respondents emphasised Sri Lankan hospitality as 'self-evident', a sense of reality (Throop & Murphy, 2002) that existed prior to the pandemic.

Thus, the Covid-19 pandemic brought an unfortunate yet unforeseen destiny to prevailing host–guest interactions. From the warm hugs and orchid garlands, the hosts have moved to distant salutations and the recognition and welcome of tourists through nods. The strict rules and regulations implemented by the authorities have changed the conventional host–guest interactions. A tourism consultant identified the growing fear of the tourists and the hosts towards each other. The consultant specifies this scenario as follows:

> *We have come to a different era. The hosts are afraid of the tourists and the tourists are afraid of the hosts. No longer we can practise the liberty and goodwill.* (RES5)

These examples further reiterate the transformations of tourism doxa; how these new values, rules and regulations are internalised and turn into newly shaped habitus. For example, one of the participants reminisced about the strong friendships he had previously formed with his clients prior to the pandemic. He mentioned that this is also linked with how Sri Lankans are known worldwide for their hospitality and friendliness. He believed this would be somewhat challenging post-pandemic but that they would have to get used to keeping the distance, putting their hands together for greetings instead of handshakes.

Similarly, the pandemic has brought about new rules and regulations for the survival of the tourism industry. For instance, Sri Lankan tourism authorities have made it compulsory for tourism service providers to gear up with personal protective equipment (PPE). Similarly, tourists are required to wear masks, prompting the external parties to focus on their health concerns. Interestingly, this has become a legal requirement to control the spread of the pandemic. According to the newly issued 'Sri Lanka Tourism Operational Guidelines with Health Protocols' (Sri Lanka

Tourism Development Authority, 2020a), the tourists are required to adhere to the following procedures:

- Use only the traditional Sri Lankan greeting 'Ayubowan' at all times instead of handshaking, hugging or kissing.
- Face masks worn during the flight should be disposed of, and new face masks should be worn before entering the airport.
- Washing hands with soap and disinfecting the footwear is mandatory for all tourists before entering the airport.
- Tourists/airport staff should maintain a minimum distance of 1.5 meters between two people at all times.
- The tourists and airport staff should wear face masks at all times; surgical face masks should be changed every 4 to 6 hours, and if needed, face masks can be purchased at the airport.

(Sri Lanka Tourism Development Authority, 2020a: 12)

A tourism officer highlighted the importance of PPE and abiding by the pandemic regulation as follows:

The pandemic has introduced a masked and a distant relationship between the hosts and guests. Both hosts and guests are well equipped with personal protective gear and equipment. If they are not wearing those, the interactions are either illegal or unacceptable. (RES2)

The physical contacts have been either restricted or banned. Many occupations including the helpers, therapists, physical instructors, have lost their occupations due to the spread of COVID-19. (RES2)

Relationships With Agents of Authority

The pre-pandemic relationships between the tourism stakeholders had been business-oriented and mutually beneficial. There had been a clear line of communication between the tourism service providers and national level tour operators regarding tourism products, service standards, managing the demand, supply channels, time slots, payments and bookings. However, the pandemic created a zero-tourism era where all communications and interactions between the tourism service providers and the principals reached a standstill. A veteran tourist shop owner expressed his comparative opinion about the pre- and post-pandemic relationship.

The travel agents used to call us every other day and check on us. Even when they were visiting on familiarisation tours, they did not forget to stop at our place and have a friendly chat with us. Similarly, we had good ties with hoteliers as well. However, due to the pandemic situation, we did not receive the duty calls, possibly because they also did not receive tourists. (RES3)

On the other hand, tourism service providers had not been keen to work with the National Tourism Organization (NTO), complaining that the NTO did not pay sufficient attention to the tourism service providers before the pandemic. However, since the pandemic, they have been con-tinuously assisted and guided by the regional tourism bodies regarding registration and training.

> *Before the pandemic, we did not have a strong relationship with the national tourism bodies. They used to visit us once in a year or two, and we did not see any benefit from them. However, we work closely with the provincial council who organise different training programs for us.* (RES6)

The pandemic has brought structural changes to the interactions and rela-tionships between the tourism service providers, including hotels, travel agents, airlines, attractions, transportation companies and the NTO. Although previously ignored, tourism service providers have identified the importance of the NTO with the advent of the COVID-19 wave. When the government implemented different concessions and allowance to tourism stakeholders, the inclusion criteria registered tourism service providers with the NTO. On the other hand, the regional authorities are also working closely with the NTO. This involvement is vital as most tourism service providers have obtained loans to their businesses before the pandemic, and the NTO has introduced different measures to release them from the financial burdens. A tourism academic expressed his opin-ion on the interactions as follows:

> *Since the COVID19, the national and regional authorities are very much concerned about the tourism stakeholders and their well-being. They (NTO) made this an opportunity to register most of the unregistered tourism service providers under one umbrella to provide better facilities and solutions to the existing issues.* (RES9)

Perspectives on Tourism Resilience and Readiness

Another key theme that emerged during the data collection was tour-ism resilience and readiness. Although it has been more than five decades since tourism was officially introduced to Sri Lanka with the enactment of 'Ceylon Tourist Board Act, No.10 of 1966', 'resilience and readiness' has never been in any tourism plans or strategic documents implemented. Sri Lanka has had negative experiences in terms of the civil war and terror-ism, followed by the Easter Sunday attack and the tourism industry had survival issues for an extended period even prior to the Covid-19 threats. However, the tourism authorities had failed to introduce a 'resilience strategy'. On the other hand, the service providers were also not keen on tourism resilience since the tourist arrivals had never come to a complete halt compared to the Covid-19 situation. Tourism stakeholders inter-viewed expressed similar ideas on the absence of a tourism resilience and readiness as follows:

> *Sri Lankan Government never had a tourism recovery plan, neither they were able to forecast a disaster of this magnitude.* (RES7)

> *The main reason for us not being prepared for the worst is the absence of tourism policies and overpromises given by the government.* (RES9)

These are some of the most prominent examples of the working of doxa or deep-seated, taken for granted understandings. In other words, these doxas represent the successful 'internal' replication of structure, resulting in social agents within a field to mistake 'objective structures' as 'natural'. These tourism doxa flow from a practical sense that is initiated in the association between habitus and structure, a process that leads to the 'taken-for-grantedness' of the objective world (Throop & Murphy, 2002; Webb *et al.*, 2002).

When discussing the next steps to rejuvenate the affected tourism industry, many scholars (Bui *et al.*, 2021; Samarathunga, 2021; Sharma *et al.*, 2021) recommend adopting a disaster management strategy and a resilience plan. Thus, proper measures need to be implemented, such as introducing a tourism resilience and readiness plan or an emergency relief fund. The NTO and the government have to pay immediate attention to this to protect the tourism industry and its stakeholders. An academic who responded at the interview highlighted the importance of tourism resilience and its strategy.

> *First, Sri Lanka should adopt a tourism policy, within which tourism resilience and readiness should be addressed.* (RES9)

Most developed countries maintain an emergency relief fund to support the tourism stakeholders during a catastrophic event. International Labour Organization (ILO) and International Monetary Fund (IMF) have also stressed the importance of maintaining such a fund to secure the industry. Accordingly, the Sri Lankan government and the NTO have to establish an emergency relief fund. This idea was stressed by a tourism consultant who participated in the interview:

> *Sri Lanka should introduce an emergency relief fund to support the tourism stakeholders during the turbulence times.* (RES7)

The tourism stakeholders developed a sense of insecurity towards the tourism industry with the recent catastrophic event and considered alternative income sources for their own well-being. They include farming and agriculture, urban migration searching for jobs and entering into small-scale businesses. According to a tourist guide:

> *Tourism is no longer a reliable breadwinner. We have to depend on a different source of income to survive.* (RES8)

Although it is not the focus of this paper to discuss the capital level of stakeholders, it seems to be appropriate to discuss as tourism structural changes are considered. Through the observations and document analysis, it is noted that many micro and small tourism entrepreneurs left the tourism industry due to two major catastrophes recently: the Easter Sunday Attack and the Covid-19 pandemic. The banks have ceased providing loans to tourism projects with the fear of not recovering them. However, the Sri Lankan Government has allocated more money to compensate tourism agents during their hour of need. Many medium- and large-scale tourism and hospitality establishments have laid off their employees given their inability to pay wages. Thus, human capital has also been negatively affected during the Covid-19 pandemic in Sri Lanka. Additionally, in the absence of tourists, the tourism service providers moved away from the industry in search of alternative income sources. A tourist guide said:

> *For months, we have been suffering, and this is the high time to find an alternative job. We all have mouths to feed, and tourism is not capable of looking after us.*

The nature of tourism in Sri Lanka is changing drastically with the emergence of the pandemic. Mass tourism, which once dominated the tourism sector, makes more space for alternative tourism. A prominent number of tourism stakeholders invest in small luxury accommodation units instead of large-scale hotels. In order to survive, large- and mega-scale hotels launch massive promotional campaigns to attract local tourists with credit card companies. Further, some hotels with multiple wings have shut down operations at few wings that come up to 50 to 100 rooms to minimise the maintenance cost. Unlike in the past, both domestic and foreign tourists now have to adhere to strict health rules and regulations introduced and implemented by the 'Presidential Task Force on COVID-19' and the Ministry of Health, Sri Lanka. Similarly, most employees have lost jobs, and the tourism recreational services have stopped their operations. As a result, tourism resources, including human capital, entrepreneurial capital, technological capital and other resources, have been diverted to alternative industries such as agriculture which seems to be growing despite the pandemic threat.

Conclusion

This study paid particular attention to tourism structural changes and the habitus adaptations of agents at tourist destinations in the context of Sri Lanka with the advent of the Covid-19 pandemic. It shed light on the significance of tourism in Sri Lanka prior to the crisis and how the fundamental and commonly held understandings and practices have been transformed under the Covid-19 pandemic by employing Bourdieusian concepts doxa and habitus. The study also revealed the structural changes in the economic and human capital that have significantly changed during the Covid-19 pandemic.

Even though the impact of Covid-19 on tourist destinations and the industry has already been subject to countless debates among tourism scholars and practitioners, less consideration has been made to the structural changes that have taken place within the field of tourism and the habitus adaption of agents involved. The present study completes this gap by shedding more light on tourism structural changes under four main themes: pre-pandemic and new normal tourism, host–guest relationships, relationships with agents of authority and perspectives on tourism resilience and readiness.

In Sri Lanka, a new normal tourism is being established with alternative types of tourism taking more space from the conventional mass tourism that once dominated the industry. However, with Covid-19 controlling rules and regulations, the nature of host–guest relationships has changed from trust, companionship, mutual understanding, cross-cultural learning to fear and suspicion mainly among the general public. Though, as a positive note, we highlighted the enhanced relationship between tourism agents and the tourism authority, in which the authority endeavours to keep the tourism agents within the tourism industry.

Finally, the perspectives on tourism resilience and readiness to survive in the future were critically assessed. In doing so, the chapter examined how the prevailing doxa concerning host–guest relations have been transformed under the stress of concerns for health and safety and institutionalised by the rules and regulations imposed by the agents of power. As a result, traditional expressions and gestures of goodwill and welcome have shifted to amalgamate new practices and the generation of new doxa. It also discussed the rift created between different tourism agencies in the process but was drawn to a close with a positive note emphasising the resilience and readiness of agents to the gradually shifting practices and understandings of the field of tourism.

References

Baum, T. and Hai, N.T.T. (2020) Hospitality, tourism, human rights and the impact of COVID-19. *International Journal of Contemporary Hospitality Management.*

Bauman, Z. (1993) *Postmodern Ethics.* Oxford: Blackwell Publishers.

Bourdieu, P. (1977) *Outline of a Theory of Practice* (R. Nice, Trans. Vol. 16). Cambridge: Cambridge University Press.

Bourdieu, P. and Wacquant, L.J.D. (1992) *An Invitation to Reflexive Sociology.* Cambridge: Polity Press.

Bui, P.L., Tzu-Ling Chen, C. and Wickens, E. (2021) Tourism industry resilience issues in urban areas during COVID-19. *International Journal of Tourism Cities* 7 (3), 861–879. https://doi.org/10.1108/IJTC-12-2020-0289

Çakmak, E., Lie, R. and McCabe, S. (2018) Reframing informal tourism entrepreneurial practices: Capital and field relations structuring the informal tourism economy of Chiang Mai. *Annals of Tourism Research* 72, 37–47.

Çakmak, E., Lie, R., Selwyn, T. and Leeuwis, C. (2021) Like a fish in water: Habitus adaptation mechanisms of informal tourism entrepreneurs in Thailand. *Annals of Tourism Research* 90, 103262.

Castanho, R.A., Couto, G., Pimentel, P., Sousa, Á., Carvalho, C. and Batista, M.d.G. (2020) The impact of SARS-CoV-2 outbreak on the accommodation selection of Azorean tourists. A study based on the assessment of the Azores population's attitudes. *Sustainability* 12 (23), 9990.

Central Bank of Sri Lanka (2021) *Annual Report – 2020.*

Chew, E.Y.T. and Jahari, S.A. (2014) Destination image as a mediator between perceived risks and revisit intention: A case of post-disaster Japan. *Tourism Management* 40, 382–393.

Choe, Y., Wang, J. and Song, H. (2021) The impact of the Middle East Respiratory Syndrome coronavirus on inbound tourism in South Korea toward sustainable tourism. *Journal of Sustainable Tourism* 29 (7), 1117–1133.

COVID19 Emergency Response Center for Sri Lanka Tourism (2020) *Tourist in Country Summary Report.*

de Souza Bispo, M. (2016) Tourism as practice. *Annals of Tourism Research* 61, 170–179.

Easterby-Smith, M.T., Thorpe, R. and Lowe, A.(1991) *Management Research: An Introduction.* London: Sage.

Foo, L.-P., Chin, M.-Y., Tan, K.-L. and Phuah, K.-T. (2020) The impact of COVID-19 on tourism industry in Malaysia. *Current Issues in Tourism* 24 (19), 2735–2739.

Graburn, N.H. (1983) The anthropology of tourism. *Annals of Tourism Research* 10 (1), 9–33.

Green, J., Willis, K., Hughes, E., Small, R., Welch, N., Gibbs, L. and Daly, J. (2007) Generating best evidence from qualitative research: The role of data analysis. *Australian and New Zealand Journal of Public Health* 31 (6), 545–550.

Gunasingham, A. (2019) Sri Lanka attacks. *Counter Terrorist Trends and Analyses* 11 (6), 8–13.

Harker, R., Mahar, C. and Wilkes, C. (1990) *An Introduction to the Work of Pierre Bourdieu: The Practice of Theory.* London: Macmillan.

Jaipuria, S., Parida, R. and Ray, P. (2021) The impact of COVID-19 on tourism sector in India. *Tourism Recreation Research* 46 (2), 245–260.

Jamal, T. and Budke, C. (2020) Tourism in a world with pandemics: Local-global responsibility and action. *Journal of Tourism Futures* 6 (2), 181–188.

Jayathilaka, G.K. (2019) The Worldmaking Role of Sri Lankan Travel Writers: Negotiating Structure and Agency in the Study of Travel Representations. PhD thesis, University of Leeds.

Jiang, S., Zhang, H., Qi, J., Fang, B. and Xu, T. (2021) Perceiving social-emotional volatility and triggered causes of COVID-19. *International Journal of Environmental Research and Public Health* 18 (9), 4591.

Kenway, J. and Fahey, J. (2009) Academic mobility and hospitality: The good host and the good guest. *European Educational Research Journal* 8 (4), 555–559.

Krippendorff, K. (2004) Reliability in content analysis: Some common misconceptions and recommendations. *Human Communication Research* 30 (3), 411–433.

Lamers, M., Van der Duim, R. and Spaargaren, G. (2017) The relevance of practice theories for tourism research. *Annals of Tourism Research* 62, 54–63.

Long, N. (2020) From social distancing to social containment. *Medicine Anthropology Theory* 7 (2), 247–260.

Negacz, K. (2021) Distinction through ecotourism: Factors influencing sustainable consumer choices. *Scandinavian Journal of Hospitality and Tourism* 21 (5), 514–530.

Neuman, D. (2014) Qualitative research in educational communications and technology: A brief introduction to principles and procedures. *Journal of Computing in Higher Education* 26 (1), 69–86.

Platenkamp, V.C. (2007) *Contexts in Tourism and Leisure Studies: A Cross-cultural Contribution to the Production of Knowledge.* Wageningen: Wageningen University and Research.

Samarathunga, W.H.M.S. (2018) Exploring the relationship between beach boys and tourists using host-guest theory: The case of Bentota, Sri Lanka. *Journal of Management and Tourism Research* I (I), 1–20.

Samarathunga, W.H.M.S. (2020) Post-COVID19 challenges and way forward for Sri Lanka tourism. *ResearchGate (Preprints)*, 1–12. https://doi.org/10.13140/RG.2.2.32337.89443

Samarathunga, W.H.M.S. (2021) Restructuring tourism economies to face the 'new normal': COVID-19 and alternative tourism. *Sri Lanka Economic Research Conference 2020, January*, 21–22.

Sharma, G.D., Thomas, A. and Paul, J. (2021) Reviving tourism industry post-COVID-19: A resilience-based framework. *Tourism Management Perspectives* 37 (October 2020), 100786. https://doi.org/10.1016/j.tmp.2020.100786

Sinkovics, R.R. and Penz, E. (2009) Social distance between residents and international tourists—Implications for international business. *International Business Review* 18 (5), 457–469.

Sri Lanka Tourism Development Authority (2020a) *Sri Lanka Tourism Operational Guidelines with Health Protocols.* See https://www.sltda.gov.lk/storage/documents/SLTourism-OperationalGuidelines.pdf (accessed October 2022).

Sri Lanka Tourism Development Authority (2020b) *Tourism in Sri Lanka – 2020.*

Throop, C.J. and Murphy, K.M. (2002) Bourdieu and phenomenology: A critical assessment. *Anthropological Theory* 2 (2), 185–207.

Var, V. and Po, S. (2017) Cambodia, Sri Lanka and the China Debt Trap. *East Asia Forum* 18, 6–9. See http://www.eastasiaforum.org/2017/03/18/cambodia-sri-lanka-and-the-china-debt-trap/ (accessed October 2022).

Webb, J., Schirato, T. and Danaher, G. (2002) *Understanding Bourdieu.* London: SAGE.

Weerathunga, P. and Samarathunga, W. (2020) Are we ready for an economic meltdown? The impact of COVID19 on Sri Lanka economy. *SageAdvance (Preprint)*. https://doi.org/10.31124/advance.12230765.v1

Xiong, J., Lipsitz, O., Nasri, F., Lui, L. M., Gill, H., Phan, L. . . . Majeed, A. (2020) Impact of COVID-19 pandemic on mental health in the general population: A systematic review. *Journal of Affective Disorder* 227 (1), 55–64.

Yeh, S.-S. (2021) Tourism recovery strategy against COVID-19 pandemic. *Tourism Recreation Research* 46 (2), 188–194.

Zhang, J., Inbakaran, R.J. and Jackson, M.S. (2006) Understanding community attitudes towards tourism and host—Guest interaction in the urban—rural border region. *Tourism Geographies* 8 (2), 182–204.

10 Gendered (Im)mobilities in China: The Impacts of Covid-19 on Women in Tourism

Meghan L. Muldoon, Alexandra Witte and Yu-Hua (Melody) Xu

Introduction

The tourism and hospitality industries have experienced catastrophic losses due to the ongoing Covid-19 pandemic. As the 'world's largest industry', tourism has seen massive economic losses across the airline industry, hotels, restaurants, travel agencies, theme parks, museums and virtually every other tourist sector globally. To provide an example in a microcosm, Broadway in New York City earned $1.83 billion in revenues in the 2018–2019 season. With Broadway shuttered during the pandemic, that lost revenue multiplied exponentially out to all restaurants, hotels, taxis and street vendors reliant on Broadway patrons for income (Whitten, 2020). This is only one example among many, and while larger companies may be able to weather Covid-19 by scaling back, small and medium enterprises (SMEs) are even more vulnerable to the effects of the pandemic, frequently resulting in permanent closures (ILO, 2020). Inevitably, this has meant that the industry's workforce has been on the receiving end of job losses, reduced hours, increasingly precarious work conditions and less and less financial security, as evidenced by several studies (Baum et al., 2020). In many ways, the impacts on the industry reflect previous experiences during SARS or MERS (Choe et al., 2021; Wen et al., 2005), yet the scale of Covid-19 in terms of its geographical spread and temporal endurance is unprecedented in living memory. Tourism and hospitality are not predicted to recover until 2024 at the earliest, and even then, not everywhere (UNWTO, 2021a).

Early on in the pandemic, it became evident that many of the impacts on livelihood, employment, income and work mobilities are gendered (Assoumou Ella, 2021; Zulver et al., 2021). As women across the world are more likely to shoulder a higher share of the domestic work and caretaking, regardless of whether they are also full time employed away from home, the challenge to balance paid and domestic labour has increased for many women globally during Covid-19 (Adisa *et al.*, 2020). Moreover, evidence shows that women are also more likely to be laid off or suffer decreased hours and salaries, as well as decreased career mobilities (Tyson & Parker, 2019), with gendered cultural norms further exacerbating such impacts (Adisa *et al.*, 2020; Evertsson, 2014). With regards to tourism and hospitality, Baum *et al.* (2020) go so far as to characterise women as the 'dying canaries in the coal mine' due to pre-existing gendered disadvantages in the industry being amplified during Covid-19.

While some work has been done in various Western contexts, Baum *et al.* (2020) also identify that we know much less about the impacts of Covid-19 on gendered motilities in tourism and hospitality elsewhere. This chapter focuses on the gendered experiences of hospitality and tourism workers in three tightly bound yet differentiated regions in the Asia-Pacific region: Mainland China, Hong Kong and Macau. This research explored how experiences of work mobilities during Covid-19 within these regions' respective tourism and hospitality industries are represented and discussed online from a gendered perspective. In doing so, we aim to further our understanding of the practices of tourism workers in China, focusing on issues of inclusion, choice, (im)mobilities, (in)visibilities and power through the lens of gender during Covid-19.

We will begin by offering a brief overview of how the pandemic's impacts on hospitality and tourism and travel regulations within China, Hong Kong and Macau have framed the current situation for their respective tourism and hospitality industries, followed by a brief overview of the gendered impacts of the pandemic discussed in the literature. We will then outline our approach to data collection and analysis, focusing on critical discourse analysis of online data, before discussing our findings from the data collected to date.

Covid-19's impact on tourism and hospitality

While countries responded in various ways to the pandemic, ranging from temporary total lockdowns (e.g. Macau, Hong Kong, Mainland China) to so-called light-touch COVID-rules (e.g. Sweden), tourism mobilities have been drastically reduced globally. The UNWTO has termed 2020 the 'worst year in tourism history' (UNWTO, 2021b), with a reduction of international arrivals by 74%. The first quarter of 2021 saw a drop of 83% compared to 2020 (UNWTO, 2021a), with a return to 2019 levels to be expected only by 2024 or even later. The Asia-Pacific region has experienced the most extreme decline in international arrivals, primarily due to this region instituting some of the strictest travel restrictions in the world.

The People's Republic of China (PRC) implemented an almost complete ban on international arrivals of foreign nationals in late March 2020. A slight relaxation in September 2020 applied only to foreign nationals with valid residence permits. Concessions have started being made to travellers with certain COVID vaccines since March 2021 (China Briefing, 2021). The Special Administrative Region (SAR) Macau implemented a total ban on arrivals of non-residents (excepting Chinese nationals, including those from Hong Kong and Taiwan), which has not been lifted at the time of writing in December 2021 (exceptions apply to international arrivals serving the public interest) (Macau Government Tourism Office, 2021). This travel ban includes Macau's population of non-resident foreign workers with valid work permits. Hong Kong equally shut its borders to non-residents in March 2020 but started allowing non-Hong Kong residents in for specific purposes starting in late April 2020, with quarantine measures in place (Brazier, 2021).

Unsurprisingly, these three regions' tourism industries have suffered significantly, despite travel between Mainland China, Hong Kong and Macau and domestic travel within Mainland China not being suspended completely. Partial travel bans, frequent changes in regulations regarding vaccination requirements, testing and quarantine periods have contributed to this drop in domestic and inter-regional tourism. Mainland China has reported a decrease of 52.1% in its domestic tourism market between 2019 and 2020 (Xinhua, 2021). During the Chinese New Year, a significant travel time typically, the hotel industry in China lost 67 billion Yuan (approximately US$9.44 billion) in revenue (China Hospitality Association, 2020). According to the same report, by April 2020, 74.29% of hotels in China reportedly ceased operations. As the most dependent among the three on tourism and hospitality due to its focus on the gaming industry, Macau saw a 50% decrease in the territory GDP in the first half of 2020 (Liu et al., 2021; McCartney et al., 2021). With a decrease in visitor arrivals of 46% year-on-year in the first quarter of 2021, based on an already existing drop of 68.9% between Q1 in 2020 and 2019, Macau's overall economy and tourism and hospitality, in particular, continue to suffer (McCartney et al., 2021). Hong Kong experienced a decrease of 93.6% in visitor arrivals in 2020 compared to 2019 (Hong Kong Tourism Board, 2021).

Covid-19 and gender

With the severe repercussions the pandemic has had and still is having on the economy, labour markets have also suffered globally. Recently, the UN announced that by 2022 over 200 million people would have been pushed into unemployment, with women and young people suffering the most (UN, 2021). The same report announced that women had experienced a 5% fall in employment, compared to 3.9% for men. Moreover, among those employed, 108 million workers were categorised as 'poor' based on their earnings compared to 2019.

The UN's findings that women are on average more severely affected by the fall in employment are also supported by a survey of 129 countries by the International Labour Organization (ILO, 2020). Partially, this can be explained by the dominance of female workers in those sectors hit hardest by the pandemic, including hospitality and tourism (ILO, 2020; UN, 2020). Statistical evidence indeed suggests that to be true for Hong Kong and Macau (Statista, 2020, 2021). While no statistical evidence exists for the PRC, women tend to form the majority of staff in tourism and hospitality in most countries, especially in lower-level positions (Baum *et al.*, 2016; Kensbock *et al.*, 2016). Although China has made progress in reducing the gender wage gap in recent years, new data suggest that improvements for women in the workforce are unlikely to return to pre-COVID levels due to the pandemic (Brussevich *et al.*, 2021).

Even pre-pandemic, research has found that the nature of employment in the industry leaves workers in hospitality highly susceptible and vulnerable to crises (e.g. Robinson *et al.*, 2019; Tapia & Alberti, 2019). The industry's wages are among the lowest across industry comparisons (Casado-Díaz & Simón, 2016), meaning that many workers live paycheck-to-paycheck and have little to no financial cushion when faced with job loss or reduced working hours, in both the formal and informal tourism sectors. Further, many hospitality workers count among the less educated demographics and these workers also have relatively limited options open to them when they need to seek out alternative employment (Baum *et al.*, 2020). Therefore, Baum *et al.* (2020) argue that Covid-19 has not necessarily brought about entirely new workers in tourism and hospitality but has amplified pre-existing problems such as precarious employment, low wages and problematic working conditions in the industry.

Women in hospitality were also more likely to be laid off or have their hours reduced than men in the industry (González-Sánchez *et al.*, 2021). Losing one's job has been further found to impact present earnings and negatively affect future income and career advancement, which, once more, affects women more than men (Brand, 2006). These adverse effects increase when job loss occurs during times of crisis, such as a global pandemic (Davis & von Wachter, 2011).

Although less affected by the industry's precarious employment conditions, women in supervisory and managerial positions are also experiencing gendered impacts on their work lives. Already accounting for a relatively small percentage of senior-level workers in tourism and hospitality (Dashper, 2020), women are further likely to experience amplified gender inequalities due to persisting unequal labour divisions at home (OECD, 2014). As Costa *et al.* (2017) found pre-pandemic, women in higher-level positions were often seen as less effective hospitality managers than their male counterparts due to their perceived lesser flexibility stemming from ongoing expectations that women shoulder the majority of domestic labour (Carli, 2020). With the pandemic and resulting school closures and reduced access to help from their social circles, women's time and work dedicated to caretaking for children or elderly relatives have also increased (Chen & Mooney, 2020). Even when able to work from home, women's higher likelihood to be the primary caretakers frequently means it is disproportionately more difficult for them to find time to concentrate on their paid work from home. Though domestic labour has also increased for men, continuing inequities leave more women than men with the reduced time they may focus on their jobs (Miguel-Puga *et al.*, 2021).

Additional pressures may be experienced by tourism and hospitality workers overall due to their increased exposure to Covid-19. Those working in quarantine hotels face a higher risk of infection due to direct contact with quarantine guests (Teng *et al.*, 2020). With quite stringent and widely effected regulations for quarantine for travellers across China, Hong Kong and Macau, many hospitality companies saw a much-needed income source in becoming a designated quarantine hotel offering their workers a better chance at continued employment. However, it comes at the cost of higher infection risks for frontline workers in hospitality. These risks are also experienced by those working in the frontlines of the travel industries, including at airports, airlines, train stations and other arteries of mobility, as recent outbreaks at the Hong Kong and Nanjing airports have shown. As Teng *et al.* (2020) found, many frontline workers are experiencing added stress due to fear of being infected or carrying the infection to their families and friends.

Covid-19's impacts on the hospitality and tourism industry are significant, relating to job losses, reduced hours and income, or reduced career mobilities, which add to stresses resulting from increased domestic labour demands in addition to their paid work and the mental and physical health impacts of increased exposure to the virus. Many of these impacts are exacerbated for women (European Commission, 2021; Reichelt *et al.*, 2021). The following will offer a brief overview of our data collection and analysis approach before exploring the narratives and discourses uncovered during our research.

Methods

In order to learn more about the impacts of the Covid-19 epidemic on women's mobilities in tourism in China, we used critical discourse analysis to understand how women are represented in texts relating to tourism and Covid-19, as well as how women themselves understand and express their experiences resulting from the pandemic. Critical discourse analysis's interest lies in uncovering relationships of power embedded within texts that reflect and (re-)create real-world power imbalances (Rose, 2001; Waitt, 2005). We turned to publicly available online texts to understand better how women's experiences of the Covid-19 pandemic are being shared and structured online. Employing a Foucauldian-informed poststructural approach to discourse, we interrogated the online texts looking for how certain 'truths' are promulgated via the texts while also paying attention to silences, or discourses that are obscured or declared as 'untruths' in the prevailing discourse (Hannam & Knox, 2005; Rose, 2001; Waitt, 2005). As described by Grimwood et al. (2019: 237), we understand discourses to be 'power-laden ways of making sense of and engaging with this world'.

Discourse analysis is never neutral, and we as researchers each bring our own biases and positionalities to our understandings of the texts. We have employed several strategies to ensure credibility and transparency in this work. A team of six undergraduate student assistants at a joint Chinese-American university was responsible for the initial data collection and coding. Student assistants were trained for qualitative research and text coding. Newspaper articles, opinion pieces and blog sites from Mainland China, Macao and Hong Kong were searched using the keywords: 'women', 'gender', 'tourism', 'equalities' and 'mobility'. A total of 168 individual texts were identified over three months in the fall of 2021, in both English and Chinese, which were then sorted according to high, medium or low relevance to our research questions by one of the principal investigators. Texts included blog postings, posts on Zhihu.com (a Chinese questions and answers site), Xiaohongshu.com (the Chinese equivalent of Instagram), Baijiahao.baidu.com (a platform for independent writers, bloggers and journalists) and several online news sites located in the three regions of the study, as well as in the US and the UK.

The authors of the texts on the news sites are journalists with named credentials accompanying the texts. Residents write the texts from social media of Mainland China, Macao and Hong Kong. However, collected social media texts are concentrated in Mainland China. Although an effort was made to access blogs and discussion sites in Hong Kong and Macau, the researchers were restricted to sources written in English or Mandarin, therefore likely missing salient social media texts relevant to the Hong Kong and Macau context. Thus, future research could investigate Cantonese blogs and discussion forums to further insights into the effects Covid-19 has had on women's mobilities within tourism and hospitality. Most of the social media texts collected were posted by women, while some were posted by women's families or friends reporting their stories. However, very little other information regarding their identities is available due to the nature of these platforms.

The research assistants drew up initial line-by-line codes, and each text was coded by one research assistant and then cross-checked by another. One of our faculty members, a Chinese native speaker, supervised the students' coding process. Once the initial codes were completed, the three principal investigators, faculty members at a European, a Hong Kong and a Chinese university, undertook further coding and developed the themes presented in this chapter. The principal investigators all identify as women. All nine investigators working together on this research are women; future studies in this area could be diversified and expanded by including the voices of other genders.

In undertaking this study, we were guided by two research questions: *How are women's mobilities understood with China's tourism and hospitality industry? How have the tourism and hospitality industry impacted women's mobilities due to the Covid-19 pandemic?* Critical discourse analysis is always concerned with uncovering 'effects of truth' within the text that establish and (re-)privilege specific ways of knowing about the topic at hand. The following section describes the themes that emerged through our close reading of the online texts and what this analysis shows us about women's mobilities in China due to Covid-19.

Analysis

Through our analysis, many themes emerged pointing the fragility of the tourism industry and the particular vulnerabilities of women within that sphere. The themes that were identified are *career change, backwards mobility/immobility, uncertainty vs. faith* and *the in(visibility) of women.* We discuss each of these in turn below.

Career change

Unsurprisingly, the decimation of the tourism industry has led to several people being forced to change jobs or even careers. Within the texts, some writers conceptualise these changes as opportunities, as the unexpected shock and rapidity of the Covid-19 epidemic forced them to take a chance and perhaps pursue a dream they had always had, opening a new enterprise, or switching to a career that may have once seemed out of reach. Others have celebrated that a career in the tourism industry provides one with an array of soft skills valued in a range of industries. Several organisations are named which have been responsible for hiring a substantial number of former airline workers due to their soft skills. There is lateral mobility for some former tourism industry workers.

Unfortunately, the experiences that many women share online are of downward mobility. Not all industries recognise the skills developed through working in the tourism industry, and many workers have to start over again at the bottom in a new career pathway despite having invested in years of experience. F is a flight attendant experiencing salary cuts due to the COVID restrictions. She said:

> *Dismissal is inevitable, many colleagues who rank higher than me have resigned...I am learning knowledge and skills in cosmetic medicine, I hope I could switch my gear to that industry in the future.*

Others have turned to start-ups that have not been successful or have focused on creating online videos. As might be expected, particularly during a pandemic, none of these avenues was seen as easy solutions for being made redundant. Thirty-year-old M graduated with a tourism major and worked in the tourism industry for seven years. M had recently been laid off and was looking for opportunities outside tourism, remarking:

> It wasn't until this year when I started looking for jobs that I understood what 'despair' means. There are rare chances for an interview. Even if you got interviewed, there would be no follow-ups due to your age or lack of experience in that industry...finally a game company gave me a chance for an interview, but when I checked it online, it...looks like a fake, a shell firm.

The knock-on effects of these situations are also being made visible in women's stories. Women wrote of having had to take lower paying positions that left them unable to support their children. Others are unable to find work anywhere in the city where they live, pleading via their blogs for information about organisations hiring in other cities, willing to uproot their lives. Yet, more often than not, the comments these posts receive the original poster to remain where they are, the job situation is not better elsewhere, and they run a significant risk in relocating to a new urban centre.

Moreover, posters also spoke about a career change, ending their dream career even when successful. For example, T, who worked as a flight attendant for one of Hong Kong's airlines, found a job working as a venue manager in a restaurant. However, she commented: 'We lost not only our jobs, but also our dreams', indicating the emotional impact that this enforced lateral mobility within her career has had on her and others like her.

Furthermore, narratives regarding the increased visibility of gender role perception in society and the job market during Covid-19 emerged. Women often tended to adjust their careers for family life in two-parent working families due to the Covid-19 pandemic, and they continue to be disproportionately responsible for childcaring and caring for family members who become sick. Many of the texts examined in this study are deeply concerned with the impacts of Covid-19 on the gender wage gap and the higher levels of insecurity women face in the job market due to a remaining prevalence of traditional gender roles. For example, in an anonymous letter sent to the South China Morning Post, the writer comments:

> Many still subscribe to the outdated thinking that 'men are breadwinners, women are homemakers,' regarding men as more important and reliable in the workforce – and leaving women the first choice when it comes to the firing line.

Regarding the persistence of unequal income, Sevin Yeltekin from Carnegie Mellon University suggested that women's incomes might decline so considerably that it will now become 'impossible' to return to pre-COVID levels.

Women face additional barriers when jobs are scarce, as many job advertisements will expressly declare that available positions are for men only (a common practice despite being illegal) due to job expectations that are perceived as being incompatible for female workers, such as travel for work, long hours or physical labour. Women are also more likely to be marginalised in the hiring process due to perceptions that women will leave the workforce to marry or have children and will be unwilling to work as hard as men. Finally, an increasing emphasis on instilling 'manliness' in young boys has led to some traditionally female jobs – such as kindergarten teachers – being reframed to prioritise male workers in those positions (Hernández, 2016). While these gendered work aspects in China have been true for some time, with the combination of the Covid-19 pandemic and the significant over-representation of women in vulnerable positions in the tourism industry, many of the texts examined in this study express deep concern about the losses to gender equality in the workforce in China. Several texts, however, use the example of the Covid-19 pandemic to demonstrate how vulnerable and under-resourced women's labour is in China and that the government must use this opportunity to turn its attention to the problems women face in the workforce to protect them against future shocks to the economy.

Backwards mobility/immobilities

With job losses in many industries, financial concerns are a significant focus of many texts analysed. People speak of having significant debt loads with no relief from the government to support them with their bills. For some, this has meant making the difficult decision to return to their hometowns, where possibly the cost of living is lower and/or they can return to live with their parents, disrupting, possibly permanently, the lives that they had established for themselves. This type of backwards mobility was at times seen to present opportunities, as in the case of J, a young woman who left her job in the tourism industry in Beijing to return home and begin an export business selling local produce online. For many others, however, the lack of economic opportunity was their reason for migrating away from home in the first place. A particular group that emerges as vulnerable in this regard is migrant workers.

However, although domestic migrant workers from rural areas are an essential part of China's economic success over the past decades, the discourse surrounding migrant workers is not always a friendly one. It may even be carefully theorised that a return of female migrant workers may be considered a potential solution to China's issue regarding an oversupply of unmarried men, especially in rural areas. This has recently led the Shanxi Think Tank Development Association and the Chinese People's Political Consultative Conference of Hunan Xiangyin County to propose in 2021 that the government should incentivise urban women to move to the countryside, which was met with massive criticism in the Chinese online community e (Li, 2021; Turland, 2021). However, rural women being forced to return to rural areas may just be seen by some as a relatively acceptable solution.

Another explanation why backwards mobilities, especially among rural migrants, *may* be considered a positive development is directly related to tourism. With Covid-19 shifting the focus in China – as elsewhere – to domestic tourism pathways, there is a revitalised emphasis on the development of tourism in rural areas, especially home-sharing businesses that have attracted most leisure tourists during COVID (Huang *et al.*, 2021). The movement to 'touristify' many of China's rural villages is heavily focused on women, who are presented as content to remain at home and take care of the house and family. Moreover, these women are positioned as lacking education and therefore being 'naturally' confined to jobs focused on taking care of home and guests. Rural village tourism is perceived as a potential source of economic growth for the entire village, and this success relies upon women beautifying their homes and providing a comforting and welcoming atmosphere to guests. In Gansu province, the calls for the development of rural village tourism refer to 'her power' in the role that women must play in making the villages beautiful and desirable. The secretary of Gansu Tourism ThinkTank, Ms Gao, said:

> *Many female Minsu hosts appeared in Langjie Village, most of them were among 30-40. They need to take care of the elderly and children and cannot emigrate for work, so they cherish this opportunity. Some of the hosts only got elementary school education. They would be very satisfied with a 2000 yuan monthly income; they work devotedly and feel accomplished and happy.*

However, this equating of women's power and physical attractiveness silences anything else that women may have to contribute to developing the local tourism product. Thus, through their utter lack of mobility alternating with enforced backwards mobilities, rural women are being called upon to save the economic fortunes of entire villages.

Uncertainty versus faith

In the private blog postings included in this analysis, there are exciting juxtapositions visible in how much posters believe in the future of the tourism industry. Some advocate resilience, seemingly based on the notion that the Chinese economy is strong and that tourism and hospitality will soon recover. N, an employee of a chain hotel, explains how her company has struggled to survive since COVID. Seeing all the efforts being made, N kept positive about her job:

> *Ever since I graduated, I've been working in the hospitality industry for over ten years. I love communicating with customers and serving different customers every day. I think this is quite fun. I hope I can always do a good job in this position. Therefore, even if I am concerned, I don't have any plans to change my job…Now our occupation rate is growing, we insist on implementing all the COVID prevention steps on a daily basis …COVID is rampant overseas, so we cannot slack off. I hope the pandemic will pass soon.*

On the other hand, some seem less confident in this. Several posts indicate that the posters do not feel that their job is secure, even if they are still employed. This is supported by several online posts listing travel and hospitality companies going into liquidation or laying off workers in huge numbers. Such uncertainty has clear emotional impacts, with posters expressing fear and anxiety and feeling depressed. Most of these sentiments were expressed by workers in the aviation and international tourism industry. S, a Chinese employee at an international airline, had been grounded in China due to Covid-19 and was suspended from duty, receiving a baseline salary. In her post, she mentioned preparing for an accreditation test for translator and interpreter in response to feeling uncertain about the stability of this arrangement:

> *For individuals, the financial income has shrunk sharply. Although I got the base salary as they promised, the situation has not turned out well at all. Who knows if the paycheck will arrive on time next month? Even if my flights were recovered, I am afraid the salary and benefits will not be as good as before.*

Implied is a degree of desolation and lack of faith that the industry will recover, or perhaps simply a belief that it will recover too far in the future to be of any good to individuals now. In the case of L, the uncertainty became a certainty in the form of finally losing her job. Having worked for a tourism company that specialised in the Chinese outbound tourism visa business, her job was suspended several times due to the constant recurrence of COVID outbreaks overseas:

> *At the beginning of COVID, I believed in China's ability to control the pandemic. I believe that this might have a short-term impact on us, but not detrimental. However, after I got back to work just for a week, outbreaks happened again overseas, and now it is still not fully controlled. Then we have to go home with the base salary again. One more week passed, I received the notice of the company's dissolution. I officially lost my job.*

Feelings of uncertainty also stemmed from a perceived lack of policy support for workers by the government. One posting referred to government support for businesses, but workers were not mentioned. It is unclear whether this represents an actual lack of support in helping workers who have lost their employment or simply a perception that is being shared online. Yet, little to no attention is given in the mainstream media to questioning the government's support for working families.

While stories of uncertainty and perceived lack of support were found within social media texts, a very different narrative could be found in the news media in general, supported by several social media texts. Instead, these were focused on how China has beaten the Covid-19 through the combined efforts its people and national government and how China is surging forward while the rest of the world continues to flounder under the pandemic. H worked for a tourism training company in Shenzhen. After the initial domestic COVID outbreak, she had been laid off for six months and decided to switch her role to a Didi[1] driver. Even though she commented:

> The good news is that with the weather becoming warmer, the pandemic has been controlled well domestically, tourism is recovering. Now I have returned back to tourism and started to host some group activities. Believing in the country, the government, and the nation. We people have the determination to be united and beat the virus. After the pandemic, it is tourism that will experience an outbreak.

Much of the public media posts were about favourable policies issued to help tourism recover when it comes to tourism. While the spirit of resilience should be encouraged during hard times, we still need to question how certain groups, in this case, women in the tourism and hospitality industry, maybe marginalised both as the result of pre-existing vulnerabilities being exacerbated through crises and lack of targeted support for such groups, and through a lack of media attention bringing these issues into public consciousness.

A somewhat more critical view emerged regarding the Hong Kong and Macau media landscape, directed both at industry and government. For example, the Hong Kong news media reported that the criticism from parts of the hospitality industry directed at the government for recently implementing the mandatory use of its 'leave Home Safe' app for patrons at restaurants and similar venues. Previously, customers could also leave a paper record of their name and phone number. However, as Hong Kong is set to re-open quarantine-free travel with the mainland, the app is becoming mandatory, raising fears that many Hong Kongers who are reluctant to use the app will refrain from patronising hospitality businesses. At the same time, other restrictions also remain in place, restricting the ability of restaurants and other businesses to navigate these new requirements strategically (Yau, 2021).

The (in)visibility of women

The starkness of the Covid-19 crisis has amplified existing gender disparities, expectations and marginalisations in many parts of the globe. China is no exception. Women represent nearly 70% of the healthcare profession globally (OECD, 2020), and in the early stages of the pandemic, women and men rushed to provide medical support to the ill in Wuhan and other areas. Much of Chinese media was dedicated to lauding the selfless acts of these healthcare providers, and individual stories of bravery went viral. Images celebrating the efforts of the healthcare heroes often showed male doctors' faces, despite the more significant numbers of women working on the frontlines of the pandemic. Women's stories were highlighted. It was usually in conjunction with their role first as a woman and mother. In one instance, a female healthcare worker was lauded for working while pregnant; another received accolades for returning to work at the hospital only a few days after suffering a miscarriage. Thus, women are made visible in their sacrifices during the pandemic, but only with their roles as women. Otherwise, the heroes promoted early on were primarily male, and women's work in the crisis was overlooked to some extent. While this in and of itself is not particularly surprising in male-dominated cultures, what was astonishing was the backlash that this ignited on Chinese social media and the government's seeming inability to contain it.

Thousands of blog posts, video commentaries and other social media posts protested the invisibilisation of women on the frontlines of the fight against Covid-19 (BBC, 2020). The Chinese government can usually censor social media posts; however, the volume of this pushback was so great that the government could not contain it. In addition to the public outcry, academics and feminists in China also accused officials of not considering the needs of female health workers. The protests highlighted the inhumane conditions women were working under, such as not having access to sanitary products, which led to many citizens mobilising to ensure that the women had access to the supplies needed. A propaganda poster celebrating the healthcare heroes was changed from an image of a masked man to a masked woman. While the Covid-19 crisis has rendered many women immobile and invisible, the voices of women and supporters of women have found a powerful megaphone through social media, allowing them to become mobile in unprecedented fashion within Mainland China. While none of these texts speaks directly to women's work lives in the tourism industry, the deluge of texts demanding better working conditions for women in healthcare may be an opportunity to extend those dialogues to other industries predominately staffed by women.

The often-contradictory ways in which women are made both invisible and hypervisible in the context of the pandemic, the direction of visibility seemingly determined by the potential for news to emotionally capitalise upon (pseudo-)exclusive female traits, also became apparent in the few news articles from Hong Kong focused on women in the hospitality and tourism industry. For example, one article in this study focused its attention on shifting the blame for a particular outbreak of the virus on hostesses[2] in the city rather than their clients. The hostesses were characterised as carriers of the disease and cast as Other, being predominantly from away as Thai/Mainland Chinese/Taiwanese workers and undocumented workers. Thus, these women are made visible in how they are outside of mainstream society and are held accountable for spreading Covid-19, tacitly excusing citizen Hong Kongers (mainly the male clients of these hostesses) from being the source of this particular outbreak. Another article from Hong Kong cited the massive job losses among hotel cleaning workers in the city without noting that the vast majority of hotel cleaning staff are women, thus invisibilising the precarity of women's work in times of crisis (Leung, 2021). Similar observations can be made for mass lay-offs among airline workers in Hong Kong, which are being reported regularly (e.g. Lee & Choi, 2021). However, it remains unspoken that women make up the majority of airline's employees. For example, about two-thirds of Cathay Pacific's, Hong Kong's flagship airline, employees were female in the year before the pandemic (Cathay Pacific, 2019). Thus, the exacerbated impact on the female workforce of Hong Kong's travel and hospitality industry often remains implicit at best.

Discussion and Conclusions

It is by no means unknown that Chinese women face many inequalities in the workplace. Indeed, the China Labour Bulletin (China Labour Bulletin, 2004) goes so far as to label the treatment of working women in China as that of second-class workers. Despite the frequent references to Mao's assertion that 'women hold up half the sky', issues of gender disparity are increasingly being silenced in Chinese society (the CLB, for instance, operates out of Hong Kong). Feminist activists have been arrested for protesting sexual harassment (Yang, 2021). Under the CCP government, popular hashtags such as #MeToo and #Feminism have been censored, and many feminist voices have had their social media sites shut down by the government (Yang, 2021). What surprised us in this study was not the shortage of online texts relating to gender and mobility in the tourism industry but rather that we could locate as many texts as we did.

Women in China navigate a complicated web of societal expectations, informed at once by the neo-Confucian revival, which frames women as humble, nurturing and immobile, as well as by the more modern capitalistic forces in which women are expected to effortlessly balance work and family (Gao, 2003; Muldoon *et al.*, 2021; Wu, 2010). Covid-19 has not *made* China a problematic place to be a woman with aspirations of equality. What it has effectively done, however, is to exacerbate existing

Table 10.1 Gendered mobilities in China's tourism and hospitality industry during the Covid-19

Existing issues exacerbated during Covid-19	Women as second-class workers
	Women in general and female migrant workers in particular forming majority of lower-level workforce in the sector – low pay, insecure positions
	Invisibility of gendered issues in hospitality and tourism in public media
Emerging trends and issues during Covid-19	Lateral career mobilities
	Backward mobilities (career and physical)
	Lack of inclusive policies addressing increased demands on women as caretakers during the pandemic
	Use of women as 'performative devices' in state media

inequalities that make it challenging for women to have successful and fulfilling careers in the tourism and hospitality industries. Through this critical discourse analysis, online texts suggested that women are more likely to be employed in precarious positions, making them more vulnerable to economic shocks such as Covid-19. We effectively identify lateral, backward and immobilities narratives within the social media texts (see Table 10.1). The Covid-19 pandemic has made it more difficult for women to maintain employment and situate themselves in new positions or careers. It has caused many to lose their independence by returning to their hometowns or being unable to leave their homes for work. Many have had to leave the workforce to care for children or ailing family members in the home. Many women who continue to leave home for work are in frontline positions in the tourism and hospitality industry or healthcare, and this has them facing ongoing precarity at the risk of contracting and transmitting the virus to their loved ones.

These experiences are accompanied by effective mobilities, with netizens shifting between faith in the ability of China to remain resilient and at least do better than others, to affectivities seemingly more marked by uncertainty, worries about the individual's future and even in some cases, a feeling that the pandemic has ended individuals' dreams. However, these observations stem primarily from the narratives of private citizens expressing their concerns, experiences, fears and emotional upheavals online. At the same time, the official news landscapes remain largely silent regarding the difficulties explicitly experienced by female hospitality and tourism workers in China, instead directing attention to China's success in curbing the spread of the virus. Although the Hong Kong and Macau news explicitly articulate concerns related to the impact of Covid-19 on hospitality and travel, it remains unspoken that women as the primary workforce in the sector, especially at the lower hierarchy levels, are also primarily affected by lay-offs. We note here that the only news related to gendered inequalities in the context of tourism and hospitality during the pandemic we were able to find related to nations other than China. Herein lies the potential for future research into how Chinese news media mobilise narratives about the difficulties of other nations to present its policies as superior (albeit this is by no means a tactic only visible in China).

While women are shouldering these sacrifices, much of this work invisibly in mainstream media discourse. We are now seeing significant growth in social media platforms to protest the secondary citizen status of women in China. Advocates are increasingly turning to the keyboard to speak of their struggles and demand changes for women who want to work. It remains to be seen whether this online advocacy movement will be allowed to continue once the pandemic has subsided. Through this research, we have found that women's mobilities in the tourism and hospitality industry have come under increasing threat, and many of the gains made in terms of gender equality in China have been eroded at an astonishing pace. At the same time, we end on a hopeful note, as social media is increasingly allowing women and women's allies to speak their truth, support one another virtually and advocate for change. It is difficult to anticipate how the structural changes that women and men in the tourism and hospitality industries will have to navigate will alter their practices regarding their changing roles in the field. On one hand, after decades of (often slow) progress towards gender equality in China, this pandemic has laid bare the myriad of ways women are often treated as dispensable in the tourism and hospitality industries. On the other, the Covid-19 crisis and the light that it shone on women's inequality in the workforce led to a massive outpouring of support online, which may lead to women's increased sense of self-worth as stakeholders in the changing tourism landscape.

Notes

(1) Didi is a Chinese ride-sharing service roughly analogous to Uber or Lyft.
(2) Hostesses in Hong Kong refer to women employed by bars and clubs to entertain usually male clients. While hostesses may also be prostitutes (legal in Hong Kong), this is not always the case. The article did not clarify whether it referred to one, the other or both.

References

Adisa, T.A., Aiyenitaju, O. and Adekoya, O.D. (2021) The work–family balance of British working women during the COVID-19 pandemic. *Journal of Work-Applied Management* 13 (2), 241–260. https://doi.org/10.1108/JWAM-07-2020-0036
Assoumou Ella, G. (2021) Gender, mobility, and COVID-19: The case of Belgium. *Feminist Economics* 27 (1–2), 66–80. https://doi.org/10.1080/13545701.2020.1832240

Baum, T., Kralj, A., Robinson, R.N. and Solnet, D.J. (2016) Tourism workforce research: A review, taxonomy and agenda. *Annals of Tourism Research* 60, 1–22. https://doi. org/10.1016/j.annals.2016.04.003

Baum, T., Mooney, S., Robinson, R. and Solent, D. (2020) COVID-19's impact on the hospitality workforce – New crisis or amplification of the norm? *International Journal of Contemporary Hospitality Management* 32 (9), 2813–2829. https://doi. org/10.1108/IJCHM-04-2020-0314

BBC (2020, December 29) China COVID-19: How state media and censorship took on coronavirus. *BBC*. Retrieved October 2021 from: https://www.bbc.com/news/ world-asia-china-55355401

Brand, J. (2006) The effects of job displacement on job quality: Findings from the Wisconsin longitudinal study. *Research in Social Stratification and Mobility* 24 (3), 275–298. https://doi.org/10.1016/j.rssm.2006.03.001

Brazier, E. (2021, October 7) COVID-19 in Hong Kong: A time line. *Chatteris*. Retrieved October 2021 from: https://chatteris.org.hk/2021/02/22/covid-19-hong-kong-timeline/.

Brussevich, M., Dabla-Norris, E. and Li, G. (2021) China's rebalancing and gender inequality. *IMF Working Paper*, WP/2021/138. Retrieved October 2021 from: https://www-imf-org.proxy-ub.rug.nl/en/Publications/WP/Issues/2021/05/11/ China-s-Rebalancing-and-Gender-Inequality-50250 File:///

Carli, L. (2020) Women, gender equality and COVID-19. *Gender in Management: An International Journal* 35 (7/8), 647–655.

Casado-Díaz, J.M. and Simón, H. (2016) Wage differences in the hospitality sector. *Tourism Management* 52, 96–109. https://doi.org/10.1016/j.tourman.2015.06.015

Cathay Pacific (2019) *Sustainable Development Report 2019*. Retrieved October 2021 from: https://www.swire.com/en/sustainability/sd_reports/cx_2019.pdf

Chen, L. and Mooney, S. (2020) What happened to women working in the hospitality industry when COVID-19 struck? *Hospitality Insights* 4 (2), 11–12. https://doi. org/10.24135/hi.v4i2.84

China Briefing (2021) China's travel restrictions due to COVID-19: An explainer. Retrieved October 2021 from: https://www.china-briefing.com/news/ chinas-travel-restrictions-due-to-covid-19-an-explainer/

China Hospitality Association (2020) The impact of COVID-19 on China's lodging industry. Retrieved October 2021 from: http://www.xinhuanet.com/food/2020-03/02/c_1125652997.htm

China Labour Bulletin (2004, March 7) China Labour E-Bulletin Issue No. 16 (2004-03-07). Retrieved October 2021 from https://clb.org.hk/content/china-labour-e-bulletin-issue-no-16-2004-03-07

Choe, Y., Wang, J. and Song, H.J. (2021) The impact of the Middle East Respiratory Syndrome coronavirus on inbound tourism in South Korea: Toward sustainable tourism. *Journal of Sustainable Tourism* 29 (7), 1117–1133. https://doi.org/10.1080/0966 9582.2020.1797057

Costa, C., Bakas, F.E., Breda, Z., Durao, M., Carvalho, I. and Caçador, S. (2017) Gender, flexibility and the 'ideal tourism worker'. *Annals of Tourism Research* 64, 64–75. https://doi.org/10.1016/j.annals.2017.03.002

Davis, S.J. and von Wachter, T. (2011) Recessions and the costs of job loss. *Brookings Papers on Economic Activity* 2, 1–72. Retrieved October 2021 from: https://www. brookings.edu/wp-content/uploads/2011/09/2011b_bpea_davis.pdf

Dashper, K. (2020) Mentoring for gender equality: Supporting female leaders in the hospitality industry. *International Journal of Hospitality Management* 88, 1–8. https:// doi.org/10.1016/j.ijhm.2019.102397

European Commission (2021) 2021 Report on gender equality in the EU. Retrieved October 2021 from: https://ec.europa.eu/info/sites/default/files/aid_development_ cooperation_fundamental_rights/annual_report_ge_2021_printable_en_0.pdf

Evertsson, M. (2014) Gender ideology and the sharing of housework and child care in Sweden. *Journal of Family Issues* 35 (7), 927–949. https://doi.org/10.1177/01925 13X14522239

Gao, X. (2003) Women existing for men: Confucianism and social injustice against women in China. *Race, Gender, and Class* 10 (3), 114–125. https://www.jstor.org/stable/41675091

González-Sánchez, G., Olmo-Sánchez, M. and Maeso-González, E. (2021) Challenges and strategies for post-COVID-19 gender equity and sustainable mobility. *Sustainability* 13 (5), 1–19. https://doi.org/10.3390/su13052510

Grimwood, B.S.L., Muldoon, M.L. and Stevens, Z. (2019) Settler colonialism, Indigenous cultures, and the promotional landscape of tourism in Ontario, Canada's 'near North'. *Journal of Heritage Tourism* 14 (3), 233–248. https://doi.org/10.1080/17438 73X.2018.1527845

Hannam, K. and Knox, D. (2005) Discourse analysis in tourism research: A critical perspective. *Tourism Recreation Research* 30 (2), 23–30. https://doi.org/10.1080/02508 281.2005.11081470

Hernández, J. (2016, February 6) Wanted in China: More male teachers to make boys men. *The New York Times*. Retrieved October 2021 from: https://www.nytimes.com/2016/02/07/world/asia/wanted-in-china-more-male-teachers-to-make-boys-men.html

Hong Kong Tourism Board (2021) Retrieved October 2021 from: https://www.discover-hongkong.com/content/dam/dhk/intl/corporate/newsroom/press-release/hktb/2021/01-2020-full-year-arrivals-E.pdf (accessed October 2022).

Huang, S., Shao, Y., Zeng, Y., Liu, X. and Li, Z. (2021) Impacts of COVID-19 on Chinese nationals' tourism preferences. *Tourism Management Perspectives* 40, 1–10. https://doi.org/10.1016/j.tmp.2021.100895

ILO (2020) ILO monitor: COVID-19 and the world of work (3rd edn), Geneva. Retrieved October 2021 from: https://www.ilo.org/global/topics/coronavirus/impacts-and-responses/WCMS_743146/lang--en/index.htm

Kensbock, S., Jennings, G., Bailey, J. and Patiar, A. (2016) Performing: Hotel room attendants' employment experiences. *Annals of Tourism Research* 56, 112–127. https://doi.org/10.1016/j.annals.2015.11.010

Lam, N. (2021, November 24) Coronavirus: Hong Kong's restaurant, gym owners push for more relaxed rules in exchange for making 'Leave Home Safe' app compulsory. Retrieved October 2021 from: https://www.scmp.com/news/hong-kong/health-environment/article/3157185/coronavirus-hong-kongs-restaurant-gym-owners-push

Lee, D. and Choi, G. (2021, June 23) Nearly two-thirds of Hong Kong Airlines workers are laid off or take pay cuts. Retrieved October 2021 from: https://www.scmp.com/news/hong-kong/hong-kong-economy/article/3138427/nearly-two-thirds-hong-kong-airlines-workers-are

Leung, K. (2021, February 16) Hong Kong hotel union blasts lack of Covid-19 unemployment aid, cites dirtier rooms, heavier workloads. *South China Morning Post*. Retrieved October 2021 from: https://www.scmp.com/news/hong-kong/hong-kong-economy/article/3121888/hong-kong-hotel-union-blasts-lack-covid-19

Li, P. (2021) 鼓励女青年留乡解决大龄男择偶难" 引争议 湖南湘阴民政局回应|农村|养老|湘阴_新浪新闻, 9 October, 2021. Retrieved December 20, 2021 from: https://news.sina.com.cn/c/2021-10-09/doc-iktzqtyu0409709.shtml

Liu, M., Wang, S., McCartney, G. and Wong, I. (2021) Taking a break is for accomplishing a longer journey: Hospitality industry in Macao under the COVID-19 pandemic. *International Journal of Contemporary Hospitality Management* 33 (4), 1249–1275. https://doi.org/10.1108/IJCHM-07-2020-0678.

Macau Government Tourism Office (2021) Retrieved October 2021 from: https://www.macaotourism.gov.mo/en/announcement.

McCartney, G., Pinto, J. and Liu, M. (2021) City resilience and recovery from COVID-19: The case of Macau. *Cities* 112, 1–9. https://doi.org/10.1016/j.cities.2021.103130

Muldoon, M.L., Witte, A., Guan, S., Fang, H.Y., Xie, Y. and Zhou, L. (2021) Gendered tourism experiences in China: Exploring identity, mobility, and resistance online. *Annals of Leisure Research* 1–22. https://doi.org/10.1080/11745398.2021.1878379

OECD (2020) The gender dimension of COVID-19: A wake-up call for business. *OECD*. Retrieved October 2021 from: https://oecd-development-matters.org/2020/04/30/the-gender-dimension-of-covid-19-a-wake-up-call-for-business/

OECD (2014) Unpaid care work: The missing link in the analysis of gender gaps in labour outcomes. *OECD Development Centre*. Retrieved ctober 2021 from: https://www.oecd.org/dev/development-gender/Unpaid_care_work.pdf

Reichelt, M., Makovi, K. and Sargsyan, A. (2021) The impact of COVID-19 on gender inequality in the labor market and gender-role attitudes. *European Societies* 23 (S1), S228–S245. doi: 10.1080/14616696.2020.1823010

Robinson, R.N., Martins, A., Solnet, D. and Baum, T. (2019) Sustaining precarity: Critically examining tourism and employment. *Journal of Sustainable Tourism* 27 (7), 1008–1025. https://doi.org/10.1080/09669582.2018.1538230

Rose, G. (2001) *Visual Methodologies: An Introduction to the Interpretation of Visual Materials*. London: SAGE Publications.

Miguel-Puga, J., Cooper-Bribiesca,D., Avelar-Garnica, F., Sanchez-Hurtado, L., Colin-Martínez, T., Espinosa-Poblano, E., Anda-Garay, J., González-Díaz, J., Segura-Santos, O., Vital-Arriaga, L. and Jáuregui-Renaud, K. (2021) Burnout, depersonalization, and anxiety contribute to post-traumatic stress in frontline health workers at COVID-19 patient care, a follow-up study. *Brain and Behaviour* 11 (3), 1–9. https://doi.org/10.1002/brb3.2007

Statista (2020) Size of labour force in Macao from 2010 to 2020, by gender. Retrieved October 2021 from: https://www.statista.com/statistics/319493/macau-total-labor-force-by-gender/

Statista (2021) Number of employees in accommodation and food services in Hong Kong from 2015 to 2019, by gender. Retrieved October 2021 from: https://www.statista.com/statistics/871485/employees-in-accommodation-food-services-by-gender-in-hong-kong/

Tapia, M. and Alberti, G. (2019) Unpacking the category of migrant workers in trade union research: A multi-level approach to migrant intersectionalities. *Work, Employment and Society* 33 (2), 314–325. doi: 10.1177/0950017018780589

Teng, Y., Wu, K., Lin, K. and Xu, D. (2020) Mental health impact of COVID-19 on quarantine hotel employees in China. *Risk Management and Healthcare Policy* 13, 2743–2751. https://doi.org/10.2147/RMHP.S286171

Turland, J. (2021, October 20) Op-ed in China draws backlash for advocating women 'warm rural bachelors' beds'. *The Diplomat*. Retrieved October 2021 from: https://thediplomat.com/2021/10/op-ed-in-china-draws-backlash-for-advocating-women-warm-rural-bachelors-beds'

Tyson, L.D. and Parker, C. (2019, 8 March) An economist explains why women are paid less. *World Economic Forum*. Retreived October 2021 from: https://www.weforum.org/agenda/2019/03/an-economist-explains-why-women-get-paid-less/

UN (2020) Policy brief: The impact of COVID-19 on women. New York. Retrieved October 2021 from: https://www.un.org/%20sites/un2.un.org/files/policy_brief_on_covid_impact_on_women_9_april_2020.pdf

UN (2021) COVID crisis to push global unemployment over 200 million mark. Retrieved October 2021 from: https://news.un.org/en/story/2021/06/1093182

UNWTO (2021a) World Tourism Barometer, May 2021. Retrieved October 2021 from: https://www.unwto.org/unwto-world-tourism-barometer-data

UNWTO (2021b) 2020: Worst year in tourism history with 1 billion fewer international arrivals. Retrieved October 2021 from: https://www.unwto.org/news/2020-worst-year-in-tourism-history-with-1-billion-fewer-international-arrivals

Waitt, G. (2005) Doing discourse analysis. In I. Hayes (ed.) *Qualitative Research Methods in Human Geography* (pp. 163–191). Oxford: Oxford University Press

Wang, L. and Klugman, J. (2020) How women have fared in the labour market with China's rise as a global economic power. *Asia & the Pacific Policy Studies* 7 (1), 43–64. https://doi.org/10.1002/app5.293

Wen, Z., Huimin, G. and Kavanaugh, R.R. (2005) The impacts of SARS on the consumer behaviour of Chinese domestic tourists. *Current Issues in Tourism* 8 (1), 22–38. https://doi.org/10.1080/13683500508668203

Whitten, S. (2020, 29 September) New York City misses out on billions of tourism dollars as coronavirus keeps Broadway Dark. *CNBC*. Retrieved October 2021 from: https://www.cnbc.com/2020/09/29/coronavirus-broadway-nyc-shuttered-until-2021.html

Wu, X. (2010) From state dominance to market orientation: The composition and evolution of gender discourse. *Social Sciences in China* 31 (2), 150–164. https://doi.org/10.1080/02529201003794924

Xinhua (2021) Retrieved October 2021 from: http://www.xinhuanet.com/english/2021-02/19/c_139752621.htm

Yang, S. (2021, 7 June) China is repressing the feminist movement, but women's voices are only getting louder. *ABC News*. Retrieved October 2021 from: https://www.abc.net.au/news/2021-06-08/feminism-in-china-internet-crackdown-erase-womens-voices/100165360

Yau, C. (2021, 7 December) Hong Kong's restaurant sector calls on government to lift existing social-distancing rules if it pushes ahead with vaccine passport scheme. Retrieved October 2021 from: https://www.scmp.com/news/hong-kong/hong-kong-economy/article/3158818/hong-kongs-restaurant-sector-calls-government-lift

Zulver, J.M., Cookson, T.P. and Fuentes, L. (2021) COVID-19 and gender-based violence: Reflections from a "data for development" project on the Colombia-Venezuela border. *International Feminist Journal of Politics* 23 (2), 341–349. https://doi.org/10.1080/14616742.2021.1894208

Part 4

Emerging Perspectives on Post-Covid-19 Tourism

11 Questionable Hospitality: New Relations and Tensions Between Hosts and Guests After Covid-19

Maximiliano E. Korstanje

The recent virus outbreak which originated in the Chinese Province of Wuhan, rapidly expanded to the world escaping from the national barriers of its propagation. The Covid-19 not only ground the tourism industry but also global commerce to a halt. Regardless of its level of economic maturation, each nation adopted different restrictive steps and measures to avoid the mass-contagion. These measures included the imposition of strict lockdowns as well as the closure of borders and airspaces. The present book chapter places the tourist-centricity in the critical lens of scrutiny. Whether the British Sociologist Urry coined the term the tourist-gaze to denote a cultural matrix that mainly marks what can be gazed at or not, the post-pandemic context paves the ways for the rise of a wicked-gaze where tourists are demonised as potential carriers of a lethal virus. Here the word wicked equates to evilness. This does not mean tourists are evil-doers but they are perceived as potential threats to the local order.

Introduction

The year 2019 will be remembered in history books as the year of the Covid-19 pandemic that impacted negatively in different spheres of the global economy (Hall *et al.*, 2020; Sigala, 2020). Of course, not only the tourism industry but also the global trade has been threatened by the Covid-19. Some scholars agree that tourism is paradoxically the main carrier of Covid-19 but at the same time its main victim (Baum & Hai, 2020). The technological breakthrough that has potentiated the aviation industry connects far-away cities in hours or days. Having said this, the overcrowded cities, as well as the international travels, are fertile ground for the mass-contagion. Governments systematically disposed of the strictest measures against tourism and global travels which included the closure of borders and airspace, without mentioning the domestic lockdowns (Grech *et al.*, 2020). It is safe to say that the tourism industry came across with one of a most devastating crisis in its history; a catastrophe that today still shows long-lasting socioeconomic effects (Gössling *et al.*, 2020; Hoarau, 2020; Korstanje & George, 2021; Raj & Griffin, 2020). Nonetheless, despite this fact, experts acknowledge that the crisis opens the doors to a new opportunity for a rebirth of the industry (Galvani *et al.*, 2020; Higgins-Desbiolles, 2020; Romagosa, 2020), a new more sustainable version that demands new horizons and methodologies. To put things straight, in a post-Covid-19 world mainly marked by low mobilities, the discipline needs further epistemologies and multi-disciplinary methods (Hoque *et al.*, 2020; Wen *et al.*, 2020). As Wen *et al.* (2020) remark, many brains are better than one. In a world without tourists, epistemologists should coordinate efforts to conduct cross-disciplinary research. Other interesting studies – within the borders of social sciences – navigate on the waves of the complexity of social and psychological impact in tourism behaviour. This includes anti-Chinese sentiment or chauvinist expressions against ethnic minorities (Mostafanezhad *et al.*, 2020), radical shifts in travel behaviours (Korstanje & George, 2021), inter-state geopolitical conflicts (Seyfi *et al.*, 2020) and psychological distress and mental illness accelerated by extensive lockdowns (Buckley & Westaway, 2020). Although tourism-related scholars were familiar with other pandemics such as swine flu, Ebola and SARS, they were certainly unprepared to deal efficiently with Covid-19 (McKercher & Chon, 2004; Ratten, 2021). Doubtless, the pandemic not only showed material inequalities and contradictions finely ingrained in the capitalist system but also woke up long-dormant narratives and stereotypes oriented to demonise the foreign tourist. In the present book chapter, we explore what anthropologists dubbed as the fear of the 'Other', Korstanje's the end of hospitality or Ritzer's (2004, 2007) inhospitable hospitality (Korstanje, 2017; Ritzer, 2004, 2007). Bauman (2003) coins the term mixophobia to denote a much deeper sentiment of fear and hostility against strangers in the urban cities. Lay-citizens develop a clear mistrust in the 'Other', in the outsider, because of a manifest impossibility to create durable social ties. To put this in other terms, the 'Other' interrogates our sense of security (Franklin, 2003). The fear of the 'non-Western Other' seems not to be new it traces back to the ancient times and probably earlier but with the rise of modern nation-state the fear situated as foundational cultural value of society. Having said this, Covid-19 potentiates this fear closing West to the 'non-Western Other'.

The Culture of Fear: A Short Introduction

In Hobbesian terms, the psychological fear – far from disappearing – remains encrypted in the core of the modern nation-state. The Leviathan (the state) not only monopolises the legal use of force but also instills fear as an efficient instrument to domesticate its citizens (Hobbes, 2007). The conception of the geographical borders divides the phenomenological world in two: here-us and there-them. Borders are socially construed but politically negotiated. As Bailyn (1970) puts it, the authority emanated from the nationhood associated with its efficiency of state to impose the law. In his seminal book *The Origins of American Politics*, he toys with the belief that the US – from its outset – debated between two contrasting fears. On one hand, the fear of tyranny led Madisonians to draw the political architecture of the check and balance institutions. On the other, the fear of the stranger, which epitomised in the archetype of the noble savage, gradually consolidated the American character. The Western nation-state is based on a much deeper and manifest fear of the 'Non-Western Other'. A historical insight suggests eloquently that France and England officially arrived and expanded to colonise (index) overseas territories (colonies) over the 17th and 18th centuries. In so doing, the cultural invention of the 'Other' occupied a central position not only as an object of scientific curiosity but also as a form of entertainment. Travel writings and novels recreated the conditions of the first settlers as well as their adventures in the discovery of the new world (Lindsay, 2011; Pratt, 2007). Writing literature was widely consumed by a vast European readership. Doubtless, the figure 'non-Western Other' played a leading role in the configuration of Western rationality while reminding the superiority of European ideals (Korstanje, 2017; Said, 1985; Todorov, 1999). The mistrust for the stranger accompanied the DNA of the modern nation-state even to date (Korstanje, 2017). In a landmarked book which entitles *Governing Through Crime*, Simon (2007) calls attention to what historians dubbed as 'the culture of fear'. The invention of external and internal enemies allows policies otherwise would be rejected by citizens. Per Simon, the fear of the stranger, which embodies in a long-dormant colonial discourse, revives just after 9/11 (Simon, 2007). As Altheide (2017) notably remarks, the 'culture of fear' operates historically in two dimensions. As an authoritative voice in terrorism studies, Altheide argues convincingly that just after 2001 a new symbolic meaning of fear was brought into the foreground. This happens simply because fear is not only a powerful instrument, but it leads to major institutional challenges and changes. However, as he notes, the culture of fear seems to be far from being new. It remains encrypted in the history of the US. Although fear keeps some biological roots, which helped humans in their evolution, it can be politically manipulated. Over the recent decades, mass media successfully packaged and reproduced fear as the touchstone for a system of economic exploitation. Through fear, workers passively accept economic policies otherwise would be overtly rejected. The West closes its doors to the 'non-Western Other' imposing travel bans and migratory restrictions to newcomers. At the same time, no less true is that terrorism altered host-guest relations as never before (Korstanje, 2017; Ritzer, 2004).

The Crisis of Western Hospitality

In his book *Of Hospitality*, French philosopher Derrida (2000) (in dialogue with Anne Dufourmantelle) distinguishes two types of hospitalities: conditioned and absolute hospitality. While the former demands from the guest something in return to the host, the latter is giving asking nothing instead. Hospitality centres on the power of language that divides the native from the non-native speakers. Derrida equates hospitality to the role of translator who deciphers and adapts foreign languages to our understanding of the world.

The guest not only shakes us from the reign of dogmatism but also interrogates further our laws and customs. Per Derrida, outsiders know our lives more than we. Hospitality can be offered or not, but whatever the case may be, two questions arise: Who are you and what do you want? Hospitality takes place only when the stranger credits its identity, as Derrida concludes. If this does not happen, the guest becomes an 'a parasite', whereas hospitality takes the way to a sentiment of hostility overtly directed against the outsider (Xenos) (Derrida, 2000). Lashley (2019) baptises this as 'altruistic hospitality'. Per his viewpoint, hospitality is given to hosts for its own sake without any expectation of return. The generosity of hosting is related to the desire to place in the Other's place while meeting his needs (Lashley, 2019). Altruistic hospitality is receding given the advance of commercial hospitality. In this token, Innerarity (2017) alerts that Western hospitality is facing a serious crisis of sense because of the quest of risk-zero society. In this vein, he overtly holds that hospitality can be compared to a foreign guest who knocks on our doors asking for food and shelter. We can offer or not an appropriate lodging, but he is philosophically interlinked to us. At closing the doors to the 'Other', we are closing ourselves to the unexpected future. If this happens, the tolerance to the uncertainness declines and of course the culture ultimately perishes. Here, Innerarity means 'Other' to those outsiders who do not take part of the society. In this vein, 'the Other' should be distinguished from the 'neighbour' who is a stranger closer to me. Those societies, who are reluctant to welcome the 'non-Western Other' (migrant), are dying. Hospitality is more than a rite; rather it is based on ethics. Without going into further detail, Western social imaginary and hospitality have been inevitably entwined (Korstanje, 2017).

Over the recent years, some critical voices have emphasised the crisis of Western hospitality. One of them, Selwyn (2019) continues Derrida's debate revolving around the dichotomy between hospitality and hostility. Whether hospitality serves to engage established relationships with the 'Other', converting strangers into familiars, no less true is that the term is strictly associated with hostility. The feasting and warfare are inextricably intertwined, as Selwyn (2019) adheres. Both not only interact but also alternate in the social structure accepting but at the same negating the stranger. If hospitality makes strangers friends, hostility keeps away the newcomers negating its possibility to be transformed.

In the UK, a hostile climate against foreigners and illegal migration has come to stay. Selwyn coins the term 'hostile environment' to reflect a mobilisation of an emerging culture based on hostility against the outsider. This climate coincides not only with the social decomposition the UK faces today but also with a long-lasting economic downturn. Over years, this sentiment of apathy derived from social frustration becomes a structural hostility (Selwyn, 2019). In consonance with this, Ritzer (2019) laments that the quest for efficiency, predictability and calculability in the fields of tourism and hospitality creates a managerial culture that threatens genuine host guests' relationships. In this way, the impulse to impose a brand consistency eradicates gradually hospitality. Any act of hospitableness alludes to be hospitable for genuine motives. The need of understanding the Other's place is the key factor of hospitableness. For Ritzer (2019), commercial hospitality seems to be inhospitable simply because hosts are psychologically motivated by commercial goals (profits). There is a type of *McDonaldsised hospitality* (i.e. the fast-food restaurants) where the guest is unilaterally subject to routinised and standardised processes. The search for higher profits and efficiency is antithetical to what hospitality means. The question of whether hospitality can be deciphered as a process of solidarity characterised by diversity, differentiation, enchantment and humanisation, the introduction of technology for hosts to mediate with guests paves the ways for the emergence of *simulated hospitality*. It is difficult to resist the impression that Ritzer's diagnosis explains at least why migrants, asylum seekers and other non-productive agents are being systematically unwelcomed by the capitalist societies (Korstanje, 2017). This raises a more than a pungent question: is Covid-19 the opportunity towards a genuine conception of hospitableness or simply it is the sign of the death of hospitality?

It is tempting to say that the Covid-19, far from being a foundational event, affirms a tendency already existent since 2001 – and most certainly earlier. As Korstanje and George (2022) highlight, there are interesting commonalities between terrorism and Covid-19 that merit to be discussed; at a first glimpse, terrorism inaugurated a new climate where lay-citizens were heavily suspected to be potential terrorists. One of the frightening aspects of 9/11 associates with the idea that anyone, most probably a friend, a colleague or even a neighbour can be a terrorist. In the post-COVID 19 contexts, all are potential terrorists or carriers of a lethal virus. The War on Terror originally declared by Bush's administration has been replaced by the War against a virus. Like the terrorist who lurks in the dark side of society, the virus remains an invisible enemy which should be effaced. Governments have disposed of restrictive measures, which include the closure of borders and airspace, accompanied with internal disposition as strict lockdowns, and social distancing. Lay-citizens are considered biological weapons that should be quarantined to keep the social order. Paradoxically, the tourism industry, which prompted the expansion of globalisation, is the main victim of Covid-19. Tourists who historically were ambassadors of Western civilisation, as well as the democratic prosperity are now considered *undesired guests* (Korstanje, 2021; Korstanje & George, 2021, 2022). In the post-Covid-19 era, the world has been feudalised according to new forms of travel behaviour, travel bans and health passports. At the same time, the inter-state geopolitical tensions are widely followed by separatist movements and discourses of hostility against foreign tourists. Lastly, the tourist gaze, a term coined by Urry (2002) to denote the need of discovering landscapes or cultures to get authentic experiences, sets the pace to the wicked gaze. In a nutshell, the wicked-gaze exhibits the hostility of locals for the 'non-Western Other' in which case it marks the crisis of hospitality (Korstanje & George, 2022). This issue will be detailed in the next section.

The Future of Tourism After Covid-19

The literature about Covid-19 and its effects in the industry abounds. Most of them focus on the economic impacts of the pandemic in the industry (Brouder, 2020; Haryanto, 2020; Prideaux *et al.*, 2020). Brouder (2020) draws a parallel between Covid-19 and the effects of 11 September 2001. Both were foundational events that changed the current travel behaviour. It is noteworthy that the pandemic opens the doors to a transformative reset.

Tourism has widely shown to be a resilient activity that resisted not only terrorism but also other pandemics. There is some consensus to say that those economies that are dependent on tourism are more affected than other economies that developed less dependency. At a preliminary stage, the tourism industry, as well as other subservice sectors, revitalises underdeveloped economies through the demand stimulation and the multiplications of jobs, but sooner than later it generates some dependency while becoming the largest earner of foreign exchange (Rogerson & Baum, 2020; Rogerson & Rogerson, 2020). Some studies eloquently evidence how the economic damages in the industry vary in-country and subsectors. Those companies dealing successfully with social distancing and the health protocols have fewer probabilities to perish than other companies that failed to adopt innovative measures (Seyitoğlu & Ivanov, 2020). Digital technologies – without mentioning artificial intelligence – proved to be successful in the struggle against the pandemic (Zeng *et al.*, 2020; Zhang, 2021; Zhang *et al.*, 2021). While the profits of international cruises companies and hotels slumped down, other subsectors of the tourism industry such as rent-a-car companies remained more stable (Kar, 2021; Korstanje, 2021). The tourist system regulates itself towards a balance point where new techniques, innovative products and services ultimately surface (Dias *et al.*,

2021). Hence, the global pandemic is molding academic patterns in tourism education while reformulating new syllabuses and education programme to educate the next workers of a more resilient industry (Ratten, 2021). The fear of travelling abroad has been a theme recently investigated in the social fields (MacSween & Canziani, 2021). For example, a seminal applied research headed by Isaac and Keijzer (2021) report that part of Dutch population (based on a sample of 402 participants) have enthusiasm to travel countrywide but keep some resistance to take international travels. This coincides with the existent risk perception theory that punctuate leisure travels abroad are more sensitive to global dangers (like Covid-19) than domestic business travels.

As the previous argument is given, Niewiadomski (2020) recognises that the world is experiencing a rapid de-globalisation which includes not only the hostility to foreign tourists but also the erection of barriers and different travel bans. International global tourism evolves towards more domestic forms. In this vein, the crisis exposed the limitations and problems of neoliberal discourse to articulate successfully the multifaceted forces of a global economy. Hence, the tourism industry crystallises the triumph of revolutionary advances in transport means which fostered international traffic and the dominant logic of free trade. All these forces and factors that boosted the capitalist economy to expand are not receding because of Covid-19. As he overtly recognises, tourism, as we know it, has ceased to exist.

Given the previous backdrop, scholars investigated further on the sociological aftermaths in many studies. These include changes in the travel behaviour of tourism consumption (Korstanje & George, 2021, 2022; Wen *et al.*, 2020), separatist or right-alt movements, psychological depression and distress, geopolitical tensions, or racist discourses against Asian tourists (only to name a few) (Mostafanezhad *et al.*, 2020; Qui *et al.*, 2020; Im *et al.*, 2020). No less true seems to be not all social consequences should be defined as negative. As Carr documented, Maori aboriginals in New Zealand have recently gained further social mobilities while becoming some of the leaders in society. Their cosmologies not only help to find resilient and more integrated solutions to the pandemic but also efficient government response to recover the industry (Carr, 2020). At a closer look, an indigenous-related diagnosis would positively promote transforming business and education towards a more resilient society (Lew *et al.*, 2020).

With the benefits of hindsight, Wassler and Talarico (2021) dissect the emerging racist discourses against Chinese tourists in a post-Covid-19 context. Per their viewpoint, the social impacts of national representations and narrative remain poorly investigated. Scholars emphasise the economic effects of Covid-19 leaving this topic untouched. A much deeper stereotyping process long dormant in the colonial periods has to lead to the radicalisation of some political voices. As a result of this, some expected geopolitical discrepancies arise. More importantly, the negative representations of Asian tourists act as a catalyst effect over the higher levels of anxiety this pandemic awakens. It is important not to lose sight of the fact that xenophobia and racism have been triplicated against Chinese visitors because of the Covid-19 (Armutlu *et al.*, 2021; Reny & Barreto, 2020). In consonance with this, Roberto *et al.* (2020) coordinate efforts in offering an all-encompassing diagnosis of negative stereotypes against Chinese tourists just after Covid-19. They hold the thesis that the Covid-19 outbreak, which originates in China, was globally covered by journalism and the press. The mistreatment and prejudice against Chinese tourists were proportional to the bad advertising found in English-speaking articles and TV news. As they note, these accounts are repercussions revolving around the figure of the 'non-Western Other' that the West attributed to Asians. Such a stigmatisation process is coincident with a profound 'Orientalism' which portrays Asians as inferior, filthy or messy persons whose organisational culture or health conditions (above all in the unsanitary food treatment) are fertile ground for virus outbreaks. Starting from the premise that racism emerges in contexts of social deprivation, frustration or anxiety (so to speak volatile situations), authors acknowledge that numbers of racist incidents against Asian visitors have notably increased as long as the pandemic. Per some blog posts circulating in the media, China was blamed to exert censorship against doctors who originally reported the first virus outbreaks. Per these voices, Chinese tourists are carriers of the Covid-19. In other cases, the ethnic stigmatisation was mainly based on the responsibility of the Socialist Republic of China to exert censorship over the first voices who alerted on the possibility of a new global pandemic (Roberto *et al.*, 2020). Whatever the case may be, the anti-Chinese sentiment has become equally acute in Europe, Oceania, Africa, Latin America and North America. While some tourists were prohibited to use public transportation (i.e. trains or buses) others denounce ill-treatment at hotels or commercial flights (Roberto *et al.*, 2020). Last but not least, the anti-Chinese narratives are far from being news. Rather, they have been forged and replicated during the colonial period. To a major or minor degree, the pandemic potentiated the hostility against 'non-Western Other', epitomised in the stereotypes created in the Western nations about Chinese tourists (Mostafanezhad *et al.*, 2020), but it is not limited only to tourists. Some local Chinese communities reported countless acts of discrimination and violence in Western nations (Wassler & Talarico, 2021). Most certainly this denotes the crisis of hospitality ignited by the fear of the stranger.

The Tourism Industry in Argentina

Due to the asymptomatic nature of the virus or the mild symptoms, many silent carriers propagated and infected others during the lockdowns worldwide. This is particularly one of the frightening aspects of Covid-19. The enemy is there at the street, but we are unable to see it. This point defies directly our own Ocularcentrism which means the obsession to posses what can be gazed upon (Korstanje & George, 2022). At least this explains the desperate measures disposed by government to contain the mass contagion as well as the devastating consequences tourism industry suffered (a point hotly debated in the earlier sections). This part gives a summary of the obtained results of 30 interviews administered over front-desk tourism workers as well as tour guides, professionals and authorities of the industry. The sample was drawn by 13 females and 17 males ranging from 25 to 55 years old working for the tourism industry in Argentina. The selected method is the snow-ball technique which suggests each participant recommended a colleague to be interviewed. Because the method is not statistical, representative outcomes should not be extrapolated to other universes. Participants were met by Google meet, Skype and Zoom in view of the already-existent restrictive measure to interact vis-à-vis. Interviewees were administered in Spanish. The real names of interviewees were changed or altered to protect their intimacy.

Argentina is geographically located in the Southern region of South America, bordering Bolivia and Paraguay (north), Chile (West), Brazil (northeast) and Uruguay (east). The country is formed by 23 provinces and one autonomous city. With more than 2 million km², Argentina is the largest Spanish-speaking country in the World and the second-largest of South America. The restrictions in Argentina started just after 19 March of 2020 when President Alberto Fernandez declared a strict nationwide lockdown (known as ASPO – Social and mandatory isolation). The first lockdown spanned from the end of March to July of 2020, but it was systematically extended to date (June of 2021).

At a first glimpse, Argentina experienced one of the strictest and longest quarantine worldwide. The mandatory lockdown included the closure of airports, borders and even the airspace, followed by the cancellation of international and domestic flights as well as social distancing and serious restrictions to move freely at streets. For the state, the exceptions to the quarantine were health, drug and food production, security forces and industries. At the same time, the government created a centre of research that monitors the pandemic and its effects on society and the economy. The announcement was originally well received, but in the successive months, it generates serious economic losses leading the tourism industry to the brink of collapse. With the end of bailing out hapless tourist organisations and companies from bankruptcy, the government issued a set of different financial aids to pay the workers' wages. The interviewed professionals manifested their worries in three clear-cut directions: *the future of tourism, the fractured country and the decline of hospitality.*

The future of tourism

The negative impacts of Covid-19 on the tourism and hospitality industries are unquestionable. In numbers of the Transportation Security Administration (TSA), on 6 September of 2019, almost 2,509,000 international flights were reported. This number slumped down to 386,969 for the same day of 2020 in the US (https://www.tsa.gov/coronavirus/passenger-throughput). In Argentina, incoming tourism decreased almost 77% in 2020 leading the industry to an unparalleled standstill. Given this experts and policymakers agree that almost 12,000 restaurants and hotels have entered into bankruptcy in country-wide (Eleisegui, 2020). The dispositions to contain the pandemic have invariably devastating effects on tourism profitability. Interviewees manifested their concerns and fears to lose their jobs. Marcela (female, 48 years old), who works as a tour guide in Cordoba for more than 15 years, says:

> I am panicked about the future of the tourism industry. This job is everything I have. I have two children and I am the sole breadwinner. If you ask me, I cannot sleep for these days, I am suffering insomnia. I know the government issued some loans and give some financial support but it is only ARS 10.000 (100 USD). It is not enough because of the increasing inflation and the economic problems in the country. When I chose this career I felt in the autonomy and the climate of stability and friendship tourism generates, but tourism has a dark side, it is an activity very sensitive to post-disaster context.

Doubtless, Marcela exposes not only her worries about the future of tourism in Argentina but also give some insights on the limitations of government to cover all unemployed citizens. Jose (male, 29-year-old front desk staff at an important airline) replied:

> this government is committing flagrant abuses against freedom and liberty. They said that they work for saving lives, but it isn't true. The lockdown and the derived impositions are part of an authoritarian government to break any political opposition. Of course, I am afraid to lose my job tomorrow, but I am more worried about the future of Argentina. The new world will be feudalised, marked by a climate of ongoing political instability and hostility. Tourism is the sign and most vivid example of democracy and inter-ethnic tolerance, COVID-19 is killing tourism as well as the democratic lives.

Both participants showed their scare for the decline of tourism, but while Marcela speaks of the extreme sensitivity of the industry to the pandemic, Jose denotes a geopolitical vision, a type of neo-feudalised world where the figure of the nation-state is dismantled. Jose claims that Government has adopted authorative dispositions taking advantage of the crisis. At the same time, he lays some comparisons of tourism with democracy and free-trade.

The fractured country

The lockdown sanctioned by Alberto Fernandez inaugurated a new era of chaos and social discontent in the country. Although originally governors accepted the resolution, each one reserved the right to articulate their dispositions in the territory. While some provinces as Santa Fe or Cordoba disposed of light measures, others as Formosa erected real new barriers for the entrance of outsiders. Thousands of compatriots were stranded or unable to return to their homes. The pandemic showed the country was ultimately fractured into pieces. Each province adopted different steps and protocols to monitor outsider travellers. The inter-state borders were not only re-drawn according to the new rules but also travellers were asked of migratory requirements normally submitted by international tourists. This paved the ways for many political tensions among provinces which ushered Fernandez's administration in a misleading state of confusion and anarchy. Juan (male, 52 years old and CEO of an international hotel) expresses his discontent as follows:

> I am upset because Bolivia has closed the borders with Argentina. They impeded thousands of nationals can return successfully to their homes. They forget all the help Argentina historically gave to this country, to the migration of thousands of Bolivians yearly come to Argentina. Their children go to our hospitals, they go to our school and pay nothing for that. Bolivians are ungrateful to us. Fernandez should close all borders to strangers as well as imposing restrictions for them to access our hospitals or health system. They cross the border to be paid for the financial assistance and return to Bolivia. Do you believe it is just? I feel Bolivians abuse Argentinean hospitality it is time to change that. We need a strong president that repatriates strangers and assist Argentineans, like Donald Trump does for America.

In a similar direction, Fernanda (female, 22 years old, tourism student) energetically asked for the intervention of central administration in the humanitarian crisis of Formosa, whose governor Gildo Insfran prevents the repatriation of hundreds of stranded people.

> What is happening in Formosa is a violation of human rights. Hundreds of people are impeded to come back to Formosa, to meet their relatives, brothers, sisters or parents, they live in the borders, without sanitary attention, without food or medicine. We are the same country, why the national laws do not apply to Formosa? Is Formosa a new country with an autonomous constitution? President Fernandez failed to put things in a straight for Insfran. The issue escalated to the Supreme Court so that it can be resolved in favor of the people. Our constitution watches for the right of free circulation and trade, all these basic rights are being violated by Fernandez and Insfran. Some provinces are overtly claiming their autonomy not only to administer the lockdown but organising their territoriality.

Fernanda and Juan start from different premises. While the former is a young tourism student worried about the continuous fragmentation between the Provinces and the central administration, the latter is a successful businessman dotted with some partisan discourse oriented to demonise the strangers, above all Bolivians. Fernanda criticises the protocols of Formosa, a Northern Province which closed the borders leaving thousands of citizens stranded without any type of assistance or shelter. Insfran's scandal escalated to the Supreme Court who ordered the immediate re-opening of borders. For the Court, Insfra's resolution is simply unconstitutional because any province has the right to stop free circulation. Similar examples take place in other Provinces, Districts and Municipal Governments.

The lack of hospitality: Let me in!

As stated, the pandemic revealed not only the material inequalities of the capitalist societies but also the long-dormant prejudices against Asian countries. Patricio (25 years old, hotel concierge) energetically emphasised the needs of revising the health protocols in China.

> *This virus outbreak is a mere responsibility of China. The government not only censored the dissident voices but laid the foundations for the pandemic expansion. These things happen because the Chinese are filthy, and manipulate food in unsanitary conditions. Besides, they travel globally to the West because of their higher purchasing power. This was a combined fatality; the virus was carried by Chinese tourists to Europe and Later to the US causing a real genocide. Western countries should regulate tourism with China. We need to erect new barriers to trade with China. This country should pay for this. The first days in the origin of the pandemic I denied rooms to Chinese tourists. I said Sirs I have no further room availability.*

Natalia (female, 45 years old, housekeeper) manifested aversion to attending Chinese tourists:

> *I have nothing against Asian tourists, they seem to be nice. But I have fear, I have a little boy. I do not know what his future is if I die. I feel part of the problems of China to deal with the pandemic explains by the lack of democracy and autonomous agencies but far from that China never alerted to Europe. When they did, it was too late! I am not discriminating against Chinese tourists if you ask me, but I do not want to attend them any longer, they are carriers of a biological bomb.*

Lastly, Maximiliano (male, 29 years old, front desk staff at a rent-a-car) answers:

> *I have heard the news of the 37 Korean tourists who violated the quarantine at the hotel. I am surprised because of this indignant event. We are*

*good people who welcome strangers while giving them the possibility to
be isolated for 2 weeks. We know these Korean tourists could not come
back to their country. Despite our hospitality, they decide to break the
law and abandon the hotel without notice. Thanks to god they were
rapidly apprehended by the Police and deported. Hope they never return
to Argentina. If this mess has something positive it is that we will stimulate domestic tourism. I am not racist but often feel Asian do not respect
our customs and laws, they feel superior to us.*

As the previous argument is given, one might speculate the anti-Chinese sentiment takes two different forms. On one hand, the case of Patricio
adopts a clear anti-Chinese attitude based on racism and negative stereotyping. But the same does not apply to Natalia who overtly accepts
Chinese are nice people but is scared to attend them, as they are potential
carriers of a biological weapon! Lastly, Maximiliano comments over the
case of the South Korean tourists who violated the quarantine at the hotel.
On the first days of the ASPO (on 17 March of 2020), a tour formed by 37
Korean tourists was deported after they violated the quarantine. President
Fernandez disposed all stranded strangers to be compulsorily lodged without costs at hotels for two weeks. Once that time elapsed, they should be
returned to their homelands. Korean tourists breached this resolution and
were rapidly seized and deported by migratory officers and Police.

Conclusion

In this chapter, we focused on the anti-Chinese discourses we found
in professionals, students and workers of the tourism industry. Having
said this, Covid-19 generated devastating economic consequences for the
tourism industry, but at the same time, some social maladies surfaced in
the light. To the reviewed economic effects as the economic downturn, the
untrammeled unemployment and tourism companies' bankruptcy, we
must add the rise of partisan and chauvinist expressions long dormant in
the Western social imaginary. We coined the term 'wicked gaze' to denote
the sentiment of antipathy for foreigner (Asian) tourists because of the
pandemic. If the globalised world witnessed the prosperity of free trade
and international tourism, in the post Covid-19 era, a new feudalised
(fractured) world make foreign tourists the object of its hostility. Tourists
who were historically considered ambassadors of prosperity and democracy are now mistreated as undesired guests (Korstanje & George, 2021,
2022). This evinces, without any doubt, the crisis of hospitality, as this
chapter discussed.

Beyond the anti-tourist narratives, there is a much deeper fear of strangers culturally encrypted in the Western nation-state. Basically, some parallels
between 9/11 and Covid-19 can be drawn, but in fact, the fear of strangers
seems to be the touchstone of Western hospitality. With a study-case based

on Argentina, we provided a new conceptual basis to understand the psycho-sociological effects of Covid-19 in the anti-Chinese narratives. It is very interesting to beg the question to what extent these anti-Chinese expressions are at the best a much deeper sentiment of hostility against Asian tourists, but this moot point should re-approached in future research.

Last, but not least, the future of tourism denotes a manifest sentiment of uncertainty that all interviewees feel because of the sector crisis; this variable is assessed in combination to the fracture of geographical borders as well as the problems of central administration to manage the functioning of the provinces. Each province not only adopted different containing measures but also reserved federal rights which appertain to the central administration. The decline of hospitality can be found in an emerging anti-tourist movement which overtly rejects foreign visitors. Following Derrida, hospitality results from the dogmatic thinking given by the language, if it is true also its decline would be seen a sign of more freedom or the triumph of a more open society.

Doubtless, Covid-19 has accelerated radical shifts in society, as well as travel behaviour. The changes include the concept of the 'Other' and the human relationships. The present chapter was orientated to discuss the transformations within the tourism industry after COVID in a new fractured world.

References

Altheide, D.L. (2017) *Terrorism and the Politics of Fear.* New York: Rowman & Littlefield.

Armutlu, M.E., Bakır, A.C., Sönmez, H., Zorer, E. and Alvarez, M.D. (2020) Factors affecting intended hospitable behaviour to tourists: Hosting Chinese tourists in a post-Covid-19 world. *Anatolia* 32 (2), 218–231.

Baum, T. and Hai, N.T.T. (2020) Hospitality, tourism, human rights and the impact of COVID-19. *International Journal of Contemporary Hospitality Management* 32 (7), 2397–2407.

Bauman, Z. (2003) *City of Fears, City of Hopes* (p. 5). London: Goldsmith's College.

Bailyn, B. (1970) *The Origins of American Politics* (Vol. 604). London: Vintage.

Brouder, P. (2020) Reset redux: Possible evolutionary pathways towards the transformation of tourism in a COVID-19 world. *Tourism Geographies* 22 (3), 484–490.

Buckley, R. and Westaway, D. (2020) Mental health rescue effects of women's outdoor tourism: A role in COVID-19 recovery. *Annals of Tourism Research* 85, 103041.

Carr, A. (2020) COVID-19, indigenous peoples and tourism: A view from New Zealand. *Tourism Geographies* 22 (3), 491–502.

Derrida, J. and Dufourmantelle, A. (2000) *Of Hospitality.* Stanford: Stanford University Press.

Dias, Á.L., Silva, R., Patuleia, M., Estêvão, J. and González-Rodríguez, M.R. (2021) Selecting lifestyle entrepreneurship recovery strategies: A response to the COVID-19 pandemic. *Tourism and Hospitality Research* 22 (1), 115–121.

Eleisegui, P. (2020, 23 June) Miles de establecimientos estan a un paso de cerrar definitivamente sus puertas. Buena parte del empresariado no recibió ninguna ayuda oficial. *Iprofesional.* See https://www.iprofesional.com/negocios/318320-colapsan-hoteles-en-la-argentina-cuantos-cerrarian-para-siempre (accessed October 2021).

Franklin, A. (2003) The tourist syndrome: An interview with Zygmunt Bauman. *Tourist Studies* 3 (2), 205–217.

Galvani, A., Lew, A.A. and Perez, M.S. (2020) COVID-19 is expanding global consciousness and the sustainability of travel and tourism. *Tourism Geographies* 22 (3), 567–576.

Gössling, S., Scott, D. and Hall, C.M. (2020) Pandemics, tourism and global change: A rapid assessment of COVID-19. *Journal of Sustainable Tourism* 29 (1), 1–20.

Grech, V., Grech, P. and Fabri, S. (2020) A risk balancing act–tourism competition using health leverage in the COVID-19 era. *International Journal of Risk & Safety in Medicine* (Preprint), 1–5.

Hall, C.M., Scott, D. and Gössling, S. (2020) Pandemics, transformations and tourism: Be careful what you wish for. *Tourism Geographies* 22 (3), 577–598.

Haryanto, T. (2020) COVID-19 pandemic and international tourism demand. *JDE (Journal of Developing Economies)* 5 (1), 1–5.

Higgins-Desbiolles, F. (2020) Socialising tourism for social and ecological justice after COVID-19. *Tourism Geographies* 22 (3), 610–623.

Hoarau, J.F. (2020) Is international tourism responsible for the pandemic of COVID-19? A very preliminary assessment with a special focus on small islands. *Economics Bulletin* 40 (3), 2395–2407.

Hobbes, T. (2007) *Leviathan* (pp. 399–415). Durham: Duke University Press.

Hoque, A., Shikha, F.A., Hasanat, M.W., Arif, I. and Hamid, A.B.A. (2020) The effect of Coronavirus (COVID-19) in the tourism industry in China. *Asian Journal of Multidisciplinary Studies* 3 (1), 52–58.

Im, J., Kim, J. and Choeh, J.Y. (2021) COVID-19, social distancing, and risk-averse actions of hospitality and tourism consumers: A case of South Korea. *Journal of Destination Marketing & Management* 20, 100566.

Innerarity, D. (2017) *Ethics of Hospitality*. Abingdon: Routledge.

Isaac, R.K. and Keijzer, J. (2021) Leisure travel intention following a period of COVID-19 crisis: A case study of the Dutch market. *International Journal of Tourism Cities* 7 (3), 583–601. https://doi.org/10.1108/IJTC-08-2020-0158

Kar, M. (2021) Financial leasing and operational leasing: An early assessment of the impact of COVID-19 pandemic. In M. Korstanje (ed.) *Socio-Economic Effects and Recovery Efforts for the Rental Industry: Post-COVID-19 Strategies* (pp. 20–44). Hershey: IGI Global.

Korstanje, M. (2017) *Terrorism, Tourism and the End of Hospitality in the West*. Basingstoke: Palgrave Macmillan.

Korstanje, M.E. (2021) The impact of COVID-19 on the rent-a-car industry: A study case with focus in Argentina. In M. Korstanje (ed.) *Socio-Economic Effects and Recovery Efforts for the Rental Industry: Post-COVID-19 Strategies* (pp. 111–133). Hershey: IGI Global.

Korstanje, M. and George, B. (2021) *The Nature and Future of Tourism: In a Post COVID19 Context*. Palm Beach: Apple Academic Press.

Korstanje, M. and George, B. (2022) *Mobility and Globalisation in the Aftermath of COVID19: Emerging New Geographies in a Locked World*. Basingstoke: Palgrave Macmillan.

MacSween, S. and Canziani, B. (2021) Travel booking intentions and information searching during COVID-19. *International Hospitality Review* 35 (2), 208–224. https://doi.org/10.1108/IHR-08-2020-0046

McKercher, B. and Chon, K. (2004) The over-reaction to SARS and the collapse of Asian tourism. *Annals of Tourism Research* 31 (3), 716.

Mostafanezhad, M., Cheer, J.M. and Sin, H.L. (2020) Geopolitical anxieties of tourism: (Im)mobilities of the COVID-19 pandemic. *Dialogues in Human Geography* 10 (2), 182–186.

Niewiadomski, P. (2020) COVID-19: From temporary de-globalisation to a re-discovery of tourism? *Tourism Geographies* 22 (3), 651–656.

Lashley, C. (2019) Towards a theoretical understanding of hospitality. In B. Rowson and C. Lashley (eds) *Experiencing Hospitality* (pp. 1–24). Hauppauge: Nova Science Publishers.

Lew, A.A., Cheer, J.M., Haywood, M., Brouder, P. and Salazar, N.B. (2020) Visions of travel and tourism after the global COVID-19 transformation of 2020. *Tourism Geographies* 22 (3), 455–466. https://doi.org/10.1080/14616688.2020.1770326

Lindsay, C. (2011) Beyond imperial eyes. In J. Edwards and R. Graullund (eds) *Postcolonial Travel Writing* (pp. 17–35). London: Palgrave Macmillan.

Pratt, M.L. (2007) *Imperial Eyes: Travel Writing and Transculturation*. Abingdon: Routledge.

Prideaux, B., Thompson, M. and Pabel, A. (2020) Lessons from COVID-19 can prepare global tourism for the economic transformation needed to combat climate change. *Tourism Geographies* 22 (3), 667–678.

Qiu, R.T., Park, J., Li, S. and Song, H. (2020) Social costs of tourism during the COVID-19 pandemic. *Annals of Tourism Research* 84, 102994.

Raj, R. and Griffin, K. (2020) Reflecting on the impact of COVID-19 on religious tourism and pilgrimage. *The International Journal of Religious Tourism and Pilgrimage* 8 (7), 1–8.

Ratten, V. (2021) COVID-19 and entrepreneurship: Future research directions. *Strategic Change* 30 (2), 91–98.

Reny, T.T. and Barreto, M.A. (2020) Xenophobia in the time of pandemic: Othering, anti-Asian attitudes, and COVID-19. *Politics, Groups, and Identities* 1–24.

Ritzer, G. (2004) The inhospitable hospitality industry. *Hospitality Review* 6 (3), 40–46.

Ritzer, G. (2007) Inhospitable hospitality. *Hospitality: A Social Lens* 1 (10), 129–139.

Ritzer, G. (2019) Inhospitable hospitality? In B. Rowson and C. Lashley (eds) *Experiencing Hospitality* (pp. 73–90). Hauppauge: Nova Science Publishers.

Roberto, K.J., Johnson, A.F. and Rauhaus, B.M. (2020) Stigmatization and prejudice during the COVID-19 pandemic. *Administrative Theory & Praxis* 42 (3), 364–378.

Rogerson, C.M. and Baum, T. (2020) COVID-19 and African tourism research agendas. *Development Southern Africa* 37 (5), 727–741.

Rogerson, C.M. and Rogerson, J.M. (2020) COVID-19 and tourism spaces of vulnerability in South Africa. *African Journal of Hospitality, Tourism and Leisure* 9 (4), 382–401.

Romagosa, F. (2020) The COVID-19 crisis: Opportunities for sustainable and proximity tourism. *Tourism Geographies* 22 (3), 690–694.

Said, E.W. (1985) Orientalism reconsidered. *Race & Class* 27 (2), 1–15.

Seyitoğlu, F. and Ivanov, S. (2020) Service robots as a tool for physical distancing in tourism. *Current Issues in Tourism* 24 (12), 1631–1634.

Selwyn, T. (2019) Hostility and hospitality: Connecting Brexit, Grenfell & Windrush. In B. Rowson and C. Lashley (eds) *Experiencing Hospitality* (pp. 51–72). Hauppauge: Nova Science Publishers.

Seyfi, S., Hall, C.M. and Shabani, B. (2020) COVID-19 and international travel restrictions: The geopolitics of health and tourism. *Tourism Geographies*. https://doi.org/10.1080/14616688.2020.1833972

Sigala, M. (2020) Tourism and COVID-19: Impacts and implications for advancing and resetting industry and research. *Journal of Business Research* 117, 312–321.

Urry, J. (2002) *The Tourist Gaze*. London: Sage.

Simon, J. (2007) *Governing Through Crime: How the War on Crime Transformed American Democracy and Created a Culture of Fear*. Oxford: Oxford University Press.

Todorov, T. (1999) *The Conquest of America: The Question of the Other*. Oklahoma: University of Oklahoma Press.

Wassler, P. and Talarico, C. (2021) Sociocultural impacts of COVID-19: A social representations perspective. *Tourism Management Perspectives* 38, 100813.
Wen, J., Wang, W., Kozak, M., Liu, X. and Hou, H. (2020) Many brains are better than
one: The importance of interdisciplinary studies on COVID-19 in and beyond
tourism. *Tourism Recreation Research* 46 (2), 310–313.
Wen, J., Kozak, M., Yang, S. and Liu, F. (2020) COVID-19: Potential effects on Chinese
citizens' lifestyle and travel. *Tourism Review* 76 (1), 74–87.
Zhang, Y. (2021) A big-data analysis of public perceptions of service robots amid COVID-
19. *Advances in Hospitality and Tourism Research (AHTR)* 9 (1), 234–242.
Zhang, H., Song, H., Wen, L. and Liu, C. (2020) Forecasting tourism recovery amid
COVID-19. *Annals of Tourism Research* 87, 103149.
Zeng, Z., Chen, P.J. and Lew, A.A. (2020) From high-touch to high-tech: COVID-19
drives robotics adoption. *Tourism Geographies* 22 (3), 724–734.

12 Covid-19 and the Host Community: Towards an Uncertain Future?

Philipp Wassler

Introduction

This chapter takes a close look at the resident community, which classify as 'hosts' in a tourism context as they are expected to host their 'guest' counterparts. The author investigates the role of residents as hosts, their role during the Covid-19 pandemic and their likely role in the future concurrently. A case study conducted by Wassler and Talarico (2021) in the Italian city of Pisa is given as an example of the already evident impacts of the pandemic on resident attitudes towards tourists and tourism.

This chapter highlights problems such as the increasing need for risk management by the resident stakeholder throughout the pandemic and underlines the delicate role which local governments might play in guaranteeing a safe reprisal of the tourism industry for the host community. Economic, health and sociocultural impacts of the Covid-19 pandemic on the resident stakeholder are also discussed.

A look in the future is finally offered, where residents should not only be allowed to reprise their role as hosts safely, but also where they will most likely face a reality of 'revenge tourism' which exposes them to major health risks. This will complicate their relationship with tourists and governments, while economic sustainability and Covid-19 vaccine uptake will most likely play crucial roles.

Finally, a worrying reality is delineated based on recent studies, where residents were found to not only suffer economic impacts from the pandemic but also to demonstrate increasing signs of xenophobia towards tourists. A recent study by Williams *et al.* (2021) found that tourism-dependent residents showed a lower intention to uptake a Covid-19 vaccine than other parts of the population.

As this volume aims at exploring the practices of tourism stakeholders affected by Covid-19 from a sociological and anthropological perspective, the role of residents as hosts in a tourism context and the relevant resulting practices need to be reconsidered during and after the pandemic. Residents' everyday lives as the local community living in a destination, as well as their involvement in the tourism industry, are likely to be conditioned by Covid-19. This unprecedented 'super-shock' for the local community needs thus to be examined through sociological and anthropological lenses.

The Role of Residents as 'Hosts'

Although approaches to resident studies in tourism vary, common denominators can be summarised as reliance on anthropological and psychological perspectives; an assumption that communities are heterogeneous and may show varying levels of tourism support; and sociocultural impacts deriving from the tourism-resident relationship (Mason & Cheyne, 2000). In other words, residents should ideally, as hosts, be willing to welcome tourists and support the tourism industry as a 'host community'.

Studies have succeeded in identifying a wide range of those variables influencing residents' attitudes. These include extrinsic variables, such as the level and density of tourism development, the type of tourism, the seasonality of the destination and the level of national development. Intrinsic variables, on the other hand, include economic/employment dependency on tourism, community attachment, distance from the tourism zones, interaction with tourists, personal values, social identity/status and demographics (Rasoolimanesh et al., 2015). Harrill (2004) summarises related variables in an extensive review and identifies the most salient. Socioeconomic variables such as age, gender, income and length of residence have additionally been linked to resident attitudes, but with mixed and contradictory results (Mason & Cheyne, 2000; Perdue et al., 1990).

Spatial variables assume that the closer the residents live to tourism activities, the more negative their attitude will be (Harrill, 2004). Related studies include geographical proximity (Belisle & Hory, 1980; Brougham & Butler, 1981; Harrill & Potts, 2003); use of recreational areas (Gursoy et al., 2002) and location of residential areas (Wassler et al., 2018). Findings here have also been contradictory, with studies showing that residents living closer to tourism centres may have less favourable attitudes (Harrill & Potts, 2003), more favourable attitudes (Belisle & Hoy, 1980) or may show no difference in attitude at all (Wassler et al., 2018).

Economic variables are perhaps the most consistent factors in related literature since residents who benefit financially from tourism often tend to be more in favour of it (Williams & Lawson, 2001). Economic dependency is thus known to, at least in parts, influence residents' attitudes towards tourism development (Jurowski et al., 1997; McGehee & Andereck, 2004). Harrill (2004), however, points out that this relationship is far from simple since residents may seek to enjoy the economic benefits while minimising sociocultural impacts (Evans-Pritchard, 1989). Alternatively, they may equate economic benefits from tourism with dis-benefits such as increased cost of living (Cooke, 1982). In some cases, residents who are directly involved in the tourism business were also found to show more negative attitudes than others (Haukeland, 1984).

The contradictory nature of many of these findings is thought to stem from a variety of reasons, among the most salient being the treatment of residents as a homogeneous population, rather than a mixture of different attitude segments (Andriotis & Vaughan, 2003; Sharpley, 2014). Hence, several studies have sought to segment resident attitudes based on cluster analysis, taking a heterogeneity of relevant subgroups into account (Presenza & Sheehan, 2013).

In a seminal study, Davis *et al.* (1988) identified five clusters of Florida residents with increasingly positive attitudes towards tourists: 'haters', 'cautious romantics', 'in-betweeners', 'love 'em for a reason' and 'lovers'. Subsequently, researchers have found resident clusters ranging in attitude from very negative to very positive (Aguilo Pérez & Rosselló Nadal, 2005; Andriotis & Vaughan, 2003; Brida *et al.*, 2010; Fredline & Faulkner, 2000, 2001; Madrigal, 1995; Ryan & Montgomery, 1994; Wassler *et al.*, 2018; Williams & Lawson, 2001; Zhou & Ap, 2009). Although there are notable differences in cluster denominations and the strength of empirical evidence, commonalities among the most extreme clusters are common (Fredline & Faulkner, 2000). Furthermore, the most positively motivated cluster usually regards the economic benefits of tourism to be of the highest importance, while the most negative highlight its negative social and environmental impacts (Andriotis & Vaughan, 2003).

Recent studies have shown that the perceived risk of hosting tourists during the pandemic might affect local attitudes negatively as host communities are exposed to increased risk (e.g. Joo *et al.*, 2021) and that xenophobia and negative stereotyping among residents have been rising (Wassler & Talarico, 2021). Last, the complicated role of residents as 'safe hosts' during the Covid-19 mass vaccinations campaigns has also been highlighted (Williams *et al.*, 2020, 2021).

The Host Community During Covid-19

Hosting tourists during the pandemic has exposed residents to previously unknown levels of health and safety risks, often forcing them to decide whether to prioritise their economic livelihood or their physical health (Joo *et al.*, 2021). In addition to these very real concerns, newly strengthened stereotypes, xenophobia and even racism observed in resident communities have raised concerns about restarting the tourism industry safely (Wassler & Talarico, 2021). This poses thus a multifold risk for destination managers, attempting to protect residents' economic and physical well-being while limiting cross-cultural conflicts among host and guest communities.

Risk is commonly conceptualised as 'perceived risk', or the awareness and assessment of the uncertainty of potentially negative outcomes of decision-making (Dowling & Staelin, 1994). Risk is an intrinsic feature of tourism and has mostly been related to health risks (e.g. Lepp & Gibson, 2008; Rittichainuwat & Chakraborty, 2009) and psychological risks such as crosscultural issues and perceived vulnerability (Reisinger & Mavondo, 2005; Wassler & Kuteynikova, 2020). These have however largely been related to tourists rather than the host communities (Joo *et al.*, 2021).

However, residents risking their economic livelihood and physical health during the pandemic is a new situation and widely evident. Generally speaking, the ongoing pandemic has had unprecedented impacts on the health systems and economies on a global scale, at least if this is to be considered in a modern age. Scholars and practitioners have been overwhelmed by the collapse of the tourism industry and its subsectors, including the airline and cruise industries and the food and beverage sectors. Tourism has been one of the hardest-hit industries, where even timid signs of recovery have been stopped in their tracks and many related businesses are believed to have closed their doors forever. In certain destinations, residents were put in a position to choose whether their economic livelihood or physical health should be privileged (Burleigh, 2020). Butler (2021) states that vaccine passports, rapid and cheaper tests for the virus are a key to resume travel safely, but that the pandemic might permanently change how tourism is perceived as an industry and that certain destinations might 'opt-out' from resuming the industry entirely. Joo *et al.* (2021) add that residents' exposure to risk due to the tourism industry is now to be considered as real and substantial, hinting towards a need for residents' safety and health risk management if travel resumes.

In addition to risk, sociocultural impacts of the pandemic have been observed across communities. This has largely been evident through finger-pointing. Initially, China was almost universally blamed for the advent of the virus. Most famously, former US president Donald Trump and former US secretary of state Mike Pompeo repeatedly referred to the virus as 'Wuhan virus', 'Chinese virus' or 'Wuhan flu' (Jaipragas, 2020). The World Health Organization (WHO) has heavily condemned such denominations, as they would limit the responsibility to certain locations and might cause frictions and conflicts. From other parts of the world, similar accusations have come. Iran accused the USA and Israel of the creation of the virus, China suspected the American military and Italy at different points in time, and most recently, the so-called 'vaccine war' has caused further friction (Choi, 2021; Zhou, 2021).

These political tensions have also reflected on the general population(s). Initially, when most virus cases were assumed to be imported from China, Chinatowns around the world found themselves deserted as patrons refused to visit Chinese restaurants (Watsky, 2021). This has also been reflected in other East Asian enterprises and individuals. According to Wassler and Talarico (2021), a Singaporean man reported being attacked in London during the early phase of the pandemic, and a Hong Kong student was refused service in Bologna, Italy at the same time. When Italy became one of the hardest-hit countries in Europe during the first wave, Italians also reported experiencing discrimination abroad, such as an Italian couple who were refused the use of a taxi in London due to their nationality and the risk that they might bring for spreading the virus. Western tourists in Kenya reported having been threatened and asked to leave the country, as they were seen as 'white spreaders' of the disease (Wassler & Talarico, 2021).

This creates problems for the tourism industry, as commonly it has been assumed that positive local attitudes towards tourism and tourists were largely motivated by financial gains. Past studies have looked at several motivators for positive resident attitudes towards tourists and financial benefits have been identified as the most stable factors (Williams & Lawson, 2001).

While this is assumed to hold also during the pandemic, examples have shown that financial factors might have taken the backseat to risks concerns during the pandemic (Joo et al., 2021). A recent study by Wassler and Talarico (2021) highlights how sociocultural fears among the host community have increased during the early stages of Covid-19 in Italy, and this example is highlighted next.

Sociocultural Fears of a Host Community: The Case of Pisa, Italy During Covid-19

Wassler and Talarico (2021) took the case of the Italian city of Pisa and investigated how Chinese tourists were represented among the local population during the first wave of the Covid-19 pandemic to understand potentially changing attitudes within the host community.

In their study, they found a predominant image to be that of 'The goose that laid the golden eggs' (it. 'la gallina dalle uova d'oro') and 'The anointer' (it. 'l'untore').

Based on the data and the identified anchoring, the gallina dalle uova d'oro can be described as a hegemonic representation, shared by the majority, and emerging from groups with power and dominating public opinion and the media (Moscovici, 1988, 2001).

The national Italian tourism board (ENIT) had promised in early 2020 to be a 'magnet for Chinese visitors in 2020', with the marketing director stating that 'New challenges and new routes will stem from the China-Italy Year -- a beneficial nourishment for the (Italian) peninsula, which is launching new strategies for innovation that place culture center-stage within the offers dedicated to Chinese travelers' (Xinhua, 2021: n.p) Accordingly, ENIT (2020) also announced pre-Covid-19 that it planned to open two new offices in the Chinese mainland: one in Shanghai and one in Guangzhou, to 'reinforce the growing interest in Italy'. Respondents of the study had also mentioned that they were aware of the Chinese market bringing benefits to 'various sectors of the local tourism industry'. Even during the early stages of the pandemic in Italy, when most infection cases were assumed to be imported from China, this representation stayed predominant.

This was largely anchored in economics and official media. Local media have reported that out of 3 million tourist arrivals in central Pisa, 2 million per year are from China (Bartolini, 2020). Estimates on the impact of Covid-19 have also shown that Pisa alone could lose up to 10 million euros due to the decrease in Chinese tourist arrivals (Bartolini, 2020). Accordingly, the Chinese market is highly economically profitable, with an estimated per capita expenditure of 143 euros spent per night in Pisa and the regional government has called for continuous investment in Chinese tourism for future expansion of the industry (Bartolini, 2020).

Wassler and Talarico (2021) found the representation of the gallina dalle uova d'oro to be firmly anchored in personal experience. Respondents have mentioned mostly that they also personally experienced Chinese tourists to be high spenders and interested in the local culture, although they had experienced them to be culturally distant. The Pisan authorities have made a conscious effort to promote tourism to the Chinese market (Salemi, 2020), and most of the residents had personally interacted with them and were conscious of the economic benefits which this market brings.

The 'l'untore', on the other hand, referred originally to 15th- and 16th-century rumours of 'plague-spreaders' in Italy; individuals who supposedly spread the disease purposefully by anointing public places with 'infectious ointments' and dusting the clothes of the infected with 'contagious powders' (Cardano, 1558). This concept is deeply rooted in Italian folklore and culture, and its origins can be traced back to Ancient Roman times (Calimani, 2013). The so-called 'nightmare of the untore' has been vividly revived throughout the Covid-19 pandemic in Italy (La Repubblica, 2020b). This image has been anchored in art and literature. Alessandro Manzoni (1785–1873), one of Italy's most famous novelists and poets, has immortalised the concept in his 1840 historical novel *History of the Column of Infamy*. He re-tells the stories of real-life suspects Guglielmo Piazza and Gian Giacomo Mora, both of them executed by the breaking wheel during the 1630 plague epidemic in Milan. Through a historical, juridical and psychological lens, Manzoni criticises concepts such as abuse of power and popular paranoia. The book takes its name from the so-called 'column of infamy', a monument to shame the memory of two presumed anointers. Albertini (2020) writes that the psycho-character symptoms experienced by the local population during Covid-19 in Italy and apocalyptic scenarios which were painted can be compared to characters in Manzoni's novel.

Wassler and Talarico (2021) show that in the case of Pisa, certain characteristics that were already attributed to the Chinese tourist, such as 'culturally different', took new forms in the historically revived 'mystique' of the historical plague-spreader (Cantù, 1854; Cardano, 1558). The same shift was largely expressed through linguistic choices, such as the resurfacing of the controversial term untore (La Repubblica, 2020b), hunt for the untori (La Repubblica, 2020a) and the concept of pestis manufacta (Calimani, 2013). Common terminologies used in hegemonic representations such as 'different' and 'distant' were found to co-exist with 'incomprehensible', 'unhealthy' and related to issues such as 'hygiene' and 'food'. Similar terminologies have at the same time resurfaced in Italian media and among public personalities in the country (Merelli, 2020; Palma, 2020; Pegoraro, 2020; RAI News, 2020), while mainstream media still point to the importance of the Chinese tourist market (Bartolini, 2020). The findings of their study can constitute a warning to the possibly uncertain future of the tourism industry following Covid-19. The World Travel and Tourism Council (2020) has long warned that there will be devastating impacts on the tourism industry as fewer people can travel, and the WHO has made the devastating sanitary impacts very clear. Although a rise in xenophobia and nationalism had been observed (e.g. Habibi *et al.*, 2020), the impacts of this on the future of the tourism industry can only be hypothesised. As an industry that depends highly on a favourable understanding of a positive relationship between host and guest, tourism is likely going to be damaged in the long term by negative representations of the 'other' emerging during Covid-19. While governments are pointing fingers at each other (Aarabi, 2020; Mangan, 2020), the emergence of the untore representation shows that this is also happening to the local people. More worryingly, while the gallina dalle uova d'oro representation has been found as rooted in what tourism scholars would traditionally call rational Social Exchange principles, the untore is deeply anchored in century-long historical and cultural factors (Calimani, 2013; Farinelli & Paccagnini, 1988). Based on the increasing tension among nations that have emerged during Covid-19, it can thus be assumed that negative Social Representations are likely to arise or re-emerge across the globe, threatening the tourism industry with an uncertain future of xenophobia, stereotyping, and conflict.

A Look Into the Future

Although impacts of the pandemic on resident communities are already evident in economic, health, sociocultural and psychological terms, the tourism industry and its actors face an uncertain future and the role of the resident stakeholder in the upcoming years can only be speculated upon.

Literature shows that residents' attitudes towards the tourism industry (and the subsequent role they play in it) develop throughout phases of the tourism life cycle and tend to be context-dependent. In a recent publication, Butler (2021) applied the original Tourism Area Life Cycle model to the pandemic context, demonstrating that the impacts are likely to vary on destinations based on their stage of development. From this, several inferences on the resident stakeholders' future role can be made.

First, some destinations are likely to resume tourism normally as the pandemic eventually eases up or comes to an end, while in others, the industry might suffer permanent damages (Zenker & Kock, 2020). Butler (2021) underlines that this might largely depend on how 'safe' countries will be perceived in the handling of their pandemic, particularly on a government level. It can be assumed that in destinations that put sufficient safety measures in place to minimise the risk of infection, the tourism industry can resume with more ease, and residents might be able to resume receiving economic benefits from the industry with minimal risk to their health. This is likely to shift the focus not only on the traditional host–guest paradigm but will also heavily play into residents' relationships with their respective governments. Recent studies have shown that residents in tourism destinations tend to have more favourable attitudes towards the industry if they feel empowered by and trust in their respective government bodies (Wassler *et al.*, 2021). Furthermore, this could lead to residents' outrage over an irresponsible amount of tourism inbound which is allowed by government bodies, or over the excessive relaxing of safety measures.

If risk management for the resident stakeholder is to be a key topic for the upcoming years (Joo *et al.*, 2021), this is likely to be made more difficult by the rise of eventual 'revenge tourism'. The term 'revenge tourism' was coined in a paper by Wassler and Fan (2021: 6) based on interviews with tourism professors in different countries and refers to *tourists traveling more to make up for the time lost [during the pandemic] when this will be possible again.* In other words, tourism experts are expecting an aggressive and (maybe) uncontrolled rebound of the tourism industry, sustained by aggressive marketing efforts to restart tourism as fast and numerous as possible.

This will likely not come without negative consequences for the local host communities in tourist destinations. An unsustainable increase in tourist numbers, coupled with surviving negative stereotypes, fear and xenophobia induced by the pandemic, could lead to a long-lasting negative impact on global host–guest relations. Not only this, but revenge tourism is also likely to increase health risks for the resident population. While tourists might be able to leave or avoid Covid-19 hot spots (Karl *et al.*,

2020), residents might not have that luxury and be left with no options (Joo *et al.*, 2021). Tourists could be seen as possible 'anointers' or even as privileged individuals who get priority for hospital treatment and vaccination, increasing potential hostility and conflict among hosts, government bodies and guests.

On a similar line, health measures put in place might heavily influence residents' attitudes in destinations and complicate their relevant risk management. This is particularly problematic concerning the mass campaigns against Covid-19 vaccination. In a recent publication, Williams *et al.* (2020) raise related issues. Accordingly, initial survey findings suggest that a significant percentage of the population of the US, France and the UK exhibit vaccine hesitancy and will not take a COVID vaccine even if widely available (DeRoo *et al.*, 2020), creating issues for travellers and destinations. For the former, countries that have not eliminated the virus may be a health risk and increased costs as their home country may apply quarantining and other health checks on return. For the latter, there may be a renewed risk of infection from countries with non-mandatory vaccine rules, along with social discomfort from natives who may perceive tourists as infection vectors (Williams *et al.*, 2020). Since health risk perceptions and vaccine take-up can vary by background, monitoring schemes may become discriminatory if not properly designed, and an understanding of risk perceptions will be crucial.

Williams *et al.* (2020) mention that this could lead to different types of homophily, influencing the host and guest relationship. Technological Country Travel Homophily refers to countries that have adopted similar types of vaccines. The current 'vaccine race' with multiple types under development and in use exacerbates geopolitical issues in terms not only of different safety standards but also in using the vaccine as a possible political weapon for alliances or accusations of espionage and sabotage (LaFraniere *et al.*, 2020). This differs from the scenario for yellow fever, for example, for which there is a single vaccine. Russia has recently faced criticism for allegedly skipping testing phases for its locally produced vaccine, while China has already administered a vaccine to army personnel (Westcott, 2020). There may be the emergence of travel corridors between locations that have adopted similar types of vaccines. Tourists' risk perceptions may be affected by a destination's adoption (or lack) of a certain vaccine type. Further, public health organisations in host destinations may not trust the efficacy of a vaccine that cannot be easily verified by local officials. These factors suggest that there may be emergent preferential travel patterns between countries based on the adoption of vaccine technology.

Regulatory Country Travel Homophily refers to countries with similar legal frameworks according to vaccines. In addition to the type of vaccine, the veracity of Covid-19 vaccine certificates will need to be established and monitored. At the time of writing, the European Union has installed a vaccine passport which is not only necessary for border crosses but in some cases also delineates access to public venues, restaurants, public transport and work permits (Warren & Lofstedt, 2021). This issue will be further complicated where there are border crossings, spaces of transit (such as cruise ships, airplanes, or airports) or if tourists enter international waters where national laws do not necessarily apply. A related issue is tourist tracking via contact tracing apps. While countries like South Korea have been highly successful with their contact tracing application, in Europe, most efforts have had only partial success, mostly due to low download rates of the necessary app and data. Since countries have taken differing approaches to respond to the pandemic, host countries may set up preferential travel corridors for visitors from similar health regimes. For example, Swedish tourists' recent exclusion from travel to Denmark shows that certain origins and destinations are likely to be excluded from travel corridors. In this case, concepts such as cultural distance in travel choice and risk perception might change or be added to a 'vaccine regime' distance, where tourists incorporate health regulatory risks that are accessed via an examination of vaccine laws and regulation when choosing a destination, possibly influencing future tourism development at destinations (Lee & Chen, 2022). This might be particularly delicate if inbound travel requires the download of a tracking app. The risk perception of tourists to expose their data to another government might be particularly high, especially if this is related to smartphone tracking and other types of smart technologies.

Behavioral Country Travel Homophily relates to 'vaccine compliant behavior' by the host and guest communities and the willingness to uptake vaccines. Conspiracy theorists have stated that the pandemic was engineered with the purpose to create totalitarian surveillance states (Williams et al., 2020), and the cultural traits of Western countries might make the application of mass vaccination and monitoring difficult. While during the pandemic, countries have promoted themselves as a relatively COVID-free zone (Beirman, 2020) with rigorous testing (e.g. New Zealand, Faroe Islands), this might lead to others branding themselves as COVID-restrictions-free zones, where sckeptics are not requested for tests, quarantines or vaccine passports. This is likely to be initially economically beneficial for residents but could put them at long-term health risks.

Finally, and arguably most worryingly, a recent publication by Williams et al. (2021) carried out a large-scale study about the willingness to uptake a Covid-19 vaccine in Italy and found that residents with more involvement in the tourism industry were less likely to uptake a vaccine. While the reasons for this are not entirely clear, the predominance of lower-skilled service personnel in tourism and the high financial dependency of rural and remote areas on the sector might be a possible explanation (Williams et al., 2021). While this study is based on only one destination (Italy) and the effects of the pandemic on host communities across the world are likely to vary (Butler, 2021), the findings are anyhow worrying. If there are significant numbers of residents with high tourism dependency who will not undertake a vaccine, health risks for the host and guest communities are likely to increase and the rebound of the tourism industry might be slowed down (Williams *et al.*, 2021). While some destinations might make vaccinations mandatory, the role of residents and vaccine-compliant stakeholders will thus be crucial for the safe restarting of tourism on a global scale.

Conclusion

This chapter shows the delicate role that residents are required to play during the Covid-19 pandemic and highlights problems that will likely need to be confronted in the upcoming years. This volume aims at exploring the practices of tourism stakeholders affected by Covid-19 from a sociological and anthropological perspective, and it was found that the residents' role, both as inhabitants of a destination and as potential hosts for the tourist community, changes due to the pandemic.

First, it needs to be underlined that the pandemic has disrupted conventional tourism life cycles of destinations, and this might likely impact the future of the tourism industry in different locations (Butler, 2021). Residents' attitudes often follow the stages of tourism development linearly, and positive attitudes allow them to follow their role as 'hosts' appropriately. Economic variables were found as the most important in predicting residents' attitudes towards the tourism industry and that negative impacts on the local communities would mostly be spurred by a decrease in local quality of life due to tourism (e.g. Andriotis & Vaughan, 2003; Harrill, 2004).

The role of residents as hosts during the pandemic has followed a much less predictable pattern. Locals often had to decide whether to prioritise their economic survival or physical health when hosting tourists (Joo *et al.*, 2021) and resulting cross-cultural conflicts have been evident. Joo *et al.* (2021) highlight that this opens a wholly new debate on risk management for residents in tourism destinations, a field of study that was in the past largely concerned with tourists only. If residents perceive that tourists might put their physical health at risk, they will most likely develop negative attitudes expressed through stereotypes and xenophobia (Wassler & Talarico, 2021), resulting in a potential conflict between hosts and guests. Government bodies need thus be not only concerned with residents and their willingness to host tourists during and past the pandemic, but also with their role as citizens – guaranteeing them a tourism industry that poses minimal risks to their health.

This chapter has shown that maintaining a safe hosting role for residents will face increasing challenges, as 'revenge tourism' is likely to result in crowding of tourist destinations (Wassler & Fan, 2021) and will expose locals to the risk of infection. Similar problematics will be relevant in managing the mass vaccination campaigns, where not only safety for residents and tourists needs to be guaranteed, but residents should be vaccinated to safely resume their hosting role (Williams *et al.*, 2020). The recent findings by Williams *et al.* (2021) showing that economic benefits from tourism are likely not enough to lead residents to undertake the vaccine, pose a further problem for relevant governing bodies.

Thus, it needs to be concluded that the pandemic has strongly questioned the role of residents as compliant hosts, putting their economic and physical risks inherent in tourism ito the forefront. Likely, the inherent complexities of the resident stakeholder and the additional strain that the pandemic has put on their management processes will result in the above-discussed challenges, which need to be successfully addressed by academics and practitioners alike.

References

Aarabi, K. (2020, March 19) Iran knows who to blame for the virus: America and Israel. *Foreign Policy.* See https://foreignpolicy.com/2020/03/19/iran-irgc-coronavirus-propaganda-blames-america-israel/ (accessed October 2022).

Aguilo Pérez, E. and Rosselló Nadal, J. (2005) Host community perceptions A cluster analysis. *Annals of Tourism Research* 32 (4), 925–941.

Albertini, S. (2020, April 1) The new coronavirus psycho-character syndromes come from Manzoni. *VNY – La voce di New York.* See https://www.lavocedinewyork.com/en/arts/2020/04/01/the-new-coronavirus-psycho-character-syndromes-come-from-manzoni/ (accessed October 2022).

Andriotis, K. and Vaughan, R.D. (2003) Urban residents' attitudes toward tourism development: The case of Crete. *Journal of Travel Research* 42 (2), 172–185.

Bartolini, S. (2020, February 2). Pisa, addio turisti cinesi: mille disdette in sette giorni per il coronavirus. In *Il Tirreno.* See https://iltirreno.gelocal.it/regione/toscana/2020/02/02/news/pisa-addio-turisti-cinesi-mille-disdette-in-sette-giorni-1.38415085

Beirman D. (2020, July 29) "The Trouble with Travel Bubbles." New Europe: London. See https://www.neweurope.eu/article/the-trouble-with-travel-bubbles/

Belisle, F.J. and Hoy, D.R. (1980) The perceived impact of tourism by residents: A case study in Santa Marta, Colombia. *Annals of Tourism Research* 7 (1), 83–101.

Brida, J.G., Osti, L. and Barquet, A. (2010) Segmenting resident perceptions towards tourism—A cluster analysis with a multinomial logit model of a mountain community. *International Journal of Tourism Research* 12 (5), 591–602.

Brougham, J.E. and Butler, R.W. (1981) A segmentation analysis of resident attitudes to the social impact of tourism. *Annals of Tourism Research* 8 (4), 569–590.

Butler, R. (2022) COVID-19 and its potential impact on stages of tourist destination development. *Current Issues in Tourism* 25 (10), 1682–1695.

Burleigh, N. (2020, August) The Caribbean dilemma. The New York Times. Retrieved November 25, 2020 from https://www.nytimes.com/2020/08/04/travel/coronavirus-caribbean-vacations.html

Calimani, R. (2013) *Storia degli ebrei italiani.* Milan: Mondadori.

Cantù, C. (1854) *Scorsa di un lombardo negli archivi di Venezia.* Archivi di Venezia: Venice.

Cardano, G. (1558) *De rerum varietate.* M. Vincentius: Avignon.

Choi, S.H. (2021) *How the Pandemic Undermined US Hegemony in Asia-Pacific: The COVID-19 Vaccine War and the South China Sea.* Atlas Institute for International Affairs: New York. See https://www. internationalaffairshouse. org/

how-the-pandemic-undermined-us-hegemony-in-asia-pacific-the-covid-19-vaccine-war-and-the-south-china-sea (accessed October 2022).

Cooke, K. (1982) Guidelines for socially appropriate tourism development in British Columbia. *Journal of Travel Research* 21 (1), 22–28.

Davis, D., Allen, J. and Cosenza, R. (1988) Segmenting local residents by their attitudes, interests, and opinions toward tourists. *Journal of Travel Research* 27 (2), 2–8.

DeRoo, S.S., Pudalov, N.J. and Fu, L.Y. (2020) Planning for a COVID-19 vaccination program. *Jama* 323 (24), 2458–2459.

Dowling, G.R. and Staelin, R. (1994) A model of perceived risk and intended risk-handling activity. *Journal of consumer research* 21 (1), 119–134.

ENIT (2020) L'Italia calamita per il dragone nel 2020. Retrieved from https://www.enit.it/it/litalia-calamita-per-il-dragone-nel-2020.

Evans-Pritchard, D. (1989) How "they" see "us": Native American images of tourists. *Annals of Tourism Research* 16 (1), 89–105.

Farinelli, G. and Paccagnini, E. (1988) *Processo agli untori. Milano 1630: cronaca e atti giudiziari*. Milan: Garzanti.

Fredline, E. and Faulkner, B. (2000) Host community reactions: A cluster analysis. *Annals of Tourism Research* 27 (3), 763–784.

Fredline, E. and Faulkner, B. (2001) Residents' reactions to the staging of major motorsport events within their communities: A cluster analysis. *Event Management* 7 (2), 103–114.

Gursoy, D., Jurowski, C. and Uysal, M. (2002) Resident attitudes: A structural modeling approach. *Annals of Tourism Research* 29 (1), 79–105.

Habibi, R., Burci, G.L., de Campos, T.C., Chirwa, D., Cinà, M., Dagron, S., ... Negri, S. (2020) Do not violate the International Health Regulations during the COVID-19 outbreak. *The Lancet* 395 (10225), 664–666.

Harrill, R. (2004) Residents' attitudes toward tourism development: A literature review with implications for tourism planning. *Journal of Planning Literature* 18 (3), 251–266.

Harrill, R. and Potts, T.D. (2003) Tourism planning in historic districts: Attitudes toward tourism development in Charleston. *Journal of the American Planning Association* 69 (3), 233–244.

Haukeland, J.V. (1984) Sociocultural impacts of tourism in Scandinavia: Studies of three host communities. *Tourism Management* 5 (3), 207–214.

Jaipragas, B. (2020, March 7) Coronavirus: US secretary of state Mike Pompeo switches disease name to "Wuhan virus" as it spreads in the US. *South China Morning Post*. See https://www.scmp.com/news/china/politics/article/3074050/coronavirus-us-secretary-state-mike-pompeos-wuhan-virus (accessed October 2022).

Joo, D., Xu, W., Lee, J., Lee, C.K. and Woosnam, K.M. (2021) Residents' perceived risk, emotional solidarity, and support for tourism amidst the COVID-19 pandemic. *Journal of Destination Marketing & Management* 19, 100553.

Jurowski, C., Uysal, M. and Williams, D.R. (1997) A theoretical analysis of host community resident reactions to tourism. *Journal of Travel Research* 36 (2), 3–11.

Karl, M., Muskat, B. and Ritchie, B.W. (2020) Which travel risks are more salient for destination choice? An examination of the tourist's decision-making process. *Journal of Destination Marketing & Management* 18, 100487.

LaFraniere, S., Thomas, K., Weiland, N., Gelles, D., Stolberg, S.G. and Grady, D. (2020, November 21) Politics, Science, and the Remarkable Race for a Coronavirus Vaccine. New York Times: New York. See https://www.nytimes.com/2020/11/21/us/politics/coronavirus-vaccine.html

La Repubblica (2020b) Coronavirus, non usate il termine untore, è dispregiativo. See https://www.repubblica.it/salute/2020/03/29/news/_coronavirus_non_usate_il_termine_untore_e_dispregiativo_-252651451/

Lee, C.C. and Chen, M.P. (2022) The impact of COVID-19 on the travel and leisure industry returns: Some international evidence. *Tourism Economics* 28 (2), 451–472.

Lepp, A. and Gibson, H. (2008) Sensation seeking and tourism: Tourist role, perception of risk and destination choice. *Tourism Management* 29 (4), 740–750.

Madrigal, R. (1995) Residents' perceptions and the role of government. *Annals of Tourism Research* 22 (1), 86–102.

Mangan, D. (2020, March 19) Trump blames China for coronavirus pandemic: 'The world is paying a very big price for what they did'. *CNBC*. See https://www.cnbc.com/2020/03/19/coronavirus-outbreak-trump-blames-china-for-virus-again.html (accessed October 2022).

Mason, P. and Cheyne, J. (2000) Residents' attitudes to proposed tourism development. *Annals of Tourism Research* 27 (2), 391–411.

McGehee, N.G. and Andereck, K.L. (2004) Factors predicting rural residents' support of tourism. *Journal of Travel Research* 43 (2), 131–140.

Merelli, A. (2020, February 24). Hysteria over coronavirus in Italy is reminiscent of the black death. *QUARTZ*. See https://qz.com/1807049/hysteria-over-coronavirus-in-italy-is-reminiscent-of-the-black-death/ (accessed October 2022).

Moscovici, S. (1988) Notes towards a description of social representations. *European Journal of Social Psychology* 18, 211–250.

Moscovici, S. (2001) *Social Representations. Explorations in Social Psychology*. New York: New York University Press.

Palma, C. (2020, March 20) Arrivano gli untori 'necessari', ma anche questa volta non esistono. *Strade*. See https://www.stradeonline.it/scienza-e-razionalita/4138-arrivano-gli-untori-necessari-ma-anche-questa-volta-non-esistono (accessed October 2022).

Pegoraro, A. (2020, March 16) Coronavirus, Meloni: "A me non mi fregano. I cinesi ci hanno portato il virus". *Il Giornale*. See https://www.ilgiornale.it/news/politica/coronavirus-meloni-me-non-mi-fregano-i-cinesi-ci-hanno-1841454.html (accessed October 2022).

Perdue, R.R., Long, P.T. and Allen, L. (1990) Resident support for tourism development. *Annals of Tourism Research* 17 (4), 586–599.

Presenza, A. and Sheehan, L. (2013) Planning tourism through sporting events. *International Journal of Event and Festival Management* 4 (2), 125–139.

RAI News (2020, February 29). *Zaia: "I cinesi mangiano topi vivi". L'ambasciata di Pechino protesta, lui si scusa*. See http://www.rainews.it/dl/rainews/articoli/zaia-cinesi-mangiano-topi-vivi-ambasciata-protesta-lui-si-scusa-6630af83-073d-49b3-8e60-0f47339f672d.html (accessed October 2022).

Rasoolimanesh, S.M. and Seyfi, S. (2020) Residents' perceptions and attitudes towards tourism development: A perspective article. *Tourism Review* 76 (1), 51–57.

Rasoolimanesh, S.M., Jaafar, M., Kock, N. and Ramayah, T. (2015) A revised framework of social exchange theory to investigate the factors influencing residents' perceptions. *Tourism Management Perspectives* 16, 335–345.

Reisinger, Y. and Mavondo, F. (2005) Travel anxiety and intentions to travel internationally: Implications of travel risk perception. *Journal of Travel Research* 43 (3), 212–225.

Rittichainuwat, B.N. and Chakraborty, G. (2009) Perceived travel risks regarding terrorism and disease: The case of Thailand. *Tourism Management* 30 (3), 410–418.

Ryan, C. and Montgomery, D. (1994) The attitudes of Bakewell residents to tourism and issues in community responsive tourism. *Tourism Management* 15 (5), 358–369.

Salemi, G. (2020, March 17) L'Italia punta al turismo cinese. Il Foglio. See https://www.ilfoglio.it/economia/2019/03/17/news/l-italia-punta-al-turismo-cinese-242618/ (accessed October 2022).

Sharpley, R. (2014) Host perceptions of tourism: A review of the research. *Tourism Management* 42, 37–49.

Warren, G.W. and Lofstedt, R. (2021) COVID-19 vaccine rollout management and communication in Europe: one year on. *Journal of Risk Research* 9, 1–20.

Wassler, P. and Fan, D.X. (2021) A tale of four futures: Tourism academia and COVID-19. *Tourism Management Perspectives* 38, 100818.

Wassler, P. and Kuteynikova, M. (2020) Living travel vulnerability: A phenomenological study. *Tourism Management* 76, 103967.

Wassler, P. and Talarico, C. (2021) Sociocultural impacts of COVID-19: A social representations perspective. *Tourism Management Perspectives* 38, 100813.

Wassler, P., Schuckert, M., Hung, K. and Petrick, J.F. (2018) You're welcome? Hong Kong's attitude towards the Individual Visit Scheme. *International Journal of Tourism Research* 20 (5), 637–649.

Wassler, P., Wang, L. and Hung, K. (2021) Residents' power and trust: A road to brand ambassadorship? *Journal of Destination Marketing & Management* 19, 100550.

Watsky, A. (2021) The effects of COVID-19 on Chinatown: An analysis of ethnic enclave participation and immigrant entrepreneurship in the restaurant industry.

Westcott, B. (2020, June 30) Beijing approves experimental Covid-19 vaccine for use in Chinese military. BBC London. See https://edition.cnn.com/2020/06/30/health/china-coronavirus-military-vaccine-intl-hnk-scli/index.html

Williams, J. and Lawson, R. (2001) Community issues and resident opinions of tourism. *Annals of Tourism Research* 28 (2), 269–290.

Williams, N.L., Wassler, P. and Ferdinand, N. (2019) Tourism and the COVID-(Mis)infodemic. *Journal of Travel Research* 61 (1), 214–218.

Williams, N.L., Nguyen, T.H.H., Del Chiappa, G., Fedeli, G. and Wassler, P. (2021) COVID-19 vaccine confidence and tourism at the early stage of a voluntary mass vaccination campaign: A PMT segmentation analysis. *Current Issues in Tourism* 25 (3), 475–489.

World Travel and Tourism Council (2020, March 13) Coronavirus puts up to 50 million travel and tourism jobs at risk says WTTC. See https://www.wttc.org/about/media-centre/press-releases/press-releases/2020/coronavirus-puts-up-to-50-million-travel-and-tourism-jobs-at-risk-says-wttc/ (accessed October 2022).

Xinhua (2021) Italy "a magnet" for Chinese tourists in 2020: ENIT. See http://www.xinhuanet.com/english/2020-01/24/c_138730061.htm (accessed 23 November 2021).

Zenker, S. and Kock, F. (2020) The coronavirus pandemic – A critical discussion of a tourism research agenda. *Tourism Management* 81, 104164.

Zhou, Y.J. and Ap, J. (2009) Residents' perceptions towards the impacts of the Beijing 2008 Olympic Games. *Journal of Travel Research* 48 (1), 78–91.

Zhou, Y.R. (2021) Vaccine nationalism: contested relationships between COVID-19 and globalization. *Globalizations* 19 (3), 450–465.

13 Rethinking Tourism for the Long-Term: Covid-19 and the Paradoxes of Tourism Recovery in Australia

Phoebe Everingham

Introduction

Australia's response to the Covid-19 pandemic has been one of suppression and imposition of highly regulated restrictions on international mobility through tough international border restrictions. Australia has had considerable advantages in terms of geographic isolation and population density as an island nation, with quarantining the key strategy for containing the virus coming in from overseas. While the rest of the world had to alter their lifestyles to avoid contagion dramatically, Australia's strict border control meant that life went on relatively normally. As a BBC report states in June 2021:

> For the past year, Australia has been coasting along almost blissfully detached from the global pandemic. It had achieved a "Covid normal" where people could visit restaurants and nightclubs and join crowds at festivals and theatres. (Mao, 2021)

While the first part of 2020 saw lockdowns and restrictions on domestic travel, consumer confidence related to domestic travel lifted in the second half of 2020–2021. Businesses took advantage of high pent-up demand, and spending increased 45% in the first half of 2020–2021 (Austrade, 2021). The relative freedom of movement throughout the country saw Australians 'explore their own backyard' in newfound ways. Increased acceptance of flexible working and easy access to world class tourism options drove a spike in domestic-led tourism with key tourism industry players like Tourism Australia conducting marketing campaigns such as 'Holiday here this year' and 'There's still nothing like Australia'. A survey conducted by KPMG in 2020 showed that 61% of Australian respondents planned to book a domestic holiday between January and June 2021, and

72% said they would book a holiday between July and December 2021 (KPMG, 2021). These initiatives offered possibilities for rethinking tourism consumption more broadly, with local and proximity tourism leading to less carbon-intensive and more equitable forms of tourism (Higgins-Desbiolles & Bigby, 2022). However, while 2020 saw Australia as relatively virus-free, the Delta outbreak that began in June 2021 saw 80% of the population living under the toughest restrictions since the start of the pandemic, and sporadic border closures between states and even between cities, suburbs and regions have had drastic implications for these domestic-led tourism initiatives.

The Delta outbreak that began in June 2021 highlighted the complacency of Australia in relation to vaccination targets, as well as being crisis-prepared more generally. The zero approach to Covid meant Australia was ill-prepared when it came to Delta. Patient Zero in the Delta outbreak was a limo driver in his 60s who caught the virus from a newly arrived international passenger at Sydney international airport on 16th June 2021. The driver was neither vaccinated, nor wearing a mask, nor being tested regularly (none of which he was required to do under the rules at the time) (Mao, 2021). The rapid spread of Delta shone a light on the failures in Australia's vaccine programme – among one of the last of the OECD countries to rollout vaccines. Mixed messages over the Astra Zeneca vaccine fuelled vaccine hesitancy (which was why the limo driver remained unvaccinated – despite having access to Astra Zeneca) (Mao, 2021). The ill-prepared nature of Australia concerning the Delta outbreak thus highlights the ineptitude of the Australian government and some of the key industry players in preparation for new virus strains and societal and global crises more broadly with increasingly uncertain futures.

In this chapter, I situate the Covid-19 pandemic alongside climate change – as the 'twin crises of the Anthropocene' – where the unsustainable growth of human activities has led to catastrophic changes in the global environment (Asayama et al., 2021). The Anthropocene is a term used to describe the detrimental effect of human activity and the resultant devastating environmental impacts, increasingly being taken up by critical tourism scholars (Cheer et al., 2019; Fletcher, 2018; Gren & Huijbens, 2016; Mostafanezhad & Norum, 2019). The Anthropocene calls into question the modern Western conceptual divide between 'nature' and 'culture', demonstrating the intricate links between human, social, cultural and economic activity and the destruction of natural ecosystems (Fletcher, 2018). As Mostafanezhad and Norum (2019: 422) point out, 'in many parts of the world natural systems are effectively becoming another element of regional and global systems', where human and societal relationships with the environment have irrevocably changed the very nature of bioecological conditions creating a new epoch in planetary history.

Linking the Covid-19 health pandemic to the relationalities between human systems and natural systems is key for the long-term resilience of tourism, as long-term recovery practices cannot be disconnected from the more-than-human relationalities and configurations that negate human dependency on nature. Long-term resilience also needs to consider the broader social, cultural, economic and environmental inequalities. Drawing on the work of Turner and the 'Man-made Disasters model', Mostafanezhad (2020: 2) posits that disasters rarely develop instantaneously but rather accumulate over time, resulting in a number of events (both natural and social). In the context of the COVID pandemic, the vulnerabilities and consequences that societies have experienced are not one of mere 'nature', but also politics and economy as the 'risk of illness and disease are socio-economically mediated' (Mostafanezhad, 2020: 2).

Seeing the Covid crises through the lens of the 'Anthropocene' situates the pandemic as a consequence of unbalanced relationships between humans and nature rather than an isolated 'natural' incident. 'Solutions' to the pandemic thus require a denaturalisation of 'the political and economic drivers of disasters and their human and non-human consequences' to offer holistic solutions that go beyond short-term band-aid models (Mostafanezhad, 2020: 5). There is no doubt that the Covid-19 pandemic has led to unprecedented crises for the tourism industry worldwide. However, from a planetary health perspective to Covid-19, some infectious disease and environmental health experts argue that the Covid-19 and climate/biodiversity crises are deeply connected. It is widely acknowledged by scientists that Covid-19 is a Zoonotic disease, the latest new infectious disease arising from human interdependence with nature (Armstrong et al., 2020). While a lab leak has not been ruled out as an origin (Maxmen & Mallapaty, 2021), either way, Covid-19 is a paradigmatic example of an 'Anthropocene disease', resultant from human interference with nature (O'Callaghan-Gordo & Antó, 2020: 187).

In this chapter, I build on these perspectives of Covid-19 as 'a disease of the Anthropocene' causing an 'unnatural disaster' (Mostafanezhad, 2020; Sheller, 2021) to highlight the importance of taking holistic systems perspectives to post-pandemic recovery. The pandemic contains important lessons, not only in relation to immediate crises such as the spread of the disease itself but also potentially more devastating global challenges such as climate change (Gössling et al., 2020). Sheller (2021) argues that in the face of the 'emergency of the pandemic', tourism futures also need to be considered more broadly in relation to historical perspectives that underpin 'the ongoing disasters brought about by climate change, and the chronic "slow disasters" of indebtedness, neoliberal austerity, and poverty'. These processes will all impact pandemic recovery, in turn impacting tourism recovery.

This chapter puts forward an analysis that centres the broader historical, social, economic, cultural and political systems in the management of the Covid-19 pandemic (as an 'unnatural disaster') from the Australian context. From this perspective, Covid-19 is not an isolated crisis but rather embedded within broader systems resulting in socially, environmentally unsustainable practices – all of which are causing societal crises. The chapter argues that holistic systems perspectives are needed for crisis management and tourism recovery, which centre resilience and adaptation in the face of these increasingly challenging futures.

A Disease of the Anthropocene: Covid-19 and Implications for the Future of Tourism

It is important to be cognisant of the inequalities that underpin tourism development and mobility so that reconstruction after disasters does not reproduce and/or exacerbate existing inequalities (Sheller, 2021). As Prideaux *et al.* (2020) point out, the tourism literature rarely looks beyond the bubble of tourism activity, and consideration must also be given to global geopolitics in relation to tourism recovery. In the context of the Caribbean, Sheller (2021) points out that past post-disaster reconstructions have too often sought 'quick-fix' policies that benefit the privileged few at the expense of the many. These kinds of quick-fix policies prevent 'alternative visions of development from taking root' and local communities from reimagining 'regenerative economies and resilient ecologies that are grounded in more just relations of mobility and connection' (Sheller, 2021: 1445).

While controlling the pandemic appropriately focuses on mobilising human and financial resources to provide health care for patients and prevent human-to-human transmission, it is equally important that investments are made in tackling underlying causes of the problems, such as unsustainable human activity. Baker *et al.* (2021) point out that 'anthropogenic climatic, demographic and technological changes have altered the landscape of infectious disease risk in the past two decades'. In an era of unprecedented global connectivity, the spread of diseases between populations can differentially affect the risk of emergence and the dynamics of disease within a local population. The world has already seen this in relation to the Covid variants. In the context of international travel, the total number of airline passengers globally doubled from just below two billion in 2000 to more than four billion in 2019, inevitability bringing with it new risks from emerging pathogens such as Covid-19 and now, further variants of the virus. Public experts have warned us from the beginning of the pandemic that a global response is necessary to contain the virus. Yet, issues such as vaccine inequity, for example, impedes the reduction of virus variants – which we are now seeing with the emergence of Omicron, a variant that originated in the continent of Africa where vaccination levels are just 20% to 30% of the population (Jacoby, 2021). The spread of Covid-19 is just one of many global challenges in the era of the Anthropocene, which will likely continue unless planetary boundaries are considered and social, economic inequalities are addressed.

In relation to Covid-19 and tourism, Tomassini and Cavagnaro (2020) argue that the only guarantee of well-being, safety and security is to refocus on the local dimension of tourism space. In light of global challenges more broadly, such as climate change, the impacts on destinations and tourism infrastructures are already happening, and the tourism industry will need to be prepared for further mitigation and adaptation (Hall *et al.*, 2016). However, rather than seeing this in a negative light, Covid-19 recovery could be seen as a 'transformative opportunity' to 'reimagine and reform the next normal and economic order' (Sigala, 2020: 312). Sustainable transformations that have already commenced on smaller scales, such as the increased use of renewables and initial acceptance of models such as the circular economy, may accelerate and become more widely accepted and utilised (Prideaux *et al.*, 2020).

Local tourism or proximity tourism may become more popular (and necessary) as tourism consumption adapts to changing social/environmental circumstances. A local turn in critical tourism studies is emerging that aims to address these environmental challenges and contemporary power imbalances and injustices in tourism in light of future challenges (see Higgins-Desbiolles & Bigby, 2022; Ingram *et al.*, 2020; Rantala *et al.*, 2020; Russo & Richards, 2016; Tomassini & Cavagnaro, 2020). Proximity tourism emphasises local destinations, short distances and lower-carbon modes of transportation approached through 'questions of attractiveness cultural and physical distance walkability and transportation and accessibility' (Rantala *et al.*, 2020: 3948). These slower forms of tourism can enhance social and environmental well-being by rethinking leisure time more holistically and engaging with the locals in more meaningful, fulfilling ways (Everingham & Chassagne, 2020; Everingham & Francis-Coan, forthcoming).

However, these (re)imagined futures in the face of pandemic recovery are not given. As Prideaux *et al.* (2020: 678) point out, 'as change accelerates, groups of winners and losers will emerge'. Crises can also be used 'as a political tool to stabilise existing structures and diminish the possibility of collective mobilisation' (Sigala, 2020: 313). The transformation will likely be contested by various interest groups and conflicting discourses around 'development, the ethical dimensions of development and use of tourists vs locals' space' (Prideaux *et al.*, 2020: 678). This may lead to 'conflict between local communities, the tourists use the local community for their touristic activities and the business and government elites who control the shape and form of development' (Prideaux *et al.*, 2020: 678). As Sigala (2020: 3013) points out, the transformative potentials of pandemic recovery will depend on how various stakeholders such as 'tourists, operators, destination organisations, policy makers, local communities, employees' are 'affected by, respond to, recover and reflect on the crises' (Sigala, 2020: 313).

The Paradoxes and Possibilities of Tourism Recovery in Australia During Covid

Situating the Covid crises as an 'unnatural' disaster expands understandings of crises management towards addressing the underlying root causes of the pandemic. This includes the dominance of 'growth' mindsets that situate the pandemic as outside of social, economic and political systems. While the Australian context has rightly seen priority given to managing the immediate health crises and economic fallouts, there have also been many negative flow-on effects that will require longer-term strategies. Crises management 'needs to be implemented before, during and after crises' (Sigala, 2020: 315).

Crises management involves building resilience – however, the effectiveness of resilience-building activities for tourism ultimately relies on understanding and addressing the underlying sociopolitical processes and environmental linkages that form the foundations of vulnerability (Calgaro *et al.*, 2014). Tourism destinations and tourism systems do not exist in a vacuum. It is, therefore, important to 'understand the socially constructed and dynamic spatial-temporal context within which vulnerability and resilience manifest in the tourism destination/system' (Victoria University, 2021: 23).

A 2021–2022 report by Tourism Australia states that Australian tourism's recovery will be very much domestic-led. In relation to rethinking tourism more broadly in the context of the increasing global crisis the localisation and proximity tourism agenda offers possibilities for preparing tourism beyond immediate pandemic recovery towards more sustainable systems that are future-orientated. However, as the following section highlights, the ill-prepared nature of Australia in relation to the Delta variant (and at the time of writing the Omicron variant) has thwarted the domestic-led tourism recovery in Australia, undermining economic recovery more broadly and tourism operators more specifically.

State bordering practices in Australia – A fragmented response to crises

Australia is the largest country in Oceania and the world's sixth-largest country. Much of the population lives on the coast and in cities, with states and territories containing vast underpopulated regions. The remote nature of Australia means that settlements often cross borders and/or the nearest facilities to a town are in a different state. While the domestic-led travel initiatives boomed during the international border closures that began in 2020, these initiatives were hampered by Australia's eight states and territories closing their borders from other states and cities at various stages throughout 2020 – and in an even more extreme manner after the introduction of the Delta strain of the virus in 2021, despite only very small increases in new infections. The two largest states (in population), New South Wales and Victoria, who receive the bulk of returned international residents, were particularly affected by the negative impacts on interstate travel. The impact of these state border restrictions is crucial considering that domestic-led travel in Australia accounted for 80% of total trips and spent in Australia in recent years (Tourism Economics, 2021).

The pandemic, particularly after the Delta strain arrived in June, revealed that states in Australia are more potent than people realised, undermining the national government response, which was already fragmented and uncoordinated. The lack of national coordination and infighting between states and territories has affected broader economic recovery that may have occurred through a more unified national response.

There is no doubt that the fragmented and non-unified approach to the Covid crises from differing state policies led to consumer uncertainty that undermined the domestic-led tourism recovery. Many of the state border closures happened just before the school holidays. This had followed on effects in other states and territories that were virus free and was particularly felt in border regions. For example, while South Australia saw few cases of Covid, the high numbers in Victoria led to rash border closures keeping Victorians out. However, most cases occurred in Melbourne, while regional towns in Victoria that share border regions with South Australia had zero cases. The closure of the border meant that tourism operators in regional areas near border areas bore the brunt of cancelled holidays. For example, a tourism operator on the South Australia/ Victoria border says:

> It looks like we've lost about 80 per cent of our business overnight basically, so if we're lucky we're going to have 20 per cent left of people coming for these school holidays," she said. "It's not only our accommodation and tours, it's a total roll-on effect that we have here, so that if people aren't staying or they're not touring, it's going to affect the wineries, the restaurants, the shops, all the local businesses out there. (Tlozek, 2021)

Essentially, the small- to medium-sized tourism, transport and hospitality businesses have been hit the hardest, with many potentially closing for good, as visitation numbers may not support the ability to operate at a 30%–40% demand capacity level (Stafford Strategy, 2021).

The state and territory 'go-it-alone' approach undermined consumer confidence for booking interstate holidays, where holidays had to be cancelled at the last minute, and interstate travellers were sometimes stranded in one state, unable to make it back to their home states. Strict border quarantining meant that getting from one side of the country to the other was almost impossible, for example, with NSW and Victoria relaxing restrictions while other state and territories tightened them. Conflicting health advice and snap lockdowns within and between states meant that people became stranded, even unable to visit sick and dying relatives in other states. In light of these problems, the tourism and travel industry suffered enormously, with calls such as Tourism Australia managing director Phillipa Harrison urging 'governments to accept a higher risk threshold of Covid-19 and learn to live with the virus' (Dye, 2021). Qantas chief marketing officer Jo Boundy called for 'a national consistent approach to borders' due to the constantly changing restrictions causing too much uncertainty: 'People actually aren't so worried about the health and safety of travelling anymore. Its about flexibility and disruption, where people are more worried about becoming stranded due to snap border closures than they are about contracting Covid while travelling' (Dye, 2021).

The JobKeeper payment scheme

The JobKeeper payment was a measure introduced by the federal government in March 2020 to keep the economy afloat during the crisis, providing a $1500 fortnightly payment (IOOF, 2021). JobKeeper had the right intentions – to keep workers in employment through lockdowns. The payment was designed to subsidise employers to keep them on their books, providing the equivalent of about 70% of the median wage. However, JobKeeper was criticised for being too narrowly defined, and failing in the very thing it aimed to do – to keep people in the labour force (Jericho, 2020). While JobKeeper did help keep more people employed than otherwise would have been the case, the narrow definition of legibility meant that many casual workers, contract workers (working 25 hours or less) and those who could not afford reduced hours due to the cost of childcare were disproportionately excluded.

Both employees and employers discovered problems with JobKeeper which cannot be seen in isolation from the deeply unequal relationship between employers and employees, the growing divide between the rich and the poor and the increasing casualisation in all sectors of Australian workplaces. The following issues were identified by the Independent Order of Odd Fellows (IOOF, 2021):

(1) JobKeeper arrangements were unaffordable for many employers (particularly small/medium enterprises): Employers first had to pay their employees the $1500, then claim the money back from the tax office at the end of each month. Many SMEs could not afford to pay this money out of their own pocket before they were paid back by the government.

(2) The set rate of $750 a week meant that for some workers the rate was too low, while for others, it was too high – casual workers, for example, were expected to work longer hours than they were sometimes

able to or wanted to, in order to receive the $750 a week. If they protested due to study or family commitments, they were fired (although technically in the context of Australia casual worker do not need to be fired – they just aren't given more shifts).

(3) Some employees were reclassified and pay rates reduced: Some employers utilised their position of power to demand employees could only keep their job if they handed them back part of the JobKeeper payment. Others had their work hours reduced and/or their position reclassified from full-time to part-time employment. Others were told their leave entitlements would only accrue on their new lower work hours, with pay rate reduced to $750 a week.

While JobKeeper did keep many afloat in the first lockdowns of 2020, it also worked to benefit the top tiers of wealth holders the most where at least 11 billionaires received dividends totalling tens of millions of dollars from companies that received JobKeeper despite doing quite well in the pandemic (Butler, 2021). Crown Casino in Sydney, for example, received $111million in JobKeeper despite only paying dividends of $203 million. Other big companies had similar returns (Leigh, 2020). While giant homeware company Harvey Norman was shamed by the public into giving back $6 million in JobKeeper wages, the repayments were less than a third of the estimated $22m the company and its franchises claimed in total (Karp, 2021).

JobKeeper has consequently been criticised for merely providing a '$6.2b "sugar hit" for businesses that didn't make a big revenue hit during the pandemic' (Khadem, 2021). Small businesses complained that they were honest with their earnings to the taxation department, foregoing the payment once profits increased. However, other big companies including foreign-controlled companies were accused of legally pocketing JobKeeper while increasing wages and profits. The government was accused of rolling out the scheme with a lack of transparency and accountability – especially for firms that already achieved more than $10 million in turnover. There was no accountability for firms to pay back money despite making profits (Khadem, 2021).

While many small- and medium-sized tourism organisations were impacted to the point of closure, the Australian aviation industry was bailed out with a $715 million relief package. Although many countries see airline mobility and the competitive aerospace sector as a non-negotiable, many economists argue that airline bailouts are an inefficient use of taxpayer money when fiscal recovery is desperately needed (O'Callaghan & Hepburn, 2020).

The JobKeeper payment programme ended on 28th March 2021, ironically just as the worst impacts of the Covid hit Australia in June 2021 with the Delta strain (and at the time of writing, now the Omicron strain that is creating further chaos). The NSW Tourism Industry Council petitioned a survey where they found the loss of industry capacity to be much worse should no further government support eventuate with the devastating flow-on effects within supply chains. They found:

- 1/3 tourism businesses anticipate needing to close, either permanently or temporarily, once the JobKeeper ends.
- Of those who close permanently, 36% say they will leave the industry for good, and 52% simply don't know what they will do. Only 11% of those who will close temporarily believe they'll be able to re-establish their business without financial support.

When JobKeeper ended, a $1.2 billion tourism stimulus package was introduced. Australians were encouraged to visit far-flung destinations within national borders, enticed by half price airfares and other such incentives. However, Flight Centre managing director Graham Turner argued in April 2021 that the $1.2 billion package would do little for the tourism industry without taking a nationally unified strategy in relation to keeping national state and territory borders open for domestic travel:

> I don't think this is going to help at all, really. It is about the borders. Keeping the domestic borders open and getting the international borders open as soon as possible. (Coughlan & McCulloch, 2021)

Being Crisis Prepared – Resilience and Implications for Tourism Futures

Resilience can be defined in relation to a range of spatial scales and is a necessary strategy for underpinning sustainable communities (Hopkins & Becken, 2014). Resilience depends on the social capital of the community or society, flexibility and innovation of governance structures and industries and the underlying health and well-being of individuals and groups facing a crisis (Hopkins & Becken, 2014). The tourism sector often has high resilience capacity to adapt and recover from unexpected and catastrophic events (Romagosa, 2020). However, as Romagosa (2020: 691) points out, while analysts believe that when the worst moments of Covid-19 have passed, life will go back to normal, and the tourism sector 'will have a very severe stress test to pass'.

Taking a place-specific approach of tourism and Covid from the South Eastern coast of Australia, tourism geographer Gibson (2021) points out that the Covid crises should not be situated as a singular unprecedented crisis where normality is suspended for the duration of the crisis, and afterwards life continues as 'normal'. Multiple temporalities underpin crises and disruption in uneven ways – 'socially, spatially and temporally' (Gibson, 2021: 87). There is growing recognition among tourism research and disaster studies for the necessity of 'moving beyond normative assessments of preparedness and recovery towards more nuanced analyses of asymmetries in power relations and micro-scale complexities' (Gibson, 2021: 88). In the case of tourism, this means taking a critical approach to the broader societal, economic systems and power dynamics that tourism is embedded within. Holistic focus on planetary health, environmental justice and social equality are all needed for resilient tourism systems.

Discussion and Conclusions

Lost opportunities?

Australia's tourism industry is one of Australia's leading export income generators – only just behind coal, iron ore and higher education (Gibson, 2021). While Australia at large has been sheltered from the most extreme effects of Covid-19, particularly in relation to deaths and hospitalisation, the examples in this chapter demonstrate some of the lost opportunities for Australia to be truly crises prepared and resilient in the face of increasingly uncertain futures in the Anthropocene. As Gibson (2021) notes, crises are multiple – and in the Australian context, Covid-19 arrived on the back of the devastating effects of the 2020 bushfire crises – where many small communities along the East Coast of Australia are utterly dependent on tourism were already devastated. Attempts to rebuild livelihoods after the fires were also hampered by Covid restrictions. Bringing together disaster research with a critical tourism studies agenda, Gibson (2021) also draws attention to the slower temporalities of crises – such as eco-system collapse and drought. Without addressing these underlying problems, the long-term resilience of Australian tourism will be inevitably be undermined.

Tourism development and consumption in the Anthropocene is underpinned by unsustainable anthropocentric binary relations of nature, culture and humanity. Cheer *et al.* (2019) argue that resilience in tourism needs to 'transform and recalibrate to adapt to the evolving status quo and integrate policy approaches' to ensure 'equitable and environmentally conservative development' (Cheer *et al.*, 2019: 559). While Cheer *et al.* (2019) are explicitly talking about these challenges pre-Covid, in relation to overtourism, it is clear that as planetary health deteriorates, adaptive and resilience measures are desperately needed. Precautionary action is needed around resource use and consumption practices. Increased global and societal risks in relation to climate disruption (and follow-on effects such as the global health pandemic of Covid-19) require dealing with vulnerability and promoting ecological integrity into the future (Cheer *et al.*, 2019: 561). As Cheer *et al.* (2019: 561) argue, humans are 'testing the upper limits of the social-ecological ceiling in the Anthropocene' and adaptive and resilience measures are pressing. Greater social-ecological resilience 'centres on not only halting further change, but instead assessing how the human-in-nature might best adapt to and mitigate the rate and pace of change'.

Yet, as the Australian context shows, there have been numerous lost opportunities for being crises prepared, resilient and thinking through future challenges in holistic ways.

For Marshall *et al.* (2012: 2), transformational change 'involves crossing ecological or social thresholds. It fundamentally changes some of the biophysical or socioeconomic components of a system from one form, function, nature or location to another'. From this perspective, as this chapter has argued, tourism cannot be isolated from the broader structural dynamics of economics, politics and society. From a 'systems science perspective', resilience is viewed as a subset of broader notions of sustainability and as a way of implementing sustainability policies (Lew *et al.*, 2017).

While 2020 saw a push towards sustainable strategic directions within the Australian tourism industry, Australia's economic recovery has also led to bailing out airlines undermining long-term strategies for rethinking carbon futures. In the face of climate change, the world requires rapid progress to net-zero emissions. Lost opportunities for incentivising sustainable strategies is evident here. For example, O'Callaghan and Hepburn (2020) argue that airline bailouts should include conditions that airlines reach net-zero carbon emissions by 2050. This would provide incentives for airlines to reach for climate-related targets, meeting climate commitments, where bailout funding could also be converted to equity, where taxpayers also become stakeholders.

The failings of JobKeeper demonstrate how Australia also missed the opportunity to deal with the unequal spread of accumulated wealth which ultimately undermines the resilience of small- and medium-sized operations. According to official figures, the distribution of wealth in Australia – such as property and shares – is roughly twice as unequal as the spread of incomes. The introduction of JobKeeper also saw general welfare unemployment payments rise from $550 to $1100 a fortnight. For Australia's most economically disadvantaged, this was a welcome relief. A Current Affair news report (2021) states; single mum Mandy Weber says:

> *The last couple of nights since I received my first payment, I've actually slept. I've not gone to bed worried about how I'm going to make the budget stretch.*

Australian Council of Social Services emphasised the overdue nature of these changes to the welfare system, arguing that Australia can't afford to have a decent social security system. Junaakar from the University of New South Wales argues it makes economic sense to increase welfare payments in the face of pandemic recovery, which will ultimately see a massive decline in jobs and recession/depression. Boosted welfare payments would enable the economy to grow faster as part of recovery.

However, despite these promising shifts in government policy, JobKeeper ended in March 2021 and welfare payments saw a permanent rise of only $50 per fortnight. Moreover, more than 11,000 people were sent debt letters claiming they were overpaid due to JobKeeper and were told they had an obligation to report JobKeeper as 'ordinary income'. If payments were delayed, they were told they would need to also pay back interest. While thousands of Australians anxiously navigate the confusing roll out of JobKeeper, no such initiatives were taken to claw back money from businesses who got the wage subsidy despite making profits (Henriques-Gomes, 2021).

These uneven and inequitable responses to the Covid crises have also fuelled the anti-vaccine movement in Australia. Research on vaccine hesitancy demonstrates a direct link to a decline in public trust in institutions and government policy (Chen, 2021). As Chen (2021) argues, as long as governments continue to ignore structural injustices driving political radicalisation vaccine resistance will unlikely reduce without increasing polarisation. Errors made in pro-vaccine communication have also raised additional concerns about vaccine safety and efficacy, as seen in the mixed messages about AstraZeneca. In Australia, Aboriginal communities are incredibly vulnerable to diseases such as Covid-19. The mixed messaging over the AstraZeneca vaccine has driven further mistrust between Aboriginal and Torres Strait Islander people and the government. Traumatic historical events, barriers to access and supply and misinformation turned the vaccine into a tool of fear – particularly in light of the violent history within Australia involving government officials and scientists medically experimenting on Aboriginal people (Jash, 2021).

Social inequities related to gender also need to be recognised: global data from the UN Women (European Commission, 2020) suggests that the Covid-19 pandemic could erase 25 years of increasing gender equality. School closures led to a significant increase in the burden of unpaid domestic labour, where home schooling tasks were disproportionally tasked to women. This has also had a significant impact on women's health (see Chapter 10, this volume, Muldoon *et al.*). It is recognised that globally, tourism and hospitality work largely fails to provide decent work for many women, who are often at 'the lowest levels of the occupational pyramid' (Alarcón & Cole, 2019: 904). Gendered inequalities are not only unjust, they also affect broader economic recovery. Monitoring such inequalities can help inform the implementation of national recovery and resilience plans and actions. Gender and development literature highlights the importance of connecting gender equality to resilience, as women are typically the 'glue that keeps the social fabric of communities together', and are driving forces for economic activities that underpin social provisioning and care work (Bakas, 2017: 61). As the World Bank Group's

Women, Business, and the Law points out, *'equality of opportunity is good economics'* (Bossoutrot, 2020). It is estimated that a 'full potential scenario' where women participate in the economy identically to men can add $28 trillion (26%) to annual global GDP by 2025 (Bossoutrot, 2020). It is clear that holistic approaches to equality are needed for pandemic recovery. Taking a holistic approach, an OECD (May 2021) report on 'the territorial impact of Covid-19: Managing the crises and recovery across levels of government' makes several key recommendations for managing Covid.

- Ensure safe and fair access to vaccines across regions within countries through effective coordination mechanisms between national and sub-national governments.
- Consider adopting a 'place-based' or territorially sensitive approach to recovery policies.
- Support cooperation across municipalities and regions to help mini-mise disjointed responses and competition for resources during a crisis.
- Strengthen national and subnational-level support to vulnerable groups.
- Avoid withdrawing abruptly fiscal support.
- Ease administrative burden on core regional and local services and those helping SMEs and the self-employed.
- Coordinate public investment recovery packages across levels of government.
- Balance short-term stimulus objectives with long-term priorities (e.g. sustainability, resilience, smart infrastructure).
- Support subnational public investment over the medium-term to avoid the massive cuts that occurred after the 2008 crisis.
- Reconsider regional development policy to build more resilient regions, better able to address future shocks.

Looking ahead, the report states that the Covid-19 crises have both revealed and accelerated new trends in regional development. On one hand, the crises reveal the lack of regional resilience, amplifying existing weaknesses related to social inequality. On a more positive note, however, the crisis has accelerated several megatrends, such as the imperative to transition to a low carbon economy. However, opportunities for transi-tioning to more equitable and sustainable economies need to be seized in the existing momentum of crises 'recovery'. It remains to be seen then how Australia will pull through in the face of such crises. Indeed, comprehen-sive policy and strategy is needed that addresses planetary health and social-economic inequality. Without such holistic responses, the tourism industry will ultimately continue to suffer. The challenges the tourism industry faces in relation to Covid-19 cannot be separated from the prob-lems of unsustainable growth models. Covid-19 as a virus of the Anthropocene cannot be seen in isolation from working holistically towards more equitable social and environmentally sustainable futures. The elements that makeup tourism development go beyond 'hotels, airlines or the so-called tourist industry' (Martin *et al.*, 2020: 281). Rather, tourism needs be understood as an entire 'system' complex and dynamic and part of the bigger planetary system, and social, cultural, economic and political system(s).

References

A Current Affair (2021) Calls for welfare payment boost to become permanent. See https://9now.nine.com.au/a-current-affair/coronavirus-calls-for-covid19-welfare-payment-boost-to-become-permanent/e7ffb189-9769-4a6e-8233-696144808c21 (accessed October 2022).

Alarcón, D.M. and Cole, S. (2019) No sustainability for tourism without gender equality. *Journal of Sustainable Tourism* 27 (7), 903–919.

Armstrong, F., Capon, A. and McFralene, R. (2020) See https://theconversation.com/coronavirus-is-a-wake-up-call-our-war-with-the-environment-is-leading-to-pandemics-135023 (accessed October 2022).

Asayama, S., Emori, S., Sugiyama, M., Kasuga, F. and Wantanabe, C. (2021) Are we ignoring a black elephant in the Anthropocene? Climate change and global pandemic as the crisis in health and equality. *Sustainability Science* 16, 695–701.

Austrade (2021) Insight. See https://www.austrade.gov.au/news/insights (accessed October 2022).

Bakas, F.E. (2017) Community resilience through entrepreneurship: The role of gender. *Journal of Enterprising Communities: People and Places in the Global Economy* 11 (1), 61–77.

Baker, R.E., Mahmud, A.S., Miller, I.F., Rajeev, M., Rasambainarivo, F., Rice, B.L. … Metcalf, C.J.E. (2021) Infectious disease in an era of global change. *Nature Reviews Microbiology* 20 (4), 1–13.

Bossoutrot, S. (2020) *Gender Equality: Why it Matters, Especially in a Time of Crisis.* The World Bank. See https://www-worldbank-org (accessed October 2022).

Butler, B. (2021) Billionaires receive tens of millions in dividends from companies on JobKeeper. *The Guardian.* See https://www.theguardian.com/australia-news/2021/feb/17/billionaires-receive-tens-of-millions-in-dividends-from-companies-on-JobKeeper(Leigh 2021

Calgaro, E., Lloyd, K. and Dominey-Howes, D. (2014) From vulnerability to transformation: A framework for assessing the vulnerability and resilience of tourism destinations. *Journal of Sustainable Tourism* 22 (3), 341–360.

Chassagne, N. and Everingham, P. (2019) Buen vivir: Degrowing extractivism and growing wellbeing through tourism. *Journal of Sustainable Tourism* 27 (12), 1909–1925.

Chassagne, N. and Everingham, P. (2021) Buen Vivir: A guide for socialising the tourism commons in a post-COVID era. In F. Higgins-Desbiolles, A. Doering and B.C. Bigby (eds) *Socialising Tourism: Rethinking Tourism for Social and Ecological Justice* (pp. 214–229). Abingdon: Routledge.

Cheer, J.M., Milano, C. and Novelli, M. (2019) Tourism and community resilience in the Anthropocene: Accentuating temporal overtourism. *Journal of Sustainable Tourism* 27 (4), 554–572.

Chen, S. (2021) The anti-vax movement is being radicalized by far-right political extremism. *The Conversation.* See https://theconversation.com/the-anti-vax-movement-is-being-radicalized-by-far-right-political-extremism-166396 (accessed October 2022).

Coughlan, M. and McCulloch, D. (2021) Morrison defends tourism rescue offering. *Northern Beaches New Review.* See https://www.northernbeachesreview.com.au/

story/7162148/morrison-defends-tourism-rescue-offering/None/ (accessed November 2021).

Dye, J. (2021) Australia state border closures: Tourism Australia boss calls for Australians to live with the virus. See https://www.traveller.com.au/australia-state-border-closures-tourism-australia-boss-calls-for-australians-to-live-with-virus-h1u2bx (accessed October 2022).

Everingham, P. and Chassagne, N. (2020) Post-COVID-19 ecological and social reset: Moving away from capitalist growth models towards tourism as Buen Vivir. *Tourism Geographies* 22 (3), 555–566.

Everingham, P. and Francis-Coan, S.E. (forthcoming) Rethinking tourism post COVID-19: Towards a 'more-than-tourism' perspective. In P. Mohanty, J. Nivas, A. Sharma and J. Kennell (eds) *The Emerald Handbook of Destination Recovery in Tourism and Hospitality*. Bingley: Emerald Publishing.

European Commission (2020) Focus on: Is home-schooling during the pandemic exacerbating gender inequalities? See https://eacea.ec.europa.eu/national-policies/eurydice/content/focus-home-schooling-during-the-pandemic-exacerbating-gender-inequalities_en (accessed July 2021).

Fletcher, R. (2018) Ecotourism after nature: Anthropocene tourism as a new capitalist "fix". *Journal of Sustainable Tourism* 27 (4), 522–535.

Gibson, C. (2021) Theorising tourism in crisis: Writing and relating in place. *Tourist Studies* 21 (1), 84–95.

Gössling, S., Scott, D. and Hall, C.M. (2020) Pandemics, tourism and global change: A rapid assessment of COVID-19. *Journal of Sustainable Tourism* 29 (1), 1–20.

Gren, M. and Huijbens, E.H. (eds) (2016) *Tourism and the Anthropocene*. Abingdon: Routledge.

Hall, C.M., Baird, T., James, M. and Ram, Y. (2016) Climate change and cultural heritage: Conservation and heritage tourism in the Anthropocene. *Journal of Heritage Tourism* 11 (1), 10–24.

Henriques-Gomes, L. (2021) JobKeeper recipients to pay back 32m while profitable businesses allowed to keep funds. *The Guardian*. See https://www.theguardian.com/australia-news/2021/aug/10/centrelink-orders-JobKeeper-recipients-to-pay-back-32m-while-profitable-businesses-allowed-to-keep-funds

Higgins-Desbiolles, F. and Bigby, B.C. (2022) A local turn in tourism studies. *Annals of Tourism Research* 92, 103291.

Hollenhorst, S., Houge-Mackenzie, S. and Ostergren, D.M. (2014) The trouble with tourism. *Tourism Recreation Research* 39 (3), 305–319.

Hopkins, D. and Becken, S. (2014) Sociocultural resilience and tourism. In A.C. Lew, C.M. Hall and A.M. Williams (eds) *The Wiley Blackwell Companion to Tourism* (pp. 490–499). West Sussex: John Wiley & Sons Ltd.

Husabø, I. (2020) 1% of people cause half of global aviation emission. Most people in fact never fly. See https://partner.sciencenorway.no/climate-change-global-warming-transport/1-of-people-cause-half-of-global-aviation-emissions-most-people-in-fact-never-fly/1773607 (accessed October 2022).

Ingram, L., Slocum, S. and Cavaliere, C.T. (eds) (2020) *Neolocalism: Understanding a Global Movement*. Oxford: Goodfellow Publishers.

IOOF (Independent Order of Odd fellows) (2021) The governments job keeper payment explained.See https://www.ioof.com.au/about-us/news-and-updates/talkingsuper/talking-super-articles/the-governments-JobKeeper-payment-explained (accessed October 2021).

Jacoby, S. (2021) Vaccine inequity will lead to more coronavirus variants. See https://www.today.com/health/vaccine-inequity-will-lead-more-coronavirus-variants-experts-say-t241200 (accessed October 2022).

Jash, T. (2021) What's behind COVID-19 vaccine hesitancy in Indigenous communities? ABC News. See https://www.abc.net.au/news/health/2021-09-13/covid-19-vaccine-hesitancy-indigenous-communities/100451174 (accessed October 2022).

Jericho, G (2020) JobKeeper has failed, and it's hitting women and young people the hardest. *The Guardian*. See https://www.theguardian.com/business/commentisfree/2020/jun/20/JobKeeper-has-failed-and-its-hitting-women-and-young-people-the-hardest (accessed October 2021).

Karp, P. (2021) Harvey Norman repays 6m of the 22m it claimed in JobKeeper after record profits. *The Guardian*. See https://www.theguardian.com/australia-news/2021/aug/31/harvey-norman-repays-6m-of-the-22m-it-claimed-in-JobKeeper-after-record-profits

Karp, P. (2020) Australian airline industry to receive 715m rescue package. *The Guardian*. See https://www.theguardian.com/australia-news/2020/mar/18/australian-airline-industry-to-receive-715m-rescue-package (accessed August 2021).

Khadem, N. (2021) JobKeeper subsidy turnover. *ABC News*. See https://www.abc.net.au/news/2021-09-21/JobKeeper-subsidy-turnover-small-business-covid-pandemic-pbo/100477492 (accessed October 2022).

KPMG (2021) Beyond Covid-19: Rise of domestic travel. See https://home.kpmg/au/en/home/insights/2020/12/beyond-covid-19-rise-of-domestic-travel-tourism-australia.html (accessed October 2022).

Leigh, A. (2020) JobKeeper needs to reduce inequality not increase it. See https://www.andrewleigh.com/JobKeeper_needs_to_reduce_inequality_not_increase_it_speech_house_of_representatives (accessed March 2021).

Lew, A.A., Ni, C.-C., Wu, T.-C. and Ng, P.T. (2017) The Sustainable and Resilient Community: A new paradigm for community development. In A.A. Lew and J. Cheer (eds) *Tourism Resilience and Adaptation to Environmental Change* (28–47). Abingdon: Routledge.

Lew, A.A., Cheer, J.M., Haywood, M., Brouder, P. and Salazar, N.B. (2020) Visions of travel and tourism after the global COVID-19 transformation of 2020. *Tourism Geographies* 22 (3), 455–466.

Marshall, N.A., Park, S.E., Adger, N., Brown, K. and Howden S.M. (2012) Transformational capacity and the influence of place and identity. *Environmental Research Letters* 7 (3). Bristol: IOP Publishing.

Martin, FY.R., Rivera, J.P.R. and Gutierrez, L.M. (2020) Framework for creating sustainable tourism using systems thinking. *Current Issues in Tourism* 23 (3), 280–296.

Mao, F. (2021) Covid: How Delta exposed Australia's pandemic weaknesses. *BBC News*. See https://www.bbc.com/news/world-australia-57647413 (accessed August 2021).

Maxmen, A. and Mallapaty, S. (2021) The COVID lab-leak hypothesis: What scientists do and don't know. News Explainer. *Nature* 594 (7863), 313–315.

Moore, J.W. (2017) The Capitalocene, Part I: On the nature and origins of our ecological crisis. *The Journal of Peasant Studies* 44 (3), 594–630.

Mostafanezhad, M. and Norum, N. (2019) The anthropogenic imaginary: Political ecologies of tourism in a geological epoch. *Journal of Sustainable Tourism* 27 (4), 421–435.

Mostafanezhad, M. (2020) Covid-19 is an unnatural disaster: Hope in revelatory moments of crisis. *Tourism Geographies* 22 (3), 639–645.

NSW Tourism business Council (2021) See https://www.businessnsw.com/content/dam/nswbc/businessnsw/media-releases

O'Callaghan-Gordo, C. and Antó, J.M. (2020) COVID-19: The disease of the Anthropocene. *Environmental Research* 187, 109683.

O'Callaghan, B. and Hepburn, C. (2020) Why airline bailouts are so unpopular with economists. *The Conversation*. See https://theconversation.com/why-airline-bailouts-are-so-unpopular-with-economists-137372 (accessed March 2021).

Prideaux, B., Thompson, M., and Pabel, A. (2020) Lessons from Covid-19 can prepare global tourism for the economic transformation needed to combat climate change. *Tourism Geographies* 22 (3), 667–668.

Rantala, O., Salmela, T., Valtonen, A. and Höckert, E. (2020) Envisioning tourism and proximity after the Anthrprocene. *Sustainability* 12 (10), 3948.

Romagosa, F. (2020) The COVID-19 crisis: Opportunities for sustainable and proximity tourism. *Tourism Geographies* 22 (3) 690–694.

Rowe, D. (2021) Feuding states create roadblock to Australia's recovery. See https://www.afr.com/politics/federal/feuding-states-create-roadblock-to-australia-s-recovery-20200814-p55lnu (accessed October 2022).

Russo, A.P. and Richards, G. (eds) (2016) *Reinventing the Local in Tourism: Producing, Consuming and Negotiating Place.* Bristol: Channel View Publications.

Schmude, J., Zavareh, S., Schwaiger, K.M. and Karl, M. (2018) Micro-level assessment of regional and local disaster impacts in tourist destinations. *Tourism Geographies* 20 (2), 290–308.

SBS News (2021) Prime Minister Scot Morrison defends $1.2 billion tourism plan against criticism of 'very meagre package'. See https://www.sbs.com.au/news/prime-minis-ter-scott-morrison-defends-1-2-billion-tourism-plan-against-criticism-of-very-mea-gre-package/4bd8efb3-e80d-4beb-ae96-c563c354966d (accessed October 2022).

Sheller, M. (2021) Reconstructing tourism in the Caribbean: Connecting pandemic recov-ery, climate resilience and sustainable tourism through mobility justice. *Journal of Sustainable Tourism* 29 (9) 1436–1449.

Sigala, M. (2020) Tourism and COVID-19: Impacts and implications for advancing and resetting industry and research. *Journal of Business Research* 117, 312–321.

Stafford Strategy (2021) See https://www.ttf.org.au/wp-content/uploads/2021/01/2021_0121-Case-for-extending-JobKeeper-Program-for-Tourism-2001_21-1.pdf (accessed October 2022).

Tlozek, E. (2021) Coronavirus border closure impact on funerals and tourism. See https://www.abc.net.au/news/2021-06-28/sa-coronavirus-border-closure-impact-on-funer-als-and-tourism/100250462 (accessed July 2021).

Tomassini, L. and Cavagnaro, E. (2020) The novel spaces and power-geometries in tour-ism and hospitality after 2020 will belong to the 'local'. *Tourism Geographies* 22 (3), 713–719.

Tourism Economics (2021) Australian domestic tourism limited by state border closures. See https://www.tourismeconomics.com/about/economist-perspectives-2/australian-domestic-tourism-limited-by-state-border-closures/ (accessed October 2022).

Victoria University (2021) Building the resilience of tourism destinations to disasters: The 2020 Victorian bushfires and COVID-19 pandemic. A report by Victoria University, Melbourne in collaboration with Victoria Tourism Industry Council.

14 Conclusion: Reflections and Revanche

Rami K. Isaac, Erdinç Çakmak and Richard Butler

Introduction

The chapters in this volume deal with different perspectives and issues of changing practices of a wide range of tourism stakeholders in a variety of Covid-19-affected destinations that represents a global mix of different situations. Our authors examine the changes in the subfields of tourism, the transition of attitudes in spiritual tourism, seek answers for how perceptions and habitus of tourism stakeholders changed during this health-related crisis, and reflect on the emerging perspectives on post-Covid-19 tourism. To date, many future projections and viewpoints on the impact of Covid-19 on tourism have appeared, often based on relatively little empirical research. Our authors provide some of the first empirical data from different parts of the globe in support of their conclusions. They draw attention to the questions: What has happened in tourism during this health-related crisis and what might be the future of tourism? Drawing attention to the changes in stakeholders' practices is not only of interest in academia but also in practice for both the private and public sectors. No sectors will be unaffected, and the tourism sector can act both as a catalyst for socioeconomical impact at destinations, and also as a force for economic recovery and increased resilience (Becken & Khazai, 2017). This final chapter reflects on some of the immediate effects of Covid-19 and reviews 'what could happen in tourism?' briefly in these concluding remarks, along with some discussion of implications for future handling of such events.

One of the features of the response to Covid-19 has been the great variety in extent and depth of adjustments. Part 1 examined impacts in specific subfields of tourism, ranging from airlines to small-scale operators.All faced the problems of uncertainty and lack of precedence on which to base their responses and to change behaviour and practices. Airlines are still attempting to deal with a rapidly changing situation, with airports now appearing to face greater problems than before as passenger numbers begin to recover from the pandemic levels, requiring airlines to futher adjust their schedules and approach. At the small scale of operation, day-to-day survival is still the key issue and the one dominating specific responses.

Pilgrimage and religious travel represent some of the oldest forms of travel, motivated by spiritual beliefs and demands, and these have not changed during the pandemic but have been met with differing responses, with specific adjustments required by financial obligations where agencies offer accommodation in religious settings, while in other situations, the pilgrims have demonstrated great reliance on their faith to overcome disease and still engaged in personal visits rather than adopt virtual alternatives. In all these cases, the responses were dominated by spiritual factors rather than more wordly ones as in the first group of chapters in Part 1.

At the more conceptual level, the permanence or otherwise of behaviour changes remains to be seen, and it is difficult as the pandemic continues, even while it diminishes in effect, to decide if modifications, such as those described in Part 3, will translate into new forms of habitus. In some jurisdications, state control has clearly focused on forcisng changes in behaviour to meet political requirements, a pattern seen in many countries on a clearly temporary basis in the form of quarantines, but something which may become more common if such events as the current pandemic continue to occur. In that respect, the chapters in Part 4 explore some of the least acceptable impacts of Covid-19, such as increasing xenophobia, the assignment of blame and restrictions based in race and ethnic origin. Hopefully, such actions do not become accepted habitus but begin to disappear along with the pandemic itself. At the nation-state level, the number of factors involved in trying to lead countries from a lockdown situation to one of normal freedom of movement are clearly illustrated in the final chapter of Part 4.

Where the world, and tourism in particular, goes from this point is moot. The pandemic appears to be continuing but in a less severe, if more contagious form, and many restrictions, including quarantines have been removed except in a few cases. One can perhaps expect that in any future pandemic, there will be calls for actions to be taken earlier on the basis of the speed with which Covid-19 spread globally, and restrictions, quarantines and lockdowns are likely to be more speedily imposed, recognising that travel, not all of it tourism motivated, was a key agent in the rapidity of the spread of the pandemic. Such impositions, including most likely, a ban on conferences and business related meetings, shown to be key spreading agents, are almost certainly to be temporary and not creating new habitus, although the use of virtual meetings through the various forms of media may well become a permanent change in behaviour. Allied to the reduction in spreading disease are economic benefits to companies so involved, and this is one area in which behaviour change may be long term, despite the apparent dislike of such alternatives on a permanent basis by many participants. It is highly likely that short-term personal behaviour change is more likely to occur in future cases, particularly in rural areas and in the case of small-scale operators, where central assistance is often not as available as it may be in major urban centres and for large multinational operators. In the former cases, based on the findings in this volume, adaptations in behaviour such as untact hospitality may reappear rapidly despite some clear negative impacts on destination attractiveness and competitiveness. One may conclude that while individual choice for tourists may again be severely curtailed in similar pandemics, individual responses in the supply side of tourism may continue to be innovative, opportunistic and temporary, to be abandoned as soon as deemed practical.

The Impact of Covid-19 on Tourism Economies and Stakeholders' Livelihoods

The health-related crisis has had a major impact on the global economic life and labour markets. Tourism is one of the most affected sectors, and the Covid-19 pandemic has caused massive suffering in all parts of tourism value chains. The latest data from the World Travel and Tourism Council (2021) show a 49.1% decline in total global travel and tourism GDP contributions, equating to a downturn of almost 3.86 billion EUR compared to 2019. Such a large drop had a strong effect on employment. From 2014 to 2019, one in four new jobs was related to travel and tourism, with over 330 million jobs in the industry roughly equating to 1 in 10 jobs on a global scale. In 2020, that number was reduced to 272 million jobs. UNWTO (2021a) data for 2020 show a global drop of 74% in terms of international tourist arrivals, and a loss of 1.1 billion international tourists compared to 2019. The number of international tourist arrivals in 2020 was equal to the figures recorded in 1990.

In Europe, Travel and Tourism (T&T) contributions to GDP have fallen by 51%. T&T contributions to overall GDP in Europe fell from a 9.5% share in 2019 to 4.9% in 2020. International tourism arrivals in Europe in 2020 dropped by 70% in comparison to 2019. The highest reductions were recorded in Central/Eastern Europe (74.9%), followed by Northern Europe (73.4%) and South Mediterranean Europe (72.4%), while results in Western Europe were less severe (56.2%) (UNWTO, 2021b). At the same time, in Europe, the domestic travel share of total travel increased from 55% in 2019 to 69% in 2020. WTTC data from June 2021 report that employment in tourism fell by 9.3%, corresponding to 3.6 million lost jobs in Europe, a loss that could have been far worse if governments across Europe (and elsewhere) had not supported employees and introduced job retention schemes to save millions of jobs under threat. As stated by the OECD (2020), women, young people, rural communities and local people living on tourism-related activities are likely to have been affected the most. Job losses among seasonal and part-time workers are expected to have been severe.

Destinations have to consider their recovery and normalisation process initially in the short term. Particularly, destinations in developing countries and small island states, which are reliant on tourism income for a significant contribution to their GDPs, have been affected most severely by this health-related crisis. Designing and implementing crisis management strategies are complex and vary depending on each destination's time pressure, the scale of the crisis and the degree and nature of control (Ritchie, 2004). Recent data from the European Travel Commission (2021) were more optimistic and outlined a prospect for recovery after the summer season of 2021 at an unexpectedly faster pace. Vaccine rollout has increased travel confidence not just for Europeans but also for tourists coming from North America at the beginning of summer 2021. Nevertheless, the threat of the recent Delta variant has hindered a steady recovery as many EU countries had to put into force travel protocols that limited the benefits of the adoption of the EU Digital COVID Certificate, adding more requirements to be followed in destinations. Travellers coming from third countries may be subject to different requirements and protocols across the Member States. Reaching significant vaccination rates amongst the adult population by autumn 2021 has helped travel to resume and the tourism industry recovers to an extent. However, the lack of uniformity of protocols and the different applications of 'health passes' (as extensions of the EU Digital COVID Certificate) within the EU Member States have generated uncertainty, especially with regards to unvaccinated children and teenagers. Furthermore, tourism businesses, primarily hoteliers, were experiencing a workforce shortage during the summer season of 2021 and 2022. Finding workers was a challenge for many tourism businesses for two reasons: (1) the summer season was picking up quickly, and it was better than expected in many destinations; (2) tourism businesses were losing employees during the lockdown despite the governments' job protection schemas. Workforce shortage and brain drain will be one of the largest challenges for the industry in the post-COVID recovery period.

Outside the EU, the situation also remained chaotic and dynamic. Canada and the United States created confusion among travellers within North America with different regulations regarding border crossings, while in Australia, various states closed and opened their borders several times. Western Australia has remained closed to all incomers, including fellow Australians, and Australia only opened its borders in February 2022. New Zealand remained closed to all visitors, including nationals until early 2022, and will not be open to non-nationals until late 2022, as the Omicron variant is rapidly spreading through that country. Several Asian countries such as Thailand have opened borders in 2021, but China still controlled entry tightly, even during the Winter Olympic Games. Quarantines were generally abandoned by the beginning of 2022, but remain a potential threat to full recovery and freedom to travel.

The Covid-19 pandemic had a massive impact on livelihoods. Due to the characteristics of the tourism sector (e.g. cyclical, seasonal and including many small-sized enterprises), tourism jobs are mainly labour intensive and involve many women, youth and vulnerable people in developing countries (Çakmak & Çenesiz, 2020). Importantly, this group has faced a higher risk of losing their jobs and income. Newsome (2021) stated that approximately 75 million people had lost their job in the tourism and hospitality industry by this time, which may result in a global economic recession, and further noted that by April 2020, the Covid-19 had collapsed the global tourism industry. This has been due to government interventions into protecting their nations against the spread of Covid-19. In developing countries, for example, in Palestine, many companies within Bethlehem's tourism sector are cutting down on the number of staff by either sending them on unpaid leave or cutting their jobs entirely. There is no doubt that the Covid-19 pandemic has resulted in unprecedented job losses, pay cuts and forced unpaid leave, as the Palestinian government does not offer stimulus packages to businesses operating in the tourism sector to take care of costs and losses they experienced during the Covid-19 pandemic (Isaac & Abu Aita, 2021).

The impact of the pandemic, the behavioural changes of future travellers and the measures adopted by the sector have led to several emerging trends which represent both challenges and opportunities to relaunch tomorrow's tourism. Short-term consumer trends include 'staycations' (taking holidays closer to home), longer holidays, short booking windows (confirmed by an increase of last-minute bookings), travellers searching for local experiences, special attention to safety and hygiene, and renewed interest in outdoor and nature-based activities. Long-term industry trends are related to achieving greater sustainability and further digitalisation. These trends were emerging before the pandemic, but the health emergency has accelerated the speed of change and represented a good moment to reflect on the potential future of tourism. This is an opportunity to reflect, and an opportunity to plan and perhaps reform the industry. It is a time that can provide numerous opportunities for organisations, both in the public and the private sectors, to review their business models, assess current strategies and plan for relevant adjustments to be made in adaptations to the 'new normal'.

Bounce Back or Bounce Forward ?

In a global context, numerous studies related to the evaluation of the consequences of Covid-19 and potential transformations of the tourism sector started to appear at the beginning of 2020 and arguably even before the pandemic was in full swing. Several studies were conducted on tourism trends and renewal scenarios after the end of the Covid-19 pandemic (e.g. Zhang *et al.*, 2021), tourism adaptation, and opportunities during a pandemic (Collins-Kreiner & Ram, 2021; Liutikas, 2021) studies on the impact of a pandemic on the tourism sector (Hall *et al.*, 2020; Higgins-Desbiolles, 2020; Škare *et al.*, 2021) and the analysis of problems of post-pandemic tourism sector renewal (El-Said & Aziz, 2021; Hussain & Fustè-Fornè, 2021; Sharma *et al.*, 2021). Interesting and relevant though many of these studies are, most were based on projections and viewpoints with relatively little empirical data to support the conclusions. Such has been the nature and scale of the COVID pandemic that there has been no comparable example on which to draw. Spanish Flu was too long ago, well before the age of airborne travel, and represented a very different, much more localised, if more lethal, threat to life. No other epidemic, such as SARS or avian flu, has reached the global scale and coverage of the COVID pandemic. For the first time since figures have been published, all forms of tourism, both domestic and international, have recorded severe declines throughout the world, and thus, academics are in an unprecedented situation in terms of experience.

As the attention of the media and the political stage suddenly shifted from over-tourism to the absence of tourism in the first few months of 2020, the tourism industry, academics and activists started to wonder whether the path towards recovery would involve a return to the old 'normal' or a transformation towards a more sustainable paradigm (Ateljevic, 2020) and indeed many destinations are nowadays exploring if and how they may be able to 'bounce forward' and take the crisis as an opportunity to plan and develop in a more sustainable form of tourism. The collapse of the tourism industry triggered myriad discussions on how the crisis could be seen as an opportunity to 'build back better' and to spark a positive transformation of tourism towards a more responsible and sustainable direction (e.g. Ateljevic, 2020; Higgins-Desbiolles, 2020). Even preceding this pandemic, which has forced the travel industry to a halt, a growing number of academics were calling for a shift towards degrowth strategies, particularly in the case of cities affected by excessive growth and the negative impacts of overtourism (Romagosa, 2020).

Such attitudes, however, are somewhat at variance with industry views, and as Mostafanezhad comments in the concluding article (Brouder *et al.*, 2020) in the special issue of *Tourism Geographies* (titled 'Visions of Travel and Tourism after the Global Covid-19 Transformation of 2020'): 'the papers in this issue highlight the tension among tourism industry practitioners to, on one hand, "return to normal" and by tourism academics to recreate a "new normal"' (2020: 740). Haywood in the same paper notes 'It is perhaps telling that so few of the papers and comments in this conclusion acknowledge where the groundswell of actual change (demand- and supply-related) is occurring and will continue to occur' (2020: 743). Whichever viewpoint, a return to normality or a new normal, emerges as correct, it is wise to consider the note of caution in another of those papers in *Tourism Geographies*, by Hall *et al.* (2020), which had the title 'Pandemics,

Transformations and Tourism: Be Careful What You Wish For', which drew attention to the difficulties of bringing about massive change and transformation without causing other problems.

In this vein, two opposite approaches have emerged and been proposed in the tourism literature. Some scholars (Gössling *et al.*, 2020; Rogerson & Baum, 2020) highlight the expectations of destinations and companies to return to 'as normal' and to compensate for turnover losses through financial measures offered by various national governments. For example, Hall *et al.* (2020) highlight the importance of the resilience of the tourism business and essentially the political intervention that can support the recovery, without any commitment from different stakeholders to sustainable climate change mitigation obligations. The other approach proposed explains how the pandemic has contributed to the growth of a 'global consciousness' that is more in harmony with the United Nations Sustainable Development Goals (Galvani *et al.*, 2020). For these authors, the crisis is an opportunity, a moment of 'transformations' and better address the objectives of inclusion and sustainability. Ionnides and Gyimóthy (2020) see the crisis as a chance to escape the unsustainable growth of pre-Covid-19 tourism and offer the prospect of a community-focused framework as a potential mechanism for tourism growth (Higgins-Desbiolles, 2020).

Other scholars also followed the second approach. For example, Milano and Koens (2022: 5) have stressed, 'tourism degrowth argues for a political paradigm shift towards a more balanced redistribution of benefits and rights among different players and agents' rather than a simple shift towards less or no tourism. In this sense, it represents a very different approach to what the world is currently experiencing, namely, a 'bounce back' to pre-crisis growth levels (Ioannides & Gyimóthy, 2020) rather than activate systemic change (Milano & Koens, 2022). Data from the present pandemic show a strong drive in most locations to restore the industry as quickly and strongly as possible to help businesses, entrepreneurs and the economy recover (Koens, 2021).

The Mediterranean regions are among those most affected by the crisis, especially the countries located on both sides of the sea, which represent almost a third of the overall income of international tourism (UNWTO, 2021b). Rethinking tourism in these areas represents a necessity for a sector of vital importance for local communities and businesses. Accordingly, it is essential to start a process of redefinition and planning the future of tourism for these countries, to secure and sustain their competitiveness in a global and uncertain scenario (Ateljevic, 2020; Baum & Hai, 2020; Bianchi, 2020; Carr, 2020). Some examples emerged in the literature with the recent book *Post COVID-19 Tourism: A Pathway Towards Sustainable Development in the Mediterranean Region* (Buonincontri *et al.*, 2022). This book offers 14 chapters, which cover a variety of topics related to the sustainable development of tourism in the 'post-pandemic' era. These chapters illustrate best practices in various regions in the Mediterranean, which also include innovation for sustainability, the role of agritourism, circular economy, the role of residents and Palestine tourism recovery, *Jahzeen plan* (we are ready) for welcoming back tourists among others.

While many industries and academics are seeing the pandemic as an opportunity for transformation, Richards (2021), for example, argues that to achieve a radical transformation, the tourist – rather than the industry – should be the core of such a transformation. As Ioannides and Gyimóthy (2020: 627) suggest, perhaps this human tragedy will encourage a form of 'patriotic consumption', whereby people voluntarily choose domestic destinations over travel to far-distant places, while multinational companies may have to start refocusing their products more locally (Ioannides & Gyimóthy, 2020: 628). The main social factors that will influence tourism in the future include changes in attitudes, preferences, lifestyle, changes in mobility, awareness of global health and climate, demographic shifts, aging and migration. Travellers may begin to reassess their impact on the planet and demand that businesses and governments provide more sustainable options. According to a recent study conducted by the European Commission *et al.* (2022) overall, travellers are most likely to adopt sustainable practices in the behavioural category of interacting with the local community and immersing in local life, learning about the local traditions and trades, buying local products and choosing locally owned restaurants while in the destination. The report presents the findings of a large-scale study across five European countries – Germany, the UK, France, Italy and the Netherlands. The survey focused on the pre-pandemic and forthcoming travel plans of Europeans, the potential impact of the pandemic on their projected behaviour, the behavioural constraints that would keep them from adopting sustainable travel practices as well as statements related to the underlying value system, beliefs and norms that are likely to guide travellers' actions.

Another social trend that has emerged during the pandemic is the opportunity to combine tourist entertainment with work and/or studies. The ability to work or study virtually allows some people to live on work holidays. Some authors (Walia *et al.*, 2021) proposed that involvement of both business and leisure components in travelling can be defined as 'bleisure'. Another category of such travellers could be digital nomad tourists (Chevtaeva, 2021). These tourists use attractive tourism destinations as co-working and co-living spaces (Chevtaeva, 2021). An increasing number of destinations, such as Bali, Las Palmas and Slovenia, market themselves as digital nomad-friendly destinations.

Higgins-Desbiolles and Bigby (2022: 1) argue that a local turn in tourism could serve 'to address contemporary power imbalances and injustices in tourism by focusing on and empowering local communities'. Communities have to decide about the rate, scale and intensity of tourism development. Koens (2021: 36) perceives new urban tourism as a 'regenerative' form of urban tourism after the Covid-19 crisis 'due to its emphasis on collaboration, giving local stakeholders collective ownership over what they want to share, and allowing for new creative tourism experiences that have arisen out of local interests'.

Other discussions by the industry emphasised that Covid-19 offers an opportunity to 'reset', bringing about an acceleration towards a fair and equitable transition to a low carbon world. There is a critical need for transformative, not incremental, changes towards sustainability for transformation to emerge. All actors – from government, business, philanthropy, civil society, to individuals, and more – must engage in transformative action for this to be successful.

Another phenomenon that has emerged in the tourism academia is 'proximity tourism', which emphasises local destinations, short distances and lower-carbon modes of transportation approached through 'questions of attractiveness cultural and physical distance, walkability and transportation and accessibility' (Rantala *et al.*, 2020: 3948). 'Staycation' is yet another term used in academia, as shown, for example, by Wong *et al.* (2021) who illustrate how Macau residents who were distressed during the pandemic experienced restorative benefits from local tours of Macau, rather than travelling abroad.

These discussions, albeit fascinating, remain philosophical and speculative with little evidence so far emerging that either the tourists or the travel industry are indeed embracing proximity tourism, staycation, 'new urban tourism', or the more recently developed idea of a 'local turn' in tourism studies as practical long-term approaches (Higgins-Desbiolles & Bigby, 2022). Few can argue that such alternative approaches would be a positive move towards both a more sustainable and less consumptive form of tourism that would have obvious benefits for other mega-problems such as climate change. They would also have impacts on the transfer of funds from northern developed countries to less-developed other parts of the world (a process which tourism does somewhat effectively, although far from perfectly), on employment and income generation in current tourism destinations, and perhaps a balance of payments issues. It is clear that there is a movement towards measuring success in tourism in more than only financial terms (Butler, 2022; Dwyer, 2020), and for placing a higher premium on the quality of life in destinations for their residents. Whether such trends will continue post-Covid or suffer a setback as financial priorities yet again assume dominance remains to be seen, but current failings to resolve problems such as overtourism (Butler & Dodds, 2021) because of a combination of economic priority and lack of implementation of suitable policies do not inspire confidence.

In their variety of chapters, our authors strive to question some of the changing practices of tourism stakeholders around the globe. The focus on the changing practices of tourism stakeholders in the book was intended to seek answers to the questions of what did the tourism stake-holders do during this health-related crisis and what might/could be possible in the future for tourism. The aim was not to make projections or forecasts but to explain the changes made to the everyday lives of tourism stakeholders in attempting to respond to the Covid-19 pandemic. We hope that this book inspires the reader to undertake new intellectual and physical journeys and continue to explore the boundaries in tourism research.

References

Ateljevic, I. (2020) Transforming the (tourism) world for good and (re)generating the potential 'new normal'. *Tourism Geographies* 22 (3), 467–475.

Baum, T. and Hai, N.T. (2020) Hospitality, tourism, human rights and the impact of COVID-19. *International Journal of Contemporary Hospitality Management* 32 (7), 2397–2407.

Becken, S. and Khazai, B. (2017) Resilience, tourism and disasters. In R.W. Butler (ed.) *Tourism and Resilience* (pp. 96–104). Wallingford: CABI.

Bianchi, R.V. (2020) COVID-19 and the potential for a radical transformation of tourism. *ATLAS Tourism and Leisure Review* 2, 1–8.

Brouder, P., Teoh, S., Salazar, N., Mostafenezhad, M., Pung, J.M., Lapointem D., Higgins-Desboilles, F., Haywood, M., Hall, M.C. and Clausen, H.D. (2020) Conclusions: Reflections and discussions: Tourism matters in the new normal post-COVID-19 *Tourism Geographies* 22 (3), 735–746.

Buonincontri, P., Errichiello, L. and Micera, R. (eds) (2022) *Post Covid-19 Tourism: A Pathway Towards Sustainable Development in the Mediterranean Region*. Milano: McGraw Hill.

Butler, R.W. (2022) Measuring tourism success: Alternative considerations *World Hospitality and Tourism Themes* 14 (1), 11–19.

Butler, R.W. and Dodds, R. (2022) Overcoming overtourism: a review of failure. *Tourism Review*, Vol. ahead-of-print. https://doi.org/10.1108/TR-04-2021-0215

Çakmak, E. and Çenesiz, M.A. (2020) Measuring the size of the informal tourism economy in Thailand. *International Journal of Tourism Research* 22 (5), 637–652.

Carr, A. (2020) COVID-19 indigenous peoples and tourism: A view from New Zealand. *Tourism Geographies* 22 (3), 491–502.

Chevtaeva, E. (2021) Coworking, and coliving: The attraction for digital nomad tourists. In W. Wörndl, C. Koo and J.L. Stienmetz (eds) *Information and Communication Technologies in Tourism 2021* (pp. 202–209). Cham: Springer. https://doi.org/10.1007/978-3-030-65785-7_17.

Collins-Kreiner, N. and Ram, Y. (2021) National tourism strategies during the COVID-19 pandemic. *Annals of Tourism Research* 89, 103076. https://doi.org/10.1016/j.annals.2020.103076

Dwyer, L. (2020) Tourism development and sustainable well-being: A beyond GDP perspective. *Journal of Sustainable Tourism* 7 (10), 1–18. https://doi.org/10.1080/09669582.2020.1825457

El-Said, O. and Aziz, H. (2021) Virtual tours a means to an end: An analysis of virtual tours' role in tourism recovery post COVID-19. *Journal of Travel Research*. https://doi.org/10.1177/0047287521997567

European Travel Commission, CELTH, EFTI, and Breda University of Applied Science (2022) *Sustainable Travel in an Era of Disruption: Assessing the Impact of the COVID-19 Pandemic on Travelers' Sustainable Tourism Attitudes and Projected Travel Behavior*. Brussels: ETC Market Intelligence Report.

European Travel Commission (2021) European tourism: Trends and prospects. Quarterly report (Q1/2021). See https://etc-corporate.org/reports/european-tourism-2021-trends-prospects-q1-2021/

Galvanie, A., Lew, A.A. and Perez, M.S. (2020) COVID-19 is expanding global consciousness and the sustainability of travel and tourism. *Tourism Geographies* 22 (3), 567–576,

Gössling, S., Scott, D. and Hall, C.M. (2020) Pandemics, tourism and global change: A rapid assessment of COVID-19. *Journal of Sustainable Tourism* 29 (1), 1–20.

Hall, C.M., Scott, D. and Gössling, S. (2020) Pandemics, transformations, and tourism: Be careful what you wish for. *Tourism Geographies* 22 (3), 577–598.

Higgins-Desbiolles, F. (2020) Socializing tourism for social and ecological justice after COVID-19. *Tourism Geographies* 22 (3), 610–623.

Higgins-Desbiolles, F. and Bigby, B.C. (2022) A local turn in tourism studies. *Annals of Tourism Research* 2, 103291.

Hussain, A. and Fusté-Forné, F. (2021) Post-pandemic recovery: A case of domestic tourism in Akaroa (South Island, New Zealand). *World* 2 (1), 127–138.

Ioannides, D. and Gyimóthy, S. (2020) The COVID-19 crisis as an opportunity for escaping the unsustainable global tourism path. *Tourism Geographies* 22 (3), 624–632.

Isaac, R.K. and Abu Aita A. (2021) Can you imagine Bethlehem without tourism: The impacts of COVID-19 on Bethlehem, Palestine. *Current Issues in Tourism* 24 (24), 3535–3551.

Koens, K. (2021) Reframing urban tourism. Inaugural Lecture Dr. Ko Koens. Inholland University of Applied Sciences. See https://pure.buas.nl/ws/files/15652793/koens_2021_inaugural_lecture.pdf (accessed 2 February 2022).

Liutikas, D. (2021). Conclusions: Pilgrimage during and after the pandemic crisis. In D. Liutikas (ed.) *Pilgrims: Values and Identities* (pp. 239–250). Wallingford: CABI.

Milano, C. and Koens, K. (2022) The paradox of tourism extremes. Excesses and restraints in times of COVID-19. *Current Issues in Tourism* 25 (2), 219–231.

Newsome, D. (2021). The collapse of tourism and its impact on wildlife tourism destinations. *Journal of Tourism Futures* 7 (3), 295–302.

OECD (2020) OECD tourism trends and policies 2020 | OECD iLibrary. See https://www.oecdilibrary.org/sites/6b47b985-en/index.html?itemId=/content/publication/6b47b985-e (accessed October 2022.)

Rantala, O., Salmela, T., Valtonen, A. and Höckert, E. (2020) Envisioning tourism and proximity after the Anthropocene. *Sustainability* 12, 3948. https://doi.org/10.3390/su12103948

Richards, G. (2021) Transforming tourism in a post-Covid world. *Vita Magazine* 5 (May), 62–63.

Ritchie, B.W. (2004) Chaos, crises and disasters: A strategic approach to crisis management in the tourism industry. *Tourism Management* 25 (6), 669–683.

Rogerson, C.M. and Baum, T. (2020) COVID-19, and African tourism research agendas. *Development Southern Africa* 37 (5), 727–741.

Romagosa, F. (2020) The COVID-19 crisis: Opportunities for sustainable and proximity tourism. *Tourism Geographies* 22 (3), 690–694.

Škare, M., Soriano, R.D. and Porada-Rochon, M. (2021) Impact of COVID-19 on the travel and tourism industry. *Technological Forecasting and Social Change* 63, 120469.

Sharma, D.G., Thomas, A. and Paul, J. (2021) Reviving tourism industry post-COVID-19: A resilience-based framework. *Tourism Management Perspectives* 37, 100786. https://doi.org/10.1016/j.tmp.2020.100786.

UNWTO (2021a) Tourist arrivals down 87% in January 2021 as UNWTO calls for stronger coordination to restart tourism. See https://www.unwto.org/news/tourist-arrivals-down-87-injanuary-2021-as-unwto-calls-for-stronger-coordination-to-restart-tourism

UNWTO (2021b) 2020 worst year in the tourism history with 1 billion few international arrivals. See https://www.unwto.org/news/2020-worst-year-in-tourism-history-with-1-billion-fewer-international-arrivals (accessed 3 March 2022).

Walia, S., Kour, P., Choudhary, P. and Jasrotia, A. (2021) COVID-19 and the bleisure travellers: An investigation on the aftermaths and future implications. *Tourism Recreation Research*. https://doi.org/10.1080/02508281.2021.1946653

World Travel & Tourism Council (2020) Economic impact from COVID-19: Europe. November. See https://wttc.org/Research/Economic-Impact/RecoveryScenarios/moduleId/1905/itemId/205/controller/DownloadRequest/action/QuickDownload (accessed October 2022).

Wong, I.A., Lin, Z. and Kou, I.E. (2021) Restoring hope and optimism through staycation programs: An application of psychological capital theory. *Journal of Sustainable Tourism* 31 (1), 91–110. https://doi.org/10.1080/09669582.2021.1970172

Zhang, H., Song, H., Wen, L. and Liu, Ch. (2021) Forecasting tourism recovery amid COVID-19. *Annals of Tourism Research* 87, 103149. https://doi.org/10.1016/j.annals.2021.103149

Index

Figures and boxes are shown in *italics*, tables in **bold**.